DEPOSITIONS

PRACTICE AND PROCEDURE IN FEDERAL AND NEW YORK STATE COURTS

The New York State Bar Association wishes to acknowledge the generous contribution of Mead Data Central, Inc. in donating access to the LEXIS®/NEXIS® services and Auto-Cite® feature for our use in the preparation of our reference materials. For information about NYSBA's Membership Group discount program on the LEXIS®/NEXIS® services or other NYSBA membership benefits, call (518) 487-5577.

TABLE OF CONTENTS

DETAILED TABLE OF CONTENTS

CHAPTER 6   PROTECTIVE ORDERS

CHAPTER 7 MOTIONS TO COMPEL AND FOR SANCTIONS

CHAPTER 8 CORRECTIONS TO THE DEPOSITION

CHAPTER 9 USE OF THE DEPOSITION

CHAPTER 10 DEPOSITIONS AND MOTIONS FOR SUMMARY JUDGMENT

CHAPTER 11 DEPOSITION ON WRITTEN QUESTIONS

PART TWO: STRATEGIC AND PRACTICAL CONSIDERATIONS

CHAPTER 2   AT THE DEPOSITION

CHAPTER 3   CORRECTING THE TRANSCRIPT

CHAPTER 4   USE OF DEPOSITIONS

PREFACE

This volume is intended to be helpful to all practitioners. One of our particular aims, however, is to provide assistance to the young practitioner, especially the young attorney in a solo or small practice. In our view, over the last decade, and for a lot of reasons not worth going into here, more and more young men and women have hung up their shingle alone or with a classmate, or perhaps with another young former associate from the same law firm. That phenomenon has provided lots of bright, well-intentioned lawyers, but frequently they pursue the practice of law without the supervision and training that working in a large law firm over time might provide. It has been concern about this reality that in part at least has motivated us to write this volume.

Although we hope this book will be helpful to all lawyers, especially when they are expanding their field of endeavor from one jurisdiction to the other, or from another field of law to litigation, we cannot emphasize enough how important, in our view, to the working life of the younger practitioner is the information we have tried to set forth here. We hope that, once you have read this book, you share our view of its utility.

PART ONE

JURISPRUDENCE

CHAPTER ONE

THE DISCOVERY PROCESS AND THE DEPOSITION

Broadly speaking, the attitude toward depositions and discovery in general in the state and federal systems is similar: Disclosure is not limited to matter that will be admissible at trial, but it includes information that may lead to the discovery of admissible evidence.

I. STATE PRACTICE

A. Scope of Discovery

The scope of discovery allowable in depositions and other discovery devices in New York State practice is broad: "There shall be full disclosure of all matter material and necessary in the prosecution or defense of an action, regardless of the burden of proof."[1] Disclosure can be obtained from parties and the officers, directors, members, agents or employees of parties; it can also be had from nonparties "upon notice stating the circumstances or reasons such disclosure is sought or required."[2]

The scope of disclosure in New York is "very broad, consistent with New York's policy of permitting 'open and far-reaching pretrial discovery.'"[3] Section 3101(a) of the CPLR reflects New York's "policy determination that liberal discovery encourages fair and effective resolution of disputes on the merits, minimizing the possibility for ambush and unfair surprise."[4] In the well-known case of *Allen v. Crowell-Collier Publishing Co.*,[5] the late Chief Judge Fuld wrote:

> The words, "material and necessary," are, in our view, to be interpreted liberally to require disclosure, upon request, of any facts bearing on the controversy which will assist preparation for trial by sharpening the issues and reducing delay and prolixity. The test is one of usefulness and reason. CPLR 3101 (subd. [a]) should be construed . . . to

---

1   N.Y. Civil Practice Law & Rules 3101(a) (hereinafter "CPLR").

2   CPLR 3101(a)(4). CPLR 3101(a)(2) and (3) provide for disclosure from, among others, persons located outside New York, residing more than 100 miles from the place of trial, or so sick or infirm as to afford reasonable grounds for belief that the person will not be able to attend the trial. CPLR 3101(a)(4) addresses nonparties other than those covered in subdivisions (a)(2) and (3). For a discussion of CPLR 3101(a) and deposition of nonparties, see chapter 2.

3   *Kavanagh v. Ogden Allied Maint. Corp.*, 92 N.Y.2d 952, 954, 683 N.Y.S.2d 156, 705 N.E.2d 1197 (1998) (quoting *DiMichel v. S. Buffalo Ry. Co.*, 80 N.Y.2d 184, 193, 590 N.Y.S.2d 1, 604 N.E.2d 63 (1992)).

4   *Spectrum Sys. Int'l Corp. v. Chem. Bank*, 78 N.Y.2d 371, 376, 575 N.Y.S.2d 809, 581 N.E.2d 1055 (1991).

5   21 N.Y.2d 403, 288 N.Y.S.2d 449, 235 N.E.2d 430 (1968).

permit discovery of testimony "which is sufficiently related to the issues in litigation to make the effort to obtain it in preparation for trial reasonable."[6]

As one would expect, the rule of broad disclosure is not unlimited. The court must balance conflicting considerations—the need for the disclosure must be weighed against competing interests, such as any special burden the discovery might impose on the other party, a need for unusual expedition or a requirement of confidentiality.[7] It is important that discovery not become a source of unreasonable annoyance or tend to harass or overburden the other party or a witness.[8]

Matter discoverable under CPLR 3101(a) is not limited to that which is admissible in evidence. It is therefore not a valid objection at a deposition that the question seeks an answer that could not be used at trial. The standard, rather, is whether the discovery sought may *lead* to the disclosure of admissible evidence.[9]

---

6. *Id*. at 406–407. The word *necessary* should be interpreted to mean *needful*, not *indispensable*. *Id*. at 407. *See Town of Pleasant Valley v. New York State Bd. of Real Prop. Servs.*, 253 A.D.2d 8, 685 N.Y.S.2d 74 (2d Dep't 1999); *Dolback v. Reeves*, 265 A.D.2d 625, 696 N.Y.S.2d 270 (3d Dep't 1999); *Santiago v. Pyramid Crossgates Co.*, 243 A.D.2d 955, 663 N.Y.S.2d 367 (3d Dep't 1997); *DeDivitis v. IBM*, 228 A.D.2d 963, 644 N.Y.S.2d 594 (3d Dep't 1996); *Williams Real Estate Co. v. Viking Penguin, Inc.*, 216 A.D.2d 27, 628 N.Y.S.2d 267 (1st Dep't 1995); *Robinson v. Meca*, 214 A.D.2d 246, 632 N.Y.S.2d 728 (3d Dep't 1995).

7   *Kavanagh*, 92 N.Y.2d at 954; *Town of Pleasant Valley*, 253 A.D.2d at 16; *Conrad v. Park*, 204 A.D.2d 1011, 612 N.Y.S.2d 524 (4th Dep't 1994).

8   *Conrad*, 204 A.D.2d 1011.

9   *See Allen*, 21 N.Y.2d 403; *Humiston v. Grose*, 144 A.D.2d 907, 534 N.Y.S.2d 604 (4th Dep't 1988); *Dattmore v. Eagan Real Estate, Inc.*, 112 A.D.2d 800, 492 N.Y.S.2d 302 (4th Dep't 1985); *Shapiro v. Levine*, 104 A.D.2d 800, 479 N.Y.S.2d 1006 (2d Dep't 1984); *Wiseman v. Am. Motors Sales Corp.*, 103 A.D.2d 230, 232–33, 479 N.Y.S.2d 528 (2d Dep't 1984); *Hawkins v. Genesee Hosp.*, 86 A.D.2d 971, 448 N.Y.S.2d 288 (4th Dep't 1982); *see also Hickman v. Taylor*, 329 U.S. 495, 507 (1947) ("No longer can the time-honored cry of 'fishing expedition' serve to preclude a party from inquiring into the facts underlying his opponent's case. Mutual knowledge of all the relevant facts gathered by both parties is essential to proper litigation.").

The trial judge has broad discretion over the disclosure process. The supervision of discovery and the imposition of reasonable limits and conditions are matters left to the sound discretion of the judge.[10]

Notwithstanding the CPLR's broad approach to discovery, the statute establishes three categories of protected material: (1) privileged matter, (2) attorney work product and (3) trial preparation materials. These protections have a long history in American and English jurisprudence and are based upon important principles.[11] Attorney work product and matter covered by the attorney-client privilege and other recognized privileges are immune from discovery.[12] Trial preparation materials may be obtained only upon a showing that the inquiring party has substantial need for the materials and is unable without undue hardship to obtain their substantial equivalent by other means.[13]

New York law takes a broad and liberal approach to the search for information in depositions. With regard to depositions, as is discussed in greater detail in chapter 5, the general principles summarized here lead to the following rules:

1. A question posed at a deposition need not be objected to except when the defect in the question could be cured by a timely objection; otherwise, objections are preserved for determination at trial.

2. The possibility that an answer might be hearsay or otherwise inadmissible is not a basis for making an objection.

3. Counsel may not direct the witness not to answer a question unless such question infringes upon a constitutional right or recognized privileged or protection or seeks information that is palpably irrelevant.

---

10 *Andon v. 302–304 Mott St. Assocs.*, 94 N.Y.2d 740, 709 N.Y.S.2d 873, 731 N.E.2d 589 (2000); *McMahon v. Aviette Agency, Inc.*, 301 A.D.2d 820, 753 N.Y.S.2d 605 (3d Dep't 2003); *Kozuch v. Certified Ambulance Group, Inc.*, 301 A.D.2d 840, 753 N.Y.S.2d 612 (3d Dep't 2003); *Daniels v. City of New York*, 291 A.D.2d 260, 737 N.Y.S.2d 598 (1st Dep't 2002); *Palermo Mason Constr., Inc. v. AARK Holding Corp.*, 300 A.D.2d 460, 751 N.Y.S.2d 599 (2d Dep't 2002); *Saratoga Harness Racing Inc. v. Roemer*, 290 A.D.2d 928, 736 N.Y.S.2d 811 (3d Dep't 2002); *Provident Life & Cas. Ins. Co. v. Brittenham*, 284 A.D.2d 518, 727 N.Y.S.2d 142 (2d Dep't 2001); *Doe v. Merck & Co.*, 283 A.D.2d 543, 725 N.Y.S.2d 356 (2d Dep't 2001); *Andrews v. Trustco Bank, N.A.*, 289 A.D.2d 910, 735 N.Y.S.2d 640 (3d Dep't 2001).

11 *Spectrum Sys. Int'l Corp. v. Chem. Bank*, 78 N.Y.2d 371, 376–77, 575 N.Y.S.2d 809, 581 N.E.2d 1055 (1991).

12 CPLR 3101(b), (c).

13 CPLR 3101(d)(2).

B. Scheduling and Judicial Supervision of Depositions and Discovery in New York

Although the CPLR provides for discovery to frame a complaint, typically the discovery process begins with the service of an answer or after resolution of a motion to dismiss when at least one cause of action survives. Although New York is a filing jurisdiction, the document that initiates the case in the state court system—the request for judicial intervention (RJI)[14]—generally need not be filed at any particular time.[15] A case may come to court for the first time by way of a motion for summary judgment or even a note of issue.

This is one of many ways in which state practice differs (in this instance, dramatically) from federal practice. In most cases, there is no automatic disclosure in state practice, nor is there a mandatory initial discovery conference at a fixed stage during the life of the case, measured from commencement.[16]

In a broad class of actions for damages, including those that account for the bulk of judicial business (i.e., personal injury, commercial, and real property cases), a system of differentiated case management (DCM)

---

14   Uniform Rules for the New York State Trial Courts, Rule 202.6. The Uniform Rules are set forth in N.Y. Comp. Codes, R. & Regs. tit. 22 (hereinafter "N.Y.C.R.R."), with the rule number corresponding to the N.Y.C.R.R. section number. Subsequent references herein are to "Uniform Rule ____." See Appendix, "Request for Judicial Intervention (UCS-840)" (state form).

15   Matrimonial cases are an exception. An RJI must be filed in a contested case within 45 or, if "both parties file a notice of no necessity with the court," 120 days from service of the summons and complaint or summons with notice. Uniform Rule 202.16(d).

16   A preliminary conference in a matrimonial case, however, must be held within 45 days after assignment of the case to a justice. Uniform Rule 202.16(f)(1).

applies. In such cases, a preliminary conference must be held within 45 days from filing of the RJI.[17]

At the preliminary conference, the court will address the question of what discovery is appropriate and what the discovery schedule should be. Thus, counsel appearing for such a conference must be fully prepared to discuss the discovery that each party believes will be needed or reasonably required. Depositions usually will constitute a key part of the discovery desired by each side.

First, counsel need to consider how much time should be allotted to discovery overall. The court will confirm or modify an assignment of the case to a DCM track: expedited (discovery must be completed within 8 months), standard (12 months) or complex (15 months).[18] The court system monitors these deadlines closely.[19]

In addition to this calculus, counsel must develop a discovery plan before the preliminary conference. What discovery does counsel need for the case? What does the adversary reasonably require? In what order should the discovery proceed? If discovery is to be comprehensive, it may be advisable that it unfold in a particular sequence.

---

17 Uniform Rule 202.19(b). The rule does not define the groups of cases to which it applies beyond stating, in effect, that it applies when the chief administrative judge says it applies. Uniform Rule 202.19(a). It appears to apply to the three principal groups of cases mentioned above, at least in the New York metropolitan area. It appears further that damage actions against the city of New York are excluded. The rule requires a preliminary conference irrespective of the stage at which the RJI is filed or the nature of the intervention sought. Read literally, the rule requires that a conference be held in a case in which the RJI is filed with a note of issue or with a motion to dismiss or with a motion for summary judgment. Obviously, a conference to fix a discovery schedule is never needed when an RJI is filed with a note of issue (unless the note of issue is stricken) and will usually be premature when an RJI is filed with a motion that brings about a stay. CPLR 3214. It appears that, in practice, the rule does not come into play in cases of RJIs accompanied by notes of issue (a small percentage of the filings) and that its application may be postponed until decision on the motion when the RJI is accompanied by a nondiscovery motion (a much more common situation).

18 Uniform Rule 202.19(b)(2). The rule states that the court shall designate the appropriate track at the conference. However, in busier counties the assignment is made upon filing of the RJI in accordance with the filer's designation or standing rules of the court. At the preliminary conference (or PC, as it is commonly called), the court confirms that designation or modifies it.

19 The rule does not expressly state that the note of issue is to be filed by the discovery deadline in the track assignment. However, when discovery is complete, the note of issue and certificate of readiness should be filed, as nothing stands in the way of trial at that point. The preliminary conference order will often contain a deadline for the filing of the note of issue. A summary judgment motion may be in the wings, but the deadline for that motion is linked to the note of issue. CPLR 3212(a). In many counties, cases apparently are monitored by checking whether the note of issue is filed within the DCM deadline. If not, the case is commonly said to be "beyond standards and goals."

In most personal injury cases, much of the discovery sought is clear and the sequence standard: a bill of particulars; medical authorizations; employment information when lost wages are claimed; other documents, including information as to notice; depositions of plaintiff and defendant; physical examination of plaintiff; exchange of medical reports. In some cases, however, preliminary or targeted discovery may appropriately be allowed when the completion of such discovery first might narrow the issues or lead to an early resolution, as when the discovery is in support of an early motion.

In commercial cases, it will usually promote efficient and effective processing of the case if the discovery proceeds in stages: interrogatories, document production, depositions, a possible motion for summary judgment. Again, in some cases, preliminary or targeted discovery might help narrow the scope of the disclosure.

The court may be called upon at the preliminary conference to resolve disputes as to how many depositions can be conducted, who may reasonably be deposed, the order in which depositions should proceed (to the extent not resolved by the rules on priority), the time period to be covered and other relevant aspects.

The court's determinations at the conference will be embodied in a preliminary conference order. At the conference, the court is to set a date for a compliance conference at which the court will monitor compliance with the discovery schedule set forth in the preliminary conference order. The compliance conference must be held no later than 60 days before the date set for the completion of discovery.[20]

Should problems arise in connection with depositions, they generally are handled by the justice to whom the case is assigned.[21] Such problems may involve the production of documents needed to prepare for and to use at a deposition, the convening of a deposition or objections raised during a deposition.

The court may order the appointment of a referee to supervise discovery.[22] A judicial hearing officer may be designated to fulfill this role, or all

---

20   Uniform Rule 202.19(b)(3).

21   This is the Individual Assignment System (IAS) justice.

22   CPLR 3104. This appointment may be made upon motion or upon the court's own initiative. CPLR 3104(a).

parties may agree to have a private attorney do so.[23] A referee is accorded all the powers of the court, with a few exceptions.[24] An order of the referee may be reviewed by the IAS justice upon motion.[25] Generally, this power of appointment is exercised infrequently. It occurs in cases involving extremely disputatious attorneys or obstructionist parties.[26] It might also happen in a commercial case when large numbers of documents and claims of privilege or other protections are at issue, or when numerous depositions require many rulings.

As noted, filing the note of issue normally signifies completion of disclosure. It is accompanied by a certificate of readiness reciting that disclosure is complete.[27] If a party believes that disclosure is not complete, it should move to vacate the note of issue.[28] The court may vacate a note on its own motion. Absent special or extraordinary circumstances, discovery is not allowed after a note of issue is filed.[29]

II. FEDERAL PRACTICE

A. Scope of Discovery

In federal practice, "[p]arties may obtain discovery regarding any matter, not privileged, that is relevant to the claim or defense of any party."[30] Beyond this, the rule states that, "[f]or good cause, the court may order discovery of any matter relevant to the subject matter involved in the action."[31] This distinction between party-directed, claim-related disclosure and court-ordered discovery, for which there is no similar provision in state practice, is intended to narrow the scope of discovery and to "involve the court more actively in regulating the breadth of sweeping or conten-

---

23   CPLR 3104(b).

24   The exceptions are the powers to punish for contempt, to appoint a successor and to relieve himself or herself of duties. CPLR 3104(c).

25   CPLR 3104(d).

26   David D. Siegel, New York Practice 550–51 (3d ed. 1999).

27   Uniform Rule 202.21. See Appendix, "Note of Issue," "Certificate of Readiness" (state forms).

28   Uniform Rule 202.21(e).

29   Uniform Rule 202.21(d). *See Rinker v. Oberoi*, 288 A.D.2d 873, 732 N.Y.S.2d 787 (4th Dep't 2001); *Edbauer v. Bd. of Educ.*, 286 A.D.2d 999, 731 N.Y.S.2d 309 (4th Dep't 2001); *Ferris v. Marchese*, 284 A.D.2d 998, 727 N.Y.S.2d 227 (4th Dep't 2001); *Gould v. Marone*, 197 A.D.2d 862, 604 N.Y.S.2d 867 (4th Dep't 1993).

30   Fed. R. Civ. P. 26(b)(1) (hereinafter "FRCP").

31   *Id.*

tious discovery."[32] Parties and the court should focus on claims and defenses actually involved in the case.[33] *Relevance*, as so defined, is to be broadly construed.[34] Relevant information need not be admissible at trial "if the discovery appears reasonably calculated to lead to the discovery of admissible evidence."[35]

When the discovery sought appears relevant, the party resisting disclosure has the burden of establishing lack of relevance. This burden is met by showing that the discovery in fact is of marginal relevance and that the harm that could be occasioned by the discovery would outweigh the usual presumption in favor of broad disclosure.[36]

The court shall limit the frequency or extent to which discovery devices are used if (1) the discovery sought is unreasonably cumulative or duplicative or can be obtained from some other source that is more convenient, less burdensome or less expensive; (2) the party seeking the discovery has had ample opportunity to obtain the information; or (3) the burden or expense of the discovery outweighs its likely benefit.[37] All discovery is

---

32   Notes of Advisory Committee on 2000 Amendments, FRCP 26. *See Sanyo Laser Prods. v. Arista Records, Inc.*, 214 F.R.D. 496, 498 (S.D. Ind. 2003); *Chavez v. Daimler Chrysler Corp.*, 206 F.R.D. 615, 619 (S.D. Ind. 2002).

33   Notes of Advisory Committee on 2000 Amendments, FRCP 26. In *Sanyo Laser Prods.*, 214 F.R.D. at 500, the court stated that the rule changes in 2000 had somewhat narrowed the scope of discovery. The change, though meaningful, was not dramatic, with broad discovery remaining the norm. "The revised rule simply provides one additional justification for the Court to put the brakes on discovery that strays from the claims or defenses being asserted." *Id.*

34   *Transcor, Inc. v. Furney Charters, Inc.*, 212 F.R.D. 588, 591 (D. Kan. 2003); *Johnson v. Olathe Dist. Schs.*, 212 F.R.D. 582, 586 (D. Kan. 2003); *Goodyear Tire & Rubber Co. v. Kirk's Tire & Auto*, 211 F.R.D. 658, 663 (D. Kan. 2003); *Topo v. Dhir*, 210 F.R.D. 76, 77 (S.D.N.Y. 2002); *Chavez*, 206 F.R.D. at 619; *In re Theragenics Corp. Sec. Litig.*, 205 F.R.D. 631, 636 (N.D. Ga. 2002).

35   FRCP 26(b)(1). *See United States ex rel. Schwartz v. TRW, Inc.*, 211 F.R.D. 388, 392 (C.D. Cal. 2002); *Chavez*, 206 F.R.D. at 619; *United States ex rel. [Redacted] v. [Redacted]*, 209 F.R.D. 475, 483 (D. Utah 2001).

36   *Sanyo Laser Prods.*, 214 F.R.D. at 498.

37   FRCP 26(b)(2). *See United States v. Duke Energy Corp.*, 214 F.R.D. 392, 393 (M.D.N.C. 2003) (minimal relevance was far outweighed by the burden and expense of requiring Cabinet agency to search all files); *Chavez*, 206 F.R.D. at 619.

subject to these limitations.[38] The court has broad discretion to supervise discovery.[39]

B. Scheduling and Judicial Supervision of Discovery

The parties should immediately arrange for the mandatory disclosure required by FRCP 26(a). That provision, for which there is no generally applicable parallel in state practice, mandates that, without waiting for a discovery request, a party must make certain disclosures. Mandatory disclosures include information about persons the disclosing party may use to support his or her position and a copy of or a description of documents upon which the disclosing party may rely.

This mandatory disclosure is very different from discovery sought by a party. Generally speaking, absent a court order or stipulation, a party may not seek discovery from any source before a FRCP 26(f) conference takes place.[40]

The district judge or a magistrate judge shall issue a scheduling order as soon as practicable, but at least within 90 days after the appearance of the defendant and within 120 days after the complaint has been served.[41] Before a scheduling conference is held or an order is due under FRCP 16(b), the parties must confer, pursuant to FRCP 26(f), to consider the nature of the case and the possibilities for settlement and to develop an approach to discovery for the case. At the FRCP 26(f) conference, the parties will generally confer further and develop a proposed discovery plan. A written report of the plan may be submitted to the court.[42] These steps are not generally required in state practice.

Based upon the written report submitted by the parties or after a pretrial conference, the district judge or magistrate judge shall issue the FRCP 16(b) scheduling order. This order shall set forth the deadline for

---

38   FRCP 26(b)(2).

39   *Perez v. Miami-Dade County*, 297 F.3d 1255, 1263 (11th Cir. 2002); *Hallett v. Morgan*, 296 F.3d 732, 751 (9th Cir. 2002); *Univ. of W. Va. v. Van Voorhies*, 278 F.3d 1288, 1304 (Fed. Cir. 2002); *Vica Coal Co. v. Crosby*, 212 F.R.D. 498, 504 (S.D. W. Va. 2003); *Suntrust Bank v. Blue Water Fiber, L.P.*, 210 F.R.D. 196, 199 (E.D. Mich. 2002); *Topo v. Dhir*, 210 F.R.D. 76, 79 (S.D.N.Y. 2002); *In re Buspirone Antitrust Litig.*, 208 F.R.D. 516, 522 (S.D.N.Y. 2002).

40   FRCP 26(d).

41   FRCP 16(b). See Appendix, "Pretrial Scheduling Order" (federal form).

42   If necessary to meet an expedited schedule for a FRCP 16(b) conference, a court may allow submission of an oral discovery plan in lieu of the standard written report. FRCP 26(f).

completion of discovery and will usually include the date for dispositive motions, the date of another pretrial conference when one is sought by the parties or by the court, and a trial date or month.[43]

Because of the FRCP 26(f) requirements, counsel for the parties must carefully consider the discovery requirements of the case very early in the life of a case. As in the state courts, counsel needs to consider what depositions are necessary from the client's point of view and the likely need for depositions of the adversary. The effect of the limitations upon the number of depositions set forth in FRCP 30(a)(2)(A)[44] must be taken into account. Scheduling of depositions between the parties and in relation to other forms of discovery also must be evaluated. The utility of a staged approach to discovery, as related to likely motion practice, must be considered. Many judges accept only fully briefed motions, and the date for motions should account for such a practice. All these elements should form part of the FRCP 26(f) conference, be included in the discovery plan and be addressed with the court at the FRCP 16(b) conference.

In some districts, a magistrate judge is automatically assigned to supervise disclosure from the beginning of the litigation. In others, the magistrate judge, while assigned to the case, manages discovery at the instance of the Article III judge. Often, the Article III judge will resolve discovery disputes, at least until the need for more supervision becomes manifest. This participation ensures a level of judicial intervention that the state system unfortunately cannot provide because of a lack of resources.

---

43   FRCP 16(b). The scheduling order is mandatory except in categories of cases exempted by local rule.

44   See discussion in chapter 2.

CHAPTER TWO

NOTICING AND ARRANGING
THE DEPOSITION

I. STATE PRACTICE

A. Noticing the Deposition

1. Generally

The formal notice of deposition on oral questions is governed by CPLR 3107. The rule authorizes a party to take the deposition of any person. A written notice is required.[1] Unless the court orders otherwise, 20 days' notice shall be given to each party. The notice must set forth (1) the time and place for the deposition, (2) the name and address of each person to be examined, if known, and (3) if the name is unknown, a general description sufficient to identify the person or the class or group to which he or she belongs.

Rule 3107 expressly provides that the notice need not enumerate the matters on which the person is to be examined. This provision parallels FRCP 30(b), with the significant exception of FRCP 30(b)(6), which governs depositions of corporations and other entities.

Except in matrimonial actions, a party may not serve written interrogatories on another party and demand a bill of particulars from that same person.[2] In actions for personal injury, injury to property and wrongful death based on claims of negligence, a party may not serve interrogatories on a party *and* conduct a deposition of the party without leave of court. Thus, the standard practice in personal injury cases is that a bill of particulars is served and depositions are taken, but there are no interrogatories.

If a party wishes to depose a corporation, municipality or other entity,[3] that corporation, municipality or entity may decide whom to produce as its representative(s). The party seeking the deposition cannot name any particular person to be deposed on the entity's behalf,[4] with one qualification. If the person produced by the corporation, municipality or entity lacks

---

1   See Appendix, "Notice of Deposition" (state form).

2   CPLR 3130.

3   The term *any person* in CPLR 3106(a) encompasses any entity legally recognized as a person, including corporations, partnerships and associations. See Appendix, "Notice of Deposition—Corporation" (state form).

4   *D & S Realty Dev., L.P. v. Town of Huntington*, 295 A.D.2d 306, 743 N.Y.S.2d 147 (2d Dep't 2002); *vanBergen v. Long Beach Med. Ctr.*, 277 A.D.2d 374, 717 N.Y.S.2d 191 (2d Dep't 2000); *Harris v. Town of Islip*, 268 A.D.2d 459, 703 N.Y.S.2d 45 (2d Dep't 2000); *Pisano v. Door Control, Inc.*, 268 A.D.2d 416, 702 N.Y.S.2d 307 (2d Dep't 2000); *Barone v. Great Atl. & Pac. Tea Co.*, 260 A.D.2d 417, 687 N.Y.S.2d 718 (2d Dep't 1999).

adequate knowledge of the facts, then the party seeking the deposition can depose someone else. Such subsequent depositions may and ought to be agreed upon by the parties after the first deposition.

As always, motion practice may follow if there is discord on the point. On such a motion, the party seeking an additional deposition must make a "detailed showing of the necessity for taking such depositions."[5] The movant must show that the representative(s) already deposed had insufficient knowledge of the relevant facts or were otherwise inadequate and that there is a substantial likelihood that the person(s) sought will have information to offer that is material and necessary to the case.[6]

A party may designate a particular officer, director, member or employee of a person by setting forth in the notice or subpoena the identity, description or title of the proposed deponent.[7] This individual shall be produced unless the person served notifies the party seeking the deposition—ten days or more in advance of the deposition—that another person will be produced and indicates the identity, description or title of that other person. If this notification is given, the other person shall be produced.[8] The corporation or other entity thus controls the production in the first instance if it complies with the simple procedures in CPLR 3106(d).

---

5   *Colicchio v. City of New York,* 181 A.D.2d 528, 529, 581 N.Y.S.2d 36 (1st Dep't 1992); *accord Defina v. Brooklyn Union Gas Co.,* 217 A.D.2d 681, 630 N.Y.S.2d 533 (2d Dep't 1995).

6   *Saxe v. City of New York,* 250 A.D.2d 751, 671 N.Y.S.2d 1002 (2d Dep't 1998); *see Brown v. Home Depot, U.S.A.,* 304 A.D.2d 699, 758 N.Y.S.2d 378 (2d Dep't 2003); *D & S Realty Dev.,* 295 A.D.2d 306; *Harris,* 268 A.D.2d 459 (witness produced had insufficient knowledge); *Pisano,* 268 A.D.2d 416 (showing not made); *Arendt v. Gen. Elec.,* 270 A.D.2d 622, 704 N.Y.S.2d 346 (3d Dep't 2000) (inadequate showing that numerous persons produced lacked necessary knowledge or that the CEO demanded had information to offer bearing on case); *Barone,* 260 A.D.2d 417 (showing not made); *Weiner v. Jewish Home & Hosp. for the Aged,* 243 A.D.2d 403, 663 N.Y.S.2d 195 (1st Dep't 1997) (additional witnesses ordered); *Prince v. DiBenedetto,* 189 A.D.2d 757, 592 N.Y.S.2d 388 (2d Dep't 1993) (additional deposition justified); *Colicchio,* 181 A.D.2d 528 (showing not made so as to justify deposition of New York City Commissioner of Transportation); *Joseph P. Day Realty Corp. v. Aeroxon Prods., Inc.,* 148 A.D.2d 499, 538 N.Y.S.2d 843 (2d Dep't 1989).

7   CPLR 3106(d).

8   *See Weiner,* 243 A.D.2d 403; *Hendrick Hudson Cent. Sch. Dist. v. Falinski,* 232 A.D.2d 454, 648 N.Y.S.2d 930 (2d Dep't 1996); *Bridges v. 725 Riverside Dr., Inc.,* 119 A.D.2d 789, 501 N.Y.S.2d 414 (2d Dep't 1986). The Advisory Committee on Civil Practice had proposed that the party seeking the deposition be permitted to designate the corporate official it wished to depose. The legislature in 1984 adopted the current subdivision (d) instead, which seems to have been intended to prevent harassment of high-level corporate officials. Siegel, McKinney's Practice Commentary, CPLR 3106, at 436–37 (1991).

In state practice, parties or officers, directors, members or employees of a party should generally be deposed in that person's county of residence in New York or where a business office is located or where the action is pending.[9] Generally, a nonresident plaintiff, having invoked the jurisdiction of New York, will be expected to appear for deposition in the state. The nonresident defendant too will generally be deposed in New York.[10] Of course, situations may arise in which attendance for a deposition in New York may work a hardship, in which event the protective order under CPLR 3103 can be used to craft an appropriate solution.[11]

A party who is served with a notice to be deposed may serve, on at least ten days' notice, its own notice for an examination[12] of any other party, its agent or employee.[13] This deposition is to be noticed for and shall follow at the same time and place.[14]

2. Nonparty Witnesses

If the prospective deponent is neither a party nor at the time of the deposition an officer, director, member or employee of a party, then the party seeking the deposition must serve a subpoena on the witness.[15] Service shall be made at least 20 days prior to the deposition unless the court, on motion with or without notice, orders otherwise.[16]

In considering the possible deposition of a nonparty witness, counsel must take into account CPLR 3101(a). This provision, which is directed to the scope of discovery in general, limits the persons who can be deposed as nonparty witnesses. Subdivision (a)(3) imposes certain geographic limits,

---

9   CPLR 3110.

10   *Id. Rogovin v. Rogovin*, 3 A.D.3d 352, 770 N.Y.S.2d 342 (1st Dep't 2004); *Swiss Bank Corp. v. Geecee Exportaciones, Ltda.*, 260 A.D.2d 254, 688 N.Y.S.2d 539 (1st Dep't 1999); *Farrakhan v. N.Y.P. Holdings Inc.*, 226 A.D.2d 133, 135–36, 640 N.Y.S.2d 80 (1st Dep't 1996); *Bristol-Myers Squibb Co. v. Chen*, 186 A.D.2d 999, 588 N.Y.S.2d 672 (4th Dep't 1992); *Kahn v. Rodman*, 91 A.D.2d 910, 457 N.Y.S.2d 480 (1st Dep't 1983); Siegel, McKinney's Practice Commentary, CPLR 3110, at 483–84 (1991).

11   Protective orders are discussed in chapter 6.

12   See Appendix, "Cross-Notice of Deposition" (state form).

13   CPLR 3107.

14   *Monaco v. Camie-Campbell, Inc.*, 256 A.D.2d 1214, 682 N.Y.S.2d 510 (4th Dep't 1998).

15   See Appendix, "Notice of Deposition—Nonparty Witness" and "Subpoena" (state forms).

16   CPLR 3106(b); *Lewis v. Baker*, 279 A.D.2d 380, 720 N.Y.S.2d 26 (1st Dep't 2001); *Frybergh v. Kouffman*, 119 A.D.2d 541, 500 N.Y.S.2d 552 (2d Dep't 1986).

permits discovery when the person is so ill that there are reasonable grounds to believe that he or she will be unable to attend the trial and permits the deposing party to obtain discovery from his or her medical professionals or experts. Subdivision (a)(4) authorizes discovery of "any other person, upon notice stating the circumstances or reasons such disclosure is sought or required."

On its face, CPLR 3101(a)(4) may seem straightforward. However, it is actually quite complex. Prior to 1984, the rule contained a requirement for a showing by motion of "adequate special circumstances" in order for a nonparty deposition to be taken. If, for example, a proposed deponent had a relationship with a party that might create hostility between said deponent and the party seeking the deposition, such potential hostility was deemed sufficient to meet the "special circumstances" requirement. Over time, a trend seemed to develop, with courts construing subdivision (a)(4) liberally.[17]

Then, a 1984 amendment removed the requirement for a finding on motion of "adequate special circumstances" and inserted the current formulation. The legislature's aim was to achieve greater liberalization, such as obtained in this area in the federal courts. On the face of the amended statute, the party seeking disclosure need no longer show "special circumstances"; "inasmuch as the 'circumstances' no longer have to be 'special,'" it was thought, "the interpretation of the amended paragraph (4) should be even more generous."[18] Thus, "[i]f a witness holds the key, or merely a key, to any substantial fact involved in the case, a lawyer should not be compelled to go to trial without knowing intimately what that witness is going to say."[19]

This interpretation of the revised CPLR 3101(a)(4) has not, however, been universally accepted. It was, for example, held in 1988 (after the amendment) that a showing is necessary beyond merely that the testimony

---

17   *See BAII Banking Corp. v. Northville Indus. Corp.*, 204 A.D.2d 223, 612 N.Y.S.2d 141 (1st Dep't 1994) (discussing the liberal interpretation of the pre-1984 version of CPLR 3101(a)(4) and citing *Slabakis v. Drizin*, 107 A.D.2d 45, 485 N.Y.S.2d 270 (1st Dep't 1985), which applied the pre-1984 statute); Siegel, McKinney's Practice Commentary, CPLR 3101, at 32–34 (1991).

18   *BAII Banking Corp.*, 204 A.D.2d at 225.

19   Siegel, McKinney's Practice Commentary, CPLR 3101, at 33 (1991). "Disclosure against a nonparty witness should be virtually as broad in the state practice as it is in the federal. The only barrier is CPLR 3101(a)(4), and that is truly a nominal one." *Id. See* 6 Jack B. Weinstein, et al., New York Civil Practice ¶ 3101.33a, at 31-78 (2004) (noting aim of Advisory Committee on Civil Practice to liberalize disclosure by eliminating need for a court order finding special circumstances).

sought would be relevant and material.[20] Various decisions, particularly in the Second Department, have held that a showing of "special circumstances" is still required despite the legislature's deletion of that phrase.[21] Such circumstances can be shown, one decision stated, by a demonstration that the information cannot be obtained from any other sources.[22] In mid-2004, the Second Department continued to adhere to a "special circumstances" requirement.[23]

Significantly, the First Department has expressly rejected the Second Department's approach to this issue. The First Department specifically adheres to its own line of cases, which say that after 1984 there is no longer any necessity for *special* circumstances. However, it has also held that a subpoena *duces tecum* with notice of deposition is facially defective if it fails to comply with the CPLR 3101(a)(4) mandate to set forth any "circumstances or reasons" the disclosure is sought or required.[24]

When it comes to objecting to the form of a deposition notice, counsel cannot be complacent, as all "errors and irregularities" in the deposition

---

20   *Dioguardi v. St. John's Riverside Hosp.*, 144 A.D.2d 333, 533 N.Y.S.2d 915 (2d Dep't 1988).

21   *Bostrom v. William Penn Life Ins. Co.*, 285 A.D.2d 482, 727 N.Y.S.2d 160 (2d Dep't 2001); *Provident Life & Cas. Ins. Co. v. Brittenham*, 283 A.D.2d 629, 725 N.Y.S.2d 84 (2d Dep't 2001); *Cavaretta v. George*, 270 A.D.2d 862, 706 N.Y.S.2d 291 (4th Dep't 2000); *Mikinberg v. Bronsther*, 256 A.D.2d 501, 682 N.Y.S.2d 416 (2d Dep't 1998); *Maxwell v. Snapper, Inc.*, 249 A.D.2d 374, 671 N.Y.S.2d 127 (2d Dep't 1998); *Sand v. Chapin*, 246 A.D.2d 876, 667 N.Y.S.2d 800 (3d Dep't 1998).

22   *Bostrom*, 285 A.D.2d 482 (deposition of medical examiner allowed where autopsy report and amended death certificate did not contain bases for conclusion of suicide); *see Provident Life & Cas. Ins. Co.*, 283 A.D.2d 629 (plaintiff failed to show special circumstances); *Mikinberg*, 256 A.D.2d 501 (special circumstances shown as to nonparty physician who had referred plaintiff to other doctors for the medical problem at issue and who had originally been sued but as to whom the case had later been discontinued); *Maxwell*, 249 A.D.2d 374; *Sand*, 246 A.D.2d 876 (plaintiff failed to show special circumstances to justify deposing former co-workers).

23   *Tannenbaum v. Tenenbaum*, 8 A.D.3d 360, 777 N.Y.S.2d 769 (2d Dep't 2004) (defendant failed to show special circumstances). *See also Brooklyn Floor Maint. Co. v. Providence Wash. Ins. Co.*, 296 A.D.2d 520, 745 N.Y.S.2d 208 (2d Dep't 2002) (special circumstances shown where plaintiff's principal had been unable at his deposition to answer basic questions regarding bookkeeping practices and entries).

24   *Schroder v. Consol. Edison Co.*, 249 A.D.2d 69, 670 N.Y.S.2d 856 (1st Dep't 1998); *see also Ilas v. Nihagen & Co.*, 303 A.D.2d 298, 756 N.Y.S.2d 573 (1st Dep't 2003); *Crespo v. Monterey Assocs. Ltd.*, 302 A.D.2d 206, 753 N.Y.S.2d 373 (1st Dep't 2003) (testimony material and necessary as to plaintiff's physical condition); *Capati v. Crunch Fitness Int'l, Inc.*, 295 A.D.2d 181, 743 N.Y.S.2d 474 (1st Dep't 2002). For a similar holding in the Fourth Department, see *Catalano v. Moreland*, 299 A.D.2d 881, 750 N.Y.S.2d 209 (4th Dep't 2002) (special circumstances not required; plaintiffs failed to demonstrate that the discovery they sought was material and necessary).

notice are waived unless a written objection is served on the deposing party at least three days prior to the deposition date.[25]

B. Priority in State Practice

Rule 3106(a) of the CPLR governs the normal priority in the taking of depositions once an action is instituted. Until the defendant's time for serving an answer has expired, the plaintiff may not obtain a deposition of the defendant by notice; rather, a court order for the deposition of a party is required. The defendant, however, may obtain a deposition by notice alone, either with or prior to service of the answer. If the defendant seeks a deposition of plaintiff, the plaintiff may serve a cross-notice without a court order.[26] If the defendant's time to answer expires without either party having demanded a deposition, the priority is accorded to the first party who notices a deposition.[27]

Priority is accorded the defendant on the theory that defendant is blameless of the accusations made in the complaint until plaintiff proves otherwise. Thus, absent special circumstances, the defendant should be able to take depositions first to find out what the case is about.[28]

Plaintiff may serve a notice of deposition on a nonparty prior to the expiration of defendant's time to answer,[29] although this does not occur frequently.

A party with priority cannot use this right to obstruct discovery. The party cannot serve a notice for a date inordinately far in the future. A party cannot seek to maintain priority yet fail to pursue the discovery dili-

---

25   CPLR 3112.

26   Siegel, McKinney's Practice Commentary, CPLR 3106, at 431 (1991).

27   *Scalone v. Phelps Mem'l Hosp. Ctr.*, 184 A.D.2d 65, 591 N.Y.S.2d 419 (2d Dep't 1992); *Hakim Consultants, Ltd. v. Formosa, Ltd.*, 175 A.D.2d 759, 573 N.Y.S.2d 510 (1st Dep't 1991); *Church & Dwight Co. v. UDDO & Assocs., Inc.*, 159 A.D.2d 275, 552 N.Y.S.2d 277 (1st Dep't 1990); *SPA Realty Assocs. v. Springs Assocs.*, 155 A.D.2d 839, 548 N.Y.S.2d 100 (3d Dep't 1989), *modified on other grounds*, 178 A.D.2d 817, 577 N.Y.S.2d 536 (3d Dep't 1991); *Preferred Equities Corp. v. Ziegelman*, 155 A.D.2d 424, 547 N.Y.S.2d 355 (2d Dep't 1989); *Bucci v. Lydon*, 116 A.D.2d 520, 497 N.Y.S.2d 669 (1st Dep't 1986); *Rapillo v. Saint Barnabas Hosp.*, 93 A.D.2d 760, 461 N.Y.S.2d 319 (1st Dep't 1983). The defendant's priority continues if the time to answer is extended.

28   *Rapillo*, 93 A.D.2d 760; *Allis-Chalmers Corp. v. United States Steel Corp.*, 94 Misc. 2d 865, 405 N.Y.S.2d 924 (Sup. Ct., N.Y. Co. 1978).

29   Siegel, McKinney's Practice Commentary, CPLR 3106, at 431 (1991).

gently.[30] The priority does not mean that another party may undertake no discovery until the party with priority has substantially or entirely completed its discovery or its depositions.[31] These matters will frequently be regulated by agreement of the parties, by a preliminary conference or by a court's discovery order. The court also may regulate the priority of depositions through the use of protective orders.[32] Upon a showing of special circumstances, as when the facts in the case are wholly within the knowledge of one party, priority of deposition may be given to the other party.[33]

As noted in chapter 1, the normal discovery period concludes on the filing of the note of issue,[34] which places the case on the trial calendar. The filing party must also file a certificate of readiness.[35] This certificate is, in effect, a declaration that discovery has been completed and the case is ready for trial. Depositions should no longer be an issue at this point.[36] Some additional discovery may occur but only upon a showing of special or extraordinary circumstances.

---

30 *Grosso Moving & Packing Co. v. Damens*, 261 A.D.2d 339, 691 N.Y.S.2d 426 (1st Dep't 1999); *Bucci*, 116 A.D.2d 520; *Allis-Chalmers Corp.*, 94 Misc. 2d 865.

31 *Fox v. Fox*, 96 A.D.2d 571, 573, 465 N.Y.S.2d 260 (2d Dep't 1983) (party with priority "may clearly not maintain . . . priority indefinitely by conducting protracted depositions"). In *Allis-Chalmers Corp.*, 94 Misc. 2d at 867, Justice Kassal stated:

> To permit a defendant to indefinitely depose a plaintiff's witnesses while barring reciprocal action, may well delay the resolution of many issues which could be resolved by plaintiff deposing defendant. This is so since plaintiff's deposition of the defendant may reveal that the plaintiff sued the wrong party or some other legal infirmity, warranting discontinuance of one or more of the claims in the complaint. . . . The test of reasonableness in disclosure dictates the conclusion that "[a]n adversary need not remain inactive in terms of trial preparation while his opponent completes his disclosure proceedings."

> *See Erwin Pearl, Inc. v. Burroughs Corp.*, 95 Misc. 2d 157, 407 N.Y.S.2d 101 (Sup. Ct., N.Y. Co. 1978) (Kassal, J.).

32 *Scalone*, 184 A.D.2d 65; *Church & Dwight Co.*, 159 A.D.2d 275 (defendant relied on promises by plaintiff with regard to responses to certain invoices).

33 *Preferred Equities Corp. v. Ziegelman*, 155 A.D.2d 424, 547 N.Y.S.2d 355 (2d Dep't 1989); *NOPA Realty Corp. v. Cent. Caterers, Inc.*, 91 A.D.2d 991, 457 N.Y.S.2d 851 (2d Dep't 1983); *Halitzer v. Ginsberg*, 80 A.D.2d 771, 436 N.Y.S.2d 738 (1st Dep't 1981).

34 See Appendix, "Note of Issue" (state form).

35 Uniform Rule 202.21(a). See Appendix, "Certificate of Readiness" (state form).

36 *See Kozuch v. Certified Ambulance Group, Inc.*, 301 A.D.2d 840, 753 N.Y.S.2d 612 (3d Dep't 2003); *Andujar v. Benenson Inv. Co.*, 299 A.D.2d 503, 750 N.Y.S.2d 636 (2d Dep't 2002).

C. Depositions by Nonstenographic Means

A few decades ago, nonstenographic means for the taking of depositions were rarely employed. Technology, of course, has come a long way since then. Court rules, both federal and state, reflect this reality.

Although the CPLR has for some time allowed for recording of depositions by stenographic or other means,[37] it was expanded only recently to provide that the parties may stipulate that a deposition be taken by telephone or other remote electronic means and that a party may participate electronically.[38] *Remote electronic means* would include live video conferencing, in which participants located in different places are connected together by a video link, with each being able to see and hear the others.[39] This technology, already widely used in many corporations and government agencies, is destined to become even more common in litigation.

Telephonic and other technologies give rise to technical questions as to how the deposition is to be conducted and recorded. For example, may the officer before whom the deposition is to be taken be located somewhere other than the room in which the witness and his or her counsel are present? How are documents to be presented to the witness for interrogation about them and how are they to be marked? Some attorneys will no doubt prefer to conduct depositions in the traditional deposition room rather than by remote means when many documents are involved or when the deponent is an important witness. If a key objective of the interrogating attorney is to lay the groundwork for undermining the credibility of the deponent at trial by intense questioning about documents, a deposition by remote means may not be preferable.

Under the statute, the stipulation must (1) establish reasonable procedures to ensure the accuracy of the record and the use of exhibits, (2) specify who must and who may be present and (3) address other appropriate conditions.[40] Unless the parties stipulate otherwise, the officer before whom the deposition is to be taken shall be physically present at the place of

---

37   *See* CPLR 3113(b).

38   CPLR 3113(d), added by 2004 N.Y. Laws ch. 66 (eff. Jan. 1, 2005).

39   *See Rogovin v. Rogovin*, 3 A.D.3d 352, 770 N.Y.S.2d 342 (1st Dep't 2004).

40   CPLR 3113(d).

deposition, which is consistent with what has been held to be the contemplation of CPLR 3113(b).[41]

Subdivision (d) is silent as to what is to occur if the parties are unable to agree to depositions by remote electronic means. The court has the power to issue appropriate protective orders to ensure a just and efficient discovery process depending upon the circumstances of the case,[42] which might include authorizing the use of such means. Will a protective order be available after January 1, 2005 (the effective date of CPLR 3113(d)), to authorize use of such means if all parties are not in accord? If a nonresident party seeks a protective order against a deposition in New York on grounds of serious hardship, may the court, if persuaded of the merit of the application, direct that a deposition proceed by live video conference instead?[43] Would the court's choices in such a situation be limited to denying the application or ordering the deposition to be taken at the movant's place of residence?

One might argue that by providing for depositions by telephone or other remote electronic means by stipulation but omitting provision for a court order, the legislature was impliedly indicating its wish that such means not be permitted by court order absent agreement. On the other hand, CPLR 3103, of course, was already on the books and its authority very well recognized at the time of the 2004 amendment.[44]

---

41   *See Washington v. Montefiore Hosp.*, 7 A.D.3d 945, 777 N.Y.S.2d 524 (3d Dep't 2004) (violation of procedural requirements for court reporter not to be present in the office where the deponent was located, but rather in another office participating over the phone). Under CPLR 3113(d), any additional deposition expenses shall be borne by the party who requested that the deposition be conducted by remote means, unless the parties agree otherwise.

42   CPLR 3103.

43   *See Rogovin*, 3 A.D.3d 352 (trial court properly granted a protective order directing that a deposition be conducted by live video conference of defendant, who had sole responsibility for a daughter with special needs and an elderly and ailing grandmother and thus whose travel to New York from Kansas would have been a hardship).

44   *See* Vincent C. Alexander, *New York Practice: New Legislation*, N.Y.L.J., at 2 (Sept. 20, 2004) (noting that at least one prior version of the legislation had included authorization for a court order and stating that the deletion suggests a deliberate decision to deny such authority). Compare FRCP 30(b)(7) (parties may stipulate to, or a court upon motion may order that, deposition be taken by telephone or other remote electronic means). Professor Siegel writes: "Suppose a case with a dozen parties and all but one signs the stipulation. It seems to us that with a sound exercise of discretion that meets any reasonable objection the balking party may have, the court should be able with a protective order to prevent the sour apple from spoiling the whole batch." David D. Siegel, *Siegel's Practice Review* No. 149, at 1 (May 2004).

In state court, the taking of depositions by videotape is governed by a statewide rule,[45] which authorizes the use of videotape to record depositions, provided the taping is done in compliance with the rule. An inquiring party does not have to show special need in order to take a deposition by videotape. The deposition can be taken on tape even if the deponent is bashful or reluctant.[46] When some genuine abuse or harm may be threatened, the deponent may move for a protective order. The court has broad discretion to limit a deposition in order to avoid prejudice or undue burden or annoyance.[47]

Each notice or subpoena for a videotaped deposition must state that the deposition is to be recorded by videotape and must include the name, address and employer's name of the videotape operator, who may be an employee of the inquiring attorney.[48] Rules generally applicable to depositions shall apply.[49]

At the outset of the deposition and each new tape, the operator shall provide identifying information. The deposition shall be timed and the time recorded. More than one camera may be used. The witness shall be sworn on camera by an authorized officer.[50]

---

45   Uniform Rule 202.15.

46   *Jones v. Maples*, 257 A.D.2d 53, 691 N.Y.S.2d 429 (1st Dep't 1999); *Liebman & Charme v. Lanzoni*, 164 Misc. 2d 302, 303, 624 N.Y.S.2d 752 (Civ. Ct., N.Y. Co. 1995) (court refused to prohibit a deposition from being taped where the defendant deponent was a celebrity, but the court did indicate that dissemination of the recording might be barred on a showing (lacking here) of an actual risk of public dissemination); *Roche v. Udell*, 155 Misc. 2d 329, 588 N.Y.S.2d 76, 80 (Sup. Ct., Nassau Co. 1992).

47   CPLR 3103(a); *Jones*, 257 A.D.2d at 56. In *Jones*, unusual circumstances were held to require not only that the plaintiff be barred from videotaping defendant's deposition, but that he be required to proceed by written interrogatories instead.

48   Uniform Rule 202.15(c). See Appendix, "Notice of Deposition by Video" (state form).

49   Uniform Rule 202.15(b). In *Fajardo v. St. Joseph's Med. Ctr.*, 192 Misc. 2d 369, 746 N.Y.S.2d 779 (Sup. Ct., Bronx Co. 2002), the defendant noticed the deposition of plaintiff. Plaintiff served a notice pursuant to Uniform Rule 202.15 for the videotaping of her deposition, which she had previously reserved in a preliminary conference order. At the deposition, defendant refused to proceed to depose plaintiff on tape, though not objecting to plaintiff's taping of her own counsel's questioning of her. The court ruled that the entire deposition should have been taped and rejected the defendant's contention that it was being deprived of its right to depose plaintiff as it wished. The court found unduly cumbersome the bifurcation of the deposition into taped and stenographically recorded portions that defendant's position required. In view of plaintiff's illness and the fact that defendant had had an opportunity to question her, the court declined to order a second deposition.

50   Uniform Rule 202.15(d).

The officer must certify in writing to the accuracy of the video. The video must be shown to the witness as soon as possible after the taking of the deposition (unless the witness and parties waive doing so). The witness shall sign the certification.[51]

The rule contemplates that objections made at the deposition shall be resolved by a ruling rather than a formal motion. The tape, an audio version or a transcription of relevant portions, as the court directs, shall be submitted to the court upon the request of a party within ten days after the deposition, within such time as the parties stipulate or as soon as the objections may be heard. The court must rule on the objections prior to trial.[52]

The parties are advised to resolve the matter of objections soon after the deposition is completed. The rule does not specifically address this issue, but an objection ruled upon may have been accompanied by a direction not to answer (ideally, one made in good faith and with reasonable justification), and if the objection is overruled, the deposition may need to be reconvened. Early resolution of objections is generally helpful to all parties, to the discovery process and with respect to preparing for trial. Additionally, in some courts, cases may be reassigned upon the filing of the note of issue to a settlement part or a coordinating part and may well be tried before a different justice than the one who presided over the discovery process.

As discussed in chapter 5, objections at deposition should be limited to those directed to curable defects. Otherwise, objections are preserved until trial. Directions not to answer are highly restricted. Objections on the ground of irrelevance need not be made because they are preserved. Counsel should not direct the deponent not to answer on relevancy grounds unless the questions reach the level of being palpably irrelevant. Therefore, when the court is called upon to rule on the objections pursuant to Uniform Rule 202.15(g)(2), its determinations would not constitute a definitive declaration of the admissibility at trial of the parts of the transcript to which objections were not made.

The rules and procedures generally applicable to depositions and their admissibility shall govern the use of videotaped depositions at trial.[53]

---

51   Uniform Rule 202.15(d), (f). Parties may obtain copies of the tape or audio copies or may arrange to have a stenographic transcription made. Uniform Rule 202.15(e).

52   Uniform Rule 202.15(g).

53   Uniform Rule 202.15(i).

When the court rules on the objections raised at a videotaped deposition, it shall provide the parties with notice of its rulings and of any instructions it may make regarding editing. After the proponent of the deposition completes editing in accordance with the court's directions, he or she shall allow the adversary to view the edited tape.[54]

The procedures set out in Uniform Rule 202.15 also generally apply to audiotaped depositions. The notice of deposition must indicate that audiotaping will be used.[55] The cost of video- or audiotaping shall be borne by the noticing party. This would include the cost of furnishing a free copy of the tape to the opposing party.[56] The cost shall be a taxable disbursement unless the court orders otherwise.[57]

D. Depositions Outside New York

To depose nonparty witnesses in another state,[58] a party may use a commission, which may provide assistance should that party need to resort to the courts of the locality.[59] Of course, a commission may not be needed if the witness is willing to appear and testify voluntarily. If, however, an attorney in a New York action were to serve a subpoena upon a nonparty resident of another state and that person refused to appear for deposition, the New York court could not take action to enforce the subpoena. The New York court's writ would not run to residents of other jurisdictions that are not parties to the case. One would need to enforce the subpoena through a court of the other state.[60] Hence, the commission is used.

---

54   Uniform Rule 202.15(g)(3). The court may direct that portions ruled improper be deleted or that those portions be marked so that they can be skipped over by the operator at trial. *Id.* Producing an edited video may be more expensive than marking it, but, on the other hand, would avoid the potential for an error at trial, resulting in the jury's seeing and hearing improper material.

55   Uniform Rule 202.15(j). At least five days before the deposition date, any party may apply for an order establishing additional or alternate procedures. *Id.* A party might object and seek a video deposition instead.

56   *Kamp v. Miller*, 175 Misc. 2d 516, 670 N.Y.S.2d 670 (App. Term 1997).

57   Uniform Rule 202.15(k).

58   Deposition of nonresident parties is discussed *supra* in I.A.1.

59   CPLR 3108; *Meckert v. Sears Roebuck & Co.*, 275 A.D.2d 308, 712 N.Y.S.2d 56 (2d Dep't 2000); *Kekis v. Park Slope Emergency Physician Serv., P.C.*, 244 A.D.2d 463, 664 N.Y.S.2d 609 (2d Dep't 1997); *Mifsud v. City of New York*, 208 A.D.2d 701, 617 N.Y.S.2d 823 (2d Dep't 1994); *Stanzione v. Consumer Builders, Inc.*, 149 A.D.2d 682, 540 N.Y.S.2d 482 (2d Dep't 1989); Siegel, McKinney's Practice Commentary, CPLR 3108, at 461–62 (1991). See Appendix, "Commission" (state form).

60   *Wiseman v. Am. Motor Sales Corp.*, 103 A.D.2d 230, 479 N.Y.S.2d 528 (2d Dep't 1984).

A commission may be obtained by stipulation of the parties or by motion.[61] The issuance of a commission is a matter within the sound discretion of the court. The so-called open commission is one directed to an officer of another state requesting cooperation in carrying out a deposition on oral questions. A sealed commission is one providing for a deposition on written questions.[62] The party seeking the deposition generally will prefer an open commission because it provides a greater scope and opportunity for questioning.[63] The court also has broad discretion as to which sort of commission to authorize.[64] The commission is issued by the clerk of the court under the seal of the court upon order of the justice.

To depose nonparties abroad, one can use letters rogatory.[65] One may also seek depositions of nonparties or documents from them by means of the Hague Evidence Convention[66] and other international agreements.

The parties generally pay their own expenses for depositions taken outside the state. The prevailing party may tax costs and disbursements at the conclusion of the matter.[67]

II. FEDERAL PRACTICE

A. Disclosure Plans; Deposition Schedules; Limitations on Depositions

A party may orally depose any person without leave of court, except under certain circumstances.[68] However, generally speaking, depositions shall not be taken until the parties have conferred to map out a disclosure

---

61   *Kekis*, 244 A.D.2d 463; *Morgan v. Dell Publ'g Co.*, 185 A.D.2d 876, 586 N.Y.S.2d 1004 (2d Dep't 1992). See Appendix, "Motion for a Commission" (state form).

62   *Goldblatt v. Avis Rent A Car Sys.*, 223 A.D.2d 670, 637 N.Y.S.2d 188 (2d Dep't 1996); *Stanzione v. Consumer Builders, Inc.*, 149 A.D.2d 682, 540 N.Y.S.2d 482 (2d Dep't 1989); *Wiseman*, 103 A.D.2d 230.

63   *Wiseman*, 103 A.D.2d 230.

64   6 Jack B.Weinstein et al., New York Civil Practice ¶ 3108.05 (2002).

65   CPLR 3108; *Cavaretta v. George*, 270 A.D.2d 862, 706 N.Y.S.2d 291 (4th Dep't 2000); *Wiseman*, 103 A.D.2d 230; Siegel, McKinney's Practice Commentary, CPLR 3108, at 463–64 (1991).

66   Hague Convention on the Taking of Evidence Abroad in Civil or Commercial Matters, 23 U.S.T. 2555, T.I.A.S. No. 7444, *reprinted under* 28 U.S.C. § 1781; *see Societe Nationale Industrielle Aerospatiale v. United States Dist. Court*, 482 U.S. 522 (1987); *Wilson v. Lufthansa German Airlines*, 108 A.D.2d 393, 489 N.Y.S.2d 575 (2d Dep't 1985).

67   Siegel, McKinney's Practice Commentary, CPLR 3108, at 462 (1991).

68   FRCP 30(a).

plan, unless leave of court is granted or the parties stipulate.[69] As mentioned in chapter 1, the parties must confer at least 21 days before a scheduling conference is held or a scheduling order is due under FRCP 16(b) and, when appropriate, they must submit a plan to the court within 14 days after the conference.[70] The result is a discovery schedule that fits the case—either a comprehensive schedule or one involving stages or discrete disclosure elements. Generally, depositions or a series of them will form a major part of this plan.

Absent court order otherwise, methods of discovery may be used in any sequence, and the conduct of discovery by one party, including depositions, does not operate to delay discovery by any other party.[71] The current rule was enacted to eliminate a priority system for the taking of depositions and the resulting race to depose.[72] Most frequently, the timetable for discovery is reviewed at the initial pretrial conference. In any event, an outside date for completion is made part of the order. Most of the priority issues are usually resolved between counsel and without the need for the court's intervention.

If a party seeks to depose a person who has already been deposed, leave of court or a stipulation is required.[73] Repetitive depositions should be avoided. Therefore, the party seeking to re-depose a witness must demonstrate a true need for doing so. Decisions with regard to discovery requests are in the discretion of the court, including with respect to whether a witness should be re-deposed.[74] If there is a second deposition, the court may well limit the areas to be covered, excluding those covered in the first session as well as the time allotted.[75]

The number of depositions that plaintiffs, defendants or third-party defendants may take without court approval or a stipulation is ten.[76] The limitation applies to a "side." In considering a request to exceed the limit,

---

69　FRCP 26(d) generally bars depositions and other discovery before the FRCP 26(f) conference unless the court orders otherwise or the parties agree. FRCP 30(a)(2)(C) is to like effect.

70　FRCP 26(f).

71　FRCP 26(d).

72　*Keller v. Edwards*, 206 F.R.D. 412, 415 (D. Md. 2002).

73　FRCP 30(a)(2)(B).

74　*Innomed Labs, LLC v. Alza Corp.*, 211 F.R.D. 237, 239–40 (S.D.N.Y. 2002); *Keller*, 206 F.R.D. at 416; *Tri-Star Pictures, Inc. v. Unger*, 171 F.R.D. 94, 101–103 (S.D.N.Y. 1997).

75　*Tri-Star Pictures, Inc.*, 171 F.R.D. at 102–103.

76　FRCP 30(a)(2)(A).

the court will evaluate cumulativeness, duplicativeness, convenience, burden, expense and other factors set out in FRCP 26(b)(2). A party seeking to exceed the limit must demonstrate the necessity for each deposition taken without leave of court.[77] The party must demonstrate in specific fashion that the proposed depositions are needed and will not be cumulative or repetitive; conclusory assertions of necessity will not suffice.[78]

The time allotted for each deposition is also limited:

> Unless otherwise authorized by the court or stipulated by the parties, a deposition is limited to one day of seven hours. The court must allow additional time consistent with Rule 26(b)(2) if needed for a fair examination of the deponent or if the deponent or another person, or other circumstance, impedes or delays the examination.[79]

When a party seeks after the close of discovery to take depositions beyond the allowed ten or the number set forth in the discovery schedule, that party must show, in addition to the need for more depositions, diligence in pursuit of the discovery.[80] One court observed: "A magistrate judge's scheduling order 'is not a frivolous piece of paper, idly entered, which can be cavalierly disregarded by counsel without peril.'"[81] The flouting of discovery deadlines will cause serious harm not only to the parties, the court noted, but also to the stature and integrity of the judicial system. Therefore, the court denied a request to take depositions after the

---

77 *Barrow v. Greenville Indep. Sch. Dist.*, 202 F.R.D. 480, 482–83 (N.D. Tex. 2001); *Dixon v. Certainteed Corp.*, 164 F.R.D. 685, 692 (D. Kan. 1996).

78 *Barrow*, 202 F.R.D. at 483–84; *Advanced Sterilization Prods. v. Jacob*, 190 F.R.D. 284 (D. Mass. 2000) (must state particular number of additional depositions sought, not merely request extension of discovery period); *Archer Daniels Midland Co. v. Aon Risk Servs., Inc.*, 187 F.R.D. 578, 586 (D. Minn. 1999); *see Pedraza v. Holiday Housewares, Inc.*, 203 F.R.D. 40, 42 (D. Mass. 2001) (motion denied; "possible fishing expedition").

79 FRCP 30(d)(2); *see Miller v. Waseca Med. Ctr.*, 205 F.R.D. 537, 538–39 (D. Minn. 2002).

80 *Mitchell v. AMTRAK*, 208 F.R.D. 455, 462 (D.D.C. 2002) (though plaintiff knew about witnesses before, plaintiff had been limited to five depositions and the two supervisors deposed had had little knowledge); *Integra Lifesciences I, Ltd. v. Merck KgaA*, 190 F.R.D. 556, 558–60 (S.D. Cal. 1999) (diligence not shown).

81 *Widhelm v. Wal-Mart Stores*, 162 F.R.D. 591, 593 (D. Neb. 1995) (quoting *Gestetner Corp. v. Case Equip. Co.*, 108 F.R.D. 138, 141 (D. Me. 1985)).

close of discovery where the plaintiff failed to show good cause why she had not complied with the scheduling order.[82]

Although a court will usually set a deadline for the completion of all discovery, it can permit, either initially or at a later stage, a particular deposition to be concluded by a date beyond the general deadline. A court might go beyond the deadline, for example, in admiralty cases, in which witnesses are frequently abroad and, as a result, delays in taking a deposition are anticipated. A court need not so extend the deadline, however; this extension is a matter within the court's broad discretion over discovery and case scheduling. If the court sets the deadline for all depositions and a party fails to complete a deposition within that period, a court might well be unpersuaded by an argument that the deposition now sought is essential to the conduct of the trial. The argument that it is a "trial deposition" may not work, because the rules do not distinguish between *regular* (i.e., discovery) depositions and *trial* depositions.[83]

A party is not excluded from taking a deposition even of counsel for the adversary, as FRCP 30 authorizes a deposition of "any person." As one would expect, however, depositions of opposing counsel are discouraged.[84] The party seeking the deposition must establish a basis for this unusual form of discovery.[85] In *Shelton*, the court stated that it viewed the "practice of taking opposing counsel's deposition as a negative development in the area of litigation, and one that should be employed only in limited circumstances."[86] The circumstances, the court concluded, should be confined to instances in which the party seeking the deposition has shown

---

82 *Id.*; *see Wayne v. Jarvis*, 197 F.3d 1098, 1106–1107 (11th Cir. 1999) (plaintiff failed to pursue deposition in timely fashion during scheduled discovery period); *Zhou v. Pittsburg State Univ.*, 252 F. Supp. 2d 1194, 1206–1207 (D. Kan. 2003); *West v. Media Gen. Operations, Inc.*, 250 F. Supp. 2d 923, 939–40 (E.D. Tenn. 2002).

83 *See, e.g., Chrysler Int'l Corp. v. Chemaly*, 280 F.3d 1358, 1359–62 (11th Cir. 2002); *Integra Lifesciences I*, 190 F.R.D. at 558–60.

84 *United States v. Yonkers Bd. of Educ.*, 946 F.2d 180, 185 (2d Cir. 1991).

85 *Shelton v. Am. Motors Corp.*, 805 F.2d 1323, 1327 (8th Cir. 1986); *Epling v. UCB Films, Inc.*, 204 F.R.D. 691, 693 (D. Kan. 2002); *Jennings v. Family Mgmt.*, 201 F.R.D. 272, 276–77 (D.D.C. 2001).

86 *Id.* at 1327.

that no other means exist to obtain the information and the information sought is relevant, not privileged and crucial to preparation of the case.[87]

In *In re Subpoena to Dennis Friedman*,[88] the Second Circuit concurred with the notion that depositions of opposing counsel are disfavored but declined to adopt the *Shelton* test, stating that "the disfavor with which the practice of seeking discovery from adversary counsel is regarded is not a talisman for the resolution of all controversies of this nature" and articulating instead the need for "a flexible approach to the issue of lawyer depositions."[89]

B. Deposition Notice

"Reasonable" written notice of the deposition must be provided to all parties.[90] The notice must state (1) the time and place of the deposition; (2) the name and address of each deponent, if known, or a description, if not; and (3) the method of recording to be used. The notice need not set forth the matters about which the witness will be examined.

A notice directed to a party may be accompanied by a request for the production of documents at the taking of the deposition.[91] Such request shall be made in accordance with FRCP 34.[92]

---

87   *Id.* (showing not made); *compare In re Tutu Water Wells Contamination*, 184 F.R.D. 266, 267 n.1 (D.V.I. 1999) (deposition of attorney allowed where involved in underlying transactions). *See Pamida, Inc. v. E.S. Originals, Inc.*, 281 F.3d 726 (8th Cir. 2002) (information concerning prior completed lawsuit); *New York v. Solvent Chem. Co.*, 214 F.R.D. 106, 111–12 (W.D.N.Y. 2003) (showing not made); *Epling*, 204 F.R.D. at 695 (plaintiffs failed to show that the proposed witness was the exclusive repository of the information sought); *Jennings*, 201 F.R.D. 272 (deposition allowed where counsel was a guardian and the best and perhaps sole source of information on the ward's past state of mind and abilities); *Frazier v. S.E. Pa. Transp. Auth.*, 161 F.R.D. 309, 313 (E.D. Pa. 1995).

88   350 F.3d 65 (2d Cir. 2003).

89   *Id.* at 71–72 (*dicta*).

90   FRCP 30(b)(1). See Appendix, "Notice of Deposition" (federal form).

91   FRCP 30(b)(5).

92   Document production at, as well as in preparation for, depositions is discussed in detail in chapter 3. See Appendix, "Notice of Deposition and Document Request" and "Document Request (FRCP 34)" (federal forms).

A written notice of deposition is required. It can be dispensed with only in very unusual circumstances.[93] An improper notice can invalidate the deposition.[94]

When the plaintiff is the deponent, the deposition generally will take place in the forum where the litigation is pending. The deposition of the nonresident defendant generally will occur at the place of residence. The deposition of a corporate party usually will be taken at its principal place of business. The district court, however, has great discretion over questions of place and timing for depositions.[95] Absent stipulation, these matters may be resolved by protective order.[96]

In order to depose a person who is not a party to the case, counsel must, of course, serve a subpoena on the person pursuant to FRCP 45.[97] That rule limits the place of deposition of such a witness, absent consent, to a location within 100 miles of the person's place of employment or residence. If a subpoena *duces tecum* is to be served on a person to be examined, the document list as set forth in the subpoena shall be attached to or included in the notice.[98]

A deposition of a corporation or other entity may be taken pursuant to FRCP 30(a)(1) and 30(b)(1). The notice should identify the entity as the deponent and name the person through whom it is to testify.[99] This person must be an officer, director or managing agent. The notice need not identify the matters on which the person is expected to testify.[100] If the examiner is unaware of the proper person to depose on the entity's behalf, he or she may proceed by FRCP 30(b)(6). As discussed in greater detail later in this chapter,[101] this rule requires the examiner to identify in the notice of

---

93   *Lauson v. Stop-N-Go Foods, Inc.*, 133 F.R.D. 92 (W.D.N.Y. 1990); *C&F Packing Co. v. Doskocil Cos.*, 126 F.R.D. 662, 678 (N.D. Ill. 1989).

94   *Howard v. Everex Sys., Inc.*, 228 F.3d 1057 (9th Cir. 2000); *Lauson*, 133 F.R.D. 92; *C&F Packing Co.*, 126 F.R.D. at 680.

95   *In re Standard Metals Corp.*, 817 F.2d 625, 628 (10th Cir. 1987).

96   See discussion in chapter 6.

97   See Appendix, "Subpoena" (federal form).

98   See Appendix, "Subpoena Duces Tecum" (federal form).

99   *Operative Plasterers' & Cement Masons' Int'l Ass'n v. Benjamin*, 144 F.R.D. 87, 90 (N.D. Ind. 1992).

100   *Id.*

101   See *infra* II.D.

deposition the matters on which testimony is sought from the entity and requires the entity to produce the appropriate knowledgeable person(s).[102]

C. Means for Taking the Deposition

The notice of deposition must state the means by which the deposition will be recorded.[103] The usual method, of course, is the traditional stenographic transcript. The rule, though, expressly authorizes recording by sound or sound-and-visual means unless the court orders otherwise. A court might direct that a particular method be used, depending on the circumstances of a given case. The cost of recording the deposition must be borne by the party taking it.[104]

The parties can stipulate to the taking of a deposition by telephone or other remote electronic means. The court may also order this method upon motion.[105] Attorneys using such means should be alert to the question of where the reporter should be located.[106]

Videotaped depositions, the federal courts recognize, are quite useful: "In general, video depositions provide greater accuracy and trustworthiness than a stenographic deposition because the viewer can employ more of his senses in interpreting the information from the deposition."[107] A written transcript is a cold record; a videotape, on the other hand, provides a unique report of the witness's demeanor and appearance.[108] Although a video deposition may be important when the deponent will be unavailable at trial, it can also be most useful even when the witness will certainly be present. Because it reveals "body language," gestures, inflection and other visual and sound clues that bear on credibility, it can be most helpful to an attorney seeking to impeach the deponent. On the other hand, it can also

---

102 *Operative Plasterers' & Cement Masons' Int'l Ass'n*, 144 F.R.D. at 89–90.

103 FRCP 30(b)(2).

104 *Id.*

105 FRCP 30(b)(7).

106 *Aquino v. Automotive Serv. Indus. Ass'n*, 93 F. Supp. 2d 922, 923–24 (N.D. Ill. 2000) (strict compliance with the federal rules probably requires that the court reporter be located in the same place as the deponent).

107 *Burlington City Bd. of Educ. v. U.S. Mineral Prods. Co.*, 115 F.R.D. 188, 189 (M.D.N.C. 1987). See Appendix, "Notice of Deposition by Video" (federal form).

108 *Fanelli v. Centenary College*, 211 F.R.D. 268, 270 (D.N.J. 2002).

limit the chances for impeachment if the witness testifies credibly at the deposition.[109]

A party or witness may seek a protective order against the use of videotape. However, the burden is on the movant to establish good cause for barring use of videotape. In this regard, vague assertions of harm will be insufficient; rather, concrete and serious harm must be identified with specificity.[110] A generalized concern for privacy will not suffice.[111] When concerns about privacy of particular testimony are raised, they may be addressed by means of a confidentiality order and, if necessary, the sealing of particular portions.[112]

Telephonic depositions lack the advantages of the video deposition but can minimize expenses and may be useful as a cost-saving measure for less important witnesses and in cases of modest size. Some courts have held that telephonic depositions should be liberally allowed.[113] Others hold that, absent extreme hardship, a nonresident plaintiff should appear in the forum for deposition.[114]

A party may arrange for a transcription to be made from a nonstenographic record of a deposition.[115] A party on notice may designate another method in addition to that specified in the notice of deposition.[116]

---

109   *Id.; Wilson v. Olathe Bank*, 184 F.R.D. 395 (D. Kan. 1999); *Alexander v. FBI*, 186 F.R.D. 123, 127 (D.D.C. 1998); *Riley v. Murdock*, 156 F.R.D. 130 (E.D.N.C. 1994); *Burlington City Bd. of Educ.*, 115 F.R.D. at 189.

110   *Fanelli*, 211 F.R.D. at 270 (showing found wanting where plaintiff suffering from clinical depression asserted that a videotaped deposition would cause increased anxiety); *Wilson*, 184 F.R.D. at 397.

111   *Flaherty v. Seroussi*, 209 F.R.D. 295, 299 (N.D.N.Y. 2001); *Burlington City Bd. of Educ.*, 115 F.R.D. at 191.

112   *Alexander*, 186 F.R.D. at 127; *see Flaherty*, 209 F.R.D. at 299 (no showing of intent to use video for commercial purpose; public interest in case involving government official; court refused to bar release of video to news media); *Burlington City Bd. of Educ.*, 115 F.R.D. at 191 (showing of intent to use video for ulterior purpose might bar that recording method).

113   *Rehau, Inc. v. Colortech, Inc.*, 145 F.R.D. 444 (W.D. Mich. 1993) (two telephonic depositions ordered of witnesses in Europe who were officers, directors or managing agents of plaintiff); *Jahr v. IU Int'l Corp.*, 109 F.R.D. 429 (M.D.N.C. 1986).

114   *United States v. Rock Springs Vista Dev.*, 185 F.R.D. 603 (D. Nev. 1999); *Clem v. Allied Van Lines Int'l Corp.*, 102 F.R.D. 938 (S.D.N.Y. 1984) (foreign country plaintiff).

115   FRCP 30(b)(2).

116   FRCP 30(b)(3).

The deposition must take place before a FRCP 28 officer.[117] The rule prohibits distortions of the appearance or demeanor of deponents at non-stenographic depositions.

D. Depositions of Corporations and Other Entities

The procedures for depositions of public or private corporations, partnerships, associations or governmental entities are set forth in FRCP 30(b)(6). This provision was added in 1970 to address certain problems. For example, a party seeking to depose a corporation might not know the name of an individual in the corporation having pertinent knowledge of the events or transactions at issue in the case or knowledge of record-keeping and document-retention procedures that might be important to the discovery process. The deposing party might try to guess at the right deponent in a deposition notice. Or, the party might simply name the corporation as the deponent. An opportunity would then arise, which was not always rejected, for the corporation to respond with a game of movable witnesses, with each referring at his or her deposition to someone else as the proper person to testify.[118] This sort of practice was unfair, expensive and inefficient. The prior procedure also burdened corporations acting in good faith by subjecting them to unnecessarily large numbers of depositions of officers and agents. Hence, the current provision was drafted.[119]

Under FRCP 30(b)(6), a party may name, say, a corporation as the deponent. The party's notice must then "describe with reasonable particularity the matters on which examination is requested."[120] In response, the corporation must designate one or more officers, directors, managing agents or others who consent to testify on its behalf. The corporation may set forth, as to each designee, the matters on which the person will testify. The designee "shall testify as to matters known or reasonably available to the organization."[121] A nonparty entity will also have to follow this designation

---

117   FRCP 30(b)(4). This rule also sets forth some mechanical aspects of the proceedings.

118   The Advisory Committee referred to this practice as "bandying." Notes of Advisory Committee on 1970 Amendments, FRCP 30. *See, e.g., Dwelly v. Yamaha Motor Corp.*, 214 F.R.D. 537, 540 (D. Minn. 2003).

119   Notes of Advisory Committee on 1970 Amendments, FRCP 30; *Folwell v. Sanchez Hernandez*, 210 F.R.D. 169, 172 (M.D.N.C. 2002); *Starlight Int'l Inc. v. Herlihy*, 186 F.R.D. 626, 638 (D. Kan. 1999); *United States v. Taylor*, 166 F.R.D. 356, 360 (M.D.N.C.), *aff'd, motion denied*, 166 F.R.D. 367 (M.D.N.C. 1996).

120   FRCP 30(b)(6). See Appendix, "Notice of Deposition (FRCP 30(b)(6))" (federal forms). The FRCP 30(b)(6) notice is discussed in more detail *infra* at II.D.2.

121   FRCP 30(b)(6).

and production procedure if served with a subpoena naming it as the deponent and advising it of this duty. By this rule, "a party may be assured that it will obtain the corporation's knowledge and position with respect to the case."[122] This reasoning applies even if the corporation no longer employs the persons who were involved in the events at issue.[123]

Basically, FRCP 30(b)(6) requires a two-step process. The rule only works well when both steps are carried out. "[T]he Rule only operates effectively when the requesting party specifically designates the topics for deposition, and when the responding party produces 'such number of persons as will satisfy the request,' and 'prepares[s] them so that they may give complete, knowledgeable and binding answers on behalf of the corporation.' "[124]

If an entity produces persons lacking knowledge or who are unprepared, that production is tantamount to a failure to appear at a deposition.[125] This failure is a result an attorney should most energetically wish to avoid, as it may justify a sanction under FRCP 37(d).[126]

A number of aspects of FRCP 30(b)(6) are worth emphasizing. The corporation or other entity must designate more than one person if necessary to provide information on the matters particularized by the inquiring

---

122 *Folwell*, 210 F.R.D. at 172; *see JPMorgan Chase Bank v. Liberty Mut. Ins. Co.*, 209 F.R.D. 361 (S.D.N.Y. 2002) (depositions, including 30(b)(6) depositions, are intended as means to discover facts, not contentions or legal theories).

123 As one court held:

> Rule 30(b)(6) is expressly designed to help plaintiffs in the situation . . . where employees who had knowledge of the facts are no longer employed or have been shifted elsewhere. A Rule 30(b)(6) deposition requires the corporation to obtain sufficient information to prepare an individual to testify on behalf of the corporation.

Folwell, 210 F.R.D. at 172.

124 *Dwelly v. Yamaha Motor Corp.*, 214 F.R.D. 537, 540 (D. Minn. 2003) (quoting *Marker v. Union Fid. Life Ins. Co.*, 125 F.R.D. 121, 126 (M.D.N.C. 1989)).

125 *Calzaturficio S.C.A.R.P.A., s.p.a. v. Fabiano Shoe Co.*, 201 F.R.D. 33, 37 (D. Mass. 2001); *Starlight Int'l Inc. v. Herlihy*, 186 F.R.D. 626, 639 (D. Kan. 1999); *Marker*, 125 F.R.D. at 126. If a party fails to prepare properly for its FRCP 30(b)(6) deposition, it may find that, should it attempt in response to a motion for summary judgment to provide a contradictory affidavit that contains the information that it should have been prepared for at the deposition, the court may disregard the affidavit. *Hyde v. Stanley Tools*, 107 F. Supp. 2d 992, 993 (E.D. La. 2000).

126 See discussion in chapter 7.

party.[127] The corporation may designate persons who are not officers, directors or managing agents, but their consent is required. A party is not prevented from taking a deposition pursuant to FRCP 30(a)(1) and 30(b)(1), provided the persons named are officers, directors or managing agents of the corporation.[128]

1. Corporate Designees

The mandate of FRCP 30(b)(6) that the corporation designate a person or persons to testify on its behalf is an affirmative and significant duty, which did not exist prior to 1970 and one which some entities may find uncomfortable even at this late date.[129] If the entity has no one already knowledgeable and able to testify about the matters listed, or has no one other than an attorney (whose knowledge may be limited to information covered by the attorney-client privilege or work product protection),[130] it nevertheless cannot avoid the deposition altogether. Rather, the entity must identify and prepare someone to testify as to the matters particularized in the notice.[131]

---

127 *Dwelly*, 214 F.R.D. at 540; *Starlight Int'l Inc.*, 186 F.R.D. at 638; *United States v. Taylor*, 166 F.R.D. 356, 360–61 (M.D.N.C.), *aff'd, motion denied*, 166 F.R.D. 367 (M.D.N.C. 1996); *Dravo Corp. v. Liberty Mut. Ins. Co.*, 164 F.R.D. 70, 75 (D. Neb. 1995); *Marker*, 125 F.R.D. at 126.

128 FRCP 30(b)(6). This rule "supplements the existing practice whereby the examining party designates the corporate official to be deposed." Notes of Advisory Committee on 1970 Amendments, FRCP 30; *see Folwell*, 210 F.R.D. at 173; *A.I.A. Holdings, S.A. v. Lehman Brothers, Inc.*, 2002 U.S. Dist. LEXIS 9218 (S.D.N.Y. May 23, 2002); *In re Honda Am. Motor Co.*, 168 F.R.D. 535, 540 (D. Md. 1996). The fact that the principal of an entity has been deposed in his or her individual capacity does not mean that there can be no FRCP 30(b)(6) deposition. An individual deposition provides the testimony and knowledge of the witness. A FRCP 30(b)(6) deposition represents the knowledge of the entity and is binding on it. *A.I.A. Holdings, S.A.*, 2002 U.S. Dist. LEXIS 9218, at *13–14; *Taylor*, 166 F.R.D. at 361–62. However, in the case of a small, closely held entity, there may be no difference between the knowledge of the entity and its principals. When a showing of such overlap is made, an entity could adopt as its own the testimony of a witness in an individual capacity. *A.I.A. Holdings, S.A.*, 2002 U.S. Dist. LEXIS 9218, at *13–14; *Twentieth Century Fox Film Corp. v. Marvel Enters., Inc.*, 2002 U.S. Dist. LEXIS 14682 (S.D.N.Y. Aug. 8, 2002); *Sabre v. First Dominion Capital, LLC*, 2001 U.S. Dist. LEXIS 20637 (S.D.N.Y. Dec. 12, 2001).

129 *In re Vitamins Antitrust Litig.*, 216 F.R.D. 168, 172–74 (D.D.C. 2003) (corporation mistaken in view that mere authentication of documents coupled with disavowal of their truth or accuracy satisfied FRCP 30(b)(6) obligation); *Starlight*, 186 F.R.D. 626 (failure twice to prepare witness adequately; plaintiff made to travel to England to depose a poorly prepared representative). It is not proper for an entity to seek to evade its duty by trying to force the party seeking a deposition to name the person(s) who ought to be designated. The burden rests on the entity. *Foster-Miller, Inc. v. Babcock & Wilcox Can.*, 210 F.3d 1, 17 (1st Cir. 2000).

130 *New York v. Solvent Chem. Co.*, 214 F.R.D. 106, 110–12 (W.D.N.Y. 2003).

131 *Dwelly*, 214 F.R.D. at 540; *Prokosch v. Catalina Lighting, Inc.*, 193 F.R.D. 633, 639 (D. Minn. 2000).

The person or persons named by the entity will not testify as individual witnesses. Rather, they will testify on behalf of the entity named in the deposition notice.[132] "In a Rule 30(b)(6) deposition, there is no distinction between the corporate representative and the corporation. 'The Rule 30(b)(6) designee does not give his personal opinion. Rather, he presents the corporation's "position" on the topic.' The designee testifies on behalf of the corporation and holds it accountable accordingly."[133] For this reason, the deposition of the entity counts as *one* for the purpose of the limit set forth in FRCP 30(a)(2)(A), regardless of how many persons the entity produces.[134] The testimony of the designated person(s) pursuant to FRCP 30(b)(6) will accordingly be binding upon the entity.[135]

Because the designees must testify as to matters "known or reasonably available to the organization," the entity must research what it knows or what is available to it. The persons to testify need not have personal knowledge of all issues at the outset but must educate themselves so as to be able to testify fully and unevasively and in a manner binding the entity.[136] "Corporations, partnerships, and joint ventures have a duty to make a conscientious, good-faith effort to designate knowledgeable persons for Rule 30(b)(6) depositions and to prepare them to fully and unevasively answer questions about the designated subject matter."[137] If a particular person is not suitable, the entity must designate someone else in addition to or in lieu of that person, if the knowledge exists or is reasonably available.[138] One court put it thus:

---

132   *Hyde v. Stanley Tools*, 107 F. Supp. 2d 992 (E.D. La. 2000); *Taylor*, 166 F.R.D. at 361.

133   *Hyde*, 107 F. Supp. 2d at 992–93 (citations omitted) (quoting *Taylor*, 166 F.R.D. at 361).

134   *Quality Aero Tech., Inc. v. Telemetrie Elektronik, Gmbh*, 212 F.R.D. 313, 319 (E.D.N.C. 2002).

135   *Hyde*, 107 F. Supp. 2d 992; *Taylor*, 166 F.R.D. at 361.

136   *Dwelly v. Yamaha Motor Corp.*, 214 F.R.D. 537, 540 (D. Minn. 2003); *Sanyo Laser Prods. Inc. v. Arista Records, Inc.*, 214 F.R.D. 496, 502–503 (S.D. Ind. 2003); *Starlight Int'l Inc. v. Herlihy*, 186 F.R.D. 626, 638–39 (D. Kan. 1999); *Nevada Power Co. v. Monsanto Co.*, 891 F. Supp. 1406, 1418 (D. Nev. 1995); *Marker v. Union Fid. Life Ins. Co.*, 125 F.R.D. 121, 126 (M.D.N.C. 1989); *see Gucci Am., Inc. v. Exclusive Imports Int'l*, 2002 U.S. Dist. LEXIS 14837 (S.D.N.Y. Aug. 13, 2002) (the witness must be knowledgeable, but need not be the most knowledgeable person possible); Sidney I. Schenkier, *Deposing Corporations and Other Fictive Persons: Some Thoughts on Rule 30(b)(6)*, Litig., Vol. 29, No. 2, at 20, 23 (Spring 2003) (the entity need not produce the "most knowledgeable" witness). The "burden of preparation is not required by the Rule, when another deponent, who does not require such preparation, may be designated as a successive deponent." *Dwelly*, 214 F.R.D. at 540 (successive deponents from abroad offered).

137   *Starlight Int'l Inc.*, 186 F.R.D. at 639.

138   *Prokosch v. Catalina Lighting, Inc.*, 193 F.R.D. 633, 638 (D. Minn. 2000).

> Rule 30(b)(6) explicitly requires [the company] to have persons testify on its behalf as to all matters known or reasonably available to it and, therefore, implicitly requires such persons to review all matters known or reasonably available to it in preparation for the Rule 30(b)(6) deposition. This interpretation is necessary in order to make the deposition a meaningful one and to prevent the "sandbagging" of an opponent by conducting a half-hearted inquiry before the deposition but a thorough and vigorous one before the trial. This would totally defeat the purpose of the discovery process.[139]

It is also necessary that the corporation or other entity prepare and testify so that the other parties to the case can understand the entity's version of the facts and conduct meaningful discovery in preparation for trial.[140] The obligation to review facts and to prepare requires examination of the depositions of previous fact witnesses, documents and exhibits and consultation with former employees.[141] It is not an acceptable answer for the deponent to state that corporate documents have been produced and that preparation of the witnesses was not necessary.[142] As noted, if relevant persons review the facts and documents and are unable to provide complete answers on issues designated, other persons should be made available in addition to or in lieu of those.

2. Notice

The notice is central to a deposition under FRCP 30(b)(6). The notice will determine the scope of preparation for the deposition and of the deposition itself.

The obligation that the deposing party identify with "reasonable particularity" the matters into which inquiry will be directed is important. Vague,

---

139 *United States v. Taylor*, 166 F.R.D. 356, 362 (M.D.N.C.), *aff'd, motion denied*, 166 F.R.D. 367 (M.D.N.C. 1996). At trial, a corporation can certainly argue against the factual conclusions asserted by an adversary from the adversary's evidence. But it cannot have its attorney contend "that the facts show a particular position on a topic when, at the Rule 30(b)(6) deposition, the corporation asserts no knowledge and no position." The corporation would have to make an evidentiary showing supporting such a change in position. *Id.* at 362 n.8.

140 *Calzaturficio S.C.A.R.P.A., s.p.a. v. Fabiano Shoe Co.*, 201 F.R.D. 33, 37 (D. Mass. 2001).

141 *Id.* at 37–39; *Prokosch*, 193 F.R.D. at 639; *Bank of New York v. Meridien Biao Bank Tanz.*, 171 F.R.D. 135, 151 (S.D.N.Y. 1997); *Taylor*, 166 F.R.D. at 362.

142 *Calzaturficio S.C.A.R.P.A. s.p.a.*, 201 F.R.D. at 38. *Compare United States v. Mass. Indus. Fin. Agency*, 162 F.R.D. 410, 412 (D. Mass. 1995).

generalized descriptions do not suffice.[143] Attorneys who skate very close to the line may prove themselves too clever and may, regrettably, witness the striking of the notice.

Also, lawyers have a tendency to cover many bases by incorporating in documents the phrase "including, but not limited to" or a variation on this theme; some courts have found such language deficient.[144] Such a notice may place the corporation or other entity in a difficult, or even impossible, position, because it effectively may require the corporation or entity to designate a person or persons to address the identified issues *and all other possible issues, whatever they might be.* The supposedly particularized notice is thus transformed into one of unlimited generality.

Beyond vagueness, the notice may contain defects of one sort or another, which may create problems for the preparation process, as well as the deposition itself. A notice might be overly extensive and burdensome or contain many irrelevant matters. The solution for such difficulties may lie in a motion for a protective order.[145]

A question that arises is, to what extent is the questioner bound by the FRCP 30(b)(6) designation of subjects to be covered? May the inquiry extend into matters not covered in the notice of deposition but relevant to the case? One court ruled that the FRCP 30(b)(6) notice of deposition limits the scope of questioning at the deposition.[146] The court reasoned that such a limitation is implied by the procedures set forth in the rule. The court also held, however, that counsel could not direct the witness not to answer questions beyond the scope of the notice.[147]

Other courts take the view that the notice should not be construed to limit the scope of questions at the deposition. These courts have read the "reasonable particularity" requirement as a way to ensure that a witness with knowledge is produced, making "the description of the scope of the

---

143 *Banks v. Office of Senate Sergeant-at-Arms*, 222 F.R.D. 7, 18–19 (D.D.C. 2004) (list of topics "absurdly overbroad"; stricken); *Dwelly v. Yamaha Motor Corp.*, 214 F.R.D. 537, 540 (D. Minn. 2003); *Innomed Labs, LLC v. Alza Corp.*, 211 F.R.D. 237, 240 (S.D.N.Y. 2002); *Steil v. Humana Kansas City, Inc.*, 197 F.R.D. 442, 444 (D. Kan. 2000); *Reed v. Nellcor Puritan Bennett & Mallinckrodt*, 193 F.R.D. 689, 692 (D. Kan. 2000).

144 *Innomed Labs, LLC*, 211 F.R.D. at 240; *Steil*, 197 F.R.D. at 444; *Reed*, 193 F.R.D. at 692.

145 *Calzaturficio S.C.A.R.P.A. s.p.a.*, 201 F.R.D. at 37; *Starlight Int'l Inc. v. Herlihy*, 186 F.R.D. 626, 639 (D. Kan. 1999); *Dravo Corp. v. Liberty Mut. Ins. Co.*, 164 F.R.D. 70, 75–76 (D. Neb. 1995).

146 *Paparelli v. Prudential Ins. Co.*, 108 F.R.D. 727, 729–30 (D. Mass. 1985).

147 *Id.*

deposition in the notice . . . the minimum about which the witness must be prepared to testify, not the maximum."[148]

Of course, if opposing counsel were to inquire into matters not listed in the notice, the entity may have grounds for believing it was tricked or ambushed. The solution to this problem, it has been suggested, is for counsel for the witness to object on this ground, state that the answers do not bind the entity but allow the witness to answer the questions. If the court later finds that the questions went beyond the notice, it could rule that they could be considered the individual answers of the witness, not binding on the entity at trial.[149] The scope of the examination, once a proper witness is produced, is governed by FRCP 26.

E. Depositions Outside the District

An attorney may issue, or cause to be issued, a subpoena to take the deposition of a nonparty witness or to require the production of documents by a nonparty to be used in preparation for, or in connection with, a deposition.[150] Because a federal case takes place in a national system, the attorney has greater reach than does a counselor in a state case.

A subpoena *ad testificandum* shall issue from the court for the district in which the deposition is noticed to take place.[151] If separate from a deposition subpoena, a subpoena to produce documents shall issue from the court for the district in which document production is to be made.[152] The clerk may issue a subpoena. An attorney may sign a subpoena on behalf of the court in which he or she is authorized to practice or a court for a district in which the deposition or document production is to occur, as long as the deposition or production pertains to an action pending in the

---

148 *Detoy v. City & County of San Francisco*, 196 F.R.D. 362, 366 (N.D. Cal. 2000); *accord Cabot Corp. v. Yamulla Enters., Inc.*, 194 F.R.D. 499 (M.D. Pa. 2000); *Overseas Private Inv. Corp. v. Mandelbaum*, 185 F.R.D. 67 (D.D.C. 1999); *King v. Pratt & Whitney*, 161 F.R.D. 475 (S.D. Fla. 1995), *aff'd*, 213 F.3d 646 (11th Cir. 2000).

149 *Detoy*, 196 F.R.D. at 367; Sidney I. Schenkier, *Deposing Corporations and Other Fictive Persons: Some Thoughts on Rule 30(b)(6)*, Litig., Vol. 29, No. 2, at 20, 26 (Spring 2003). *See Starlight Int'l Inc.*, 186 F.R.D. at 639; *King*, 161 F.R.D. at 476.

150 FRCP 45.

151 FRCP 45(a)(2).

152 *James v. Booz-Allen Hamilton, Inc.*, 206 F.R.D. 15, 19 (D.D.C. 2002); *Echostar Communications Corp. v. News Corp.*, 180 F.R.D. 391, 397 (D. Colo. 1998); *McNerney v. Archer Daniels Midland Co.*, 164 F.R.D. 584, 588 (W.D.N.Y. 1995).

court in which that attorney is authorized to practice.[153] Thus, the attorney may issue a subpoena nationwide.[154]

A subpoena for attendance at a deposition may be served at any place within the district of the court by which it is issued, or at any place outside the district that is within 100 miles of the place of deposition or production.[155] A subpoena may be quashed if it requires a nonparty witness, including a person who is not an officer of a party, to travel to a place more than 100 miles from the place of residence, employment or business of the person.[156]

Depositions may be taken before an officer authorized to administer oaths under United States law or the law of the place of the examination, or before an officer appointed by the court where the action is pending.[157] Depositions may be taken abroad pursuant to the Hague Evidence Convention,[158] by a letter of request (letter rogatory) to a foreign court or agency, on notice before a person empowered to administer oaths in the place of deposition by local or United States law or by a commission by the American court, usually to an American consular officer.[159]

Letters of request are a means by which a United States court can speak to a court of a foreign country and request assistance in effectuating discovery. A witness who does not wish to appear voluntarily may be made to appear in this way.[160] The taking of depositions and the obtaining of discovery abroad can be a quite protracted process, so attorneys should act expeditiously in a case in which they wish to pursue it.

---

153   FRCP 45(a)(3).

154   9A Charles A. Wright & Arthur R. Miller, Federal Practice and Procedure § 2543, at 22–23 (2d ed. 1995).

155   FRCP 45(b)(2). This rule further addresses service within a state and by statute of the United States.

156   FRCP 45(c)(3)(A).

157   FRCP 28(a).

158   Hague Convention on the Taking of Evidence Abroad in Civil or Commercial Matters, 23 U.S.T. 2555, T.I.A.S. No. 7444, *reprinted under* 28 U.S.C. § 1781. *See Societe Nationale Industrielle Aerospatiale v. United States Dist. Court*, 482 U.S. 522 (1987).

159   FRCP 28(b); 6 James W. Moore, Federal Practice § 28.10 (3d ed. 2003).

160   6 Moore, *supra* note 159, § 28.12[1].

CHAPTER THREE

DOCUMENTS AND DEPOSITIONS

Documents naturally play an important role in deposition practice. Because documents are at the heart of many cases, they are routinely inquired about at depositions. Documents are commonly produced in response to a demand either at or, preferably, prior to depositions for use in preparation for and at the depositions. Some depositions occur for the very purpose of inquiring about and identifying the existence and location of relevant documents; many depositions involve this aim at least in part. Depositions also can be used to authenticate documents for use at trial.

I. STATE PRACTICE

A. Documents and Other Things for Use at Depositions

Documents and other things may be obtained at the deposition for use at that time.[1] They also may be obtained independently of the deposition.[2]

The production of documents and other things may be required at the deposition.[3] This production can be accomplished by including the demand for documents in a notice of deposition to a party or in a subpoena to a nonparty.[4] The documents and things must be in the possession, custody or control of the person to be deposed. The production is of documents and things "to be marked as exhibits, and used on the examination," and the reasonable production expenses of a nonparty shall be defrayed by the party seeking the documents.[5]

The purpose of CPLR 3111 is to permit the interrogating attorney to learn and inquire about relevant documents and to identify and authenticate them so that they can be admitted into evidence at trial. It may also matter significantly that the documents are properly authenticated, should they later become necessary in regard to a motion for summary judgment.

---

1   CPLR 3111.

2   CPLR 3120; *Timoney v. Newmark & Co. Real Estate*, 299 A.D.2d 201, 750 N.Y.S.2d 271 (1st Dep't 2002); *Wilson v. City of Buffalo*, 298 A.D.2d 994, 997, 747 N.Y.S.2d 657 (4th Dep't 2002); *Matthews v. McDonald*, 241 A.D.2d 808, 661 N.Y.S.2d 80 (3d Dep't 1997); *Butler v. Am. Fed'n of State, County & Mun. Employees*, 72 A.D.2d 720, 422 N.Y.S.2d 74 (1st Dep't 1979).

3   CPLR 3111.

4   See Appendix, "Notice of Deposition—CPLR 3111 Document Request," "Notice of Deposition—Nonparty Witness" and "Subpoena" (state forms).

5   CPLR 3111. If the inquiring party wishes to identify or otherwise inquire at a deposition about documents that are not in the possession, custody or control of the deponent, the inquiring party will need to obtain them pursuant to CPLR 3120 before the deposition.

The inquiring party must identify the documents sought in a CPLR 3111 demand, but such identification need only be reasonable—"'as detailed as is reasonable to expect under the circumstances.'"[6] The degree of particularization required under this rule is less than that required in the demand under CPLR 3120.[7] Unlike CPLR 3120, CPLR 3111 does not require that the materials be specifically identified.[8] It may be enough for the party seeking the documents to follow the wording of the rule,[9] perhaps adding thereto a specific reference to particular documents known or believed to exist. Scattershot notices are improper.[10]

Documents produced in response to the demand under CPLR 3111 are available in a limited way to the attorney taking the deposition.[11] Docu-

---

6   *Batchie v. Travelers Ins. Co.*, 110 A.D.2d 864, 864, 488 N.Y.S.2d 420 (2d Dep't 1985) (quoting *Orange & Rockland Utilities, Inc. v. Town of Clarkstown*, 64 A.D.2d 919, 920, 408 N.Y.S.2d 132 (2d Dep't 1978)); *Carella v. Carella*, 97 A.D.2d 394, 394, 467 N.Y.S.2d 215 (2d Dep't 1983) (request for "all books and financial records, and financial statements" overbroad); *see Kaufman v. Kaufman*, 134 A.D.2d 407, 521 N.Y.S.2d 33 (2d Dep't 1987).

7   *Bartl v. Robert Half of Long Island, Inc.*, 150 A.D.2d 747, 542 N.Y.S.2d 197 (2d Dep't 1989); *Batchie*, 110 A.D.2d 864; *Early v. County of Nassau*, 98 A.D.2d 789, 469 N.Y.S.2d 809 (2d Dep't 1983); *Weiss v. Rae*, 87 A.D.2d 629, 448 N.Y.S.2d 233 (2d Dep't 1982); *Melnick v. Melnick*, 85 A.D.2d 531, 444 N.Y.S.2d 649 (1st Dep't 1981).

8   *Barnes v. Barnes*, 96 A.D.2d 894, 466 N.Y.S.2d 61 (2d Dep't 1983); *Prep v. State*, 91 A.D.2d 863, 458 N.Y.S.2d 378 (4th Dep't 1982); *J.K. Sales, Inc. v. Coburn Corp. of Am.*, 33 A.D.2d 514, 303 N.Y.S.2d 893 (1st Dep't 1969).

      In many instances, a proper specification in advance of the taking of any testimony would be impossible or impracticable. . . . The witnesses produced by respondents should, however, produce for use on their examination such books and records as are available and as are necessary to enable the witnesses to properly depose on matters relevant and material in the prosecution of the action.

      Id. at 514. *Accord Melnick*, 85 A.D.2d 531.

9   *Melnick*, 85 A.D.2d 531.

10   *Barnes*, 96 A.D.2d 894. "Although the use of such phrases as 'any and all' has been judicially disapproved of with respect to notices to produce, such broad descriptions have, on occasion, been condoned where reasonable under the circumstances." *Id.* at 894–95 (citation omitted). The CPLR 3111 notice in *Barnes* used the words "[a]ll books, papers, records and statements of accounts pertaining to" and "all," and the words were linked to fairly narrow categories of documents, with one exception. The court found the "descriptions of the material sought with respect to those items . . . sufficiently detailed and limited in scope so as not to render their production unduly onerous to plaintiff. Moreover, their relevance to the issues presented is clear." *Id.* at 895.

11   CPLR 3111 is "a more limited device" than CPLR 3120. *Matthews v. McDonald*, 241 A.D.2d 808, 809, 661 N.Y.S.2d 80 (3d Dep't 1997); *see Intex Co. v. Motorola Semiconductor Prods., Inc.*, 114 A.D.2d 1007, 496 N.Y.S.2d 344 (2d Dep't 1985); *Butler v. Am. Fed'n of State, County & Mun. Employees*, 72 A.D.2d 720, 422 N.Y.S.2d 74 (1st Dep't 1979); *Rios v. Donovan*, 21 A.D.2d 409, 250 N.Y.S.2d 818 (1st Dep't 1964).

ments are not simply piled upon the table in the deposition room for the interrogating counsel to study at leisure. There is no leisure, because the documents are to be produced at the deposition, and the deposition is to proceed at that time.

Further, a document is produced only as called for in the course of the deposition.[12] As noted, CPLR 3111 authorizes production of documents and things "to be marked as exhibits, and used on the examination." If the deposition concludes without certain documents having been discussed, the attorney for the deponent is allowed to pack his bag and go home without having to show the documents to the interrogating attorney.[13] A party producing under CPLR 3111 "need only bring pertinent records to the examination to be disclosed when 'the oral examination turns toward them and they can be identified with some degree of particularity.'"[14] In other words, CPLR 3111 does not mandate broad inspection of documents produced. In contrast, CPLR 3120 provides for inspection and copying of documents without regard to their potential use at a deposition.[15]

On the other hand, CPLR 3111 clearly is not restricted to items needed by the witness to refresh his recollection.[16] The use of documents at depositions may cover a range of things. Generally, when the deposition touches on a document, "the party seeking the examination is entitled to peruse the paper or inspect the item and is even permitted to copy it or make any other use of it that is feasible at a deposition session."[17] A narrow and rigid interpretation of the use of documents at depositions seems inappro-

---

12 *Matthews*, 241 A.D.2d 808; *Weiss v. Rae*, 87 A.D.2d 629, 448 N.Y.S.2d 233 (2d Dep't 1982); *Della Valle v. City of Niagara Falls*, 54 A.D.2d 143, 388 N.Y.S.2d 395 (4th Dep't 1976); *Wolfram v. Stokes*, 51 A.D.2d 690, 379 N.Y.S.2d 98 (1st Dep't 1976); *Kenford Co. v. County of Erie*, 41 A.D.2d 587, 340 N.Y.S.2d 303 (4th Dep't 1973); *Ramo v. Gen. Motors Corp.*, 36 A.D.2d 693, 318 N.Y.S.2d 951 (1st Dep't 1971); *see J. K. Sales, Inc.*, 33 A.D.2d 514. The party seeking discovery cannot evade the limited nature of a CPLR 3111 production by seeking discovery and inspection pursuant to CPLR 3120 together with a deposition. *Kenford Co.*, 41 A.D.2d at 587.

13 *Prudential Ins. Co. v. Ward Prods. Corp.*, 57 A.D.2d 259, 394 N.Y.S.2d 480 (3d Dep't 1977).

14 *Id.* at 261 (quoting *Columbia Gas of New York, Inc. v. New York State Elec. & Gas Corp.*, 35 A.D.2d 620, 621, 312 N.Y.S.2d 615 (3d Dep't 1970)).

15 *See Timoney v. Newmark & Co. Real Estate*, 299 A.D.2d 201, 750 N.Y.S.2d 271 (1st Dep't 2002); *Wilson v. City of Buffalo*, 298 A.D.2d 994, 997, 747 N.Y.S.2d 657 (4th Dep't 2002). A party cannot seek to circumvent CPLR 3120 by serving a subpoena for documents. *Id.*

16 Siegel, McKinney's Practice Commentary, CPLR 3111, at 490 (1991).

17 *Id.*

priate, Professor Siegel suggests, since CPLR 3120 and other tools would, in any event, be available to assist the examiner.[18]

Rule 3111 requires production of documents in the direct possession of the deponent. It also requires production of documents under the deponent's control.

Of course, a demand for the production of documents and things pursuant to CPLR 3111 raises the potential for problems for the producing person in light of the attorney-client privilege and work product protection.[19] The complexities of the privilege and the protection are beyond the scope of this text. Any 3111 production, however, must be screened in advance so that the privilege or protection can be invoked at the deposition as needed.

If a subpoena is to be served on a nonparty for a deposition and the production of records pursuant to CPLR 3111, the party seeking the discovery must provide notice to all parties.[20]

Generally, documentary evidence or exhibits used during the deposition should be annexed to and returned with the transcript. Upon request, the officer will mark the documents, give each party an opportunity to copy or inspect them, and return them to the party who offered them, with the documents then being usable as though annexed to the deposition.[21]

B. Documents and Other Things in General

A party may serve a demand for the production of documents and other things on any other party or serve a subpoena *duces tecum* on any other

---

18   *Id.*

> If the item and the activity sought to be carried out in connection with it are relevant and would be available by a direct discovery application under CPLR 3120, the deponent's refusal to permit such activity at a deposition session will only result in a CPLR 3120, 3124, or 3126 application by the seeking party afterwards.

> *Id.* The possibility that the activity might delay the deposition unduly or disrupt it would have a bearing on its appropriateness. *Id.*

19   *Della Valle v. City of Niagara Falls*, 54 A.D.2d 143, 388 N.Y.S.2d 395 (4th Dep't 1976).

20   *In re Beiny*, 129 A.D.2d 126, 517 N.Y.S.2d 474 (1st Dep't 1987).

21   CPLR 3116(c).

person (nonparty).[22] This demand or subpoena may be served at any time after commencement of an action.

The notice served by the party or a subpoena *duces tecum* in the case of a nonparty "shall set forth the items to be inspected, copied, tested or photographed by individual item or by category, and shall describe each item and category with reasonable particularity."[23]

The party issuing a subpoena must simultaneously serve a copy upon all other parties to ensure that all have notice of what is taking place. Within five days after the documents or things are produced, in whole or in part, the party shall also give notice to all other parties that the items produced are available for inspection and copying at a stated time and place.[24]

A custodian or other qualified person shall produce original documents for inspection and copying at the place where they are usually maintained if the subpoena calls for such production. Otherwise, the custodian or other qualified person may deliver complete and accurate copies of the items to be produced. The party seeking discovery must defray the "reasonable production expenses" of a nonparty witness.[25]

Because the documents or other things must be in the possession, custody or control of the party or person served,[26] that party or person is not obliged to create documents that do not exist in order to satisfy the demand.[27]

The rule aims at allowing documents to be produced in the first instance and depositions to occur thereafter, once there has been an opportunity to

---

22   CPLR 3120. For an excellent discussion of the revisions to CPLR 3120, see Connors, McKinney's Practice Commentary, CPLR 3120, 217–36 (2005) (incorporating earlier commentaries by Professor David Siegel).

23   CPLR 3120(2).

24   CPLR 3120(3). A party seeking to serve a subpoena *duces tecum* on a library, department or bureau of a municipal corporation or the state or an officer thereof must proceed first by motion on notice. CPLR 3120(4).

25   CPLR 3122(d).

26   CPLR 3120(1)(i). The rule also provides for entry on property to inspect, measure, etc. CPLR 3120(1)(ii).

27   *Gen. Elec. v. Macejka,* 252 A.D.2d 700, 675 N.Y.S.2d 420 (3d Dep't 1998); *Lear v. N.Y. Helicopter Corp.,* 190 A.D.2d 7, 597 N.Y.S.2d 411 (2d Dep't 1993); *Corriel v. Volkswagen of Am., Inc.,* 127 A.D.2d 729, 512 N.Y.S.2d 126 (2d Dep't 1987).

study the documents with care. This process is both fair and efficient. The result is that CPLR 3120 provides a tool for preparation of depositions and for the effective conduct of depositions that is, as a general rule, far preferable to CPLR 3111. Where document demands are concerned, there is, to be sure, a risk of abusive tactics by some attorneys, and permitting use of categorical demands certainly does not diminish that potentiality. However, a party identifying documents sought by category still must describe each item and category with "reasonable particularity."[28]

1. Objections to Document Requests and Withholding of Documents

Rule 3122 of the CPLR sets out the procedures by which the recipient of a document demand may object to all or parts of the demand. Within 20 days from service of a document demand, the recipient, if objecting to the disclosure called for, is required to serve a response stating "with reasonable particularity the reasons for each objection."[29] If objection is made to part of an item or category, the part must be specified.

If reasonable, the response may persuade the requesting party to revise the demand or to compromise on certain points and perhaps certain documents. The rule thus encourages parties to resolve disputes about document demands and production on their own,[30] thereby reducing litigation costs and the burden on the courts.

If the party seeking disclosure of the documents or things believes its original request was reasonable, it is authorized to move for an order to compel, pursuant to CPLR 3124 or 2308, with respect to any objection or any failure to respond.[31] Thus, the burden is on the demanding party to

---

28   *Konrad v. 136 E. 64th St. Corp.*, 209 A.D.2d 228, 618 N.Y.S.2d 632 (1st Dep't 1994); *cf.* *MacKinnon v. MacKinnon*, 245 A.D.2d 690, 665 N.Y.S.2d 123 (3d Dep't 1997).

29   CPLR 3122(a). When a subpoena is served on a medical provider for production of a patient's medical records, the subpoena must be accompanied by a signed authorization by the patient or it need not be responded to. *Id.* This provision has given rise to some problems.

30   *Budhram v. City of New York*, 264 A.D.2d 796, 695 N.Y.S.2d 393 (2d Dep't 1999); *Forest Hills Gardens Corp. v. Kamp*, 165 Misc. 2d 915, 630 N.Y.S.2d 664 (Civ. Ct., Queens Co. 1995), *aff'd*, 171 Misc. 2d 334, 659 N.Y.S.2d 690 (App. Term, 2d Dep't 1997).

31   CPLR 3122(a).

ensure that its document demands are not overly broad, vague and unduly burdensome; if they are, they may be stricken in their entirety.[32]

If documents apparently called for by the demand are withheld, the withholding person shall give notice that documents are being withheld and provide certain information about the documents.[33] This notice permits the party demanding the discovery to decide in an informed manner how to address, for example, a claim of attorney-client privilege and assists the court in resolving any such claims.

Despite the clarity of CPLR 3122, some parties fail to comply with these procedures or do so in an untimely manner. The cases make clear that a party unhappy with a demand must interpose objections as provided in CPLR 3122 and must do so within the 20-day deadline set forth. Failure to comply will mean that the court may not entertain any objections except for those based on a privilege or concerning demands that are palpably improper.[34] An objecting recipient must set forth the reasons for

---

32 *Steadfast Ins. Co. v. Sentinel Real Estate Corp.*, 278 A.D.2d 157, 719 N.Y.S.2d 221 (1st Dep't 2000); *Lichtman v. Mount Judah Cemetery*, 269 A.D.2d 319, 705 N.Y.S.2d 23 (1st Dep't 2000); *Besicorp Group, Inc. v. Enowitz*, 268 A.D.2d 846, 702 N.Y.S.2d 421 (3d Dep't 2000); *Sonsini v. Mem'l Hosp. for Cancer & Diseases*, 262 A.D.2d 185, 693 N.Y.S.2d 17 (1st Dep't 1999); *Albert v. Time Warner Cable*, 255 A.D.2d 248, 680 N.Y.S.2d 499 (1st Dep't 1998); *Lerner v. 300 W. 17th St. Hous. Dev. Fund Corp.*, 232 A.D.2d 249, 648 N.Y.S.2d 439 (1st Dep't 1996); *Williams Real Estate Co. v. Viking Penguin*, 216 A.D.2d 27, 628 N.Y.S.2d 267 (1st Dep't 1995).

33 CPLR 3122(b). The responding person shall state the legal ground for withholding each document and set forth as to each the type, general subject matter and date of the document and such other information as would be sufficient to identify it for a subpoena *duces tecum. Id.* Document production shall be made as the documents are kept in the regular course of business, or the documents shall be organized and labeled to correspond to the categories in the request. CPLR 3122(c).

34 *McMahon v. Aviette Agency, Inc.*, 301 A.D.2d 820, 753 N.Y.S.2d 605 (3d Dep't 2003); *Saratoga Harness Racing Inc. v. Roemer*, 274 A.D.2d 887, 711 N.Y.S.2d 603 (3d Dep't 2000); *Garcia v. Jomber Realty, Inc.*, 264 A.D.2d 809, 695 N.Y.S.2d 607 (2d Dep't 1999); *Briand Parenteau Inc. v. Dean Witter Reynolds Inc.*, 267 A.D.2d 576, 699 N.Y.S.2d 230 (3d Dep't 1999); *Kimmel v. State*, 261 A.D.2d 843, 690 N.Y.S.2d 383 (4th Dep't 1999); *Kern v. City of Rochester*, 261 A.D.2d 904, 689 N.Y.S.2d 842 (4th Dep't 1999); *Lawrence H. Morse, Inc. v. Anson*, 251 A.D.2d 722, 673 N.Y.S.2d 796 (3d Dep't 1998); *Greico v. Albany Ambulette Serv.*, 232 A.D.2d 938, 648 N.Y.S.2d 834 (3d Dep't 1996); *Holness v. Chrysler Corp.*, 220 A.D.2d 721, 633 N.Y.S.2d 986 (2d Dep't 1995).

withholding documents[35] and must provide the "privilege log" called for by CPLR 3122(b) when seeking to invoke a privilege.[36] The same procedures apply for both a party and a person served with a subpoena in regard to privileged items.[37]

2. Certification of Business Records

Business records produced in response to a subpoena *duces tecum* pursuant to CPLR 3120 must be accompanied by a certification that the documents produced are accurate versions of those described in the subpoena and represent all the documents called for.[38] If the documents are not a complete set, the certification must explain which are missing and why. The certification also must state that the records or copies were made in the regular course of business and it was the regular course of business to make such records.[39] A proper certification is admissible and shall be presumed true.[40] Documents so certified shall be deemed to have satisfied CPLR 4518(a) unless objection is made.[41]

The purpose of this rule is to simplify the process of identifying business records at trial. It should also ease the burden on nonparties required to produce such records.

C. Use of Documents at or in Preparation for Depositions and Waiver of Privilege

The use of documents at, or in connection with, depositions may have an impact on privilege, attorney work product and protection for materials

---

35   *Field v. Rose & Sam Seelig Charitable Trust (In re Estate of Seelig)*, 302 A.D.2d 721, 724, 756 N.Y.S.2d 305 (3d Dep't 2003); *Twenty Four Hour Fuel Oil Corp. v. Hunter Ambulance*, 226 A.D.2d 175, 640 N.Y.S.2d 114 (1st Dep't 1996).

36   *Field*, 302 A.D.2d 721; *Galioto v. Sears, Roebuck & Co.*, 262 A.D.2d 1035, 691 N.Y.S.2d 838 (4th Dep't 1999); *Stenovich v. Wachtell, Lipton, Rosen & Katz*, 195 Misc. 2d 99, 756 N.Y.S.2d 367 (Sup. Ct., N.Y. Co. 2003).

37   *See* CPLR 3122(b).

38   CPLR 3122-a.

39   CPLR 3122-a(a).

40   CPLR 3122-a(b).

41   CPLR 3122-a(c). The party seeking to offer the records at a trial or hearing is required to give 30 days' notice of such intention and of the place where the records may be inspected. Ten or more days prior to trial or hearing, another party may object and shall state the grounds for such objection. If no such objection is made, and if none is made at the trial or hearing based upon evidence that could not have been discovered in time for compliance with the rule, the records will satisfy CPLR 4518(a).

prepared in anticipation of litigation. It is well recognized that if a witness uses a document to refresh his or her recollection at trial, the other party has the right to examine that writing. If the document would otherwise be privileged or protected by the work product doctrine or as material prepared for litigation, the witness's use of it to refresh his or her recollection while on the stand waives the privilege or protection. This rule has been applied to depositions as well.[42] "The reason behind this requirement is to prevent a witness from using a writing that may furnish him with a false recollection and to protect a party from 'the introduction against him of false, forged or manufactured evidence, which he is not permitted to inspect.'"[43]

The right of the adversary to inspect the writing used by a witness while on the stand is clear. Cases hold, however, that the right of inspection extends also to a writing used by a witness to refresh his or her recollection *before* testifying at trial or at deposition. "We think it a sound rule that writings used prior to testifying for the purpose of refreshing the memory of a witness be made available to the adversary whether at the trial or at pretrial examination."[44] The "'risk . . . is precisely the same whether the witness refreshes his recollection by consulting a writing before

---

42   *See Maisch v. Millard Fillmore Hosps.*, 278 A.D.2d 838, 718 N.Y.S.2d 776 (4th Dep't 2000); *Hannold v. First Baptist Church*, 254 A.D.2d 746, 677 N.Y.S.2d 859 (4th Dep't 1998); *McDonough v. Pinsley*, 239 A.D.2d 109, 657 N.Y.S.2d 33 (1st Dep't 1997); *Clark-Fitzpatrick, Inc. v. Long Island R.R. Co.*, 162 A.D.2d 577, 556 N.Y.S.2d 763 (2d Dep't 1990) (use of document covered by attorney-client and attorney work product doctrines at deposition; waiver); *Stern v. Aetna Cas. & Sur. Co.*, 159 A.D.2d 1013, 552 N.Y.S.2d 730 (4th Dep't 1990); *Grieco v. Cunningham*, 128 A.D.2d 502, 512 N.Y.S.2d 432 (2d Dep't 1987) (attorney work product and attorney-client privilege); *Merrill Lynch Realty Commercial Servs., Inc. v. Rudin Mgmt. Co.*, 94 A.D.2d 617, 462 N.Y.S.2d 16 (1st Dep't 1983); *Hermann v. Gen. Tire & Rubber Co.*, 79 A.D.2d 955, 435 N.Y.S.2d 14 (1st Dep't 1981) (attorney work product); *Doxtator v. Swarthout*, 38 A.D.2d 782, 328 N.Y.S.2d 150 (4th Dep't 1972) (material prepared for litigation); *E.B. Metal Indus. v. State*, 138 Misc. 2d 698, 525 N.Y.S.2d 516 (Ct. Cl. 1988); *E.R. Carpenter Co. v. ABC Carpet Co.*, 98 Misc. 2d 1091, 415 N.Y.S.2d 351 (Civ. Ct. 1979) (attorney-client privilege).

43   *Slotnik v. State*, 129 Misc. 2d 553, 493 N.Y.S.2d 731, 732 (Ct. Cl. 1985) (quoting *Tibbetts v. Sternberg*, 66 Barb. 201, 203 (1870)).

44   *Doxtator*, 38 A.D.2d at 782 (citations omitted); *Alfredsen v. Loomis*, 148 N.Y.S.2d 468, 470 (Sup. Ct. 1956) ("The time when the memorandum of statement was referred to by the witness, whether at the trial or examination or prior thereto, would seem unimportant. The important fact is that it was used by him to refresh his recollection and that it accomplished that purpose" (citation omitted)).

trial [or at deposition] or by consulting it while on the witness stand during trial.' "[45]

The adversary has no right to see the document unless and until the witness has actually used it to refresh recollection.[46] A party seeking access to privileged documents, material prepared in anticipation of litigation or work product of counsel must establish that the deponent in fact used those documents to refresh recollection if a waiver is to be found.[47]

II. FEDERAL PRACTICE

A. Documents for Use at Deposition

As discussed above, New York State law provides one procedure for obtaining access to documents at a deposition and another procedure for obtaining them in advance or afterward. In contrast, federal practice does not provide two distinct mechanisms for obtaining documents for use in connection with depositions.

Under federal practice, a notice of deposition directed to a party may be accompanied by a document request "for the production of documents

---

45 *Doxtator*, 38 A.D.2d at 782 (citations omitted); *see Grieco*, 128 A.D.2d 502 (claimed attorney work product and attorney-client privilege waived by use to refresh recollection prior to deposition and trial); *Rouse v. County of Greene*, 115 A.D.2d 162, 495 N.Y.S.2d 496 (3d Dep't 1985) (refreshing recollection in preparation for deposition by means of material prepared for litigation; waiver); *Merrill Lynch Realty*, 94 A.D.2d 617 (document claimed to be privileged reviewed in preparation for deposition; any privilege waived); *Hermann*, 79 A.D.2d 955 (attorney work product used to refresh recollection prior to deposition; waiver); *Slotnik*, 129 Misc. 2d 553; *E.R. Carpenter Co.*, 98 Misc. 2d 1091 (attorney-client privilege). Some cases adopt a different approach from that described here. *Geffers v. Canisteo Cent. Sch. Dist.*, 105 A.D.2d 1062, 482 N.Y.S.2d 635 (4th Dep't 1984) (attorney work product reviewed by client in preparation for deposition); *Falk v. Kalt*, 44 Misc. 2d 172, 253 N.Y.S.2d 188 (Sup. Ct. Special Term, Suffolk Co. 1964) (attorney-client privilege; refreshing of recollection during deposition); *In re Van Gorder's Will*, 10 Misc. 2d 648, 176 N.Y.S.2d 1018 (Surr. Ct., Westchester Co. 1957) (attorney-client privilege; refreshing of recollection during deposition). The last of these cases, upon which *Falk* relied, cited no authority on point. *See E.R. Carpenter Co.*, 415 N.Y.S.2d at 353. *Geffers* is an extremely brief decision, which relied on general statements about the importance of attorney work product but did not address any cases regarding waiver. Although the client there had reviewed the memorandum in preparation for a deposition, it is not clear that it had refreshed the client's recollection. *See* Robert A. Barker & Vincent C. Alexander, Evidence in New York State and Federal Courts § 5:16, at 336 n.3 (2001) (perhaps attorney work product should be less susceptible to waiver). *See also* 6 Jack B. Weinstein et al., New York Civil Practice ¶ 3101.45, at 31-121–31-122 (2004).

46 Prince, Richardson on Evidence § 6-215, at 365 (Richard T. Farrell ed., 11th ed. 1995).

47 *Maisch v. Millard Fillmore Hosps.*, 278 A.D.2d 838, 718 N.Y.S.2d 776 (4th Dep't 2000); *Hannold v. First Baptist Church*, 254 A.D.2d 746, 677 N.Y.S.2d 859 (4th Dep't 1998).

and tangible things at the taking of the deposition."[48] This request must be made in compliance with FRCP 34, which governs the production of documents and things generally. Documents may be sought from nonparties for production at a deposition or simply sought before or after a deposition by service of a subpoena under FRCP 45, accompanied by a demand.[49]

1. FRCP 34 Document Demand

Federal Rule of Civil Procedure 34 authorizes a demand to inspect and copy designated documents and things in the possession, custody or control of the party served.[50] The requesting party must set forth "either by individual item or by category, the items to be inspected, and describe each with reasonable particularity."[51] A demand for documents and things under FRCP 34 must describe the items sought with as much particularity as can reasonably be expected given the stage of discovery involved.[52] The notice shall specify a reasonable time, place and manner of making the inspection.[53] Absent court approval or a stipulation, the request may not be served before the time specified in FRCP 26(d), which means generally not before the FRCP 26(f) conference.

The recipient of the notice has 30 days after service within which to serve a written response.[54] Since FRCP 30(b)(5) mandates that FRCP 34 procedures govern demands for the production of documents and things at the deposition, it would follow that a demand for the production of documents at a deposition must be served at least 30 days before the deposition date and, in practical terms, somewhat more than that to allow time for the adversary to serve a response.

The response to the FRCP 34 demand shall state, as to each item or category, that inspection will be provided as requested or that the demand is

---

48   FRCP 30(b)(5).

49   FRCP 34(c).

50   FRCP 34(a). Entry upon land or other property is also authorized by this subdivision. See Appendix, "Document Request (FRCP 34)" (federal form).

51   FRCP 34(b).

52   *Taylor v. Fla. Atl. Univ.*, 132 F.R.D. 304, 305 (S.D. Fla. 1990), *aff'd*, 976 F.2d 743 (11th Cir. 1992), *cert. denied*, 507 U.S. 1051 (1993); *Westhemeco, Ltd. v. N.H. Ins. Co.*, 82 F.R.D. 702, 709 (S.D.N.Y. 1979); *Mallinckrodt Chem. Works v. Goldman, Sachs & Co.*, 58 F.R.D. 348, 353 (S.D.N.Y. 1973).

53   FRCP 34(b).

54   *Id.* The court can abbreviate this period (or lengthen it) or the parties can do so by stipulation. *Id.*; *see* FRCP 29.

objected to. If there is an objection, the reasons for it shall be set forth; if the objection concerns part of an item or category, the part shall be identified and production shall go forward as to the rest.[55]

The demanding party may move for an order to compel withheld material under FRCP 37(a).[56] Since the judge relies on the pretrial scheduling order[57] to know when discovery is to conclude and when the trial is to proceed, counsel should seek such a motion under FRCP 37 (and see FRCP 30(d)(3)) if waiting for production may result in a judicial finding that supports the Durocher shibboleth that "nice guys finish last."

Documents shall be produced as kept in the ordinary course of business, or shall be organized and labeled in accordance with the categories of the demand.[58]

Documents need not literally be in the possession of the person from whom they are sought. It is sufficient if the person from whom documents are demanded has a legal right to obtain them on demand from a third party,[59] or that that person has the right, authority or practical ability to obtain the documents from a nonparty.[60]

2. Objections to Document Demand

The party objecting to the production of documents bears the burden of showing why those documents should not be produced.[61] Decisions on the simpler matters of this sort can frequently be made expeditiously by a call to the judge or magistrate judge supervising discovery. Documents can, of course, be withheld on the grounds that they are privileged or protected

---

55 FRCP 34(b). Objections are discussed in greater detail *infra* at II.A.2.

56 *Id.* Chapter 7 discusses motions to compel.

57 See Appendix, "Pretrial Scheduling Order" (federal form).

58 FRCP 34(b).

59 *Alexander v. FBI*, 194 F.R.D. 299, 301 (D.D.C. 2000); *see Novartis Pharms. Corp. v. Eon Labs Mfg.*, 206 F.R.D. 392, 395 (D. Del. 2002).

60 *Triple Five of Minn., Inc. v. Simon*, 212 F.R.D. 523, 527 (D. Minn.), *aff'd*, 2002 U.S. Dist. LEXIS 10646 (D. Minn. June 6, 2002); *SEC v. Credit Bancorp, Ltd.*, 194 F.R.D. 469, 471 (S.D.N.Y. 2000); *Prokosch v. Catalina Lighting, Inc.*, 193 F.R.D. 633, 636 (D. Minn. 2000); *Bank of New York v. Meridien Biao Bank Tanz.*, 171 F.R.D. 135, 146–47 (S.D.N.Y. 1997).

61 *Alexander*, 194 F.R.D. at 302.

under the work product doctrine.[62] The burden is on the party asserting a privilege or protection to demonstrate a factual basis therefor.[63] Documents sought must be relevant, and their production must not impose an undue burden upon the party from whom they are sought.[64]

Generalized claims of privilege or work product are improper. Objections on this score are often complex. When such objections are raised, the objecting party must provide a privilege log. The objecting party must identify each document in question and supply details about it so that the claim can be evaluated.[65] Such evaluation frequently takes place via an *in camera* inspection by the court.

Similarly, generalized or boilerplate objections do not comply with FRCP 34(b), and courts view them with disfavor.[66] An example of such an objection is the following: The demand is "vague, overly broad, unduly burdensome and seeks information that is not relevant and not reasonably calculated to lead to the discovery of relevant evidence."[67] "Such pat, generic, non-specific objections, intoning the same boilerplate language, are inconsistent with both the letter and the spirit of the Federal Rules of Civil Procedure."[68]

---

62 *Henry v. Champlain Enters.*, 212 F.R.D. 73 (N.D.N.Y. 2003); *Triple Five of Minn., Inc.*, 212 F.R.D. at 527; *United States v. Philip Morris, Inc.*, 212 F.R.D. 421 (D.D.C. 2002); *LaSalle Bank Nat'l Ass'n v. Lehman Bros. Holdings, Inc.*, 209 F.R.D. 112 (D. Md. 2002); *Bank of Am., N.A. v. Terra Nova Ins. Co.*, 212 F.R.D. 166 (S.D.N.Y. 2002); *Bank Brussels Lambert v. Credit Lyonnais (Suisse), S.A.*, 210 F.R.D. 506 (S.D.N.Y. 2002).

63 *Triple Five of Minn., Inc.*, 212 F.R.D. at 527–28; *Cobell v. Norton*, 212 F.R.D. 24, 27 (D.D.C. 2002).

64 *Wright v. AmSouth Bancorp.*, 320 F.3d 1198, 1205 (11th Cir. 2003); *Horizon Holdings, LLC v. Genmar Holdings, Inc.*, 209 F.R.D. 208, 213 (D. Kan. 2002); *Amcast Indus. Corp. v. Detrex Corp.*, 138 F.R.D. 115, 118 (N.D. Ind. 1991).

65 *Wagner v. Dryvit Sys.*, 208 F.R.D. 606, 612 (D. Neb. 2001); *Youell v. Grimes*, 202 F.R.D. 643, 649 (D. Kan. 2001); *McCoo v. Denny's Inc.*, 192 F.R.D. 675, 680 (D. Kan. 2000); *Athridge v. Aetna Cas. & Sur. Co.*, 184 F.R.D. 181, 191 (D.D.C. 1998); *Land Ocean Logistics, Inc. v. Aqua Gulf Corp.*, 181 F.R.D. 229, 237–38 (W.D.N.Y. 1998); *In re Aircrash Disaster near Roselawn*, 172 F.R.D. 295, 307 (N.D. Ill. 1997); *Obiajulu v. City of Rochester, Dep't of Law*, 166 F.R.D. 293 (W.D.N.Y. 1996).

66 *Astra Aktiebolag v. Andrx Pharms., Inc.*, 208 F.R.D. 92, 103–104 (S.D.N.Y. 2002); *Wagner*, 208 F.R.D. at 611; *Athridge*, 184 F.R.D. at 190; *Magee v. Paul Revere Life Ins. Co.*, 172 F.R.D. 627, 640 (E.D.N.Y. 1997); *In re Aircrash Disaster near Roselawn*, 172 F.R.D. at 307.

67 *In re Aircrash Disaster near Roselawn*, 172 F.R.D. at 306–307; *Obiajulu*, 166 F.R.D. at 295; *see Wagner*, 208 F.R.D. at 612.

68 *Obiajulu*, 166 F.R.D. at 295.

It is also improper to object on relevance or other grounds and then to state in the document response that documents will be produced to the extent relevant and not subject to privilege. Such a response leaves the demanding party unable to know where it stands with regard to its requests and leaves the responding party as the sole arbiter of what to produce. The court is also at a complete loss in such circumstances.[69]

Specific objections are always required. An attorney ignores this requirement at considerable peril, as failure to object in a properly specific manner may result in waiver of the objection.[70] Failure to object within the time set forth in the rule may also result in a waiver of objections.[71]

B. Use of Documents at or in Preparation for Depositions; Waiver of Privilege

As in state practice, so in federal: The use of documents to refresh recollection while a witness is on the stand waives privilege or the protection for work product.[72] The same result obtains when the refreshing of recollection occurs at a deposition.[73] Federal Rule of Civil Procedure 30(c) indicates that the Federal Rules of Evidence are to apply.[74]

---

69   *Athridge*, 184 F.R.D. at 190–91; *Starlight Int'l, Inc. v. Herlihy*, 181 F.R.D. 494, 497 (D. Kan. 1998). *See Sonnino v. Univ. of Kansas Hosp. Auth.*, 221 F.R.D. 661, 666–67 (D. Kan. 2004) (objection to a discovery request "to the extent" it seeks information protected by attorney-client privilege or work product protection is tantamount to asserting no objection at all and does not preserve privilege or protection).

70   *Anderson v. Hale*, 202 F.R.D. 548, 552–53 (N.D. Ill. 2001); *Drexel Heritage Furnishings, Inc. v. Furniture USA, Inc.*, 200 F.R.D. 255, 258 (M.D.N.C. 2001); *St. Paul Reinsurance Co. v. Commercial Fin. Corp.*, 197 F.R.D. 620 (N.D. Iowa 2000); *Pham v. Hartford Fire Ins. Co.*, 193 F.R.D. 659, 661–62 (D. Colo. 2000); *Land Ocean Logistics, Inc. v. Aqua Gulf Corp.*, 181 F.R.D. 229, 237–38 (W.D.N.Y. 1998); *Pulsecard, Inc. v. Discover Card Servs., Inc.*, 168 F.R.D. 295, 303–304 (D. Kan. 1996).

71   *Anderson*, 202 F.R.D. at 552–53; *Cotracom Commodity Trading Co. v. Seaboard Corp.*, 189 F.R.D. 655, 661 (D. Kan. 1999); *Land Ocean Logistics, Inc.*, 181 F.R.D. at 236–37; *Starlight Int'l, Inc.*, 181 F.R.D. at 497; *Coker v. Duke & Co.*, 177 F.R.D. 682, 684–85 (M.D. Ala. 1998); *Pulsecard, Inc.*, 168 F.R.D. at 303–304; *United States ex rel. Burroughs v. DeNardi Corp.*, 167 F.R.D. 680, 687 (S.D. Cal. 1996).

72   4 Jack B. Weinstein & Margaret A. Berger, Weinstein's Federal Evidence §§ 612.02, 612.05[2][a] (Joseph M. McLaughlin ed., 2d ed. 1997 & Supp. 2004) (hereinafter "Weinstein & Berger").

73   Fed. R. Evid. 612 (hereinafter "FRE"); *Sporck v. Peil*, 759 F.2d 312, 317 (3d Cir.), *cert. denied*, 474 U.S. 903 (1985); *Nutramax Lab., Inc. v. Twin Lab, Inc.*, 183 F.R.D. 458, 467 (D. Md. 1998); *Magee v. Paul Revere Life Ins. Co.*, 172 F.R.D. 627, 637 (E.D.N.Y. 1997); *Auto Owners Ins. Co. v. Totaltape, Inc.*, 135 F.R.D. 199, 202 (M.D. Fla. 1990); *S & A Painting Co. v. O.W.B. Corp.*, 103 F.R.D. 407 (W.D. Pa. 1984); 4 Weinstein & Berger, *supra* note 72, § 612.02[5] (most courts hold that FRE 612 applies at depositions).

74   *See* Sporck, 759 F.2d at 317.

Judge Weinstein's treatise states the following about refreshing recollection:

> The logic behind allowing the cross-examiner to examine and use writings employed by the witness to refresh recollection is that the practice enhances the jury's ability to assess the credibility of the witness. The same logic should be extended to writings used by the witness before taking the stand. The dangers inherent in refreshing recollection are even more pronounced before trial, when there is no bar against leading questions and no predetermined order in which questions must be asked, and there are no limitations on the way the witness may be presented materials for review.
>
> By allowing a searching inquiry on cross-examination as to how the witness reached present testimonial knowledge—other than the stock question "Did you discuss this case with anyone?"—the witness may be better enabled to separate memory from suggestion. In addition to allowing the cross-examiner to test whether the witness has present knowledge, whether discrepancies exist between the witness's testimony and the writing, and whether the writing is what the witness claims it to be, the opportunity to ascertain which writings the witness consulted before testifying may suggest to counsel an entirely new train of associations, permitting cross-examination down otherwise unanticipated avenues.[75]

In contrast with the situation that obtains under the federal rule when the witness consults a document while on the stand or in the deposition chair, disclosure of a document is not automatically required when a witness consults the document prior to testifying. Rather, disclosure will take place when the court, in its discretion, finds that disclosure is necessary in the interests of justice.[76] The "courts have struggled with the questions of

---

75   4 Weinstein & Berger, *supra* note 72, § 612.04[4][a] (footnote omitted).

76   FRE 612.

when and if waiver occurs, and how much weight to give the assertion of privilege."[77]

Clearly, there is a tension between FRE 612 as applied to documents consulted prior to testifying and the work product protection.[78] The party seeking to obtain documents used prior to testifying must show that the witness used the writings to refresh his or her memory for the purpose of testifying. Upon such a showing, the question for the court then becomes whether, in the interest of justice, the adverse party should be allowed to see the document.[79]

"[T]he work product doctrine protects legitimate efforts to prepare a case, which include preparation of witnesses for deposition and trial testimony. These efforts do not extend, however, to manufacturing favorable testimony, or concealing unfavorable testimony."[80] Judge Weinstein's treatise states that "[g]iven the liberality of disclosure and the work product exception in the discovery rules, the opponent should be required to make

---

77   4 Weinstein & Berger, *supra* note 72, § 612.05[3][a]. *See, e.g., Sporck*, 759 F.2d at 317–19; *Nutramax Lab., Inc.*, 183 F.R.D. at 467–68; *Sauer v. Burlington N. R.R. Co.*, 169 F.R.D. 120, 123 (D. Minn. 1996); *Audiotext Communications Network v. US Telecom*, 164 F.R.D. 250 (D. Kan. 1996); *Butler Mfg. Co. v. Americold Corp.*, 148 F.R.D. 275, 278 (D. Kan. 1993); *Redvanly v. Nynex Corp.*, 152 F.R.D. 460, 469–72 (S.D.N.Y. 1993); *Berkey Photo, Inc. v. Eastman Kodak Co.*, 74 F.R.D. 613, 615–17 (S.D.N.Y. 1977) (Frankel, J.).

78   In *Nutramax Lab., Inc.*, 183 F.R.D. at 461 (footnote omitted), the court stated:

> In preparing to defend depositions in cases where substantial document production has taken place, no competent counsel can afford to ignore reviewing with witnesses the documents which relate to critical issues. During a deposition, counsel questioning a witness will seldom fail to ask the witness about what he or she did to prepare for the deposition, and the identity of any documents reviewed for this purpose. Most often, this inquiry is not resisted by counsel defending the deposition, because the documents have already been produced to the opposing counsel. However, where, as here, many thousands of pages of documents have been produced and counsel have analyzed them and selected a population of "critical documents" relevant to case dispositive issues, a deposition question aimed at discovering what documents were reviewed to prepare for a deposition may draw an assertion of the work product doctrine, and an instruction not to answer. In response, the deposing attorney may contend that if the witness used the documents to prepare for the deposition, then work product immunity has been waived, and Fed. R. Evid. 612 requires the production of the documents.

79   *Sporck*, 759 F.2d at 317–19; *Nutramax Lab., Inc.*, 183 F.R.D. at 468; *Audiotext Communications Network*, 164 F.R.D. 250; *Butler Mfg. Co.*, 148 F.R.D. at 278. In analyzing whether the interest of justice requires disclosure, "the court [needs] to apply a balancing test designed to weigh the policies underlying the work product doctrine against the need for disclosure to promote effective cross-examination and impeachment." *Nutramax Lab., Inc.*, 183 F.R.D. at 468.

80   *Nutramax Lab., Inc.*, 183 F.R.D. at 469.

some showing of need to obtain materials that a witness reviewed before a deposition."[81] Most courts, though, seem to hold that refreshing recollection with attorney-client privileged documents prior to testifying results in waiver of the privilege.[82]

---

81   4 Weinstein & Berger, *supra* note 72, § 612.05[3][c].

82   *Id.* at § 612.06[2] (waiver limited to portions of the documents actually consulted); *see Audiotext Communications Network*, 164 F.R.D. 250; *Butler Mfg. Co.*, 148 F.R.D. at 278. *Compare Hiskett v. Wal-Mart Stores*, 180 F.R.D. 403, 406–408 (D. Kan. 1998) (impact of review of document was minimal; defendant had all the information that would be revealed were production ordered; production denied).

CHAPTER FOUR

EXPERT WITNESSES

Both New York State and federal practice provide for discovery with respect to experts. Expert testimony plays a critical role in many cases. The liberality with which the two systems view such disclosure could hardly be more different. The gap between the systems in New York may be as wide as in any state in the country.

I. STATE PRACTICE

Upon demand, each party must provide information regarding each person whom the party expects to call as an expert witness at trial. The party must identify the person and "disclose in reasonable detail the subject matter on which each expert is expected to testify, the substance of the facts and opinions on which each expert is expected to testify, the qualifications of each expert witness and a summary of the grounds for each expert's opinion."[1]

In a medical, dental or podiatric malpractice case, a responding party may omit the name of any medical expert but must disclose all other information required.[2]

If, for good cause, a party retains an expert an insufficient time prior to trial to furnish appropriate notice, the court shall not bar the testimony solely on grounds of noncompliance with this obligation but shall make whatever order may be just.[3] Notably, no deadline is provided for the furnishing of the CPLR 3101(d) statement.

Some important notes about these rules, most of which are discussed in detail below:

1. In contrast with FRCP 26, the rules do not expressly provide for depositions of expert witnesses, with one exception—the deposition of a treating physician or expert witness by the party who retained the witness (no. 3 below).

2. Depositions may be authorized under CPLR 3101(d)(1)(iii). However, a court order is required upon a showing of special circumstances— a standard the courts have interpreted very narrowly.

---

1   CPLR 3101(d)(1)(i).

2   *Id.* In a medical, dental or podiatric malpractice case, a party may offer to the adversary to make a trial expert available for deposition. If all parties accept, each party must produce its expert for deposition. CPLR 3101(d)(1)(ii).

3   CPLR 3101(d)(1)(i).

3. Depositions of trial experts may occur upon the voluntary written offer of any party in medical, dental and podiatric malpractice cases.[4] However, this provision is rarely employed.[5] Expense is a factor here. So is the reality that trial experts are often not retained until after filing of the note of issue and near to trial. Many attorneys also prefer to keep their experts under wraps as much as possible; the advantage to be gained from questioning the other expert often seems outweighed by the disadvantage of offering up one's own.

4. As noted, the name of an expert trial witness need not be disclosed in medical malpractice cases.

5. The CPLR 3101(d) statement is more limited than its federal counterpart.

6. As noted, there is no deadline for the furnishing of the CPLR 3101(d) statement.

A. "Special Circumstances" Limitation on Depositions of Expert Witnesses

The statute contemplates the possibility of additional expert disclosure, which could include depositions. However, such disclosure regarding the expected testimony of any expert may be obtained only by court order "upon a showing of special circumstances and subject to restrictions as to scope and provisions concerning fees and expenses as the court may deem appropriate."[6]

---

4   CPLR 3101(d)(1)(ii).

5   Richard S. Basuk, *Expert Witness Discovery for Medical Malpractice Cases in the Courts of New York: Is It Time to Take Off the Blindfolds?*, 76 N.Y.U. L. Rev. 1527, 1538 (2001) (hereinafter "Basuk").

6   CPLR 3101(d)(1)(iii).

The courts have construed the "special circumstances" requirement narrowly so that a deposition of a trial expert in New York State practice is a rare occurrence,[7] and disclosure with regard to trial experts is primarily limited to the CPLR 3101(d)(1) statement. The courts are quite reluctant to order such depositions. The fact that a testifying expert may have highly relevant and material testimony to offer is not enough to justify a deposition.[8] Nor is it enough that plaintiff's expert will present opinions that are thought to be novel, unorthodox and scientifically unsupported.[9]

Special circumstances are found when physical evidence has been lost, destroyed or changed after one side had access to it but the other did not[10] or in similar situations.[11] For example, if a fire damages or destroys property, fire experts inspect the scene shortly afterward and the scene is cleaned up before the other side can dispatch an expert, a deposition might be ordered.[12] In such situations, the courts typically will direct that

---

7   Basuk, *supra* note 5 at 1537 (the interpretation given has been so narrow as virtually to eliminate expert depositions in New York cases). *See Kaufman v. Lund Fire Prods. Co.*, ___ A.D.3d ___, 777 N.Y.S.2d 686 (2d Dep't 2004); *Brooklyn Floor Maint. Co. v. Providence Wash. Ins. Co.*, 296 A.D.2d 520, 745 N.Y.S.2d 208 (2d Dep't 2002); *Ruthman, Mercadante & Hadjis v. Nardiello*, 288 A.D.2d 593, 732 N.Y.S.2d 455 (3d Dep't 2001); *Flex-O-Vit USA, Inc. v. Niagara Mohawk Power Corp.*, 281 A.D.2d 980, 722 N.Y.S.2d 671 (4th Dep't 2001); *Taft Partners Dev. Group v. Drizin*, 277 A.D.2d 163, 717 N.Y.S.2d 53 (1st Dep't 2000); *Hallahan v. Ashland Chem. Co.*, 237 A.D.2d 697, 654 N.Y.S.2d 443 (3d Dep't 1997); *Mass. Bay Ins. Co. v. Stamm*, 237 A.D.2d 145, 654 N.Y.S.2d 752 (1st Dep't 1997); *The Hartford v. Black & Decker (U.S.) Inc.*, 221 A.D.2d 986, 634 N.Y.S.2d 294 (4th Dep't 1995); *Tedesco v. Dry-Vac Sales Inc.*, 203 A.D.2d 873, 611 N.Y.S.2d 321 (3d Dep't 1994); *232 Broadway Corp. v. New York Prop. Ins. Underwriting Ass'n*, 171 A.D.2d 861, 567 N.Y.S.2d 790 (2d Dep't 1991); *Rosario v. Gen. Motors Corp.*, 148 A.D.2d 108, 543 N.Y.S.2d 974 (1st Dep't 1989); David Paul Horowitz, *Pretrial Expert Disclosure in State Court Cases*, 75 N.Y.S.B.J. 10 (2003) (expert disclosure in state practice is "far more restrictive than expert disclosure in federal practice") (hereinafter "Horowitz").

8   *Ruthman, Mercadante & Hadjis*, 288 A.D.2d 593; *Hallahan*, 237 A.D.2d 697.

9   *Hallahan*, 237 A.D.2d at 698 (no "compelling circumstances"; a veiled assertion that plaintiffs' experts' causation theories are "bunk" and should be exposed as such is insufficient).

10   *Kaufman*, 777 N.Y.S.2d 686 (equipment changed); *Ruthman, Mercadante & Hadjis*, 288 A.D.2d 593; *Flex-O-Vit USA, Inc.*, 281 A.D.2d 980; *Hallahan*, 237 A.D.2d 697; *The Hartford*, 221 A.D.2d 986; *Tedesco*, 203 A.D.2d 873; *232 Broadway Corp.*, 171 A.D.2d 861. In *Rosario*, 148 A.D.2d at 111, Justice Wallach wrote that "the destruction of physical evidence after its inspection by an expert for one side but before its inspection by an expert for the other is per se a special circumstance justifying disclosure directly from the expert." Such disclosure should not be denied on the ground that the expert's factual observations were set forth adequately in the written report.

11   *Mass. Bay Ins. Co.*, 237 A.D.2d 145 (special circumstances found where one side completed depositions of all the other side's experts and then refused to answer interrogatories, asserting they were an improper attempt to obtain expert disclosure).

12   *Flex-O-Vit USA, Inc.*, 281 A.D.2d 980; *see Tedesco*, 203 A.D.2d 873.

the deposition be limited to the factual observations of the expert and any tests or examinations conducted by him or her.[13]

B. Exchange of Medical Reports

In personal injury and wrongful death cases, medical reports must be exchanged.[14] In state courts, personal injury actions make up a significant portion of the docket, and the exchange of medical reports thus plays an important role in state court litigation.

A party may obtain a physical, mental or blood examination of another party,[15] and the reports of such examinations must be exchanged in the appropriate circumstances.[16] Written authorizations may be obtained allowing the requesting party to receive and copy hospital records relating to

---

13 *Flex-O-Vit USA, Inc.*, 281 A.D.2d 980; *The Hartford*, 221 A.D.2d 986; *Tedesco*, 203 A.D.2d 873. This is done to protect the expert's opinions, about the disclosure of which the courts have been quite cautious. 6 Jack B. Weinstein et al., New York Civil Practice ¶ 3101.36, at 31-83 (2004) (hereinafter "Weinstein") ("the courts normally do not permit the taking of any opinion evidence from an expert who is not a party" (footnote omitted)). Indeed, in *Rosario*, 148 A.D.2d 108, the court, noting the importance of the matter, stated that the trial judge could limit a party to interrogatories even when special circumstances were present if that was necessary to protect the witness's opinions.

14 *Martinez v. KSM Holding Ltd.*, 294 A.D.2d 111, 741 N.Y.S.2d 519 (1st Dep't 2002) (expert files did not have to be produced in personal injury case where expert did tests on plaintiffs and had produced expert reports); *accord Austin v. Coastal Indus., Inc.*, 112 A.D.2d 123, 491 N.Y.S.2d 53 (2d Dep't 1985). The obligation to produce an expert report in a personal injury case cannot be circumvented by directing the expert not to prepare such a report. *Davidson v. Steer/Peanut Gallery*, 277 A.D.2d 965, 715 N.Y.S.2d 560 (4th Dep't 2000); *Pierson v. Yourish*, 122 A.D.2d 202, 505 N.Y.S.2d 165 (2d Dep't 1986); *Comunale v. Sealand Constr. Corp.*, 2 Misc. 2d 672, 771 N.Y.S.2d 631 (Sup. Ct., Monroe Co. 2004).

15 CPLR 3121(a). The examination may be obtained in any action in which the mental or physical condition or blood relationship of a party or agent, employee or person in the custody or under the control thereof is in controversy. Though not limited to such instances, this section is regularly applied to plaintiffs in personal injury actions.

16 CPLR 3121(b). Subdivision (b) mandates that a detailed written report of the examining physician setting out findings and conclusions be delivered by the examining party to any other party if the latter agrees to exchange therefor a copy of each report in that party's control of the examination made regarding the condition in issue. If a party employs a physician who studies medical records but does not conduct a physical or mental examination of the plaintiff, the physician's report does not fall under subdivision (b) but, rather, is the work of a nontestifying expert and is considered material prepared for litigation and thus is generally protected (CPLR 3101(d)(2)). 6 Weinstein, *supra* note 13, ¶ 3121.18, at 31-512. If a physical examination of plaintiff is performed at the request of plaintiff's counsel solely for litigation purposes, the plaintiff must nevertheless furnish a detailed written report of the physician's findings based on that examination. *Pierson*, 122 A.D.2d 202; *Moreno v. Greater New York Dental Admin.*, 120 A.D.2d 343, 501 N.Y.S.2d 672 (1st Dep't 1986); *Comunale*, 2 Misc. 3d 672; *Miller v. Marks*, 140 Misc. 2d 1002, 532 N.Y.S.2d 35 (Sup. Ct., Orange Co. 1988).

the condition or blood relationship involved.[17] Other medical records may be obtained pursuant to other provisions.

Uniform Rule 202.17 further provides for physical examinations and the exchange of medical reports in personal injury and wrongful death actions. The plaintiff (or other party being examined) must, prior to the physical exam, serve on the other parties copies of the medical reports of medical providers who previously treated or examined the plaintiff, together with authorizations for hospital records.[18] The reports must recite the injuries and conditions as to which testimony will be offered at trial.[19] Copies of like reports of the examining physicians shall be served on all parties after the examination.[20] Reports must be exchanged in wrongful death cases.[21]

Absent a ruling otherwise by the judge, the plaintiff will be precluded from offering at trial proof of injuries or conditions not put in issue in the medical reports previously exchanged. The court will not hear the testimony of any treating or examining providers whose reports have not been served.[22]

C. Production of Expert Reports before Trial

Apart from the requirements governing the exchange of medical reports in personal injury litigation and appraisal reports in condemnation and tax certiorari cases, the state discovery rules generally provide that the report of a testifying expert does not have to be produced prior to trial.[23] Such a report would be material prepared in anticipation of litigation or for trial and be subject to disclosure only "upon a showing that the party seeking discovery has substantial need of the materials in the preparation of the case and is unable without undue hardship to obtain the substantial equiv-

---

17   CPLR 3121(a).

18   Uniform Rule 202.17(b)(1), (2).

19   Uniform Rule 202.17(b)(1).

20   Uniform Rule 202.17(c).

21   Uniform Rule 202.17(d).

22   Uniform Rule 202.17(h).

23   CPLR 3101(d)(1)(iii); *Barrowman v. Niagara Mohawk Power Corp.*, 252 A.D.2d 947, 675 N.Y.S.2d 734 (4th Dep't), *appeal denied*, 92 N.Y.2d 817 (1998); *In re Love Canal Actions*, 161 A.D.2d 1169, 555 N.Y.S.2d 519 (4th Dep't 1990); Siegel, McKinney's Practice Commentary CPLR 3101, at 50 (1991).

alent of the materials by other means."[24] The files of a testifying expert and the tests, measurements, findings, notes and the like of such expert are likewise generally not subject to disclosure.[25] State and federal practice differ in this respect.[26]

D. Discovery of Consulting, Advisory and Nonparty Experts' Testimony

Except for examining experts in personal injury actions, what is true with regard to testifying experts is true with regard to experts retained by a party to provide consultation, assistance and advice in the prosecution or defense of an action: Experts who are retained for such purposes and who will not testify at trial do not have to provide the expert disclosure mandated by CPLR 3101(d)(1)(i) because that provision is addressed expressly to testifying experts only.[27] Disclosure from nonparties (any person not included in CPLR 3101(a)(1–3)) is authorized "upon notice stating the circumstances or reasons such disclosure is sought or required."[28]

However, as was discussed in chapter 2,[29] courts have applied CPLR 3101(a)(4) more narrowly than the words alone might suggest. The deposition of a consulting expert by an adverse party is permitted only rarely in New York practice. A report prepared by a consulting expert would constitute materials prepared for litigation and as such would generally be immune from discovery except upon a showing of substantial need and undue hardship.[30] If such a showing were made, a court ordering disclosure of such materials shall "protect against disclosure of the mental impressions, conclusions, opinions or legal theories of an attorney or

---

24   CPLR 3101(d)(2); *Barrowman*, 252 A.D.2d 947; *Marziano v. City of Yonkers*, 105 A.D.2d 832, 481 N.Y.S.2d 755 (2d Dep't 1984); David D. Siegel, New York Practice § 548, at 532 (3d ed. 1999) (hereinafter "Siegel").

25   *Barrowman*, 252 A.D.2d 947.

26   See *infra* at II. for a discussion of these differences.

27   *Casey v. Tan*, 255 A.D.2d 900, 680 N.Y.S.2d 391 (4th Dep't 1998).

28   CPLR 3101(a)(4).

29   *See* I.A.2.

30   *Richards v. Herrick*, 292 A.D.2d 874, 738 N.Y.S.2d 470 (4th Dep't 2002) (plaintiffs not required to disclose expert meteorologist's report); *Beauchamp v. Riverbay Corp.*, 156 A.D.2d 172, 548 N.Y.S.2d 215 (1st Dep't 1989) (citing *Rosario v. Gen. Motors Corp.*, 148 A.D.2d 108, 543 N.Y.S.2d 974 (1st Dep't 1989) (court can direct a party to produce a copy of an expert report where the item (a washing machine) had been disposed of and could no longer be inspected by other side's expert)).

other representative of a party concerning the litigation."[31] Similarly, the consulting expert's files, tests and the like would be material prepared for litigation.[32]

Discovery can be sought from a person with technical, scientific or other expertise when the person was a witness to relevant events and the discovery concerns that knowledge. For example, the deposition of a non-party physician might be appropriate if his or her testimony were sought on the question of how an accident occurred, rather than with regard to the physician's expert opinions as to negligence, the standard of care, causation and so forth.

In a personal injury case, the defendant cannot depose any and all non-party treating physicians as of right.[33] As discussed in chapter 2,[34] it is not enough that the testimony of the physician might be relevant and material; it must be shown that the information cannot be obtained from other sources or is otherwise necessary to prepare for trial—that there are, some courts continue to say, special circumstances sufficient to require the testimony under CPLR 3101(a)(4).[35]

In *Capati v. Crunch Fitness International, Inc.*,[36] for example, the court held that it was error to quash subpoenas directed to three nonparty treat-

---

31   CPLR 3101(d)(2).

32   6 Weinstein, *supra* note 13, ¶ 3101.52a, at 31-149–31-150 (consultants included in CPLR 3101(d)(2)). The work of a consultant might also qualify for exemption as attorney work product (CPLR 3101(c)), although this category is construed more narrowly than that of material prepared for litigation. *Id.*; Siegel, *supra* note 24, § 347, at 532. In *Russell v. City of Buffalo*, 4 A.D.3d 780, 772 N.Y.S.2d 160 (4th Dep't 2004), the court ruled that plaintiff had made a sufficient showing of substantial hardship in a case in which the defendants' experts had conducted an investigation, made measurements and prepared diagrams after a highway had been closed to permit them to do so; because plaintiffs could not shut down the highway themselves, the data would have to be provided to plaintiffs.

33   *Patterson v. St. Francis Ctr.*, 249 A.D.2d 457, 671 N.Y.S.2d 532 (2d Dep't 1998) (deposition of nonparty treating physician denied); *Roeck v. Columbia-Greene Med. Ctr.*, 248 A.D.2d 921, 670 N.Y.S.2d 269 (3d Dep't 1998); *Michalak v. Venticinque*, 222 A.D.2d 1060, 635 N.Y.S.2d 875 (4th Dep't 1995) (protective order should have been granted against deposition of treating physician); *King v. State Farm Mut. Auto. Ins. Co.*, 198 A.D.2d 748, 604 N.Y.S.2d 302 (3d Dep't 1993) (deposition of nonparty physician denied); *Dioguardi v. St. John's Riverside Hosp.*, 144 A.D.2d 333, 533 N.Y.S.2d 915 (2d Dep't 1988) (deposition of treating nonparty physician denied).

34   *See* I.A.2.

35   *See, e.g., Michalak*, 222 A.D.2d 1060. *Compare Schroder v. Consol. Edison Co.*, 249 A.D.2d 69, 670 N.Y.S.2d 856 (1st Dep't 1998) (special circumstances no longer required).

36   295 A.D.2d 181, 743 N.Y.S.2d 474 (1st Dep't 2002).

ing physicians because the testimony was material and necessary and could furnish information not available from the medical records. In that case, no autopsy had been performed on the decedent, and the medical records did not show a cause of death, nor did the death certificate.[37]

E. Discovery of Party Expert's or Treating Expert's Testimony

A party may obtain disclosure from a physician, dentist or podiatrist who provided care or diagnosis to that party or who has been retained as an expert by that party. If such disclosure is sought, any other party shall also be entitled to disclosure from that expert.[38]

Because there must be full disclosure from a party or an officer, director, member, agent or employee of a party,[39] a deposition can be required of an expert who is a defendant, for example, or the agent or employee of a party. In a medical malpractice action, for instance, the defendant physician can be deposed. The plaintiff is permitted to inquire into the standard of care ordinarily employed by such physicians and whether the defendant's actions in the case met that standard.[40]

A treating physician may testify as to his or her own observations.[41] Some cases hold that the treating physician may also give expert opinions even though he or she was not disclosed as a testifying expert and that no 3101(d) statement need be given, as that provision applies to trial experts.[42]

---

37   *Id.* Compare the dissent of two justices, 295 A.D.2d at 181, arguing that the party seeking the deposition had already had all material and necessary evidence in the medical records. In *Schroder*, 249 A.D.2d 69, the court held that a nonparty treating physician could be deposed as to plaintiff's account of the accident; there was a discrepancy between plaintiff's deposition testimony and her account of the accident as recorded by the physician and thus the deposition of the physician was material and necessary. Compare *Ruthman, Mercadante & Hadjis v. Nardiello*, 288 A.D.2d 593, 732 N.Y.S.2d 455 (3d Dep't 2001).

38   CPLR 3101(a)(3), (d)(1)(iii).

39   *See* CPLR 3101(a)(1).

40   *McDermott v. Manhattan Eye, Ear & Throat Hosp.*, 15 N.Y.2d 20, 255 N.Y.S.2d 65 (1964); *Orner v. Mount Sinai Hosp.*, 305 A.D.2d 307, 761 N.Y.S.2d 603 (1st Dep't 2003); *Johnson v. New York City Health & Hosps. Corp.*, 49 A.D.2d 234, 374 N.Y.S.2d 343 (2d Dep't 1975).

41   *Finger v. Brande*, 306 A.D.2d 104, 762 N.Y.S.2d 50 (1st Dep't 2003); *Krinsky v. Rachleff*, 276 A.D.2d 748, 715 N.Y.S.2d 712 (2d Dep't 2000).

42   *Id. Accord Mantuano v. Mehale*, 258 A.D.2d 566, 685 N.Y.S.2d 467 (2d Dep't 1999); *Overeem v. Neuhoff*, 254 A.D.2d 398, 679 N.Y.S.2d 74 (2d Dep't 1998); *Stark v. Semeran*, 244 A.D.2d 894, 665 N.Y.S.2d 233 (4th Dep't 1997), *motion for leave to appeal dismissed*, 91 N.Y.2d 956 (1998); *Rook v. 60 Key Centre, Inc.*, 239 A.D.2d 926, 660 N.Y.S.2d 238 (4th Dep't 1997).

F. Perceived Limitations of State Discovery Rules

From the perspective of those who favor more liberal expert disclosure,[43] the difficulty caused by the unfortunate virtual absence of expert depositions is compounded by several other perceived problems. The lack of a deadline for furnishing the 3101(d)(1) expert statement leads to disputes about claimed untimely production, possibly designed to secure a tactical advantage.[44] Discord also arises over the content of the statement. Whether the actions of a party justify preclusion is also a source of controversy. Even if the expert disclosure statement is produced in timely fashion, recipients often complain that it consists of largely uninformative boilerplate.[45]

Attorneys will communicate with their experts about the case and the theories being presented. Because expert witnesses are rarely deposed in state practice and, when they do testify at deposition, generally confine that testimony to observations of fact, there seems to have been little occasion in the cases to consider the possible waiver of work product protection by the presentation to the expert of protected material. The tendency seems to be to regard such communications as protected.[46]

---

43   There are, of course, two views on this matter. Arguments can be made that broader use of expert depositions in New York practice would increase the complexity and expense of litigation and delay resolution of matters. In many personal injury cases, an expert may not be retained by the plaintiff until not long before trial. Cases that settle before trial are less costly when the expert is retained in this way. Experts are very expensive as a general rule.

44   Professor Siegel writes:

> Any practitioner scanning the annotations on this statute [CPLR 3101(d)(1)(i)] must be bewildered by the many conflicting determinations it has generated. There is really no way to reconcile them all. The problem traces in most of the cases to the absence of any stated time limit on when the expert disclosure has to be made following the other side's demand. There is probably a case that can be cited for just about any position either side wants to take in a given situation, and there appears to be no end in sight.

> A legislative cure would of course be the best answer, but with the plaintiff's tort bar vehemently and vociferously opposed to the imposition of any stated time limit, no corrective amendment has been forthcoming.

Siegel, McKinney's Practice Commentary, CPLR 3101, at 7 (Supp. 2004). *See* Horowitz, *supra* note 7, at 11–12. "[T]he key to almost all court decisions made on the timeliness of an expert exchange is prejudice to the demanding party." *Id*. at 12.

45   "Very often an expert response is served that does not provide the information called for in the statute. Entire topic areas may be omitted, or the response may be so vague or jammed with boiler-plate language that no meaningful information is provided." Horowitz, *supra* note 7, at 12. *See Richards v. Herrick*, 292 A.D.2d 874, 738 N.Y.S.2d 470 (4th Dep't 2002).

46   *See People v. Edney*, 39 N.Y.2d 620, 625, 385 N.Y.S.2d 23, 26 (1976); *Holmes v. Weissman*, 251 A.D.2d 1078, 674 N.Y.S.2d 215 (4th Dep't 1998).

II. FEDERAL PRACTICE

A. Disclosure Requirements

A party must disclose the identity of any person who may be used to present expert testimony at trial.[47] Further, a party may depose anyone who has been identified as an expert whose opinions may be presented at trial.[48] A party may depose or serve interrogatories upon any nontestifying expert only as provided in FRCP 35(b) or on a showing of exceptional circumstances.[49]

With regard to a witness who is retained or specially employed to provide expert testimony or who regularly gives expert testimony as an employee of a party, the disclosure must, unless otherwise stipulated or ordered by the court, be accompanied by an expert report. This report must be prepared and signed by the witness and contain "a complete statement of all opinions to be expressed and the basis and reasons therefor," the information considered by the witness, any exhibits to be used as a summary of or in support of the opinions, the qualifications of the witness, including a list of publications, the compensation to be paid and a list of cases in which the person testified as an expert within the previous four years.[50]

A deadline for production is set forth in the rule.[51] Expert reports are generally exchanged either pursuant to the pretrial scheduling order or by directive of the court in some other fashion, but if this is not the case, such disclosure must be made 90 days or more before the trial date or the date the case is to be ready for trial.[52]

If a party fails without substantial justification to disclose information required by FRCP 26(a), that party risks a ruling that it may not use the witness or information on a motion or at trial.[53] This rule creates an incentive to produce an expert report that complies with the intent of FRCP

---

47   FRCP 26.

48   FRCP 26(b)(4)(A).

49   FRCP 26(b)(4)(B).

50   FRCP 26(a)(2).

51   FRCP 26(a)(2)(C).

52   FRCP 26(a)(2).

53   FRCP 37(c)(1).

26;[54] the drafters hoped that a detailed report would eliminate the need to depose many experts and reduce the length of the expert depositions that were taken.[55]

B. Availability of Work Product Protection for Materials Furnished to Experts

The provisions of FRCP 26 concerning discovery from testifying experts raise a question about the application of the attorney-client privilege and particularly work product protection to materials furnished to such experts to assist them in evaluating the case. There is considerable disagreement among the cases as to how to answer this question properly, especially with regard to core work product and the mental impressions, opinions or legal conclusions of counsel. This disagreement exists despite the Advisory Committee's assertion that the 1993 amendments should prevent litigants from arguing "that materials furnished to their experts to be used in forming their opinions—whether or not ultimately relied upon by the expert—are privileged or otherwise protected from disclosure when such persons are testifying or being deposed."[56]

Some cases, relying upon the language and history of FRCP 26(a)(2)(B), the comments of the Advisory Committee and policy considerations, have concluded that material furnished to a testifying expert must be disclosed whether or not it would otherwise be protected by the attorney-client privilege or as work product, including core work product.[57]

---

54   Notes of Advisory Committee on 1993 Amendments, FRCP 26, regarding subd. (a)(2).

55   *Id.*

56   *Id.*

57   *See, e.g., In re Pioneer Hi-Bred Int'l, Inc.*, 238 F.3d 1370, 1370–76 (Fed. Cir. 2001); *Lugosch v. Congel*, 219 F.R.D. 220, 247–50 (N.D.N.Y. 2003); *Baum v. Village of Chittenango*, 218 F.R.D. 36 (N.D.N.Y. 2003); *Mfg. Admin. Mgmt. Sys. v. ICT Group*, 212 F.R.D. 110 (E.D.N.Y. 2002); *Aniero Concrete Co. v. New York City Sch. Constr. Auth.*, 2002 U.S. Dist. LEXIS 2892 (S.D.N.Y. Feb. 21, 2002) (Maas, Mag. J.); *Herman v. Marine Midland Bank*, 207 F.R.D. 26, 28–29 (W.D.N.Y. 2002); *Weil v. Long Island Sav. Bank*, 206 F.R.D. 38 (E.D.N.Y. 2001) (Wall, Mag. J.); *Trigon Ins. Co. v. United States*, 204 F.R.D. 277 (E.D. Va. 2001); *TV-3, Inc. v. Royal Ins. Co.*, 193 F.R.D. 490 (S.D. Miss.), *aff'd*, 194 F.R.D. 585 (S.D. Miss. 2000); *Johnson v. Gmeinder*, 191 F.R.D. 638 (D. Kan. 2000); *Lamonds v. Gen. Motors Corp.*, 180 F.R.D. 302 (W.D. Va. 1998); *Musselman v. Phillips*, 176 F.R.D. 194 (D. Md. 1997); *B.C.F. Oil Refining, Inc. v. Consol. Edison Co.*, 171 F.R.D. 57, 62–67 (S.D.N.Y. 1997); *Karn v. Rand*, 168 F.R.D. 633 (N.D. Ind. 1996); *see* 8 Charles Alan Wright et al., Federal Practice and Procedure § 2016.2, at 252 (2d ed. 1994) ("At least with respect to experts who testify at trial, the disclosure requirements of Rule 26(a)(2), adopted in 1993, were intended to pretermit further discussion and mandate disclosure despite privilege.") (footnote omitted); *see also Monsanto Co. v. Aventis Cropscience, N.V.*, 214 F.R.D. 545 (E.D. Mo. 2002).

Federal Rule of Civil Procedure 26(a)(2) requires disclosure of an expert report that contains the data or other information *considered* by a witness in forming opinions. The committee, the courts point out, rejected the use in this context of the narrower word *relied*, intending to encompass broadly the matter taken into account (whether in the end relied upon or not) by the expert.[58] In addition, the rule's provision regarding work product[59] is, by its terms, subject to the provisions of FRCP 26(b)(4) concerning depositions of testifying experts. The courts assert that the Advisory Committee stated what it intended the provisions to mean by referring to the absence of protection for work product furnished to a testifying expert.

Furthermore, these courts note, disclosure promotes effective cross-examination, which is particularly important in an era in which experts are numerous and their opinions are accorded great weight.[60] This approach also has the advantage that bright lines do: It advances certainty in the litigation process.[61] One court added the following consideration to the analysis, which some litigators will surely find uncomfortable to contemplate:

> Some commentators argue that an attorney must be able to have free exchange with the expert because the expert is a valuable part of the "litigation team." Such proponents contend that experts should enjoy uninhibited exchange with the attorney to aid in the analysis of the case and development of litigation strategy. This argument, however, mischaracterizes the role of the expert in litigation to the extent it implies that testifying experts serve as party advocates. The expert exists to assist the judge or jury in findings of fact—not to act as an advocate from the witness stand. Therefore, mitigating the expert's role as an advocate is, in fact, desirable.[62]

---

58   *See, e.g., Mfg. Admin. Mgmt. Sys.*, 212 F.R.D. at 115.

59   FRCP 26(b)(3).

60   *In re Pioneer Hi-Bred Int'l, Inc.*, 238 F.3d at 1375–76; *Mfg. Admin. Mgmt. Sys.*, 212 F.R.D. at 116–17; *Aniero Concrete Co.*, 2002 U.S. Dist. LEXIS 2892; *Herman*, 207 F.R.D. at 28–29; *Weil*, 206 F.R.D. 38; *Trigon Ins. Co.*, 204 F.R.D. 277; *TV-3, Inc.*, 193 F.R.D. at 492 (observing that "in our present legal culture money plus the proper 'marching orders' will get an 'expert' witness who will undertake to prove almost anything"); *Johnson*, 191 F.R.D. 638; *Lamonds*, 180 F.R.D. 302; *Musselman*, 176 F.R.D. 194; *B.C.F. Oil Refining, Inc.*, 171 F.R.D. at 62–67; *Karn*, 168 F.R.D. 633.

61   *Karn*, 168 F.R.D. at 639, 641.

62   *Mfg. Admin. Mgmt. Sys.*, 212 F.R.D. at 117 (citations omitted).

Other courts take the position that the language of FRCP 26 and the remarks of the committee do not address core work product, nor do they indicate that such important material should lose its protected status. The courts also assert that the emphasis upon a need for effective cross-examination is overstated. The conclusion is that factual material provided to the expert should not be immune from disclosure but that core work product material should be.[63]

Until there is a definitive answer as to what the governing standard is in the Second Circuit, if not broader clarification by rule or consensus, attorneys must take seriously what seemingly is the preponderant opinion of judges in this circuit—that disclosure of work product, even core work product, is required. This may necessitate some careful thought from counsel as how to best go about the practical task of ensuring that the expert is educated about the case in which he or she is expected to testify.

Some courts have frankly mentioned one approach: "[I]n the first instance, an attorney can protect his work by electing not to disclose it. Obviously, that tact [sic] is less conducive to a productive relationship between attorney and expert."[64] Another approach is available, but it, too, comes at a cost, including a literal one:

> [T]he bright line rule . . . creates an incentive for a party additionally to retain a non-testifying expert, to whom an attorney may speak freely about litigation strategies and opinions without falling prey to the powerful jaws of mandatory disclosure. Retaining both a non-testifying expert

---

63　*See, e.g., Smith v. Transducer Tech., Inc.*, 197 F.R.D. 260, 262 (D.V.I. 2000); *Krisa v. Equitable Life Assurance Soc'y*, 196 F.R.D. 254 (M.D. Pa. 2000); *Moore v. R.J. Reynolds Tobacco Co.*, 194 F.R.D. 659 (S.D. Iowa 2000); *Magee v. Paul Revere Life Ins. Co.*, 172 F.R.D. 627, 641–44 (E.D.N.Y. 1997); *Haworth, Inc. v. Herman Miller, Inc.*, 162 F.R.D. 289 (W.D. Mich. 1995). *See* Gregory P. Joseph, *Emerging Expert Issues Under the 1993 Disclosure Amendments to the Federal Rules of Civil Procedure*, 164 F.R.D. 97 (1996).

64　*Baum v. Village of Chittenango*, 218 F.R.D. 36, 46 (N.D.N.Y. 2003). *See also Lugosch v. Congel*, 219 F.R.D. 220, 250 (N.D.N.Y. 2003) ("The salvable and cautionary corollary to this rule for attorneys is to be discrete and circumspect in what work product is shared with [an] expert who will be testifying."); *Mfg. Admin. Mgmt. Sys.*, 212 F.R.D. at 117 ("To escape the wide swath of discovery's net, therefore, an attorney can simply choose not to communicate such work product to a testifying expert.").

and a testifying expert, however, can increase a party's litigation costs significantly, thereby favoring flush litigants.[65]

A nontestifying expert generally cannot be deposed. It is, of course, necessary to distinguish between a fact witness and a person hired to perform services as a nontestifying expert. It may often be easy to draw this distinction, but not in every case.

As to nontestifying experts, a deposition (or interrogatories) will be allowed only upon a showing of exceptional circumstances. The party seeking such a deposition has a heavy burden. A party that retains an expert to assist in the preparation or defense of a case should not be required to perform the other side's work for it.

---

65   *Mfg. Admin. Mgmt. Sys.*, 212 F.R.D. at 118 (footnote omitted). The issue of possible disclosure of work product might be examined from a different angle. Chapter 3 summarized doctrine concerning waiver of protection when documents are used to refresh recollection of a testifying witness. With regard to this and, in particular, FRE 612 relative to expert testimony, see *Mfg. Admin. Mgmt. Sys.*, 212 F.R.D. at 118 (in this context "full reliance on Rule 612 is misplaced").

CHAPTER FIVE

CONDUCT OF THE DEPOSITION

This chapter discusses the rules that govern the actual conduct of the deposition. In a deposition, the inquiring attorney should be able to gather from the witness responsive answers to questions relevant to the issues in the case, taking the time necessary to explore these questions in reasonable and adequate detail. Although the inquiring attorney should avoid repetition, he or she should be able to examine facts from different angles if it makes sense to do so.

The deposition should not be an occasion for dancing around issues nor an exercise in terminological disputation. Although a witness need not be expansive, it is improper for a witness to be evasive and try to skip around questions rather than provide answers. The interrogator has the right to pin the witness down to specific testimony about the facts when the witness has information about those facts. The purpose of the deposition is to obtain the testimony of the witness, not that of his or her attorney or anyone else in the room. The testimony should not be gilded or molded by the interventions of counsel. The attorney whose job it is to represent a deponent at a deposition has no right to engage in conduct that artificially obstructs the questioning or inhibits the witness from providing answers to relevant questions posed.

At the same time, the process must respect the rights of the witness. The deposition should not delve into irrelevant matter, especially if it is highly personal. The deposition should seek testimony about relevant facts, not the legal opinions of the witness. The deposition should not be used as a mechanism to argue with, harass or oppress the witness. The questioner has no right to invade recognized privileges, nor to disregard limitations the judge places on questioning or on discovery in general.

Attorneys should never be rude or discourteous toward one another, the witness or anyone else present. Such behavior ought not to occur in normal daily life; it is far less acceptable in a deposition, which, though it may occur in an anonymous conference room, is part of the workings of our system of justice and thus should reflect the dignity and seriousness of that system.

The deposition should unfold efficiently, in as inexpensive a manner for both sides as possible.

This framework is the ideal. As with other legal processes, achieving the ideal represents a considerable challenge.[1] In an effort to meet the challenge, the rules strike a balance among competing considerations. Whether the right balance has been struck in every instance is a matter of some controversy.

In recent years, concern has been expressed in many quarters in our legal system about the expense and burdens associated with the discovery process. This concern has extended to deposition practice.[2] Especially in the federal system, increased attention has been given to abusive conduct at depositions.[3]

I. THE RULES—AN OVERVIEW

A. State Practice

In New York State practice, the main provisions governing the conduct of depositions are CPLR 3113 and 3115.[4] In regard to depositions, the CPLR reflects the broad approach to discovery summarized in chapter 1.[5] In general, within some important limits discussed below, questioning should proceed from beginning to end without interference or significant interruption, even if errors are made during the process. Errors are to be corrected at trial unless they are such as could be obviated if raised at the deposition. In this way, depositions can proceed to a conclusion quickly, efficiently and effectively and without the need for judicial intervention.

---

1   In the deposition,

> counsel are expected to rise above their roles as advocates for a particular party, and, acting as officers of the court, resolve their differences on the spot without outside intervention. As difficult as it is to do, and recognizing . . . that reasonable minds can differ in good faith about many discovery issues, it is nonetheless required that counsel behave appropriately during deposition discovery.

Boyd v. Univ. of Md. Med. Sys., 173 F.R.D. 143, 144 (D. Md. 1997).

2   *See, e.g.*, Federal Bar Council, *A Report on the Conduct of Depositions*, 131 F.R.D. 613 (1990). The authors note that depositions "have often become theaters for posturing and maneuvering" and "often are no longer cost-effective devices for obtaining discovery," "that improper deposition conduct is rampant" and that "there is a pervasive view that advocacy may require that improper deposition tactics be met in kind." *Id.* at 613, 621.

3   *See, e.g.*, Janeen Kerper & Gary L. Stuart, *Rambo Bites the Dust: Current Trends in Deposition Ethics*, 22 J. Legal Prof. 103 (1998).

4   CPLR 3112 provides that all "errors and irregularities" in the deposition notice are waived unless a written objection is served on the noticing party at least three days prior to the deposition date. This ensures that such errors or irregularities need not be raised at the deposition but will be waived or presumably addressed and resolved in advance.

5   David D. Siegel, New York Practice § 356, at 554 (3d ed. 1999) (hereinafter "Siegel").

Examination and cross-examination at the deposition "shall proceed as permitted in the trial of actions in open court."[6] In general, objections may be made at trial to the use of any part of a deposition just as if the witness were then present and testifying.[7] This liberality in the taking of testimony is qualified by other portions of CPLR 3115. Subdivision (b) addresses "[e]rrors which might be obviated if made known promptly" and provides that errors and irregularities

> in the manner of taking the deposition, in the form of the questions or answers, in the oath or affirmation, or in the conduct of persons, and errors of any kind which might be obviated or removed if objection were promptly presented, are waived unless reasonable objection thereto is made at the taking of the deposition.

Consistent with this provision, CPLR 3115(d) states that objections to the competency of a witness or the admissibility of testimony are not waived if not interposed prior to or during the deposition, "unless the ground of the objection is one which might have been obviated or removed if objection had been made at that time." Further, objections to the proceedings made at the time shall be noted upon the deposition by the officer before whom it is to be taken, and the deposition shall proceed "subject to the right of a person to apply for a protective order."[8] The deposition "shall be taken continuously and without unreasonable adjournment, unless the court otherwise orders or the witness and parties present otherwise agree."[9]

The purpose of these last provisions is "to prevent any objection from cancelling the whole examination if that can possibly be avoided. If the parties disagree on a question and the deponent on counsel's advice declines it, the examination . . . should continue on other matters until the questioner has exhausted all of her questions, answered or not."[10] Professor Siegel notes:

> [T]he rule permits the attorney to withhold all . . . objections except those relating to mere form. . . . Not making

---

6   CPLR 3113(c).

7   CPLR 3115(a).

8   CPLR 3113(b).

9   *Id.*

10   Siegel, *supra* note 5, § 356, at 555.

the objection at the deposition does not waive it. At the trial, when the question is read, the attorney may then and there object to it notwithstanding that it was answered without objection in the deposition. If excludible under any rule of evidence, the court will not permit the answer to be read at the trial.

* * *

The only category of defect that must be the subject of an objection at the deposition session, or risk waiver, is that which can be forthwith cured. In the questioning of the deponent, this would ordinarily embrace only the question whose form is objected to, an objection that can be cured by a rephrasing or narrowing of the question. If the objection, even though it may be said to relate only to some matter of form, is not susceptible of immediate cure, it should not be deemed to be in this category. It should fall under subdivision (a) and be available at the trial.[11]

The other immediately curable problems to which CPLR 3115(b) refers "would include the sequence in which several witnesses depose or in which a given witness is questioned by opposing sides, the manner in which the oath is administered, etc."[12] Failure to object at the time to the absence of an interpreter constitutes a waiver of a claim that the witness did not understand the questions.[13]

One court has said:

[O]ur system of unsupervised deposition is dependent on the good-faith obligation of attorneys to comply with the spirit as well as the letter of the statute and procedure, and not to make objections which are merely obstructive,

---

11   Siegel, McKinney's Practice Commentary, CPLR 3115, at 543, 544 (1991).

12   *Id.*; *see* Siegel, *supra* note 5, § 356, at 555. In *Washington v. Montefiore Hosp.*, 7 A.D.3d 945, 777 N.Y.S.2d 524 (3d Dep't 2004), the officer who administered the oath was not present in the deposition room (i.e., the deponent's location), as contemplated by CPLR 3113(b), but in another office connected by phone. The deposition notice had indicated that the deposition would be by phone. An attorney objected to the deposition generally and refused to take part. That attorney had not acted in response to the notice. The attorney did not raise a specific objection to the manner in which the oath was administered. The court held that the objection had been waived. A substitute reporter might have been brought to the site had the problem been raised.

13   *Sheikh v. Sinha*, 272 A.D.2d 465, 707 N.Y.S.2d 241 (2d Dep't 2000).

or to direct the witness not to answer questions objected to when there will be no substantial prejudice in permitting the question to be answered, reserving the objection pursuant to CPLR 3115.[14]

The rules do not so state expressly, but their spirit seems to indicate that, as objections are generally preserved and are thus unnecessary, they should be kept to a minimum since even well-founded objections have some impact on the smooth flow of a deposition; attorneys *should not* make objections that are unnecessary and thus merely obstructive in impact.[15] The making of many objections may amount to sanctionable conduct. Therefore, the rule in New York is as follows:

> [I]n an examination before trial unless a question is clearly violative of the witness's constitutional rights, or of some privilege recognized in law, or is palpably irrelevant, questions should be freely permitted and answered, since all objections other than as to form are preserved for the trial and may be raised at that time.[16]

Thus, the circumstances under which an attorney may direct a witness not to answer a question in state practice are quite narrow (as they are, with some variations, under federal procedure). Yet, improper directions have often been issued in both federal and state court litigation, with considerable disruptive effect. "There simply is no more aggravating action than a lawyer improperly instructing a deponent not to answer a question.

---

14   *White v. Martins*, 100 A.D.2d 805, 805, 474 N.Y.S.2d 733 (1st Dep't 1984).

15   *Id.* (attorneys should "not . . . make objections which are merely obstructive"). Professor Siegel writes: "The fact that substantial objections need not be made does not mean that they cannot be. . . . The courts are especially impatient with petty objections at this stage, however." Siegel, *supra* note 5, § 356, at 555.

16   *Freedco Prods., Inc. v. New York Tel. Co.*, 47 A.D.2d 654, 655, 366 N.Y.S.2d 401 (2d Dep't 1975); *accord Tardibuono v. County of Nassau*, 181 A.D.2d 879, 581 N.Y.S.2d 443 (2d Dep't 1992); *Walter Karl, Inc. v. Wood*, 161 A.D.2d 704, 555 N.Y.S.2d 840 (2d Dep't 1990); *Humiston v. Grose*, 144 A.D.2d 907, 908, 534 N.Y.S.2d 604 (4th Dep't 1988); *Byork v. Carmer*, 109 A.D.2d 1087, 487 N.Y.S.2d 226 (4th Dep't 1985); *Ferraro v. New York Tel. Co.*, 94 A.D.2d 784, 463 N.Y.S.2d 31 (2d Dep't 1983); *Watson v. State*, 53 A.D.2d 798, 385 N.Y.S.2d 170 (3d Dep't 1976). In *White*, 100 A.D.2d at 805, the court set forth the standard in a manner somewhat broader than the *Freedco* formulation, referring to questions that infringe upon a privilege, or are palpably and grossly irrelevant or "unduly burdensome" or "are so improper that to answer them will substantially prejudice the parties." A few cases overstate the restrictiveness of the rule. *See, e.g., Spatz v. World Wide Travel Serv. Inc.*, 70 A.D.2d 835, 418 N.Y.S.2d 19 (1st Dep't 1979); *Palmeri v. Island Med. Care, P.C.*, Index No. 016398/2000, 2002 N.Y. Misc. LEXIS 865 (App. Term, 1st Dep't Apr. 3, 2002).

This tactic frequently is used to frustrate new or inexperienced lawyers, and thwart legitimate discovery by more seasoned ones."[17]

Regardless of the reason for an instruction not to answer, an attorney who wishes to contest the instruction with a motion to compel must remember some important logistical matters. To order that questions be answered, the court must have a proper record to work with. Accordingly, the questioning attorney should set forth on the record each question she or he wishes to ask—even if every question is met with the same instruction not to answer. That way, the court can order answers to specific questions. In the alternative, the questioning attorney can elicit from the objecting attorney a stipulation to the effect that pursuing a whole line of questioning is futile and will be met with objection. In that event, the court can order that the line of questioning may be pursued.[18]

B. Federal Practice

The philosophy evident in CPLR 3113 and 3115 is likewise alive in federal practice, but with some additional restraints on the attorney representing the deponent. The major federal provision on the subject is FRCP 30.

In federal practice, objections may be made, but "the examination shall proceed, with the testimony being taken subject to the objections."[19] Federal Rule of Civil Procedure 32(b) preserves the right of a party to object at trial to admission into evidence of all or part of a deposition for any reason that would require exclusion of the evidence if the witness were then testifying in person.[20] Objections to the competency of a witness or to the

---

17   *Boyd v. Univ. of Md. Med. Sys.*, 173 F.R.D. 143, 144 (D. Md. 1997). Directions not to answer can be especially disruptive. A direction not to answer is obviously more disruptive than a single simple objection because it actually blocks the flow of information. Notes of Advisory Committee on 1993 Amendments, FRCP 30(d).

18   Deposition-related motions to compel are discussed in chapter 7.

19   FRCP 30(c). *See, e.g., Gall v. St. Elizabeth Med. Ctr.*, 130 F.R.D. 85 (S.D. Ohio 1990); *Int'l Union of Elec., Radio & Mach. Workers v. Westinghouse Elec. Corp.*, 91 F.R.D. 277 (D.D.C. 1981); *Lloyd v. Cessna Aircraft Co.*, 74 F.R.D. 518 (E.D. Tenn. 1977); *Preyer v. United States Lines, Inc.*, 64 F.R.D. 430 (E.D. Pa. 1973), *aff'd*, 546 F.2d 418 (3d Cir. 1976); *Shapiro v. Freeman*, 38 F.R.D. 308 (S.D.N.Y. 1965). The parallel sentence in CPLR 3113(b) is similar to the sentence in question in FRCP 30(c), except that in the former, the deposition is to proceed "subject to the right of a person to apply for a protective order."

20   *See, e.g., Reeg v. Shaughnessy*, 570 F.2d 309, 317–18 (10th Cir. 1978); *Trade Dev. Bank v. Cont'l Ins. Co.*, 469 F.2d 35, 45 (2d Cir. 1972); *Dravo Corp. v. Liberty Mut. Ins. Co.*, 164 F.R.D. 70, 74 (D. Neb. 1995); *Mark IV Props., Inc. v. Club Dev. & Mgmt. Corp.*, 12 B.R. 854, 858 n.6 (S.D. Cal. 1981).

competency, relevancy or materiality of testimony are not waived if not interposed at the deposition unless they are such as could have been corrected if raised at that time.[21] Objections based upon the manner of taking the deposition, the form of the questions or answers, or errors of any kind that could be cured if then presented are waived if not raised at the deposition.[22]

> [Objections] . . . ordinarily should be limited to those that under Rule 32(d)(3) might be waived if not made at that time, i.e., objections on grounds that might be immediately obviated, removed, or cured, such as to the form of a question or the responsiveness of an answer. . . . [O]ther objections can, even without the so-called "usual stipulation" preserving objections, be raised for the first time at trial and therefore should be kept to a minimum during a deposition.[23]

The mandate that objections to curable irregularities be made at the deposition rather than withheld until trial prevents a party from manipulating the deposition in order to gain a tactical advantage.[24]

Any objection must "be stated concisely and in a non-argumentative and non-suggestive manner."[25] Once an objection is recorded, the witness ordinarily must answer the question. No person may instruct a witness not to answer a question except "when necessary to preserve a privilege, to enforce a limitation directed by the court, or to present a motion under

---

21 FRCP 32(d)(3)(A); *Jordan v. Medley*, 711 F.2d 211, 217–18 (D.C. Cir. 1983); *Kirschner v. Broadhead*, 671 F.2d 1034, 1038 (7th Cir. 1982); *Bahamas Agric. Indus. Ltd. v. Riley Stoker Corp.*, 526 F.2d 1174, 1180–81 (6th Cir. 1975); *Dravo Corp.*, 164 F.R.D. at 74–75; *Cronkrite v. Fahrbach*, 853 F. Supp. 257, 262–63 (W.D. Mich. 1994); *Hall v. Clifton Precision*, 150 F.R.D. 525, 528 n.3 (E.D. Pa. 1993); *United States v. Irvin*, 127 F.R.D. 169, 171 n.2 (C.D. Cal. 1989); *Delco Wire & Cable, Inc. v. Weinberger*, 109 F.R.D. 680, 691 (E.D. Pa. 1986).

22 FRCP 32(d)(3)(B); *Wilmington v. J.I. Case Co.*, 793 F.2d 909, 921 (8th Cir. 1986); *Kirschner*, 671 F.2d at 1038; *Oberlin v. Marlin Am. Corp.*, 596 F.2d 1322, 1328 (7th Cir. 1979); *Bahamas Agric. Indus. Ltd.*, 526 F.2d at 1180–81; *Sims Consol., Ltd. v. Irrigation & Power Equip., Inc.*, 518 F.2d 413, 417 (10th Cir. 1975); *Ware v. United States*, 971 F. Supp. 1442, 1451 (M.D. Fla. 1997); *Boyd*, 173 F.R.D. at 147; *Associated Bus. Tel. Sys. Corp. v. Greater Capital Corp.*, 729 F. Supp. 1488, 1500 (D.N.J. 1990).

23 Notes of Advisory Committee on 1993 Amendments, FRCP 30(d).

24 *Roy v. Austin Co.*, 194 F.3d 840, 844 (7th Cir. 1999); *Kirschner*, 671 F.2d 1034.

25 FRCP 30(d)(1).

Rule 30(d)(4)."[26] Notably, this provision is framed differently from the rule governing state practice, as usually set forth in state cases.

Upon demand of the objecting party or deponent, the deposition must be suspended for the time necessary to make a motion pursuant to FRCP 30(d)(4).[27] Upon a motion and a showing that "the examination is being conducted in bad faith or in such manner as unreasonably to annoy, embarrass, or oppress the deponent or party," the court is empowered by FRCP 30(d)(4) to order that the deposition cease or limit its scope or the manner of its taking. Expenses of the motion may be awarded.

Federal Rule of Civil Procedure 37(a)(2)(B) authorizes a motion to compel if a witness at a deposition fails to answer a question. This rule also allows the inquiring party to complete the examination or adjourn it before applying for an order.

Although counsel certainly resort to motion practice under the above rules,[28] most often they obtain rulings during the deposition from the magistrate judge or the district judge, depending on which judicial officer is supervising discovery.

The Advisory Committee noted and counsel is well advised to keep in mind the following:

> In general, counsel should not engage in any conduct during a deposition that would not be allowed in the presence of a judicial officer. The making of an excessive number of unnecessary objections may itself constitute sanctionable conduct, as may the refusal of an attorney to agree with other counsel on a fair apportionment of the time allowed for examination of a deponent or a refusal to agree to a reasonable request for some additional time to complete a deposition.[29]

---

26   *Id.* The 2000 amendments made clear that the prohibition embraced nonparties and eliminated a reference to objections "to evidence" in order to minimize disputes. Notes of Advisory Committee on 2000 Amendments, FRCP 30(d).

27   *Resolution Trust Corp. v. Dabney,* 73 F.3d 262, 266 (10th Cir. 1995); *Miller v. Waseca Med. Ctr.,* 205 F.R.D. 537, 539 (D. Minn. 2002); *Kaiser v. Mut. Life Ins. Co.,* 161 F.R.D. 378, 380 (S.D. Ind. 1994).

28   Chapter 7 discusses such motions in detail.

29   Notes of Advisory Committee on 1993 Amendments, FRCP 30(d).

Except as otherwise authorized by the court or agreed to by the parties, a deposition is limited to one day of seven hours.[30] Absent consent of the parties, further deposition time requires a court order, for which good cause would be needed.[31] Although the rule assumes that a single day of testimony would be standard,[32] in some cases this mandate may not be appropriate, as when the deponent is elderly, ill or very young. Parties should attempt to "make reasonable accommodations to avoid the need for resort to the court."[33] Reasonable breaks presumably would be allowed during the deposition.[34] "Preoccupation with timing is to be avoided."[35]

The limitation placed on the length of a deposition creates a disincentive to an attorney who is tempted to ask prolix, irrelevant, repetitive or harassing questions or to take depositions without adequate preparation. Obviously, the limitation might also constitute an unsound weapon in the hands of an unscrupulous attorney representing a deponent at a deposition. Therefore, in addition to the constraints already referred to, the court *must* allow additional time "if needed for a fair examination of the deponent or if the deponent or another person, or other circumstance, impedes or delays the examination."[36] The court is authorized to impose an appropriate sanction, including reasonable costs and attorneys' fees, on any person who is responsible for any impediment, delay or other frustrating conduct.[37]

Some members of the bar may take the view that in a reasonable effort to curtail excesses in the taking of depositions, the FRCP has gone too far in imposing restrictions upon counsel for the witness that make it too difficult to protect the witness and the record against abuse by the inquiring attorney. For example, FRCP 30 does not provide for directions not to answer based upon irrelevancy. In addition, the requirement, set out in various federal cases, that counsel who directs a witness not to answer fol-

---

30   FRCP 30(d)(2).

31   Notes of Advisory Committee on 2000 Amendments, FRCP 30(d)(2).

32   *Id.*

33   Notes of Advisory Committee on 2000 Amendments, FRCP 30(d).

34   *Id.*

35   *Id.*

36   FRCP 30(d)(2). *See Malec v. Tr. of Boston Coll.*, 208 F.R.D. 23 (D. Mass. 2002); *Miller v. Waseca Med. Ctr.*, 205 F.R.D. 537 (D. Minn. 2002).

37   FRCP 30(d)(3). In presenting the latter changes, the Advisory Committee observed, with considerable understatement, that it "has been informed that overlong depositions can result in undue costs and delays in some circumstances." Notes of Advisory Committee on 2000 Amendments, FRCP 30(d).

low the direction with a request for a ruling or a motion means that counsel for the witness must shoulder the burden and expense of seeking judicial intervention with respect to what may be entirely baseless and prejudicial questioning. The burden and expense may not be trivial considerations if a reasonably prompt and efficient ruling cannot be obtained. If no motion were required, counsel for the witness might still incur the burden and expense of *defending* objections on a motion to compel. That said, a motion to compel might never be made in some instances because of the impropriety of the questioning.

Furthermore, the mandate that objections be concise, nonargumentative and nonsuggestive may, some might fear, induce some attorneys to be so cautious about raising an objection that the record and the witness may suffer. Once one says, for instance, "objection," how much more, some cautious attorneys may wonder, can one say without being accused of being nonconcise, argumentative or suggestive, or all three?[38] All this being said, it should be kept in mind that, more often than not, the judge or magistrate judge, at least in federal court, will be available to rule after listening to argument on a telephone call.

II. PROTECTIVE ORDERS IN ADVANCE OF DEPOSITION

An attorney may anticipate problems in advance of a deposition. A protective order, which is discussed in greater detail in chapter 6, may be sought against the taking of a deposition, in whole or in part.[39] A party who seeks a protective order under FRCP 26(c) must make a specific and documented showing of good cause and a specific need for some sort of protection.[40]

The court has broad, though not unlimited, discretion to control the extent of discovery in a case and the schedule on which it shall proceed, in the interests of fairness, efficiency, celerity and the limitation of expenses.[41]

---

38   *See* Federal Bar Council, *A Report on the Conduct of Depositions*, 131 F.R.D. 613, 627 (1990).

39   FRCP 26(c); CPLR 3103; *see, e.g., Jones v. Maples*, 257 A.D.2d 53, 691 N.Y.S.2d 429 (1st Dep't 1999) (plaintiff pro se not permitted to take videotape deposition of defendant; plaintiff limited to interrogatories).

40   *Schorr v. Briarwood Estates Ltd. P'ship*, 178 F.R.D. 488, 491 (N.D. Ohio 1998).

41   *Kamhi v. Dependable Delivery Serv., Inc.*, 234 A.D.2d 34, 650 N.Y.S.2d 676 (1st Dep't 1996); *Farrakhan v. N.Y.P. Holdings Inc.*, 226 A.D.2d 133, 640 N.Y.S.2d 80 (1st Dep't 1996). Under appropriate circumstances, such as when there is particular need for spontaneous, uninfluenced testimony, the court may exclude a party or a nonparty from a deposition. *Swiers v. P & C Food Mkts., Inc.*, 95 A.D.2d 881, 464 N.Y.S.2d 39 (3d Dep't 1983).

As noted, a federal judge may limit the number of depositions. The court's approval would be required if a proposed deposition is not stipulated to and would bring the number in the case to more than ten.[42] The court can restrict the length of a deposition and can adjust the deposition schedule when there is good reason for doing so.[43]

Rulings on the propriety of deposition questions in state court should ordinarily be made only after a specific question has been asked but not answered, and not before the deposition.[44] It would still seem possible, though, for a court at a preliminary or compliance conference, or on a formal motion, to issue directives as to the relevancy of certain subject matter, which would limit future questioning at depositions.[45] Most federal courts are reluctant to order that a particular deposition not be taken, since the parties are able to object to individual matters or questions and obtain relief with regard thereto.[46]

In many commercial cases, discovery into business practices, product formulae, pricing information and the like raises parties' concerns about maintaining the confidentiality of this information. Such concerns can create difficulties during depositions. A common remedy is a confidentiality order in advance of deposition. This order, which often takes the form of a "so ordered" stipulation between or among the parties, guards the confidentiality of sensitive business information. Various mechanisms are often incorporated in such orders.[47] In state court, parties must remember the

---

42   FRCP 30(a)(2).

43   *Sidari v. Orleans County*, 174 F.R.D. 275, 286–88 (W.D.N.Y. 1996); *see Farrakhan*, 226 A.D.2d 133.

44   *Tardibuono v. County of Nassau*, 181 A.D.2d 879, 581 N.Y.S.2d 443 (2d Dep't 1992). The court should not direct that all objections, whatever they might be, be reserved for the trial court, as that would deprive the party-deponent of the right to apply for a protective order. *Supama Coal Sales Co. v. Jackson*, 186 A.D.2d 1052, 588 N.Y.S.2d 493 (4th Dep't 1992).

45   Siegel, McKinney's Practice Commentary, CPLR 3124, at 264 (Supp. 2004).

46   *See, e.g., Banks v. Office of Senate Sergeant-at-Arms*, 222 F.R.D. 7, 18 (D.D.C. 2004).

47   *See* 2 Robert L. Haig, Commercial Litigation in New York State Courts § 18.11 (1995); Manual for Complex Litigation, Third § 21.432 (1995).

rule on the sealing of court files, which restricts parties' ability to shield court files from general view.[48]

III. APPLICATION OF THE RULES—COMMON ISSUES[49]

A. Privileged or Confidential Matter

Questions that seek to invade a privilege, a constitutional right or a protection against disclosure of confidential information (e.g., trade secrets) should not be asked at a deposition. The examiner, however, will not always be aware that an inquiry threatens to tread upon protected ground. If such a question is posed, counsel representing the deponent may properly object to it.[50] Further, an instruction not to answer is authorized when necessary to protect confidential information.[51]

Although FRCP 30(d)(1) speaks of "a privilege," the Advisory Committee refers to "a privilege or protection against disclosure."[52] The privilege or protection sought to be maintained must be one recognized by the law, not merely by counsel defending the deposition.[53] Examples of recognized privileges and protections are attorney work product,[54] the constitutional protection against self-incrimination[55] and the attorney-client,

---

48   Uniform Rule 216.1; *see* George F. Carpinello, *Public Access to Court Records in New York: The Experience under Uniform Rule 216.1 and the Rule's Future in a World of Electronic Filing*, 66 Alb. L. Rev. 1089 (2003); George F. Carpinello, *Public Access to Court Records in Civil Proceedings: The New York Approach*, 54 Alb. L. Rev. 96 (1989). It should be remembered, though, that state court files do not contain all papers exchanged in a litigation nor all discovery items. The same is true of federal court files. *See* FRCP 5(d) (depositions, documents, etc. not filed until they are used in the case or the court so orders).

49   The format of the following discussion concerning application of the governing rules during depositions in New York State and federal litigation departs from the usual practice in the rest of the book of examining state and federal practice separately.

50   *Byork v. Carmer*, 109 A.D.2d 1087, 487 N.Y.S.2d 226 (4th Dep't 1985).

51   FRCP 30(d)(1). The same is true in New York, as demonstrated by the case law. *See, e.g., Dibble v. Consol. Rail Corp.*, 181 A.D.2d 1040, 582 N.Y.S.2d 582 (4th Dep't 1992); *Humiston v. Grose*, 144 A.D.2d 907, 534 N.Y.S.2d 604 (4th Dep't 1988).

52   Notes of Advisory Committee on 1993 Amendments, FRCP 30(d).

53   *Gober v. City of Leesburg*, 197 F.R.D. 519, 520–21 (M.D. Fla. 2000).

54   Notes of Advisory Committee on 1993 Amendments, FRCP 30(d); *Banks v. Office of Senate Sergeant-at-Arms*, 222 F.R.D. 1, 4 (D.D.C. 2004); *Coastal Oil N.Y., Inc. v. Peck*, 184 A.D.2d 241, 584 N.Y.S.2d 564 (1st Dep't 1992).

55   *Nat'l Life Ins. Co. v. Hartford Accident & Indem. Co.*, 615 F.2d 595 (3d Cir. 1980).

physician-patient and husband-wife privileges.[56] Questions that seek to reveal trade secrets also need not be answered.[57]

Where settlement discussions are concerned, the law has long recognized the interests of parties in confidentiality and the public utility of providing that protection. Rules on the subject are now embodied in CPLR 4547 and FRE 408. It has been held that FRE 408 can provide a basis for a limitation on a deposition, although the rule is addressed to admissibility only.[58]

A mediation proceeding, court-ordered or voluntary, or other forms of alternative dispute resolution (ADR) might also give rise to claims of confidentiality.[59] New York does not now have a statute broadly protecting ADR communications, although court orders, agreements between or among parties or the rules of ADR programs may provide protection.[60] Parties to mediations might also seek refuge in the rules governing settlement negotiations.[61] Disputes at depositions might also occur as a result of statutes in other jurisdictions that grant confidentiality to ADR proceedings conducted in those jurisdictions.[62]

The rationale behind the permission given to counsel for the deponent in state and federal courts to issue an instruction not to answer a question that would infringe upon a recognized privilege or protection is apparent—the privilege or protection would be defeated by the giving of an

---

56   *See, e.g., SEC v. Thomas,* 116 F.R.D. 230, 233–34 (D. Utah 1987).

57   *See, e.g., Int'l Union of Elec., Radio & Mach. Workers v. Westinghouse Elec. Corp.,* 91 F.R.D. 277, 279–80 (D.D.C. 1981).

58   *Alcan Int'l Ltd. v. S.A. Day Mfg. Co.,* 179 F.R.D. 403 (W.D.N.Y. 1998).

59   *See In re Anonymous,* 283 F.3d 627 (4th Cir. 2002); *Sheldone v. Pa. Turnpike Comm'n,* 104 F. Supp. 2d 511 (W.D. Pa. 2000); *Folb v. Motion Picture Indus. Pension & Health Plans,* 16 F. Supp. 2d 1164 (C.D. Cal. 1998); *Cohen v. Empire Blue Cross & Blue Shield,* 178 F.R.D. 385 (E.D.N.Y. 1998).

60   *See, e.g.,* Rules of the Alternative Dispute Resolution Program, Commercial Division, Supreme Court, New York County, Rule 5 (Feb. 15, 1999), *available at* www.nycourts.gov/comdiv/ ADR_Rules.htm. N.Y. Judiciary Law § 849-b(6) provides for confidentiality of mediations conducted by the Community Dispute Resolution Centers program. The National Conference of Commissioners on Uniform State Laws has drafted a Uniform Mediation Act (approved and recommended for enactment at the annual conference, Aug. 2001), which provides for confidentiality of mediations. The act was introduced in the New York legislature on January 29, 2003, as S-01340.

61   *Cutrone v. Gaccione,* 210 A.D.2d 289, 619 N.Y.S.2d 758 (2d Dep't 1994).

62   *Olam v. Cong. Mortgage Co.,* 68 F. Supp. 2d 1110, 1120–28 (N.D. Cal. 1999); *see Bauerle v. Bauerle,* 206 A.D.2d 937, 616 N.Y.S.2d 275 (4th Dep't 1994).

answer. However, inquiring counsel should be allowed to question the deponent about the factual basis for the asserted privilege. This is not just to satisfy the attorney that the objection is well taken or at least arguable, but to ensure that, if counsel does not agree, the judge will have the information needed to make a reasoned ruling or decision on any motion.[63] In the U.S. District Courts for the Southern and Eastern Districts of New York, for instance, the local rules require that an attorney asserting a privilege, including during a deposition, provide information about the basis for the assertion in order to assist in understanding the nature and validity of the privilege being asserted.[64]

Some federal cases hold that whenever an attorney directs a deponent not to answer a question, that attorney must move for a protective order, rather than rest upon the direction and require the interrogator to make a motion to compel.[65] However, a motion to compel is authorized under the federal rules if a witness at a deposition fails to answer a question.[66] The need for such a motion would be undercut if the deponent's failure to move for a protective order amounted to a waiver of the objection.

On the other hand, FRCP 30(d)(1) is clear: Absent an objection based on privilege or a court-ordered limitation, the deponent's counsel cannot instruct the witness not to answer a question except when necessary to present a motion for a protective order under FRCP 30(d)(4). A distinction has been drawn between directions not to answer based upon a colorable claim of privilege and directions founded on other grounds:

> [T]he privilege objection must be made to avoid waiver; it implicates substantive rights of the party apart from the litigation; and it serves to prevent depositions from becoming tools for abuse. Consequently, the attorney who properly interposes a privilege objection should be able to rest on the objection without shouldering the burden of mov-

---

63   7 James W. Moore, *Moore's Federal Practice* § 30.43[2], at 30-68–30-68.1 (3d ed. 2002) (hereinafter "Moore").

64   *See, e.g.*, Local Civil Rules for the Southern and Eastern Districts of New York, Rule 26.2.

65   *See, e.g., Calzaturficio S.C.A.R.P.A., s.p.a. v. Fabiano Shoe Co.*, 201 F.R.D. 33 (D. Mass. 2001); *Gober v. City of Leesburg*, 197 F.R.D. 519, 521 (M.D. Fla. 2000); *In re Stratosphere Corp. Sec. Litig.*, 182 F.R.D. 614, 619 (D. Nev. 1998); *Furniture World v. D.A.V. Thrift Stores*, 168 F.R.D. 61, 63 (D.N.M. 1996); *Hearst/ABC-Viacom Entm't Servs. v. Goodway Mktg., Inc.*, 145 F.R.D. 59 (E.D. Pa. 1992); *Smith v. Logansport Cmty. Sch. Corp.*, 139 F.R.D. 637, 643 (N.D. Ind. 1991); *Nutmeg Ins. Co. v. Atwell, Vogel & Sterling*, 120 F.R.D. 504, 508 (W.D. La. 1988). *Compare Riddell Sports Inc. v. Brooks*, 158 F.R.D. 555, 558 (S.D.N.Y. 1994).

66   FRCP 37(a)(2)(B).

ing for a protective order. If the asserted privilege objection is frivolous, the objecting party may be sanctioned regardless of where the burden of seeking judicial resolution is placed.[67]

Distinguished commentators acknowledge that FRCP 30(d) reflects "a substantial preference for requiring that deponents apply to the court for protection rather than simply refusing to answer questions."[68] Nevertheless, "it is to be hoped that the courts will take a realistic view of the conduct of depositions rather than foreclose deponents' objections in response to motions to compel answers. . . . It would be unduly draconian to penalize the deponent for failure to make a motion under Rule 30(d)."[69]

Unlike FRCP 30, CPLR 3113 and 3115 do not expressly address directions not to answer. Rule 3113(b) does provide that all objections are to be recorded by the officer present, "the deposition shall proceed *subject to the right of a person to apply for a protective order*" and the deposition is to be "taken continuously" (emphasis added).

In *White v. Martins*,[70] the court stated that although, in general, all questions should be answered subject to objections, some questions may infringe upon a privilege and the like and thus should not be answered.[71] The court immediately added, "Thus, although the statute provides that the deposition shall proceed, it adds 'subject to the right of a person to apply for a protective order.'"[72] The order on appeal in that case was found defective because, by directing the answering of all questions prospectively without knowing what those questions would be, it had deprived the party deposed of the right to apply for a protective order. The court would seem to be saying, then, that counsel for the deponent may issue instructions not to answer a question in the limited circumstances of "substantial prejudice" described, but that counsel should go beyond that and

---

67   7 Moore, *supra* note 63, § 30.43[2], at 30-68.

68   8A Charles Alan Wright et al., Federal Practice and Procedure § 2116, at 124 (2d ed. 1994).

69   *Id.* On this interpretation, there would not be a bright line indicating a point beyond which counsel clearly cannot go on his or her own.

70   100 A.D.2d 805, 474 N.Y.S.2d 733 (1st Dep't 1984).

71   *Id.* at 805.

72   *Id.* (quoting CPLR 3113(b)).

obtain a judicial imprimatur for the action by moving for a protective order or seeking a ruling.[73]

A ruling can be sought immediately, although the parties may wish to agree to postpone bringing the matter to the justice's attention in order that the examiner may pursue other questions. If the objecting party intends instead to make a motion, that intention should be noted clearly on the record because the issue will not be fully presented to the justice for decision until at least some days have passed.

Some state cases, however, have upheld directions not to answer on motions to compel—that is, without motions for a protective order by the attorney for the deponent.[74] It is not clear whether, when it comes to the need for the deponent's attorney to seek a protective order, the state courts might draw distinctions among the permissible bases for instructions not to answer.

At a minimum, when an attorney objects to a question and interposes a direction not to answer under circumstances in which such a direction is permissible and when there is disagreement about the objection between counsel that cannot be resolved, the objecting attorney would be well advised to take affirmative action. In such a case, the objecting attorney should bring the problem before the court, rather than rest upon the objection and leave it to the adversary to move to compel or for sanctions. Counsel would also be well advised to act with dispatch. The good faith of the objecting attorney is far less subject to challenge if he or she demonstrates that a resolution of the problem was expeditiously sought on his or her initiative.

---

73   *Id.* ("Such a restrictive order may be obtained either by formal motion or by informal application for a ruling."). *See Orner v. Mount Sinai Hosp.*, 305 A.D.2d 307, 761 N.Y.S.2d 603 (1st Dep't 2003) (improper to issue directions not to answer in areas "'unilaterally'" deemed irrelevant); *Levine v. Goldstein*, 173 A.D.2d 346, 346, 569 N.Y.S.2d 715 (1st Dep't 1991) (counsel erred in ordering clients not to answer questions "in areas which counsel *unilaterally* deemed to be irrelevant") (emphasis added); *Byork v. Carmer,* 109 A.D.2d 1087, 487 N.Y.S.2d 226 (4th Dep't 1985); *Lewis v. Brunswick Hosp.*, Index No. 5007/92, 2001 N.Y. Misc. LEXIS 407, at **8 (Sup. Ct., Queens Co. May 10, 2001) ("There is simply no authority in the CPLR to direct one's witness not to answer a question. Rather, plaintiff's remedy was to interpose an objection and seek a protective order from the court."). Of course, strictly speaking, counsel must do more than merely object.

74   *See, e.g., Lobdell v. S. Buffalo Ry. Co.*, 159 A.D.2d 958, 552 N.Y.S.2d 782 (4th Dep't 1990); *see Burell v. New York City Transit Auth.*, 242 A.D.2d 504, 662 N.Y.S.2d 125 (1st Dep't 1997); *see also Roggow v. Walker*, 303 A.D.2d 1003, 757 N.Y.S.2d 410 (4th Dep't 2003); Siegel, *supra* note 5, § 356, at 555 (motion to compel).

B. Enforcing Court-Ordered Limitations

An attorney in a federal case may object if the inquiring counsel seeks to violate a limitation established by the court and may direct the witness not to answer.[75] This limitation may be directed to the scope or length of the deposition.[76] As discussed previously, the district judge or magistrate judge will issue an order establishing a discovery schedule and, as part of the process, may set limits on the substantive bounds of discovery, as well as perhaps the number and length of depositions. If a question would run afoul of the limitation, it is sensible for FRCP 30(d) to allow a direction not to answer because, in contrast with other objections, the judge has in effect already ruled on it.

Of course, attorneys may differ about whether an established limitation reaches the specific question posed. Counsel should try to come to agreement on the point. The movant must, in fact, confer with the adversary in an effort to resolve an issue regarding the deposition.[77] If the inquiring attorney is not persuaded of the merit of the objection, the objecting attorney may move for an order if the issue is important enough to justify the effort and expense. (Indeed, as just noted, certain cases require the objecting attorney to bring a motion.)

In the state courts, the cases cited above on the allowable bases for directions not to answer do not expressly address enforcement of a limitation previously established by the court. Given the volume of matters pending in the state courts, it may be less likely that court orders will be issued establishing bounds on the scope of discovery. Often, preliminary and compliance conference orders in state court are concerned largely or exclusively with deadlines for the completion of various types of discovery. However, the court may issue a directive at a conference or in a decision on a motion that certain subject matter is irrelevant to the case and outside the bounds of discovery. In such event, a question that violates that limitation might be objected to or even form the basis of a direction not to answer on the grounds that it is palpably irrelevant.[78] A motion or a request for a ruling may follow.

---

75   *Auscape Int'l v. Nat'l Geographic Soc'y*, 02 Civ. 6441, 2002 U.S. Dist. LEXIS 26318 (S.D.N.Y. Oct. 8, 2002); *SEC v. Oakford Corp.*, 141 F. Supp. 2d 435, 437 (S.D.N.Y. 2001).

76   Notes of Advisory Committee on 1993 Amendments, FRCP 30(d).

77   FRCP 37(a)(2).

78   *See Kelly v. Juskowitz*, 182 A.D.2d 677, 582 N.Y.S.2d 269 (2d Dep't 1992); Siegel, McKinney's Practice Commentary, CPLR 3124, at 264 (Supp. 2004).

Perhaps more than any other difference in the two systems, the right to appeal only from final orders helps the federal system move with dispatch. Under New York State law, a motion for a ruling may be appealed to the appellate division and cost a great deal in time and money for any litigant. The process can be ineffective, unless the objecting attorney is seeking delay. Thus, the request for a ruling will usually be preferable to all but the obstructive counsel.

C. Objections on Grounds of Relevance

Many a deposition has been conducted over the years in which counsel for the witness has objected and directed the witness not to answer because a question was deemed irrelevant. Sometimes the pleadings are sufficiently vague that the parties may have quite different understandings about the issues presented in the case. On other occasions, the parties may be in full agreement as to what the case is about but differ in good faith as to whether particular proof bears on the issues presented. There undoubtedly have been one or two instances in which an attorney has regarded the assertion of irrelevancy as merely one of a number of tools in a kit of obstructive tactics. In the hands of this last sort of lawyer, this objection can wreak havoc for the inquiring attorney and the discovery process.

On the other hand, if the inquiring attorney does not do his or her homework, the questioning can veer into and bog down in irrelevancies, wasting the time, money and energy of all concerned. Such inquiries might also be pursued by an unscrupulous attorney in an effort to harass and oppress the witness.

In light of the above, in state cases, it is improper for an attorney to direct a client-witness not to answer a question on the mere ground that it is thought to be irrelevant.[79] Moreover, because objections should be kept to a minimum and relevance objections are preserved for trial, the attorney often should not even object to such a question.[80]

Some questions may, however, go further and be "palpably irrelevant"; the witness may be directed not to answer these. By *palpably irrelevant*, the cases presumably mean a question that clearly or plainly concerns a subject not at issue in the litigation. If, however, a question is clearly irrel-

---

79   *See, e.g., Orner v. Mount Sinai Hosp.*, 305 A.D.2d 307, 761 N.Y.S.2d 603 (1st Dep't 2003); *Levine v. Goldstein*, 173 A.D.2d 346, 569 N.Y.S.2d 715 (1st Dep't 1991); *Beatty v. Donley*, 31 Misc. 2d 164, 220 N.Y.S.2d 218 (Sup. Ct., Nassau Co. 1961).

80   *Orner*, 305 A.D.2d 307; *Levine*, 173 A.D.2d 346.

evant but answering it would cause no prejudice to the client-witness, it would be best to allow the answer in order to get on with the questioning and avoid a possibly costly quarrel with the other side. As pointed out earlier, this is the philosophy of the CPLR in regard to depositions in general.

When there will be prejudice, though, the situation is different.[81] Substantial prejudice may occur if the clearly irrelevant question seeks to elicit sensitive, private information. In a contract case, for example, information about the deposing defendant's marital difficulties would clearly be irrelevant and highly personal, and counsel for the witness would be within his or her rights to direct the client not to respond.[82] Similarly, it is one thing if the interrogator over the course of hours presents a few questions that are clearly irrelevant; it is quite another if, instead, a few irrelevant questions are but a prelude to what is to be a lengthy and tortuous diversion from the matters at issue in the case.

If the attorney for the deponent has a concern, he or she may ask the questioner for an explanation of the theory of relevancy in order to gauge the direction in which the questioning counsel intends to head and so be able to act in a reasonably informed manner. A few irrelevant questions may not be enough to amount to sanctionable conduct.[83] In state court, as indicated, cases say that the attorney should not unilaterally decide what is palpably irrelevant but should seek a protective order.

In federal practice, a direction not to answer on the ground that a question is irrelevant, even palpably so, is not authorized.[84] However, a defending attorney may direct the witness not to answer in order to present a motion under FRCP 30(d)(4).[85] The attorney representing the witness may issue an objection without a direction not to answer. However, the Advi-

---

81   Indeed, to be precise, the court in *White v. Martins*, 100 A.D.2d 805, 805, 474 N.Y.S.2d 733 (1st Dep't 1984), spoke not of prejudice but of "substantial prejudice," which narrows somewhat further defending counsel's right to bar answers.

82   Siegel, *supra* note 5, § 356, at 555; *see Green v. City of New York*, 281 A.D.2d 193, 721 N.Y.S.2d 353 (1st Dep't 2001); *see also Cuthbertson v. Excel Indus.*, 179 F.R.D. 599 (D. Kan. 1998); *Int'l Union of Elec., Radio & Mach. Workers v. Westinghouse Elec. Corp.*, 91 F.R.D. 277, 280 n.5 (D.D.C. 1981). *Cf. Carney v. Wopperer*, 277 A.D.2d 1050, 715 N.Y.S.2d 263 (4th Dep't 2000) (compelling response where marital therapy was integral part of malpractice claim).

83   *See In re Stratosphere Corp. Sec. Litig.*, 182 F.R.D. 614, 618–19 (D. Nev. 1998).

84   *See* FRCP 30(d)(1).

85   FRCP 30(d)(1). *See, e.g., Plaisted v. Geisinger Med. Ctr.*, 210 F.R.D. 527 (M.D. Pa. 2002); *Gober v. City of Leesburg*, 197 F.R.D. 519, 520 (M.D. Fla. 2000); *Quantachrome Corp. v. Micromeritics Instrument Corp.*, 189 F.R.D. 697 (S.D. Fla. 1999).

sory Committee indicated that objections ordinarily should be limited to those that would be waived if not raised.[86] One court thus stated that it is arguable whether a relevancy objection is even allowed at a deposition.[87] In another case,[88] the court took a narrow view of a party's right to take action against irrelevant questions:

> [T]he federal courts do not permit a witness to refuse to answer a question that is irrelevant. Instead, the witness must answer the question subject to the objection.
>
> ***
>
> [T]he worst that can happen when a party asks a 30(b)(6) witness questions about an irrelevant topic is that the process will be unnecessarily time-consuming. While there are more pleasant ways to pass the time, that kind of "burden" has to be endured in any deposition because . . . a witness must answer even irrelevant questions in a non-30(b)(6) deposition. To have one rule for the ordinary deposition and a completely different one for 30(b)(6) depositions makes no sense, particularly when some lawyers hardly need encouragement to make discovery more expensive and when, given crowded dockets, the court may not be able to act as promptly as the parties hope on a motion to preclude the party taking the 30(b)(6) deposition from asking certain questions. Moreover, there is time and power enough after the deposition has been taken to punish the party or lawyer who wasted everyone's time.[89]

Federal Rule of Civil Procedure 30(d)(1) seeks to prevent abuse of depositions by means of irrelevancy objections. By requiring that a direction not to answer (apart from those based on privilege and prior court limita-

---

86   Notes of Advisory Committee on 1993 Amendments, FRCP 30(d).

87   *Quantachrome Corp.*, 189 F.R.D. 697. *See* 7 Moore, *supra* note 63, § 30.43[2], at 30-68 (Relevance objections are "entitled to little judicial deference." Improper relevance objections are, for the most part, "unnecessary and are interposed more to disrupt opposing counsel than to genuinely protect the witness, the adjudicatory process, or the interests of justice."); *cf. Gober*, 197 F.R.D. at 520. *See also Banks v. Office of Senate Sergeant-at-Arms*, 222 F.R.D. 1, 6 (D.D.C. 2004) (directing a witness not to answer on grounds of relevance is clear violation of federal rules and sanctionable).

88   *Banks*, 222 F.R.D. at 7.

89   *Id.* at 18. The court reserved the right to reach a different decision in a case in which there was more obvious abuse. *Id.*

tion) at most only be made in and in connection with a motion, the rule attempts to limit relevancy-based interruptions of the deposition to instances of genuine prejudice, because an objecting attorney ought not go to the trouble and expense of a motion and burden the court and other parties with it unless it involves important considerations. The rule provides protection against irrelevancy in questioning, but it is limited to cases of true need.[90]

Some practitioners may believe that the balance thus struck is not perfect because the attorney for the witness is only able to defend against inquiries that are clearly irrelevant and invasive of sensitive personal information or very detailed and protracted by incurring the expense of a motion. These critics may feel that FRCP 30(d)(1) gives an incompetent or malevolent attorney too much power to harass and oppress a witness. But it may be possible, and often is in federal court, for objecting counsel to obtain a cost-effective resolution by seeking a ruling from the court at a telephonic or in-person conference.[91]

D. Objections to Form of Questions and Similar Objections

Objections to the form of the question must be made at the deposition or they will be waived. Although objections to the form of questions are the most obvious waivable objections, they are not the only ones. The state statute refers to errors and irregularities "of any kind which might be obviated or removed if objection were promptly presented."[92] Federal Rule of Civil Procedure 32(d)(3) is to the same effect.

If an objection were raised on irrelevancy grounds, the claimed defect in the question likely could be corrected only by withdrawal of the entire inquiry, which is not the sort of "cure" contemplated here.[93] Where a claimed irrelevancy is concerned, the attorney is objecting not to the way in which the question is phrased but to the fact that the information involved is being sought at all. On the other hand, objections to the form of the question, which must be made on pain of waiver, include questions

---

90   *Ethicon Endo-Surgery v. U.S. Surgical Corp.*, 160 F.R.D. 98, 99 (S.D. Ohio 1995) (counsel does not have the right to decide unilaterally whether questions are irrelevant or repetitious by instructing the witness not to answer them; the remedy is to move for a protective order or sanctions).

91   See chapter 6 at I.B. for further discussion.

92   CPLR 3115(b).

93   *In re Stratosphere Corp. Sec. Litig.*, 182 F.R.D. 614, 618 (D. Nev. 1998).

that are compound, call for speculation, are argumentative, are unintelligible, improperly lead the witness or mischaracterize the evidence.[94]

The attorney representing the witness therefore must pay close attention to the form of questions being posed, as well as anything else that might provide the basis for a waivable objection. When necessary, an objection should be stated. Concision matters. Counsel should not engage in long-winded explanations of these objections lest they clutter the record and provide ammunition for the adversary. However, objecting counsel might wish to add a word or two in order to preclude any uncertainty about what the objection was if, at trial, counsel should need to assert that the objection has been preserved. "Objection to the form of the question" or "objection to the form of the question—compound," or the like, should suffice.[95]

Inquiring counsel should prepare well in advance and should make course corrections as needed during the deposition so that the information he or she wishes to obtain is obtained in a manner that will allow for its admissibility later—unless that does not matter to counsel. Some depositions are intended primarily as a means for learning information and others as methods for the preserving of testimony to be used at trial, either because the witness is likely for one reason or another to be unavailable or because counsel believes the deposition testimony may be usable to impeach the witness when he or she is on the stand.

Counsel should be conservative about assuming what may not be needed later, since life has an infuriating tendency to surprise us. Inquiring counsel should listen carefully to the objections raised. If an objection is unclear, counsel would be well advised to ask the adversary to elaborate briefly and to correct any errors or irregularities in form or similar shortcomings legitimately pointed out in the objections.

E. "Speaking" Objections; Suggestive Objections

On occasion, at depositions, counsel representing the witness makes objections coupled with speeches on the record. For example, counsel might say something like this:

---

94   *Id.*; *Boyd v. Univ. of Md. Med. Sys.*, 173 F.R.D. 143, 147 (D. Md. 1997).

95   Of course, if the attorney merely said "Objection," he or she might try to argue at trial all possible bases for objection to the particular question.

Objection. Mr. Smith, I do not understand your question. You have been inquiring about the shipment from July up to this point, for the most part, but I can't tell now whether you mean that shipment or the one sent from the Utica plant the following March that the witness testified to at the outset. Since the purchasing officer was not involved in the negotiations in September, there is no connection to the March shipment. Regardless, the question is completely garbled. Also, you continue to insist upon pursuing these transactions, which, as I made clear earlier, are irrelevant to this case, as Judge Jones will rule when we make our summary judgment motion. The witness is a businesswoman, and a very able one at that, but if I cannot understand your question after 20 years of law practice, I don't see how she can, and obviously a witness cannot answer a question that is confusing and not understood. I have been very indulgent and allowed you to inquire into this entire area up to this point, but if we go on chasing after irrelevant information, I'll have to direct the witness not to answer. What's more, . . .

Objections of this sort, often loosely referred to as *speaking objections*, are clearly improper.[96] They clutter the record and prolong the deposition. Even if the speaker does not issue a directive not to answer, such objections obviously interfere with the questioning. Indeed, sometimes it is precisely the purpose of the objection to throw the interrogator off stride. The attorney representing the witness has a right to protect against genuine prejudice but not to harass the questioner or inhibit reasonable inquiry. Objections of this sort also can generate a contentious atmosphere in the deposition room; consequently, everything becomes harder, longer and more expensive for everyone.

In federal practice, objections must be stated concisely.[97] State courts can be expected to be similarly inhospitable toward prolix objections.

Sometimes objections are made at excessive length simply because the attorney is loquacious and disputatious. On the other hand, verbose attorneys have been known to pose speaking objections for the purpose of sug-

---

96   *See, e.g., Plaisted v. Geisinger Med. Ctr.*, 210 F.R.D. 527 (M.D. Pa. 2002); *McDonough v. Keniston*, 188 F.R.D. 22 (D.N.H. 1998).

97   FRCP 30(d)(1).

gesting answers the witness should adopt.[98] The Advisory Committee stated in 1993 that "[d]epositions frequently have been unduly prolonged, if not unfairly frustrated, by lengthy objections and colloquy, often suggesting how the deponent should respond."[99] Sometimes the speaker will seek to convey to the witness the idea that the question is confusing or in some other respect defective in the hope or expectation that the witness will take the hint and state that he or she cannot answer for that reason. Sometimes the speaker will seek to lead the witness to provide an answer containing particular information alluded to in the objection.

It should be obvious to all, and is certainly fundamental, that the questioner is entitled to the testimony of *the witness*, not that of the attorney representing the witness. The testimony should truly be that of the witness, not the witness as advised or guided or improved upon by her lawyer. Witnesses are not supposed to be parrots, adroitly repeating someone else's words.

Further, "[e]xamination and cross-examination of deponents shall proceed as permitted in the trial of actions in open court."[100] At trial, attorneys of course cannot use speaking objections to coach witnesses. Thus, there is no basis for the interposition of suggestive objections at a deposition. Indeed, in federal practice, objections must be made not only concisely but also in a "non-suggestive manner."[101] New York State courts would undoubtedly react similarly to objections that fail to meet this standard, even though CPLR 3113 and 3115 do not expressly embody this standard. It is therefore improper, for example, for counsel representing the witness to

- interpret questions on the record.

- rephrase questions.

- summarize prior testimony of the witness that supposedly answers the question.

- interject advice to the witness (e.g., "Don't speculate.").

---

98   *See, e.g., Calzaturficio S.C.A.R.P.A., s.p.a. v. Fabiano Shoe Co.*, 201 F.R.D. 33, 39–41 (D. Mass. 2001); *Morales v. Zondo, Inc.*, 204 F.R.D. 50 (S.D.N.Y. 2001).

99   Notes of Advisory Committee on 1993 Amendments, FRCP 30(d).

100   CPLR 3113(c). *See* FRCP 30(c).

101   FRCP 30(d)(1).

- advise the witness to answer "if you know" or "if you remember."

- assert that the question is incomprehensible to counsel.

- tell the witness to answer "if you can understand the question."

- advise inquiring counsel that a different witness should be questioned about specific subjects.

- criticize the inquiring attorney's theory of discovery for the case or its merits.

- criticize the inquiring attorney's formulation of questions.[102]

As litigators are naturally combative, an attorney representing a witness may fall to arguing with the questioning lawyer. These arguments take the guise of purported objections to the questions. Federal practice expressly forbids such behavior, mandating that all objections be framed "in a non-argumentative . . . manner."[103]

F. Objections Concerning Speculation and Repetition

Questions at trial should seek testimony based upon a foundation, not speculative musings.[104] However, as discussed, the standards governing admissibility at trial and the conduct of depositions are different. There may be subjects about which a witness at a deposition is less than certain and yet which may properly be pursued. If, for example, the witness does not know with certainty who placed a certain phone call, the line of inquiry may nevertheless be properly pursued if the witness has a reasonable basis for believing the caller to have been A, B or C. The inquiry may also be productive in at least ruling some persons out.

At trial, hearsay is, of course, inadmissible (absent an exception), but it can be pursued at deposition because it may lead to the discovery of

---

102   *See Plaisted v. Geisinger Med. Ctr.*, 210 F.R.D. 527 (M.D. Pa. 2002); *Calzaturficio S.C.A.R.P.A., s.p.a.*, 201 F.R.D. at 39–41; *Morales*, 204 F.R.D. at 54–57; *Phinney v. Paulshock*, 181 F.R.D. 185 (D.N.H. 1998), *aff'd sub nom. Phinney v. Wentworth Douglas Hosp.*, 199 F.3d 1 (1st Cir. 1999); *Hall v. Clifton Precision*, 150 F.R.D. 525, 530 (E.D. Pa. 1993); *see also In re Anonymous Member of S. Carolina Bar*, 346 S.C. 177, 191, 552 S.E.2d 10 (S.C. 2001).

103   FRCP 30(d)(1). Argumentative objections are improper. *See, e.g., Freeman v. Schointuck*, 192 F.R.D. 187 (D. Md. 2000); *United States v. Kattar*, 191 F.R.D. 33 (D.N.H. 1999).

104   *See, e.g., In re Stratosphere Corp. Sec. Litig.*, 182 F.R.D. 614, 618 (D. Nev. 1998); *Boyd v. Univ. of Md. Med. Sys.*, 173 F.R.D. 143, 147 (D. Md. 1997).

admissible evidence. So, in the example given, the "speculation" about A, B or C may be helpful to the discovery process of the inquiring attorney, who, if the issue is important enough, might even wish to depose one or all of them to acquire truly admissible evidence.

A question may call for an informed estimate. This estimate is distinguishable from a mere guess. If it matters, an objection to a question calling for speculation should be interposed, as it is an objection to the form of the question.[105]

Because depositions are often lengthy, even under current federal rules, disagreements inevitably arise from time to time about the repetition of questions. The objection "asked and answered" is itself repeated frequently. Of course, any such objection would be groundless unless the question had in fact been answered *in full*. The questioner has a right to repeat the question until a fully responsive answer is given, unless a direction not to answer is allowed under the rules discussed.

Objecting attorneys sometimes will recall that a topic was raised and an answer provided but will not remember that the answer was in some respect incomplete. Even if a full answer was given, the questioner has a right to explore the surrounding facts in order to understand it. Sometimes what may seem repetitious to counsel for a witness is in fact a question that seeks some related, additional information. The questioner often must revisit areas of inquiry in order to avoid gaps that might prove harmful later on in the discovery process or at trial.

That said, the questioning attorney may not repeat the same answered question over and over again. A fully responsive answer is what it is, whether the questioning lawyer likes it or not; counsel has no right to ask the question over and over in the hope of tricking the witness into giving a "better" answer, eliciting a "better" answer by wearing down the witness's concentration or harassing the witness into being more "helpful."[106] It is not proper to pound away at answered questions to try to sow confusion in the record, perhaps in the hope of some tactical advantage on a summary judgment motion.

The attorney representing the witness should be careful about making too many objections. If the interrogator poses answered questions, coun-

---

105   *See, e.g.*, *In re Stratosphere Corp. Sec. Litig.*, 182 F.R.D. at 618; *Boyd*, 173 F.R.D. at 147.

106   *Mruz v. Caring, Inc.*, 166 F. Supp. 2d 61, 69–70 (D.N.J. 2001); *Boyd*, 173 F.R.D. at 146.

sel can object, and indeed should do so if needed to build a record for a motion. It is, however, improper in federal practice to direct the witness not to answer a question on the ground of repetition.[107] This is also improper in state practice. If the matter truly becomes serious, counsel may interrupt the deposition for a ruling or motion.

Many problems can be avoided. If a dispute of significance arises about prior testimony where the recollections of counsel differ, it may be useful to have the reporter search for a prior reference during a break. It may turn out that one attorney has inaccurately remembered the testimony.

G. Consulting with the Witness

As noted, the interrogator is entitled to the testimony of the witness. Both state and federal practice contemplate that the questioning will proceed as at trial. Thus, if it is not permissible for counsel for the witness to interpose suggestive objections during a deposition, then it is even more improper for counsel to interrupt questioning of the witness in order to consult privately with the witness for the purpose of assisting him or her to frame helpful answers. Interruptions for the purpose of coaching of this sort have certainly occurred.[108]

Although this rule seemingly is inarguable, certain complexities are worth exploring. In *Hall v. Clifton Precision*,[109] for example, the court stated:

> A deposition is meant to be a question-and-answer conversation between the deposing lawyer and the witness. There is no proper need for the witness's own lawyer to act as an intermediary, interpreting questions, deciding which questions the witness should answer, and helping the witness to formulate answers. The witness comes to the deposition to testify, not to indulge in a parody of Charlie McCarthy, with lawyers coaching or bending the

---

107 *Plaisted v. Geisinger Med. Ctr.*, 210 F.R.D. 527 (M.D. Pa. 2002); *Fondren v. Republic Am. Life Ins. Co.*, 190 F.R.D. 597, 600 (N.D. Okla. 1999); *Dravo Corp. v. Liberty Mut. Ins. Co.*, 164 F.R.D. 70 (D. Neb. 1995).

108 *See, e.g., Plaisted*, 210 F.R.D. at 534–35; *Morales v. Zondo, Inc.*, 204 F.R.D. 50, 54–57 (S.D.N.Y. 2001); *Calzaturficio S.C.A.R.P.A., s.p.a. v. Fabiano Shoe Co.*, 201 F.R.D. 33, 39–41 (D. Mass. 2001).

109 150 F.R.D. 525 (E.D. Pa. 1993).

witness's words to mold a legally convenient record. It is
the witness—not the lawyer—who is the witness.[110]

Accordingly, the court rejected the argument that the witness and his
attorney had an unfettered right to consult as they wished. The court also
rejected the contention that the attorney and his client had the right to
review together a document proffered to the witness during the questioning before any questions about it had to be answered. The court noted that
at a deposition, as at a civil trial, "a witness and his or her lawyer are not
permitted to confer at their pleasure during the witness's testimony,"[111]
nor is the witness free to initiate unlimited conferences with counsel.[112]
Indeed, the court went further, stating that counsel and client may not even
confer during breaks or recesses and that communication at such times, at
least by the lawyer to the client, would not be covered by the attorney-client
privilege.[113] Read strictly, *Hall* would seemingly extend the ban on consultation to a protracted hiatus between sessions with a witness, which
occur with some frequency during civil litigation.

1. Consultation to Determine Whether Privilege Should Be Invoked

The *Hall* court recognized that consultation with the witness should be
allowed to enable counsel to evaluate whether a privilege can or ought to
be invoked.[114] Counsel representing a witness, of course, cannot rely on
cross-examination to protect the privilege because, in that case, the barn
will have already burned down before the fire hose is unfurled. Sometimes counsel may be certain that a privilege objection and a direction not
to answer should be interposed in response to a particular question. On
other occasions, though, counsel may see that a question approaches a
possibly privileged area but be unsure whether all the facts support assertion of the privilege. Was a third party, for instance, present at a communication that would otherwise be privileged? In still other instances, the
attorney may be unaware of the possibility that the answer to a question
may invade an area of privilege, but the witness may want to confer with
her attorney to raise the issue.

---

110   *Id.* at 528 (footnote omitted).

111   *Id.*

112   *Id.* at 531–32.

113   *Id.*

114   *Id.* at 529–30.

It would not be sound to be so strict about consultations with the witness as to undermine privileges on the one hand, or, on the other, to induce counsel to make privilege objections and directions not to answer in the absence of knowledge that they are well founded. Thus, counsel can interrupt to confer for this limited purpose.[115] However, when the questioning is halted, counsel should explain on the record that consultation is necessary for this reason.[116]

2. Timing and Scope of Consultations

The *Hall* case has been the subject of controversy in the federal system,[117] although there is little authority on the issue in New York State practice. Some federal courts have taken the position that *Hall* goes too far in forbidding consultation during all breaks and recesses, even long ones, which would adversely affect the attorney-client relationship.[118]

Some courts have held that, despite *Hall*, consultation during scheduled breaks, breaks called by the interrogator, or overnight or other recesses between sessions is acceptable. The rules do not expressly forbid such consultation.[119]

There seems to be consensus that, while a question is pending, it is not proper for counsel to consult the witness about the question, the answer or a document presented to the witness, except, as noted, to protect a privilege or recognized right to confidentiality, which purpose should be stated

---

115 Rule 30.6 of the Local Civil Rules for the Southern and Eastern Districts of New York provides that, in the latter district, "[a]n attorney for a deponent shall not initiate a private conference with the deponent during the actual taking of a deposition, except for the purpose of determining whether a privilege should be asserted."

116 *Hall*, 150 F.R.D. at 530.

117 *Compare Plaisted v. Geisinger Med. Ctr.*, 210 F.R.D. 527 (M.D. Pa. 2002), *and In re Anonymous Member of S. Carolina Bar*, 346 S.C. 177, 552 S.E.2d 10 (S.C. 2001), *with McKinley Infuser, Inc. v. Zdeb*, 200 F.R.D. 648, 650 (D. Colo. 2001), *and In re Stratosphere Corp. Sec. Litig.*, 182 F.R.D. 614, 619–21 (D. Nev. 1998), *and Odone v. Croda Int'l PLC*, 170 F.R.D. 66 (D.D.C. 1997), *and Damaj v. Farmers Ins. Co.*, 164 F.R.D. 559 (N.D. Okla. 1995), *and Ethicon Endo-Surgery v. U.S. Surgical Corp.*, 160 F.R.D. 98 (S.D. Ohio 1995). *See W. Virginia ex rel. Means v. King*, 205 W. Va. 708, 520 S.E.2d 875 (W. Va. 1999); *In re PSE&G Shareholder Litig.*, 320 N.J. Super. 112, 726 A.2d 994 (N.J. Super. Ct., Ch. Div. 1998).

118 *McKinley Infuser, Inc.*, 200 F.R.D. at 649–50; *In re Stratosphere Corp. Sec. Litig.*, 182 F.R.D. at 622; *Odone*, 170 F.R.D. at 69; *see* 7 Moore, *supra* note 63, § 30.42[2].

119 *McKinley Infuser, Inc.*, 200 F.R.D. at 650; *In re Stratosphere Corp. Sec. Litig.*, 182 F.R.D. at 621; *Odone*, 170 F.R.D. at 69.

on the record.[120] Consultation during a pending question for reasons other than protection of a privilege or right would amount to coaching. Neither counsel nor the witness should be able, during the pendency of a question, to manufacture an occasion for coaching by calling an unscheduled break when tactically convenient and conferring as thought helpful. When the witness or his or her counsel calls a break, there should be no consultation, the cases seem to indicate, except with regard to privilege or similar protection. If the witness does not understand a question, he or she should ask the interrogator for clarification, not interrupt to seek "clarification" by consulting with his or her attorney.[121]

During consultations, counsel for the witness is constrained by the rules of ethics. Counsel must not coach a witness at any time in an effort to induce the witness to present false testimony or testimony that would create a false impression. However, counsel should be able to assist the witness in presenting the truth effectively. During breaks not occurring while a question is pending and not engineered by the witness or his or her counsel, counsel should be allowed, some decisions suggest, to point out that the witness's answers have, for example, often been rambling, gone beyond the question posed, been speculative or the like. Counsel, it has been suggested, should also be allowed to inquire of the client-witness whether he or she may have made an inadvertent mistake about a particular matter, the testimony being contradicted by a document, prior statements by the witness to counsel or the like.

Often it will make sense to clear up the record quickly, after a break not engineered for convenience, if the witness has misunderstood a question or misstated an answer. The examiner can explore the change of course

---

120   *See, e.g.*, *In re ML-Lee Acquisition Fund II, L.P.*, 848 F. Supp. 527, 567 (D. Del. 1994).

121   *McKinley Infuser, Inc.*, 200 F.R.D. at 650; *In re Stratosphere Corp. Sec. Litig.*, 182 F.R.D. at 621; *Odone*, 170 F.R.D. at 69.

and ask whether the change took place after consultation with counsel. Such consultations, these decisions indicate, should be privileged.[122]

Others, however, take the position that attorneys should be prohibited from consulting with client-deponents during recesses even though no question is pending. Obviously, conferences during scheduled recesses do not obstruct the progress of the deposition, but they do give rise to potential problems with regard to the crafting of testimony. In *McDermott v. Miami-Dade County*,[123] the court upheld an order of a judge of compensation claims in a workers' compensation case that prohibited the claimant's attorney from discussing with her the circumstances of her fall until the resumption of her deposition. A judge has the discretion to issue such an order, the court ruled.[124]

In light of *Hall*, one commentator has suggested that conferences ought to be permissible during recesses agreed upon by the parties, but that during such conferences, counsel and the client-deponent should not be allowed to address the substance of the deponent's past or future testimony. The interrogator may ask the witness whether he or she conferred during the recess and, if so, whether the communications concerned the substance of his or her testimony. If the witness indicates that the substance was discussed, the interrogator should be permitted to inquire into the details, and the attorney-client privilege should not bar the answers. After all other counsel have concluded their questioning, the deponent

---

122   7 Moore, *supra* note 63, §§ 30.42[2], 30.43[6].

> [W]itnesses can make honest mistakes, and one of the functions of their counsel is to call those to their attention. . . . Nothing in the Rules bars an attorney . . . from consulting with the attorney's client at an appropriate break in the proceedings to ensure that a clear and fair record has been made.

> *Id.* at 30.72. Although it would have been preferable to ascertain the facts on the record, one court refused to impose a penalty where the client and counsel had conferred during a five-minute break not called by that attorney as to whether the deponent had misunderstood a question to which he had given a response. The conference took place after the completion of the line of inquiry but before the end of the interrogation. The deponent's counsel rehabilitated the client during cross as a result of the discussion. The court refused to hold that a waiver of the attorney-client privilege had occurred. The court observed that a consultation could not be neatly segmented into communications about testimony and about other matters. *Odone*, 170 F.R.D. 66; *see W. Virginia ex rel. Means v. King*, 205 W. Va. 708, 520 S.E.2d 875, 881–82 (W. Va. 1999).

123   753 So. 2d 729 (Fla. Dist. Ct. App. 2000).

124   The deposition in that case had been interrupted by the interposition by the attorney for the claimant of an unjustified direction not to answer on grounds of irrelevance.

and counsel should be able to confer prior to cross-examination, and that consultation may include consideration of the deponent's testimony.[125]

3. Constitutional Issues

Some cases suggest that a very strict approach to the matter of consultation might raise constitutional issues. In *Geders v. United States*,[126] the U.S. Supreme Court held that an order that forbade a defendant in a criminal case from consulting his attorney about anything during an overnight recess of 17 hours between his direct examination and cross impinged upon his Sixth Amendment right to counsel.

The Court noted that judges have "broad power to sequester witnesses before, during, and after their testimony."[127] This ancient power, which apparently arose during a trial for rape in which Solomon presided, was then and is now used to prevent witnesses from tailoring their testimony to fit the story presented by other witnesses. The practice of sequestering also helped to detect testimony that was not candid and to prevent improper efforts at influencing testimony.[128] But, when the rights of the defendant in a criminal case are at stake, "the role of counsel [while witnesses are sequestered] is important precisely because ordinarily a defendant is ill-equipped to understand and deal with the trial process without a lawyer's guidance."[129] It is therefore not proper for a court to forbid such guidance during all recesses, even about matters unconnected to the testimony.

In *Perry v. Leeke*,[130] the Supreme Court further defined the issues. The Court held that judges are not constitutionally required to allow the defendant in a criminal case to consult with counsel during a short break called by the court while the defendant is testifying. The Court stated that the

---

125 A. Darby Dickerson, *The Law and Ethics of Civil Depositions,* 57 Md. L. Rev. 273, 342–46, n.195 (1998) (asserting that a conference ought not to be used by counsel to determine whether the client-deponent misunderstood questions or otherwise made an honest mistake while testifying; rather, counsel should seek to rehabilitate the witness on cross-examination); *see* Del. Super. Ct. Civ. R. 30(d)(1) (prohibiting during recesses of fewer than five days conferences regarding the substance of testimony already given or to be given except for discussion as to whether to assert a privilege or how to comply with a court order, or suggestions to the deponent as to the manner in which any question should be answered).

126 425 U.S. 80 (1976).

127 *Id.* at 87.

128 *Id.*

129 *Id.* at 88.

130 488 U.S. 272 (1989).

defendant has no constitutional right to consult counsel while testifying. The trial judge can refuse to declare a recess at the close of direct testimony or at any other point during it and also has the power to "maintain the status quo" during a brief recess by prohibiting consultation.[131] The Court contrasted long recesses, during which a consultation would normally encompass matters going beyond the content of the defendant's testimony (e.g., trial tactics, etc.), with short recesses "in which it is appropriate to presume that nothing but the testimony will be discussed."[132]

4. Civil Cases

A few cases have considered whether the due process rights of a party to a civil case limit a court's power to restrict conferences between client and counsel during the trial. Such limits might have implications for rules governing the conduct of counsel and deponent during short or extended recesses in depositions. In *Potashnick v. Port City Construction Co.*,[133] the court stated broadly:

> Notwithstanding the civil-criminal dichotomy, an analogy can be drawn between the criminal and civil litigants' respective rights to counsel. In both cases the litigant usually lacks the skill and knowledge to adequately prepare his case, and he requires the guiding hand of counsel at every step in the proceedings against him. In each instance, the right to counsel is one of constitutional dimensions and should thus be freely exercised without impingement.[134]

The judge's ruling in *Potashnick* that the court of appeals found deficient had barred the president and sole shareholder of the corporate defendant from conferring with counsel for seven days while he was testifying, including overnight recesses.[135]

---

131   *Id.* at 283.

132   *Id.* at 284; *see, e.g., Sanders v. Lane,* 861 F.2d 1033 (7th Cir. 1988), *cert. denied,* 489 U.S. 1057 (1989); *Bova v. Dugger,* 858 F.2d 1539 (11th Cir. 1988); *Mudd v. United States,* 798 F.2d 1509 (D.C. Cir. 1986).

133   609 F.2d 1101 (5th Cir.), *cert. denied,* 449 U.S. 820 (1980).

134   *Id.* at 1118 (citation omitted).

135   *Id.* at 1119–20; *see Aiello v. City of Wilmington,* 623 F.2d 845 (3d Cir. 1980); *Brake v. Murphy,* 749 So. 2d 1278 (Fla. Dist. Ct. App. 2000).

In *Reynolds v. Alabama Department of Transportation*,[136] the court wrote:

> A civil party does not have a right to consult with his counsel at any time about any matter during the course of his or her testimony. Rather, the trial court has broad power to control the progress of testimony before it. This broad power is, however, limited by a testifying party's right to engage in such non-testimonial matters as giving and receiving information and working on the presentation of his or her case through strategizing, developing tactics, and generally managing the progress of the case. Because these non-testimonial matters arise most often during extended recesses—in particular, over evenings and weekends—the court must be sensitive to allow a testifying party to confer with his or her attorney during such periods.[137]

Cases discussing the power of the court to restrict conferences between counsel and client while the latter is testifying at trial focus, as noted, upon the need to prevent the tailoring of testimony as it develops. *Geders v. United States*[138] emphasized the issues facing a defendant and counsel, other than the defendant's testimony. The U.S. Supreme Court in *Perry v. Leeke*[139] contrasted nontestimonial issues likely to be addressed during long recesses with the fact that during a short recess nothing but testimony will presumably be discussed. The Court also indicated that a judge may issue an order permitting consultation limited to nontestimonial matters during a brief recess.[140] It is not, however, always easy to draw a line

---

136   4 F. Supp. 2d 1055 (M.D. Ala. 1998).

137   *Id.* at 1066. *See United States v. Philip Morris Inc.*, 212 F.R.D. 418, 420 (D.D.C. 2002):

> [I]n general, a deponent and the deponent's attorney have no absolute right to confer during a deposition in a civil proceeding, except for the purpose of determining whether a privilege shall be asserted. This general prohibition may extend to communications occurring during breaks, lunch, or even overnight, if a deposition lasts for longer than a day. However, there is by no means a categorical prohibition on communications once a deposition has commenced. Indeed, the extent to which a court may limit communications between a deponent and her attorney during the course of a deposition requires a balancing of several countervailing factors [citations omitted].

138   425 U.S. 80, 88 (1976).

139   488 U.S. 272, 284 (1989).

140   *Id.* at 284 n.8.

between consultations about nontestimonial matters and those that involve consideration of testimony.[141]

5. Conclusions of Committee on Federal Procedure

In a report dated December 12, 2002, the Committee on Federal Procedure of the Commercial and Federal Litigation Section of the New York State Bar Association concluded that a conference during a deposition while a question is pending should always be prohibited except for the purpose of determining whether a privilege or other protection from discovery should be asserted.[142] In addition, the committee concluded that consultation should be allowed during overnight breaks.[143] The committee could not reach consensus as to any other guidelines in this area.

The committee evaluated several situations in which clients might confer with their attorneys during a deposition and considered relevant factors for and against allowing conferences in each situation. The committee agreed that conferences for the purpose of coaching a witness[144] should be prohibited because coaching would frustrate the major purpose of the deposition, which is to discover facts and preserve truthful testimony.[145] The committee also cautioned against mid-deposition conferences because they can interfere with the interrogator's examination. Part of the strategy of the interrogator is to control the pace of the questioning, and if defending counsel interferes, the interrogator's effectiveness is reduced.[146]

---

141 *Id.* at 284 ("[D]iscussions [of trial-related matters] will inevitably include some consideration of the defendant's ongoing testimony."); *see id.* at 295 n.8 (Marshall, J., dissenting). The order at issue in *Reynolds v. Alabama Dep't of Transp.*, 4 F. Supp. 2d 1055, 1057 (M.D. Ala. 1998), permitted consultations between counsel and witnesses about nontestimonial matters on evenings and weekends. The court also indicated that it would consider requests to allow consultation even about testimony.

142 New York State Bar Association Commercial and Federal Litigation Section, Committee on Federal Procedure, *Should Deposition Witnesses Be Allowed To Confer With Their Counsel During a Deposition?*, at 13–14 (2002) (hereinafter "Comm. on Fed. Procedure Report").

143 *Id.* at 14.

144 The committee was careful to distinguish coaching from preparation. Coaching occurs when counsel, directly or indirectly, tells the witness how to answer a question. *Id.* at 3 (citing *In re Stratosphere Corp. Sec. Litig.*, 182 F.R.D. 614, 621 (D. Nev. 1998)). This can harm the deposition process by allowing the witness to give untruthful answers. Preparation, on the other hand, occurs when counsel and the witness review the witness's recollection of relevant events, documents, issues in the case and deposition procedure. *Id.* (citing *Christy v. Pa. Turnpike Comm'n*, 160 F.R.D. 51, 53 (E.D. Pa. 1995)).

145 Comm. on Fed. Procedure Report, *supra* note 142, at 3–4.

146 *Id.*

The committee recognized that attorney-client consultation during depositions might arguably be appropriate for the purpose of discussing what seem to be harassing questions and determining with the client whether to seek court intervention in regard to them. The committee noted that, although counsel can explain the remedial option to the client before the deposition, it may be that an assessment of the appropriate course of action cannot realistically be made until the harassing event occurs. However, the committee urged caution in deciding whether to suspend the deposition for judicial intervention.[147] The committee indicated that the witness's counsel should make a record under FRCP 30(c) stating a basis for any consultation.

The committee's report did not come to a definite conclusion on the question of whether a mid-deposition conference should be allowed to correct inadvertent false statements. The committee was of the view that correcting errors is neither clearly acceptable nor clearly unacceptable. Weighing against acceptability is the close resemblance that a mid-deposition conference for the purpose of correction bears to coaching.[148] On the other hand, the committee found that a conference to correct a material error could arguably be warranted because if the error is not immediately corrected, it can lead to a series of irrelevant questions and a waste of everyone's time.

The committee felt that many variables factor into the decision of whether to allow mid-deposition conferences to reassure a witness. The committee found this to be an area in which workable rules that do not infringe on examination by the interrogator could be devised. Reassurance should be provided during preparation, the committee stated, no matter when the preparation occurs. Should there be an overnight break in the deposition, reassurance would likely be appropriate. Less clear is the permissibility of reassurance during normal breaks, such as for a meal. The committee suggested a possible rule based on who initiates the breaks. Another possible rule would make the content of consultations during

---

147   The committee noted that a suspension of the deposition for intervention in accordance with FRCP 30(d)(4) might, if unsuccessful, result in sanctions under FRCP 37(a)(4)(A). *Id.* at 6.

148   "Correcting errors . . . looks very much like coaching the witness." Comm. on Fed. Procedure Report, *supra* note 142, at 8. The committee dismissed efficiency concerns, stating that the goal of a deposition is not economy or efficiency but discovery of facts through truthful testimony. In addition, the committee noted that an attorney has a chance to clarify any previous incorrect statements by further examination of the witness. *Id.*

breaks initiated by the deponent or deponent's counsel discoverable, which would deter coaching.[149]

Regardless of where the line is drawn regarding consultations, counsel for the witness may seek to repair any residual damage from errors of the witness on cross-examination. If counsel for the witness does try to rehabilitate the witness by further exploration on cross, the questioner is protected by the right to redirect.

H. Questions of Law

Questions are improper when they call for legal conclusions. Such improper questions include those that relate to a party-deponent's understanding of his or her contentions in the case.[150]

I. Competency of Witness

Objections to the competency of the witness are preserved for trial unless the basis thereof is such that the objection would be obviated or removed if made at the deposition.[151] Therefore, counsel should permit the witness to answer even if he or she believes the witness is not competent to testify to a particular subject and that the testimony will be inadmissible. Even if the question is ultimately found objectionable and the answer excluded, the answer in the meantime may lead the questioner to evidence that is relevant and admissible. The answer should be allowed and the ruling left for trial.[152]

---

149 Two members of the committee and one member of the section's executive committee dissented in part from the committee's conclusion. The dissenters agreed with the majority that conferences should be prohibited while a question is pending except to consider possible assertion of privilege or other discovery protection. However, in the absence of any court rules or ethics rule, the dissenters did not believe that lawyers are or should be under any proscription against other kinds of consultation during a deposition. *Id.* at 14.

150 *JPMorgan Chase Bank v. Liberty Mut. Ins. Co.*, 209 F.R.D. 361, 362 (S.D.N.Y. 2002) (depositions are intended as a means for the discovery of facts, not contentions or legal theories); *Chattanoga Mfg., Inc. v. Nike, Inc.*, 140 F. Supp. 2d 917, 929 n.12 (N.D. Ill. 2001); *Adley Express Co. v. Highway Truck Drivers & Helpers, Local No. 107*, 349 F. Supp. 436, 450 (E.D. Pa. 1972); *Tardibuono v. County of Nassau*, 181 A.D.2d 879, 581 N.Y.S.2d 443 (2d Dep't 1992); *Lobdell v. S. Buffalo Ry. Co.*, 159 A.D.2d 958, 552 N.Y.S.2d 782 (4th Dep't 1990); *Blitz v. Guardian Life Ins. Co.*, 99 A.D.2d 404, 470 N.Y.S.2d 6 (1st Dep't 1984).

151 CPLR 3115(d); FRCP 32(d)(3)(A).

152 *United States v. Odom*, 736 F.2d 104 (4th Cir. 1984); *United States v. Gerry*, 515 F.2d 130 (2d Cir. 1975); *United States v. Crosby*, 462 F.2d 1201 (D.C. Cir. 1972); *Walter Karl, Inc. v. Wood*, 161 A.D.2d 704, 555 N.Y.S.2d 840 (2d Dep't 1990); *Watson v. State*, 53 A.D.2d 798, 385 N.Y.S.2d 170 (3d Dep't 1976).

J. Publicly Available Information

Questions at a deposition may seek information from a witness, even if that information can be located elsewhere, including in public documents.[153]

K. Evasive Answers

Just as the inquiring attorney has the right to pursue an inquiry that is not inhibited or frustrated by arbitrary or baseless objections or interruptions, so should the questioning be marked by freedom from artificial obstacles posed by the witness in the form of evasive answers. Both at trial and in depositions, witnesses are obliged to provide responsive answers to the extent of their knowledge.

It is improper for a witness to provide "answers" that seek to sidestep questions. Purported answers that engage the questioner in wordplay, seek to split verbal hairs without justification, willfully misinterpret questions in a narrow way to suit the convenience of the witness, provide incomplete responses and the like are improper. It is even worse for the witness to claim ignorance of, or pretend to have no recollection of, things the witness knows. A witness may be penalized for asserting ignorance or lack of recollection about facts of which the witness must be aware. An evasive or incomplete answer is regarded as a failure to respond.[154]

L. Walking Out of Depositions

Counsel for a witness may sometimes find that his or her patience is tested by questioning that is insufficiently focused or that wanders around in fields of irrelevancy. The attorney may feel the temptation to declare the examination over and depart with the client-deponent in tow. This course of action is improper. "The deposition shall be taken continuously and without unreasonable adjournment."[155]

If the interrogator is proceeding improperly, counsel for the witness may make an appropriate objection. When authorized by the rules discussed thus far, counsel may direct the witness not to answer invalid queries and seek a ruling or prepare to make a formal motion. However,

---

153   *See, e.g., Riddell Sports Inc. v. Brooks*, 158 F.R.D. 555, 557 (S.D.N.Y. 1994). *But see* FRCP 26(b)(2) (limitations on discovery generally).

154   FRCP 37(a)(3); *Eaves v. K-Mart Corp.*, 193 F. Supp. 2d 887, 895 (S.D. Miss. 2001); *Winn v. Associated Press*, 903 F. Supp. 575, 581 (S.D.N.Y. 1995), *aff'd*, 104 F.3d 350 (2d Cir. 1996).

155   CPLR 3113(b).

counsel should not resort to self-help and terminate the deposition without a ruling or an intention to make a motion.

When questioning is improper, counsel for the witness may interrupt for the purpose of making a motion under CPLR 3103 pursuant to CPLR 3113(b) or under FRCP 30(d)(4). This is an appropriate interruption, not a termination (unless, of course, the court concludes on the motion that no proper questions remain to be asked). It may suit the interests of all concerned if the application is made, at least in the first instance, in the form of a request for a ruling.

Under federal law, the questioning may continue on subjects not in controversy to the conclusion of the deposition, at which point a motion or application for a ruling may be made.[156] This is the philosophy of CPLR 3113 as well.[157] Counsel should be able to agree between themselves on the wisdom of continuing the deposition on questioning not in dispute.

If obtaining an immediate ruling is not possible, it may be appropriate to stop the questioning for that purpose and resume once the ruling is given at or about the point where the questioner left off. If the opportunity for a ruling will be delayed or a formal motion will be necessary, there would normally be no reason not to continue with the rest of the deposition until its completion. That course has the benefit that, in the event other problems arise requiring judicial resolution, all can be included in the one motion. There should be no occasion for, and no need for, a walk-out by counsel and the deponent.[158]

It may, of course, happen that the time allotted for the deposition expires before counsel has completed his or her questioning. Counsel for the witness needs to approach this situation in a reasonable manner. As indicated above, the federal rules, and the state courts as well, are impatient with petty disagreements between attorneys over timing. If counsel for the witness unreasonably seeks to limit questioning on the ground that time therefor has expired, the court is very likely to allow some additional

---

156   FRCP 37(a)(2)(B).

157   Siegel, McKinney's Practice Commentary, CPLR 3113, at 526 (1991).

158   *See Higginbotham v. KCS Int'l, Inc.*, 202 F.R.D. 444 (D. Md. 2001) (improper where attorney sets arbitrary limit on length of deposition and leaves with witness at end of that time); *Ebeh v. Tropical Sportswear Int'l Corp.*, 199 F.R.D. 696 (M.D. Fla. 2001); *Cuthbertson v. Excel Indus.*, 179 F.R.D. 599, 604 (D. Kan. 1998) (questioning should have continued on other topics); *see also Alexander v. FBI*, 186 F.R.D. 208, 213 (D.D.C. 1999) ("[A]bsent good cause, deponents are not free to leave a court-ordered deposition with impunity.").

time if there is good justification for doing so. The termination gambit not only is likely to fail but may well undermine the objecting attorney's standing with the court.

IV. IMPACT OF INTERRUPTIONS

The questioner should not be offended by justified objections to the form of his or her questions, followed occasionally, at least if clarification is requested, by very brief and reasonable statements of the nature of the defect,[159] together with an occasional interruption to explore the possibility of, or to make, an objection based upon a privilege recognized in law. There is no reason for a squabble under such circumstances. If the questioner is uninterested in the claimed defect and prefers to plow ahead, he or she risks that at trial the court may agree that the question is objectionable and rule the evidence inadmissible, in which event the questioner may find himself in a difficult position. Of course, as noted, the questioner sometimes is simply trying to gather information and does not care that a particular portion of the deposition cannot be used at trial.

As suggested above, however, counsel for the witness must pay attention to the cumulative impact of all objections. A large number of technically correct but petty and hypersensitive objections may have an unreasonable impact upon the deposition. "The making of an excessive number of unnecessary objections may itself constitute sanctionable conduct."[160] Also, that some objections are technically correct will not completely exonerate counsel who interposes other, less justifiable ones and whose interruptions, taken together, have interfered with or frustrated the progress of the deposition.

It is not proper, for example, for an attorney repeatedly to interrupt the questioning, occasionally direct the witness not to answer, make brief hypertechnical speeches and comment condescendingly as to how questions ought to be asked. Although some of these activities may be accompanied by objections that have a reasonable basis, there may be so much

---

159 In *Quantachrome Corp. v. Micromeritics Instrument Corp.*, 189 F.R.D. 697, 701 n.4 (S.D. Fla. 1999), the court stated that if an objection is made based on the form of a question, a brief explanation or clarification should be provided, but only if requested by inquiring counsel, and, in such case, in a succinct and nonsuggestive way.

160 Notes of Advisory Committee on 1993 Amendments, FRCP 30(d).

interruption that, in totality, the conduct amounts to an interference with the reasonable flow of the deposition.[161]

A rule of thumb can be used to discern when conduct cumulatively is troublesome, if not improper. Even if the questioner is inexperienced, unprepared, disorganized or inept, the name of counsel for the witness should appear on a minority of the deposition transcript pages. If the name of counsel for the witness appears, for example, on 75 of the 91 transcript pages[162] or on 132 of 147 pages,[163] there is reason for concern that something is amiss.

Because so many objections are preserved for trial, even questioning that is a model of how not to depose a witness should not elicit a vast number of objections that inhibit the flow, such as it is, of the deposition. If the questioner is exceptionally lacking in skill or unprepared, counsel for the witness should pay attention to avoiding interposition of objections that are not necessary, either because the matter is unimportant or because the objection is preserved for trial, and, when making objections that are necessary, should strive to be as concise, nonargumentative and nonsuggestive as possible. If, however, the situation is hopeless, the remedy lies in a request for a ruling or a motion.

V. PERSONAL ATTACKS AND ABUSE

In a perfect world, it would be unnecessary to state that it is completely unacceptable behavior for an attorney at a deposition to insult or harass opposing counsel, witnesses or others; to make snide remarks on the record; or otherwise to engage in rude or discourteous behavior. Alas, this world is not a perfect one. Over the last decade or two, the courts have grown less tolerant of such misconduct in a deposition. Now, personal attacks or abuse may well lead to the imposition of sanctions upon the

---

161 *See Morales v. Zondo, Inc.*, 204 F.R.D. 50 (S.D.N.Y. 2001); *Phinney v. Paulshock*, 181 F.R.D. 185, 206 (D.N.H. 1998), *aff'd*, 199 F.3d 1 (1st Cir. 1999); *Learning Int'l, Inc. v. Competence Assurance Sys., Inc.*, No. 90 Civ. 2032, 1990 U.S. Dist. LEXIS 16810 (S.D.N.Y. Dec. 13, 1990).

162 *Learning Int'l, Inc.*, 1990 U.S. Dist. LEXIS 16810.

163 *Unique Concepts, Inc. v. Brown*, 115 F.R.D. 292 (S.D.N.Y. 1987).

offending attorney.[164] Sanctions may be imposed even if verbal abuse is not alleged to have significantly delayed or impeded the deposition.[165]

The discovery process is, to a substantial degree, dependent upon cooperation between opposing attorneys. The courts cannot participate directly in every single step of the discovery process because they are too busy, and supervision in such detail would make the process even more time-consuming and expensive than it already is.[166] The deposition itself is a part of a judicial proceeding, and attorneys have an obligation to conduct themselves with dignity in every phase of such proceedings. "A lawyer's duty to refrain from uncivil and abusive behavior is not diminished because the site of the proceeding is a deposition room or law office, rather than a courtroom."[167] At the very heart of the legal profession is a duty of civility that attorneys owe to one another and to all others in the judicial process.

In October 1997, the New York State Unified Court System issued standards of civility for the profession.[168] The Chief Judge of the State of New York stated that incidents of incivility "can reinforce unflattering popular conceptions about the current state of the profession."[169] The standards were designed to serve as guidelines to encourage the profession "to observe principles of civility and decorum."[170] Among other things, the standards require that attorneys conduct themselves with dignity during depositions and refrain from acts of rudeness and disrespect. In particular:

---

164 *Corsini v. U-Haul Int'l*, 212 A.D.2d 288, 630 N.Y.S.2d 45, 47 (1st Dep't 1995), *appeal denied*, 87 N.Y.2d 964, 642 N.Y.S.2d 192 (1996); *Principe v. Assay Partners*, 154 Misc. 2d 702, 586 N.Y.S.2d 182 (Sup. Ct., N.Y. Co. 1992) (relying on pt. 130 of the Rules of the Chief Administrator); *see Carroll v. Jaques Admiralty Law Firm*, 110 F.3d 290 (5th Cir. 1997); *Freeman v. Schointuck*, 192 F.R.D. 187 (D. Md. 2000); *Paramount Communications v. QVC Network Inc.*, 637 A.2d 34, 51 (Del. Super. Ct. 1994) (court *sua sponte* raised issue of abusive conduct).

165 *Principe*, 154 Misc. 2d 702.

166 *See Freeman*, 192 F.R.D. at 189 ("[S]ystematic and deliberate abuses . . . cannot go unsanctioned as they are destructive of the very fabric which holds together the process of pretrial discovery—cooperative exchange of information without the need for constant court intervention" (footnote omitted)).

167 *Corsini*, 212 A.D.2d at 291.

168 New York State Unified Court System, *Standards of Civility*, Preamble (1997), *available at* www.nycourts.gov/jipl/standardsofcivility.pdf (hereinafter "*Standards of Civility*").

169 The State of the Judiciary Address 1998, at 19 (Mar. 23, 1998), *available at* www.nycourts.gov/admin/stateofjudiciary/soj98.htm.

170 *Standards of Civility*, *supra* note 168, Preamble.

(C) A lawyer should not obstruct questioning during a deposition or object to deposition questions unless necessary.

(D) Lawyers should ask only those questions they reasonably believe are necessary for the prosecution or defense of an action. Lawyers should refrain from asking repetitive or argumentative questions and from making self-serving statements.[171]

The duty to refrain from abusive conduct during a deposition extends to others in attendance and to the deponent.[172] In one case, a court revoked the *pro hac vice* admission of an out-of-state attorney because he had failed to make adequate efforts to control the abusive conduct of the client-deponent.[173]

VI. ETHICAL CONSIDERATIONS

The Lawyer's Code of Professional Responsibility admonishes attorneys against abusive behavior toward opposing counsel and others in the legal process:

> In adversary proceedings, clients are litigants and though ill feeling may exist between clients, such ill feeling should not influence a lawyer's conduct, attitude, and demeanor towards opposing lawyers. A lawyer should not make unfair or derogatory personal reference to opposing counsel. Haranguing and offensive tactics by lawyers interfere with the orderly administration of justice and have no proper place in our legal system.[174]

Some may believe that the emphasis upon civility and decorum conflicts with the ethical obligation of attorneys to represent their clients zealously. But there is no conflict. An attorney can zealously and aggressively represent his or her client at deposition and trial, and with the utmost vigor and thoroughness make appropriate motions and pursue appropriate

---

171   *Standards of Civility, supra* note 168, Lawyers' Duties to Other Lawyers, Litigants and Witnesses, Standard VII.

172   *Antonino-Garcia v. Shadrin*, 208 F.R.D. 298, 299 (D. Or. 2002) (disruptive relative).

173   *State v. Mumford*, 731 A.2d 831 (Del Super. Ct. 1999).

174   The Lawyer's Code of Professional Responsibility, EC 7-37.

discovery in order to protect the interests of the client without resorting to harassment or oppression or engaging in rude or abusive conduct.

Courts every day encounter attorneys who are outstandingly zealous on behalf of their clients and who achieve success doing so, but without resorting to rude, discourteous or abusive behavior. It is false to contend that zealousness and civility are mutually exclusive. Certainly, the ethical obligation of counsel is to represent the clients zealously, but within the framework of the law. The law makes clear that there is no place for harassment or oppression or rude or abusive conduct by lawyers during the course of litigation.[175]

As noted above, the attorney representing a client at a deposition has an ethical obligation to prepare the witnesses in a proper manner and to do the same when consulting with the witness during the course of the deposition to the extent consultation is permitted by law.[176] In preparation, the attorney may advise the client not to volunteer information not requested, not to engage in rambling or unfocused answers and to answer the precise question asked, not what the witness may believe the questioner is looking for ultimately; and the attorney should otherwise strive to assist the witness to protect his or her interests and to make as effective a presentation as possible. The attorney, however, should not coach the witness to provide answers that are false and indeed should make clear to the witness that he or she should always tell the truth.

The attorney conducting the deposition has an ethical obligation not to abuse the deposition process in an effort to harass or oppress the witness, nor to pursue questioning of the adversary-deponent simply in order to make the conduct or defense of the litigation difficult for that adversary. The attorney has an obligation reasonably to prepare for the deposition and not to conduct it in such a way that substantial amounts of time are consumed with irrelevant matters. The interrogator needs to have a reasonable basis for pursuing in good faith a line of inquiry at a deposition.

---

175   *In re Schiff*, 190 A.D.2d 293, 599 N.Y.S.2d 242 (1st Dep't 1993); *see In re Dinhofer*, 257 A.D.2d 326, 690 N.Y.S.2d 245 (1st Dep't 1999); *Alexander v. FBI*, 186 F.R.D. 21, 52–53 (D.D.C. 1998).

176   Charles W. Wolfram, Modern Legal Ethics § 12.4.3 (1986); Richard S. Wydick, *The Ethics of Witness Coaching*, 17 Cardozo L. Rev. 1 (1995).

CHAPTER SIX

PROTECTIVE ORDERS

I. STATE PRACTICE

A. Protective Orders in General

The protective order in state practice is governed by CPLR 3103. Such an order may be issued at any time, either on the court's own initiative or on motion of any party or any person from whom discovery is sought, which would include a nonparty witness. The order may deny, limit, condition or regulate the use of any disclosure device in order to "prevent unreasonable annoyance, expense, embarrassment, disadvantage, or other prejudice to any person or the courts."[1]

Service of a notice of motion suspends the disclosure in dispute, which protects the party or witness who otherwise might be prejudiced pending determination of the motion (although it can also be a tool for the party intent upon obstruction and delay). If disclosure is obtained improperly, a protective order may be issued directing that it be suppressed.[2] A motion for a protective order must be accompanied by an affirmation reflecting that an effort was made to resolve the dispute without need for court action.[3]

Section 3103 of the CPLR is aimed at a multitude of sins. It "recognizes how readily the devices can be abused, and wisely surrenders all attempts to enumerate potential abuses. The cure is an ad hoc order."[4] Of the innumerable forms of abuse that can be regulated by a protective order, some of the most common include the following:

- when and where depositions take place and which should be taken first;

- how many persons should be deposed (whether corporate representatives or others produced possess adequate knowledge of the facts or whether additional persons need to be produced, and whether a person already deposed needs to be deposed again);

---

1   CPLR 3103(a).

2   CPLR 3103(b), (c).

3   Uniform Rule 202.7; see Appendix, "Motion for a Protective Order," "Affirmation on Motion for Protective Order" and "Affirmation of Good Faith (Uniform Rule 202.7)" (state forms). A certification pursuant to 22 N.Y.C.R.R. § 130-1.1a is also required. *See* Siegel, McKinney's Practice Commentary, CPLR 3103 (1991).

4   David D. Siegel, New York Practice § 353, at 549 (3d ed. 1999); *see* Siegel, McKinney's Practice Commentary, CPLR 3103, at 356–57 (1991).

- deadlines for the completion of discovery or stages thereof, such as the document production and deposition stages, and whether a deadline extension should be granted;

- the number and kinds of questions that can be asked in interrogatories and at depositions;

- which disclosure device can be used and how devices may be used in combination;

- what matters may be inquired into (e.g., which matters are relevant and which are not and the period of time the discovery may cover);

- whether attendance at a deposition should be limited and whether the transcript should be sealed;

- whether and how trade or business secrets should be protected; and

- whether special financial arrangements to address the costs of discovery are necessary under the circumstances.[5]

As noted, the court is empowered to issue a protective order on its own initiative, which may occur at a court conference. Happily, most litigators are able to work out their discovery problems together most of the time. Although an application for a protective order covering one or more of the above items certainly is not unusual, it is, in the authors' experience, more the exception than the rule.

A motion for a protective order may be made at any time, but it generally should be made before the disclosure is due. The disclosure in issue may be suspended so that an objection may be raised in a timely manner without the objecting party having to risk prejudice from an adverse ruling.[6] An objecting attorney should proceed expeditiously, as a party must serve a response stating the reasons for each objection within 20 days from service of the demand.[7]

Because the trial court has considerable discretion in supervising disclosure, it has broad authority to grant protective orders, especially when

---

5   *See* Legislative Studies and Reports, CPLR 3103 (1991).

6   CPLR 3103(b).

7   CPLR 3122(a). A nonparty may object to a subpoena *duces tecum* in the same way. See chapter 3 for further discussion of the CPLR 3122 requirements.

the disclosure sought would be unduly burdensome.[8] "[T]he burden of establishing any right to protection is on the party asserting it; the protection claimed must be narrowly construed."[9]

B. Rulings and Applications in Connection with Conduct at Depositions

At an appropriate point in a deposition (whether right after a problem has arisen or when a suitable number of issues can be addressed together, whichever is most efficient under the circumstances of the particular case), a defending attorney can seek an application for a ruling by the court.[10] Many problems can be solved in this way, typically with little expense and no harm to the client from so proceeding rather than making a formal motion.[11]

If the deposition is being conducted in or near the courthouse or if the court can be reached by telephone, the results can be quite efficient. However, judges cannot always drop their other work or interrupt a trial to accommodate counsel. It may be possible to contact the court and, if the court is not then available, schedule a convenient time for a telephone conference and continue the deposition on other matters. Counsel should consult local rules and the individual rules, if any, of the judge assigned to

---

8   *Andrews v. Trustco Bank, N.A.*, 289 A.D.2d 910, 735 N.Y.S.2d 640 (3d Dep't 2001).

9   *Spectrum Sys. Int'l Corp. v. Chem. Bank*, 78 N.Y.2d 371, 377, 575 N.Y.S.2d 809, 581 N.E.2d 1055 (1991). Commentators have observed:

> Burden of proof considerations with respect to the grant or denial of protective orders are ancillary to the more subtle and imprecise considerations involved in balancing the litigants' entitlement to open disclosure with its abuse potentials. Reliance upon burden of proof doctrine to justify a decision in this area is often a mask for a refusal to come to grips with the problem or a reluctance to express the actual grounds for a decision.

> 6 Jack B. Weinstein et al., New York Civil Practice ¶ 3103.08, at 31-256 (2004) (footnote omitted).

10   The examining attorney also can seek to compel information or end obstruction by a request for a ruling in lieu of a formal motion to compel under CPLR 3124 or for sanctions under CPLR 3126.

11   *Am. Reliance Ins. Co. v. Nat'l Gen. Ins. Co.*, 174 A.D.2d 591, 571 N.Y.S.2d 493 (2d Dep't 1991) (a request for a ruling is perhaps preferable to a formal motion); *see Cohen v. Heine & Co.*, 39 A.D.2d 563, 331 N.Y.S.2d 751 (2d Dep't 1972). In state court, no appeal to the appellate division lies as of right from a ruling, but the notice of appeal can be considered an application for leave to appeal. *McGuire v. Zarlengo*, 250 A.D.2d 823, 673 N.Y.S.2d 200 (2d Dep't 1998); *see Kinkela v. Inc. Vill. of Mineola*, 306 A.D.2d 382, 761 N.Y.S.2d 284 (2d Dep't 2003) (no appeal as of right from order denying motion to direct witness to answer questions at deposition; notice can be considered application).

the case before the deposition begins to see if the court has issued any directives on the subject.

Disclosure is apt to be closely supervised by the federal judge or a magistrate judge. Given the very large number of cases pending in state court (at the time of this writing, for example, some 40,000 cases were pending in Supreme Court, New York County, alone) and the comparative scarcity of resources there, judicial supervision may not be as active, and the opportunity for prompt rulings may be more uncertain. On occasion, a supreme court justice may assign a special referee to supervise depositions pursuant to CPLR 3104. However, special referees are not available to the same extent as are federal magistrate judges. In state practice, the parties may also involve a private attorney on consent.[12]

If counsel for the witness concludes that judicial intervention is necessary and that a formal motion is required, he or she should move for a protective order under CPLR 3103.[13] Such motion should be made either immediately or when other lines of inquiry have been exhausted. It should be made in whatever way is most protective of the deponent's rights and, at the same time, the least disruptive to the interrogator's questioning.

C. Protective Orders in Detail

> Trial courts are vested with broad discretion to issue appropriate protective orders to limit discovery. But this discretion is to be exercised with the competing interests of the parties and the truth-finding goal of the discovery process in mind. As a consequence, the general preference for allowing discovery must be balanced against the objecting party's prerogative to be free of "unreasonable annoyance, expense, embarrassment, disadvantage, or other prejudice."[14]

The movant must make a factual showing of disadvantage, annoyance or prejudice. Conclusory or vague assertions of hardship will not be suffi-

---

12   CPLR 3104(b); *see Carpenter Envtl. Assocs. v. Horn*, 239 A.D.2d 379, 658 N.Y.S.2d 35 (2d Dep't 1997). The court may make an appropriate order for payment of the private referee's reasonable expenses.

13   *See* Siegel, McKinney's Practice Commentary, CPLR 3124, at 740 (1991).

14   *Brignola v. Pei-Fei Lee, M.D., P.C.*, 192 A.D.2d 1008, 1009, 597 N.Y.S.2d 250 (3d Dep't 1993) (citation omitted).

cient.[15] The court has broad discretion when it comes to dealing with discovery applications.[16]

Uniform Rule 202.7 indicates the importance of the attorneys attempting in good faith to work out discovery problems about such things as whom to produce, where, when and in what order. As noted, the preliminary conference order usually will set out a schedule for the taking of depositions. Should difficulties arise, these often can be resolved at a subsequent conference, the outcome of which will frequently be reflected in an order, commonly called a *compliance conference order*. Sometimes, however, discussion between the parties may fail to produce a resolution, thereby necessitating motion practice.

When the court has directed that particular document production be made or depositions taken, or that discovery occur on specified dates or by certain deadlines, the parties obliged to produce or appear at a deposition are, of course, expected to obey the orders. In a particular case a problem may arise that makes compliance unduly difficult or impossible, but the attorney affected should not simply ignore the court order, believing the court will later agree. An attorney cannot decide these questions on his or her own. Court orders must be respected if the civil justice system is to function, so courts cannot take such violations lightly.

Furthermore, even if an attorney has a reasonable excuse, the court may well have a schedule for the case that must be adhered to and that will be adversely affected if the attorney engages in self-help, perhaps thereby causing broader discord to break out. If counsel for all parties can agree that a party faces a genuine problem that requires an adjustment in the prior order, the parties should consider (1) submission of a stipulation to be approved and "so ordered" by the court, (2) a conference call or (3) a conference. If there is disagreement or it is not possible to reach the court, a motion for a protective order should be made, by order to show cause if necessary.[17] Such a motion will suspend the discovery in issue. Of course,

---

15   *Kimmel v. State*, 261 A.D.2d 843, 690 N.Y.S.2d 383 (4th Dep't 1999); *Willis v. Cassia*, 255 A.D.2d 800, 680 N.Y.S.2d 313 (3d Dep't 1998); *State v. GE Co.*, 215 A.D.2d 928, 626 N.Y.S.2d 861 (3d Dep't 1995); *Brignola*, 192 A.D.2d 1008; *Carberry v. Bonilla*, 65 A.D.2d 613, 409 N.Y.S.2d 551 (2d Dep't 1978).

16   *McMahon v. Aviette Agency, Inc.*, 301 A.D.2d 820, 753 N.Y.S.2d 605 (3d Dep't 2003); *Jordan v. Blue Circle Atl. Inc.*, 296 A.D.2d 752, 745 N.Y.S.2d 289 (3d Dep't 2002).

17   See Appendix, "Order to Show Cause for Protective Order—Continuation of Deposition" (state form).

the motion must be made in good faith and not used as an obstructive device; otherwise, the moving attorney may be sanctioned.

When it comes to depositions, problems are more likely to arise at the deposition than to be perceived and addressed in advance of it.[18] Even so, a motion for a protective order may be made in advance of a deposition.[19] Difficulties may arise when a party seeks additional depositions. If the original witnesses had the necessary, relevant information and the additional proposed deponents do not have any information beyond that already supplied, a protective order may be issued.[20]

A protective order may be granted against a further deposition of a witness already deposed. Because there is no version of FRCP 30(b)(6) in state practice, questions are raised from time to time as to whether a corporation produced the correct person for deposition—someone sufficiently knowledgeable about all the relevant facts. If there were gaps in the person's knowledge, a court may order another representative to be produced when the information sought is necessary. If a particular individual is sought, it must be clear that the person has the knowledge in question.

If new circumstances have arisen since the deposition of a witness, a further deposition of the witness may be necessary. This need may arise if, for example, the plaintiff asserts new injuries in a supplementation of a response to a bill of particulars or prior discovery responses, or if a party seeks to amend a pleading.

As to corporate parties, adversaries sometimes seek the depositions of very high-level officials. In proper circumstances, a protective order may be obtained with respect to notices of deposition directed to such persons. The official will need to show by affidavit that he or she had no involvement in the events or transactions at issue and has no information of any value to offer. If, on their face, the events or transactions were routine and not likely to have come to the attention of the proposed deponent in the ordinary course of business in view of his or her lofty position, if the case

---

18 *Feili v. City of New York*, 239 A.D.2d 297, 658 N.Y.S.2d 21 (1st Dep't 1997).

19 However, because a theme running through the state cases and the federal rules is a preference to try cases on their merits, justices and district judges likely will be circumspect about limiting discovery into certain facts in advance.

20 *Wolin v. St. Vincent's Hosp.*, 304 A.D.2d 348, 757 N.Y.S.2d 33 (1st Dep't 2003); *EIFS, Inc. v. Morie Co.*, 298 A.D.2d 548, 749 N.Y.S.2d 43 (2d Dep't 2002); *Thomas v. Benedictine Hosp.*, 296 A.D.2d 781, 745 N.Y.S.2d 606 (3d Dep't 2002); *Kobre v. United Jewish Appeal-Fed'n of Jewish Philanthropies of New York*, 288 A.D.2d 157, 733 N.Y.S.2d 184 (1st Dep't 2001); *cf. Fronczak v. Zizzi*, 295 A.D.2d 985, 743 N.Y.S.2d 788 (4th Dep't 2002).

does not involve or implicate corporate policies and if another representative with knowledge has already been produced or will be, the affidavit of the named official is more likely to elicit a favorable response from the court.[21]

Courts ordinarily will not rule on particular deposition questions on a motion for a protective order made in advance of the deposition.[22] The questions feared may not be asked. If asked, the manner in which they are posed and the extent to which they are made will assist the court in addressing them.[23] Generally, therefore, the attorney should await the deposition, object then to any question if a waiver would otherwise occur and save the questions for a ruling at trial. If a question seeks privileged information or a direction not to answer is otherwise proper in accordance with the rules discussed in chapter 5, such a direction may be interposed and a motion for a protective order made.

In some circumstances, however, it may be possible to obtain a decision in advance of a deposition about its permissible parameters. An attorney-client privilege issue may come before the court if the interrogator has served a CPLR 3111 demand or a CPLR 3120 demand for documents prior to deposition and the demand is believed to impinge on the privilege and so elicits objections.

An attorney also may seek to challenge an area of inquiry on the ground that it is irrelevant. Probably, the attorney would need to know from the nature of the case, prior discovery or communications with the adversary that the area will definitely be a subject of inquiry at the deposition, and there must be irreconcilable disagreement between or among the parties about it.

For example, certain events subsequent to those at issue in the case may be thought irrelevant by some party. If what matters is what a party actually knew at the time of a transaction, subsequently acquired informa-

---

21 *See Melohn v. Beard,* 167 A.D.2d 174, 561 N.Y.S.2d 249 (1st Dep't 1990); *Broadband Communications v. Home Box Office,* 157 A.D.2d 479, 549 N.Y.S.2d 402 (1st Dep't 1990) (protective order granted against deposition of CEO; prior CEO who had been involved had testified, as had others); *Boutique Fabrice, Inc. v. Bergdorf Goodman, Inc.,* 129 A.D.2d 529, 514 N.Y.S.2d 380 (1st Dep't 1987) (protective order granted to chairman and CEO of defendant who submitted affidavit showing absence of knowledge or contacts with plaintiffs; four other executives already deposed).

22 *Eliali v. Aztec Metal Maint. Corp.,* 287 A.D.2d 682, 732 N.Y.S.2d 98 (2d Dep't 2001); *Tardibuono v. County of Nassau,* 181 A.D.2d 879, 581 N.Y.S.2d 443 (2d Dep't 1992).

23 *Tardibuono,* 181 A.D.2d 879.

tion may be ruled of no bearing. Or, the court may have issued a decision on a motion to dismiss or for summary judgment, as a result of which the proposed deponent may contend that questions on certain subjects would no longer be relevant.[24]

If a proposed witness is elderly, ill or very young, the court may grant a protective order against the taking of that person's deposition.[25] If the attorney contends that illness or advanced age should exempt the person from being deposed, a detailed showing would have to be made, including a nonconclusory physician's affidavit.

Parties to cases pending in New York usually must appear for deposition in New York.[26] This is so even if they are nonresidents. The general presumption is that the nonresident must appear for deposition in New York at his or her own expense. However, a party who would be prejudiced by such a rule may move for and obtain a protective order in the interests of justice. To be successful, the applicant must demonstrate in a nonconclusory manner that a deposition in New York would cause genuine hardship.[27] The fact that plaintiff instituted the suit in New York will generally

---

24   *See Goldberg v. Fenig*, 300 A.D.2d 439, 751 N.Y.S.2d 546 (2d Dep't 2002).

25   *Willis v. Cassia*, 255 A.D.2d 800, 680 N.Y.S.2d 313 (3d Dep't 1998) (protective order denied as to deposition of defendant 17-year-old driver at time of fatal accident, who moved on basis of depression, anxiety and trauma that deposition would cause; no proof of incompetency or psychological inability to proceed; however, treating professionals allowed to be present); *Arroyo v. Fourteen Estusia Corp.*, 194 A.D.2d 309, 598 N.Y.S.2d 471 (1st Dep't 1993) (protective order granted with respect to deposition of child 4 years old at time of events); *Melohn*, 167 A.D.2d 174; *First London Commodity Options, Ltd. v. Shearson Hayden Stone, Inc.*, 81 A.D.2d 501, 437 N.Y.S.2d 336 (1st Dep't 1981) (deposition allowed of crucial party witness, but on conditions in view of health problems).

26   CPLR 3110 specifies where depositions are to be taken within the state. It contemplates depositions in New York of nonresident parties. *See Rogovin v. Rogovin*, 3 A.D.3d 352, 770 N.Y.S.2d 342 (1st Dep't 2004).

27   *Rogovin*, 3 A.D.3d 352 (defendant to be deposed by live video conferencing in view of hardship that would be caused by travel to New York; defendant sole caregiver of elderly ailing relative and young child with special needs); *Kimmel v. State*, 261 A.D.2d 843, 690 N.Y.S.2d 383 (4th Dep't 1999); *Nauka v. Plenum Publ'g*, 266 A.D.2d 157, 698 N.Y.S.2d 32 (1st Dep't 1999); *Yoshida Printing Co. v. Aiba*, 240 A.D.2d 233, 659 N.Y.S.2d 7 (1st Dep't 1997); *De Velutini v. Velutini U.*, 151 A.D.2d 300, 542 N.Y.S.2d 574 (1st Dep't 1989) (insufficient showing by Venezuelan defendant); *Levine v. St. Luke's Hosp. Ctr.*, 109 A.D.2d 694, 486 N.Y.S.2d 737 (1st Dep't 1985) (defendant must be deposed in New York, not in Georgia nor in New York at plaintiff's expense).

weigh against an application by plaintiff that his or her deposition be taken elsewhere.[28]

A protective order may also be sought when necessary with regard to a demand for the production of documents at a deposition under CPLR 3111 or to prepare for depositions and other aspects of the case under CPLR 3120.[29] Again, a party who objects to all or part of the demand under 3120 must, pursuant to CPLR 3122, serve a response within 20 days that sets forth with reasonable particularity the bases for any objections. Failure to do so in a timely fashion may result in a waiver. Thereafter, the demanding party may move to compel, or the party resisting disclosure may make a motion or cross-motion for a protective order.

Questions regarding attorney-client privilege or other privilege or attorney work product may be brought to a head in this way.[30] Relief also may be requested on the ground that the demand seeks documents that are irrelevant to the proceedings.[31] Tax returns are not discoverable absent a strong showing of need.[32] Not uncommonly, objections are raised on the ground that the demand imposes undue burden and expense. Commercial

---

28 *Nauka*, 266 A.D.2d 157; *Carberry v. Bonilla*, 65 A.D.2d 613, 409 N.Y.S.2d 551 (2d Dep't 1978) (protective order denied where conclusory assertion of hardship made, supported only by affidavit of attorney); *cf. Oneto v. Hotel Waldorf-Astoria Corp.*, 65 A.D.2d 520, 409 N.Y.S.2d 221 (1st Dep't 1978) (plaintiff, a resident of Argentina, granted protective order providing that plaintiff was to be deposed and appear for a physical in New York ten days prior to trial or the defendant would have to pay plaintiff's expenses for an earlier trip; showing of inconvenience and expense).

29 *Kobre v. United Jewish Appeal-Fed'n of Jewish Philanthropies of New York*, 288 A.D.2d 157, 733 N.Y.S.2d 184 (1st Dep't 2001); *Eliali v. Aztec Metal Maint. Corp.*, 287 A.D.2d 682, 732 N.Y.S.2d 98 (2d Dep't 2001); *Scinta v. Van Coevering*, 284 A.D.2d 1000, 726 N.Y.S.2d 520 (4th Dep't 2001) (protective order granted against production of quality assurance and credentials files and deposition of chief of obstetrics regarding same); *State v. GE Co.*, 215 A.D.2d 928, 626 N.Y.S.2d 861 (3d Dep't 1995) (protective order may be granted when production of documents would impose unreasonable burden and expense; *Capital Sources, Inc. v. Vital Signals, Inc.*, 191 A.D.2d 193, 594 N.Y.S.2d 221 (1st Dep't 1993) (protective order denied when documents are clearly identified, limited in scope, not burdensome or expensive to produce and material and necessary).

30 *City of New York v. Keene Corp.*, 304 A.D.2d 119, 756 N.Y.S.2d 536 (1st Dep't 2003); *Claverack Coop. Ins. Co. v. Nielsen*, 296 A.D.2d 789, 745 N.Y.S.2d 604 (3d Dep't 2002); *Kern v. City of Rochester*, 261 A.D.2d 904, 689 N.Y.S.2d 842, 843 (4th Dep't 1999).

31 *See Catalano v. Moreland*, 299 A.D.2d 881, 750 N.Y.S.2d 209 (4th Dep't 2002) (standard of care exercised by reasonable medical practitioner governs; thus, bylaws not relevant); *Jordan v. Blue Circle Atl. Inc.*, 296 A.D.2d 752, 745 N.Y.S.2d 289 (3d Dep't 2002) (entire personnel file not relevant since no allegation of negligent hiring or other issue).

32 *McMahon v. Aviette Agency, Inc.*, 301 A.D.2d 820, 753 N.Y.S.2d 605 (3d Dep't 2003) (showing not made); *Mamunes v. Szczepanski*, 70 A.D.2d 684, 416 N.Y.S.2d 406 (3d Dep't 1979) (insufficient showing made).

or other sensitivity of the information sought by document demand or deposition may form the basis for an application for a confidentiality order, sometimes on consent, and perhaps an application for an order to seal the file.[33]

II. FEDERAL PRACTICE

A. Protective Orders in Advance of Depositions

1. In General

Protective orders in federal practice are governed by FRCP 26(c).[34] Such an order may be sought on motion of a party or a person from whom discovery is sought.[35] The motion, which must be accompanied by a certification of good faith,[36] should be presented to the assigned district judge or magistrate judge or, in the case of depositions in another district, the district judge of the district in which the deposition is to be taken. For a protective order to be issued, "good cause" must be shown.

The court "may make any order which justice requires to protect a party or person from annoyance, embarrassment, oppression, or undue burden or expense."[37] The order may, among other things, direct that the disclosure not be obtained; that it be obtained only on specified terms and conditions, including designation of time or place; that it be obtained only by

---

33   Uniform Rule 216.1; *see* George F. Carpinello, *Public Access to Court Records in New York: The Experience under Uniform Rule 216.1 and the Rule's Future in a World of Electronic Filing*, 66 Alb. L. Rev. 1089 (2003); George F. Carpinello, *Public Access to Court Records in Civil Proceedings: The New York Approach*, 54 Alb. L. Rev. 93 (1989).

34   In *Seattle Times Co. v. Rhinehart*, 467 U.S. 20, 34–35 (1984) (footnotes omitted), the U.S. Supreme Court stated:

> Because of the liberality of pretrial discovery permitted by Rule 26(b)(1), it is necessary for the trial court to have the authority to issue protective orders conferred by Rule 26(c). It is clear from experience that pretrial discovery by depositions and interrogatories has a significant potential for abuse. This abuse is not limited to matters of delay and expense; discovery also may seriously implicate privacy interests of litigants and third parties. The Rules do not distinguish between public and private information. Nor do they apply only to parties to the litigation, as relevant information in the hands of third parties may be subject to discovery.

> There is also potential for abuse from document demands.

35   See Appendix, "Motion for Protective Order" (Samples 1–5) (federal forms).

36   This certification states that the movant has in good faith conferred with other affected parties, or attempted to do so, in an effort to resolve the dispute without need for court intervention. The state analogue is required by Uniform Rule 202.7.

37   FRCP 26(c).

a method of discovery other than that chosen by the party seeking discovery; that the scope of discovery be limited to certain matters; that discovery be conducted with no one present other than persons designated by the court; and that discovery be protected under seal or by other means.[38]

A motion for a protective order may be granted in part. If the motion is not granted in its entirety, the court, on appropriate terms or conditions, may order that discovery be provided. An award of expenses on the motion is governed by FRCP 37(a)(4).

On a motion for a protective order, the applicant has the burden of showing good cause to justify the granting of the motion.[39] The matter is committed to the sound discretion of the court.[40] Courts have often required

---

38   FRCP 26(c)(1)–(8).

39   *Flatow v. Islamic Republic of Iran*, 308 F.3d 1065, 1074 (9th Cir. 2002); *Dove v. Atl. Capital Corp.*, 963 F.2d 15, 19 (2d Cir. 1992); *Davidson v. Goord*, 215 F.R.D. 73, 82 (W.D.N.Y. 2003); *Topo v. Dhir*, 210 F.R.D. 76, 77 (S.D.N.Y. 2002); *Epling v. UCB Films, Inc.*, 204 F.R.D. 691, 693 (D. Kan. 2002); *Rivera v. NIBCO, Inc.*, 204 F.R.D. 647, 649 (E.D. Cal. 2001), *aff'd*, 364 F.3d 1057 (9th Cir. 2004); *Simmons Foods, Inc. v. Willis*, 191 F.R.D. 625, 630 (D. Kan. 2000); *Tuszkiewicz v. Allen Bradley Co.*, 170 F.R.D. 15 (E.D. Wisc. 1996), *aff'd*, 142 F.3d 440 (7th Cir. 1998); *Riddell Sports Inc. v. Brooks*, 158 F.R.D. 555, 557 (S.D.N.Y. 1994); *Smith v. Dowson*, 158 F.R.D. 138 (D. Minn. 1994). In *Rivera*, the court stated that factors to be considered regarding good cause were whether the information is sought for legitimate purposes, whether disclosure will violate any privacy interest, whether disclosure will cause embarrassment, whether it is important to public health and safety, whether it will promote fairness and efficiency and whether the case involves issues of public importance. 204 F.R.D. at 649.

40   *Flatow*, 308 F.3d at 1074; *Davidson*, 215 F.R.D. at 82.

the applicant to make a showing of necessity based on specific examples or articulated reasons, or particular and specific facts.[41] Generalized, speculative or conclusory assertions, it is often said, will not suffice.[42]

2. FRCP 26(c) and Depositions

a. Motion for Order to Bar Deposition

Although a movant can seek an order prohibiting the taking of a deposition, such a motion is disfavored and it is extremely rare for a court to grant it. "[I]t is exceedingly difficult to demonstrate an appropriate basis for an order barring the taking of a deposition."[43] This is so because, outside the FRCP 30(b)(6) context, the notice of deposition will not identify

---

41   *AMW Materials Testing, Inc. v. Town of Babylon*, 215 F.R.D. 67, 72 (E.D.N.Y. 2003); *Sanyo Laser Prods. Inc. v. Arista Records*, 214 F.R.D. 496, 503 (S.D. Ind. 2003); *Williams v. Greenlee*, 210 F.R.D. 577, 579 (N.D. Tex. 2002); *Low v. Whitman*, 207 F.R.D. 9, 10 (D.D.C. 2002); *Jennings v. Family Mgmt.*, 201 F.R.D. 272, 275 (D.D.C. 2001); *Static Control Components v. Darkprint Imaging*, 201 F.R.D. 431, 434 (M.D.N.C. 2001); *In re Tutu Water Wells Contamination*, 184 F.R.D. 266, 267 (D.V.I. 1999) (specific showing that inquiry will prejudice party seeking order); *Alexander v. FBI*, 186 F.R.D. 60, 63–64 (D.D.C. 1998); *Prozina Shipping Co. v. Thirty-Four Autos.*, 179 F.R.D. 41, 48 (D. Mass. 1998); *Schorr v. Briarwood Estates Ltd. P'ship*, 178 F.R.D. 488, 491 (N.D. Ohio 1998); *Bank of New York v. Meridien Biao Bank Tanz.*, 171 F.R.D. 135, 143 (S.D.N.Y. 1997); *Tuszkiewicz*, 170 F.R.D. 15 (distinct facts); *Frazier v. S.E. Pa. Transp. Auth.*, 161 F.R.D. 309, 313 (E.D. Pa. 1995), *aff'd without opinion*, 91 F.3d 123 (3d Cir. 1996); *Bucher v. Richardson Hosp. Auth.*, 160 F.R.D. 88, 92 (N.D. Tex. 1994); *Frideres v. Schlitz*, 150 F.R.D. 153, 156 (S.D. Iowa 1993); *Blum v. Schlegel*, 150 F.R.D. 38, 41 (W.D.N.Y. 1993); *Cooper v. Welch Foods, Inc.*, 105 F.R.D. 4, 6 (W.D.N.Y. 1984). In *Topo*, 210 F.R.D. at 77, the court stated that some courts have followed a "good cause" standard, while others have required specificity (noting *Seattle Times Co. v. Rhinehart*, 467 U.S. 20 (1984)). Further, the magistrate judge concluded that good cause is required in the Second Circuit without regard to specificity, at least in cases that do not involve injury to business. 210 F.R.D. at 77–78 (citing *Sterbens v. Sound Shore Med. Ctr.*, 2001 U.S. Dist. LEXIS 19987 (S.D.N.Y. Dec. 4, 2001); *Wilcock v. Equidev Capital L.L.C.*, 2001 U.S. Dist. LEXIS 11744 (S.D.N.Y. Aug. 14, 2001)).

42   *Sanyo Laser Prods.*, 214 F.R.D. at 503; *Jennings*, 201 F.R.D. at 275; *Static Control Components*, 201 F.R.D. at 434; *Alexander*, 186 F.R.D. at 63–64; *Lee v. Denver Sheriff's Dep't*, 181 F.R.D. 651 (D. Colo. 1998); *Prozina Shipping Co.*, 179 F.R.D. at 48; *Tuszkiewicz*, 170 F.R.D. 15; *Frazier*, 161 F.R.D. at 313; *Bucher*, 160 F.R.D. at 92; *Frideres*, 150 F.R.D. at 156; *Medlin v. Andrew*, 113 F.R.D. 650, 653 (M.D.N.C. 1987); *Cooper*, 105 F.R.D. at 6.

43   *Naftchi v. New York Univ. Med. Ctr.*, 172 F.R.D. 130, 132 (S.D.N.Y. 1997); *see Inv. Props. Int'l, Ltd. v. IOS, Ltd.*, 459 F.2d 705, 708 (2d Cir. 1972) (order barring taking of deposition considered unusual and viewed unfavorably); *Hughes v. LaSalle Bank, N.A.*, 2003 U.S. Dist. LEXIS 13874 (S.D.N.Y. Aug. 8, 2003), *aff'd*, 2004 U.S. Dist. LEXIS 3403 (S.D.N.Y. Mar. 4, 2004); *Fears v. Wilhelmina Model Agency Inc.*, 2003 U.S. Dist. LEXIS 12850 (S.D.N.Y. July 25, 2003); *Gen. Star Indem. Co. v. Platinum Indem. Ltd.*, 210 F.R.D. 80, 82 (S.D.N.Y. 2002); *Static Control Components*, 201 F.R.D. at 434; *Jennings*, 201 F.R.D. at 275; *Simmons Foods, Inc.*, 191 F.R.D. at 630; *Alexander*, 186 F.R.D. at 64; *Speadmark, Inc. v. Federated Dep't Stores*, 176 F.R.D. 116, 118 (S.D.N.Y. 1997); *Mike v. Dymon, Inc.*, 169 F.R.D. 376, 378 (D. Kan. 1996); *Bucher*, 160 F.R.D. at 92; *Frideres*, 150 F.R.D. at 156; *N.F.A. Corp. v. Riverview Narrow Fabrics, Inc.*, 117 F.R.D. 83, 84 (M.D.N.C. 1987); *Medlin*, 113 F.R.D. at 653; *Cooper*, 105 F.R.D. at 6.

formally the subjects to be covered at the deposition. Thus, in the absence of knowing exactly what areas will in fact be covered when the deposition proceeds, counsel likely would have difficulty showing that the deposition will unduly prejudice his or her client.

In addition, a number of protections are in place to ensure that the deponent is treated fairly. For example, the witness is protected by the preservation of most objections until trial and by the right to object at the deposition if necessary. Furthermore, if circumstances become serious enough to warrant it, the witness has the right to make a motion to limit the questioning under FRCP 30(d)(4). The record of what actually transpired at the deposition will assist the court in evaluating the issues.[44] Therefore, most motions to prohibit depositions are denied.[45]

The fact that the prospective witness professes ignorance of the facts in controversy will ordinarily be insufficient to justify issuance of a protective order since the examiner is generally entitled to test the asserted lack of knowledge.[46] The witness need not have firsthand knowledge admissible in evidence in order for that knowledge to be useful and discoverable.[47] The fact that the witness is a busy person also usually is not a basis for a prohibition of a deposition.[48] "[I]n ordinary circumstances, [it does not] matter that the proposed witness is a busy person or professes lack of knowledge of the matters at issue, as the party seeking the discovery is entitled to test the asserted lack of knowledge."[49]

A strong showing would have to be made that the person in question had no involvement in any of the events if a deposition were to be barred. If, for example, a strong showing is made that a very senior corporate officer or government official had no involvement in the events or transactions at issue or the formulation of any policy that may be relevant to the

---

44   8 Charles Alan Wright et al., Federal Practice and Procedure § 2037, at 494–95 (2d ed. 1994) (hereinafter "Wright").

45   *Medlin*, 113 F.R.D. at 653; 8 Wright, *supra* note 44, § 2037, at 496.

46   *Bynum v. Dist. of Columbia*, 217 F.R.D. 43, 51 (D.D.C. 2003); *Alexander*, 186 F.R.D. at 64-65; *Naftchi*, 172 F.R.D. at 132; *Cooper*, 105 F.R.D. at 6.

47   *Hughes*, 2003 U.S. Dist. LEXIS 13874; *Fears*, 2003 U.S. Dist. LEXIS 12850 (even hearsay may be obtained at depositions).

48   *Naftchi*, 172 F.R.D. at 132; *CBS, Inc. v. Ahern*, 102 F.R.D. 820, 822 (S.D.N.Y. 1984).

49   *Naftchi*, 172 F.R.D. at 132 (citation omitted).

case,[50] concerning which lower-level employees can testify, the officer or official may succeed on the motion to bar the deposition, particularly if the officer or official maintains an extremely busy schedule. Such a demonstration will need to be made in detail, by convincing affidavits, if the general disinclination to bar a deposition is to be overcome.[51]

In some cases, the court may conclude that a FRCP 30(b)(6) deposition may be appropriate prior to a deposition of a high-level executive.[52] One court has suggested that the preferred approach to a corporate deposition is pursuant to 30(b)(6), with the deposition of an officer, director or managing agent under FRCP 30(a)(1) to take place later if the former is unsatisfactory.[53]

In some cases, a party may seek to avoid a deposition on the ground that the information sought would be completely irrelevant to the case. However, as noted in chapter 5, the standard of relevancy during the discovery stage is quite broad; depositions in federal court allow questioning

---

50   *Gen. Star Indem. Co. v. Platinum Indem. Ltd.*, 210 F.R.D. 80, 83 (S.D.N.Y. 2002) (a high-level official who issues corporate policy will likely have knowledge of reasons therefor that a lower-level official will not).

51   *Thomas v. IBM Co.*, 48 F.3d 478, 482–84 (10th Cir. 1995) (protective order issued against deposition of chairman of board of IBM in Oklahoma in age-discrimination case brought by clerical worker, where detailed affidavit of chairman submitted and plaintiff had not sought to take depositions of her supervisors or other personnel); *Evans v. Allstate Ins. Co.*, 216 F.R.D. 515, 518–19 (N.D. Okla. 2003) (affidavits submitted by chairman, president and CEO and senior VP and CFO of major company sufficed; defendant had already produced adequate information or it could be obtained by other means); *Gen. Star Indem. Co.*, 210 F.R.D. at 83 (affidavit from another official was secondhand and insufficient, as it was not an unequivocal statement showing lack of any relevant knowledge); *Low v. Whitman*, 207 F.R.D. 9 (D.D.C. 2002) (protective order issued against deposition of high-level government official not involved in employment decision at issue); *Nyfield v. Virgin Islands Tel. Corp.*, 202 F.R.D. 192 (D.V.I. 2001), *aff'd*, 2002 U.S. Dist. LEXIS 1955 (D.V.I. Jan. 29, 2002) (protective order denied as to deposition of CEO who was a party based upon alleged individual conduct); *Detoy v. City & County of San Francisco*, 196 F.R.D. 362, 369–70 (N.D. Cal. 2000) (police chief must testify about disciplinary activities in which he was involved); *Speadmark, Inc. v. Federated Dep't Stores*, 176 F.R.D. 116, 118 (S.D.N.Y. 1997) (protective order is "most extraordinary relief" and party seeking it must show proposed deponent has nothing to contribute); *Naftchi*, 172 F.R.D. at 132 (dean of medical school failed to show total lack of familiarity with facts; protective order denied); *Johnson v. New York Hosp.*, 897 F. Supp. 83, 86–87 (S.D.N.Y. 1995) (opinion of Baer, J.) (protective order denied as to deposition of president of hospital, who was a party), *aff'd*, 96 F.3d 33 (2d Cir. 1996); 8 Wright, *supra* note 44, § 2037, at 500–502.

52   *Folwell v. Sanchez Hernandez*, 210 F.R.D. 169, 173–75 (M.D.N.C. 2002) (FRCP 30(b)(6) deposition to take place on certain topics, with other defined issues for later deposition of executive except as to those covered and answered in the 30(b)(6) deposition, which would be eliminated from the later deposition).

53   *Id.* at 173.

that may lead to relevant testimony, providing particularly broad inquiry. Thus, such a motion will usually, though not invariably, fail.[54]

b. Depositions of Physically or Mentally Fragile Witnesses

A court may grant a protective order prohibiting the taking of a deposition of a person because that person is in fragile physical or mental condition. Obviously, if the person is a party or an important nonparty witness, the court will be most reluctant to prohibit the deposition altogether. It may be possible to permit the deposition to proceed on an abbreviated schedule or by videoconference or on other conditions designed to address the frailties of the witness.[55] However, in some instances, a motion may contend that no deposition can be taken at all. If such a motion is to be granted,

---

54   8 Wright, *supra* note 44, § 2037, at 499–500; *see New York v. Solvent Chem. Co.*, 214 F.R.D. 106 (W.D.N.Y. 2003) (protective order issued barring discovery of information set out in FRCP 30(b)(6) notice and FRCP 34 demand as not relevant in view of prior court orders regarding allocation of liability); *Topo v. Dhir*, 210 F.R.D. 76 (S.D.N.Y. 2002) (protective order granted to prevent inquiry at deposition into immigration status as not relevant to case); *Rivera v. NIBCO, Inc.*, 204 F.R.D. 647 (E.D. Cal. 2001), *aff'd*, 364 F.3d 1057 (9th Cir. 2004) (protective order granted against inquiry into place of birth and employment status); *Alexander v. FBI*, 186 F.R.D. 60, 64–65 (D.D.C. 1998) (protective order denied; deposition to go forward, but plaintiffs directed not to question witness regarding certain topics not relevant to case); *Johnson v. Mortham*, 164 F.R.D. 571, 572 (N.D. Fla. 1996) (protective order granted to extent discovery sought to go beyond that demarcated in prior decision granting summary judgment as to certain issue); *Blum v. Schlegel*, 150 F.R.D. 38, 39 (W.D.N.Y. 1993) (although relevancy is broad, discovery requests can be denied by a protective order when they have no conceivable bearing on the case); *Operative Plasterers' & Cement Masons' Int'l Ass'n v. Benjamin*, 144 F.R.D. 87, 90 (N.D. Ind. 1992). In *Smith v. Dowson,* 158 F.R.D. 138 (D. Minn. 1994), the plaintiff commenced a 42 U.S.C. § 1983 action regarding his arrest and confinement. The court held that information gathered and actions taken in a later investigation, after release of the erroneously arrested plaintiff, were not relevant to whether the arrest and detainer had been accomplished with probable cause, nor did they bear on the question of qualified immunity. *See JPMorgan Chase Bank v. Liberty Mut. Ins. Co.*, 209 F.R.D. 361 (S.D.N.Y. 2002) (plaintiff barred from inquiring at FRCP 30(b)(6) deposition into what defendants had learned after issuance of bonds since such information was irrelevant; only what the defendants had known at the time the bonds were issued would be relevant).

55   See Appendix, "Motion for Protective Order (Sample 5)" and "Affidavit on Motion for Protective Order" (federal forms).

the applicant must submit detailed affidavits from appropriate medical advisers.[56]

c. Depositions of Counsel

A demand for a deposition of an attorney for a party can provide the basis for issuance of a protective order. "While the Federal Rules do not prohibit the deposition of a party's attorney, experience teaches that countenancing unbridled depositions of attorneys constitutes an invitation to delay, disruption of the case, harassment, and perhaps disqualification of the attorney."[57] Some courts state that a request for the deposition of counsel constitutes an extraordinary circumstance that would justify departure from the normal rule that prohibition of a deposition is rarely granted.[58]

d. Protective Orders to Address Forum Issues

A protective order may be sought to address difficulties arising from the place where a deposition is to be taken. Generally, the party seeking

---

56   *Jennings v. Family Mgmt.*, 201 F.R.D. 272, 275 (D.D.C. 2001) (motion by plaintiff denied where movant submitted conclusory, speculative statements rather than proof of specific harm; as against that, the defendant needed to prepare a defense and plaintiff's testimony was critical); *In re Tutu Water Wells Contamination CERCLA Litig.*, 189 F.R.D. 153 (D.V.I. 1999) (protective order granted barring second deposition of ill and aged person); *Schorr v. Briarwood Estates Ltd. P'ship*, 178 F.R.D. 488, 491–92 (N.D. Ohio 1998) (protective order granted where expert submitted detailed information about plaintiff's mental health; however, deposition permitted on conditions (two hours maximum at a time, in presence of magistrate judge, etc.)); *Bucher v. Richardson Hosp. Auth.*, 160 F.R.D. 88, 92 (N.D. Tex. 1994) (deposition allowed but on conditions in view of age and psychological health of witness); *Frideres v. Schlitz*, 150 F.R.D. 153 (S.D. Iowa 1993) (detailed, nonconclusory affidavit from a physician is required to establish a health reason to postpone or bar a deposition; information from two doctors regarding nonparty witness barred deposition until further order, with parties to receive further medical information pending a final ruling); *Medlin v. Andrew*, 113 F.R.D. 650 (M.D.N.C. 1987) (protective order granted, with plaintiff to make doctors available to defendants and for examination, if necessary, with issue to be revisited after 30 days; *see United States v. Mariani*, 178 F.R.D. 447 (M.D. Pa. 1998).

57   *N.F.A. Corp. v. Riverview Narrow Fabrics, Inc.*, 117 F.R.D. 83, 85 (M.D.N.C. 1987).

58   *Solvent Chem. Co.*, 214 F.R.D. 106; *Static Control Components v. Darkprint Imaging*, 201 F.R.D. 431, 434 (M.D.N.C. 2001); *N.F.A. Corp.*, 117 F.R.D. at 84 (protective order granted); *see Boughton v. Cotter Corp.*, 65 F.3d 823, 828–31 (10th Cir. 1995) (protective order granted against deposition of defense counsel upheld); *Epling v. UCB Films, Inc.*, 204 F.R.D. 691, 693 (D. Kan. 2002) (deposition denied as information not shown to be unavailable elsewhere); *Simmons Foods, Inc. v. Willis*, 191 F.R.D. 625 (D. Kan. 2000) (deposition denied as information not shown to be unavailable elsewhere); *In re Tutu Water Wells Contamination*, 184 F.R.D. 266, 267 (D.V.I. 1999) (deposition of one attorney allowed; another denied); *Mike v. Dymon, Inc.*, 169 F.R.D. 376, 378 (D. Kan. 1996); *S. Film Extruders, Inc. v. Coca-Cola*, 117 F.R.D. 559 (M.D.N.C. 1987) (protective order granted in part; areas of inquiry limited). *Compare In re Subpoena to Dennis Friedman*, 350 F.3d 65 (2d Cir. 2003) (favoring a flexible approach) (*dicta*).

the deposition may set the place of the deposition.[59] However, if the person being deposed is a nonparty, FRCP 45 has something to say on the subject. Generally, the place of deposition for a witness who cannot be compelled to appear at trial should be one convenient for the witness.[60] As to parties, the general rule is that the plaintiff, having selected the forum in which to commence the action, cannot seek a more advantageous venue when it comes to deposition. If the plaintiff has chosen the forum, it is difficult then to argue that the forum represents an undue burden.[61]

However, if plaintiff can demonstrate special circumstances, such as financial burdens or unusual hardship (e.g., problems caused by illness or advanced age), and these circumstances outweigh any prejudice to the defendant, a protective order may be issued.[62] Because the defendants are not before the court by choice, the nonresident defendant is generally deposed at his or her place of residence. If the defendant is a corporation, the place of deposition is generally the principal place of business.[63] However, courts retain large discretion in this area. Corporate defendants are also with some frequency deposed elsewhere than in the principal place of business for the convenience of all and in the general interests of economy and litigation efficiency.[64]

---

59 *Buzzeo v. Bd. of Educ.*, 178 F.R.D. 390, 392 (E.D.N.Y. 1998); *Bank of New York v. Meridien Biao Bank Tanz.*, 171 F.R.D. 135, 155 (S.D.N.Y. 1997); *Payton v. Sears, Roebuck & Co.*, 148 F.R.D. 667, 669 (N.D. Ga. 1993); *Sugarhill Records v. Motown Record Corp.*, 105 F.R.D. 166, 171 (S.D.N.Y. 1985).

60 *The Daiei, Inc. v. Ball Corp.*, 198 F.R.D. 658, 659 (S.D. Ind. 2001).

61 *Prozina Shipping Co. v. Thirty-Four Autos.*, 179 F.R.D. 41, 48 (D. Mass. 1998); *Grotrian, Helfferich, Schulz, Th. Steinweg Nachf v. Steinway & Sons*, 54 F.R.D. 280 (S.D.N.Y. 1971). *But see Connell v. City of New York*, 230 F. Supp. 2d 432 (S.D.N.Y. 2002) (whether plaintiff had an alternative forum to choose may be a factor; plaintiff need not come to New York for deposition; court videoconferencing technology to be used instead); *Operative Plasterers' & Cement Masons' Int'l Ass'n v. Benjamin*, 144 F.R.D. 87, 91 (N.D. Ind. 1992) (general principle loses weight where plaintiff had no choice of forum).

62 *Cobell v. Norton*, 213 F.R.D. 43, 47 (D.D.C. 2003) (detailed affidavit from the person or a physician required to demonstrate infirmities).

63 *Starlight Int'l, Inc. v. Herlihy*, 186 F.R.D. 626, 644 (D. Kan. 1999); *Chris-Craft Indus. Prods. v. Kuraray Co.*, 184 F.R.D. 605, 607 (N.D. Ill. 1999); *Buzzeo*, 178 F.R.D. at 392; *Meridien Biao Bank Tanz.*, 171 F.R.D. at 155; *M&C Corp. v. Erwin Behr GmbH & Co.*, 165 F.R.D. 65, 67 (E.D. Mich. 1996); *Payton*, 148 F.R.D. at 669; *Sugarhill Records*, 105 F.R.D. at 171.

64 *Zakre v. Norddeutsche Landesbank Girozentrale*, N.Y.L.J., Oct. 10, 2003, p. 23, col. 3 (S.D.N.Y.) (employee of German defendant need not be produced for deposition in New York, but in view of cost and inconvenience to plaintiff's counsel of travel to Germany, deposition would take place by videoconference at defendant's expense); *Buzzeo*, 178 F.R.D. at 392; *Meridien Biao Bank Tanz.*, 171 F.R.D. at 155; *Sugarhill Records*, 105 F.R.D. at 171.

e. Order to Exclude Persons from Depositions

It is possible to obtain a protective order prohibiting persons from attending depositions. Generally, of course, depositions are not open to the public.[65] Beyond that, there may be circumstances in which it is appropriate to exclude even persons who might normally be present. Here again, a showing of good cause is required. Vague generalities will not suffice.[66] Only in extraordinary circumstances will parties be excluded from each other's deposition.[67]

f. Motions Concerning FRCP 30(b)(6) Depositions

Unlike a general notice of deposition, a notice for a FRCP 30(b)(6) deposition sets forth topics or subjects for the deposition. These may generate controversy and a motion for a protective order. It might be contended, for instance, that the notice is overly broad or vague, is unduly prolix, presents an excessive burden and seeks irrelevant information.[68]

g. Order to Protect Confidentiality of Information

In some cases, a party or witness may have grounds for seeking a protective order intended to ensure the confidentiality of information. It may be, for instance, that the deposing party seeks production at the deposition of highly sensitive information about the medical condition of the witness. In business cases, sensitive commercial information, such as secret formulae or customer lists, may be involved. It may be appropriate to pro-

---

65 *Seattle Times Co. v. Rhinehart*, 467 U.S. 20, 32 (1984); *Felling v. Knight*, 211 F.R.D. 552, 553 (S.D. Ind. 2003); *New York v. Microsoft Corp.*, 206 F.R.D. 19, 22 (D.D.C. 2002).

66 *Alexander v. FBI*, 186 F.R.D. 21, 53 (D.D.C. 1998); *Tuszkiewicz v. Allen Bradley Co.*, 170 F.R.D. 15 (E.D. Wisc. 1996) (motion denied; only general statement of threat of possible prejudice presented).

67 *Galella v. Onassis*, 487 F.2d 986, 997 (2d Cir. 1973); *Lee v. Denver Sheriff's Dep't*, 181 F.R.D. 651 (D. Colo. 1998) (motion denied; plaintiff sought to exclude four parties from one another's deposition because of possible influence; plaintiff relied on speculation only; defendants had had several years to work on a common story already if so disposed); *Frideres v. Schlitz*, 150 F.R.D. 153, 158 (S.D. Iowa 1993); *see Gottlieb v. County of Orange*, 151 F.R.D. 258, 260 (S.D.N.Y. 1993).

68 *See, e.g.*, *Evans v. Allstate Ins. Co.*, 216 F.R.D. 515, 519 (N.D. Okla. 2003) (protective order granted); *Sanyo Laser Prods. Inc. v. Arista Records*, 214 F.R.D. 496, 503 (S.D. Ind. 2003) (motion for order on grounds of irrelevance denied); *Operative Plasterers' & Cement Masons' Int'l Ass'n v. Benjamin*, 144 F.R.D. 87, 90 (N.D. Ind. 1992); *see JPMorgan Chase Bank v. Liberty Mut. Ins. Co.*, 209 F.R.D. 361 (S.D.N.Y. 2002) (Rakoff, J.) (FRCP 30(b)(6) notice may not seek contentions or legal theories, nor irrelevant information).

vide for the sealing of portions of transcripts or documents if submitted to the court.[69]

The party seeking protection must demonstrate that the information sought is indeed confidential and that disclosure might be harmful.[70] In many commercial cases, the parties will agree upon a confidentiality order designed to maintain the privacy of sensitive business information.[71]

3. FRCP 26(c) and Documents

A protective order may of course be sought when the discovery being demanded is production of documents at or, more likely, in advance of a deposition (or independent thereof). Failure to raise objections pursuant to FRCP 34 may result in waiver.[72] The movant may seek to make a showing of good cause by asserting that the document demand is overbroad,[73] that it would impose an unreasonable burden on the movant[74] or that the documents requested are irrelevant to the issues in the case.[75] Good cause may be found if the documents in question are difficult and expensive to collect or very sensitive and if the documents are of marginal or no relevance to the case,[76] contain confidential commercial information[77] or are privileged or protected as work product.[78]

---

69   *See, e.g., Schofield v. Trs. of Univ. of Pa.*, 161 F.R.D. 302 (E.D. Pa. 1995).

70   *Operative Plasterers' & Cement Masons' Int'l Ass'n*, 144 F.R.D. at 91–92; *United States v. IBM Corp.*, 67 F.R.D. 40, 46 (S.D.N.Y. 1975).

71   *See Flatow v. Islamic Republic of Iran*, 196 F.R.D. 203, 205 (D.D.C. 2000), *vacated on other grounds*, 305 F.3d 1249 (D.C. Cir. 2002).

72   *Flaherty v. Seroussi*, 209 F.R.D. 300, 304 (N.D.N.Y. 2002).

73   *Wright v. AmSouth Bancorp.*, 320 F.3d 1198, 1205 (11th Cir. 2003); see Appendix, "Motion for Protective Order (Sample 2)" (federal form).

74   *Wright*, 320 F.3d at 1205.

75   *Id.*; *AMW Materials Testing, Inc. v. Town of Babylon*, 215 F.R.D. 67, 72 (E.D.N.Y. 2003) (protective order denied; relevance shown); *Tonnemacher v. Sasak*, 155 F.R.D. 193 (D. Ariz. 1994) (protective order granted); *Blum v. Schlegel*, 150 F.R.D. 38 (W.D.N.Y. 1993) (protective order granted).

76   *United States v. Duke Energy Corp.*, 214 F.R.D. 392 (M.D.N.C. 2003) (protective order granted); *Tonnemacher*, 155 F.R.D. 193 (protective order granted; internal audit manuals; GAAS and GAAP controlled standards); *Blum*, 150 F.R.D. 38 (protective order granted; sensitive information regarding faculty promotion); *see GE Capital Corp. v. Lear Corp.*, 215 F.R.D. 637, 640 (D. Kan. 2003); *Horizon Holdings, LLC v. Genmar Holdings, Inc.*, 209 F.R.D. 208 (D. Kan. 2002).

77   *Sterbens v. Sound Shore Med. Ctr.*, 2001 U.S. Dist. LEXIS 19987 (S.D.N.Y. Dec. 4, 2001); see Appendix, "Motion for Protective Order (Sample 3)" (federal form).

78   *Gulf Islands Leasing v. Bombardier Capital*, 215 F.R.D. 466 (S.D.N.Y. 2003).

As noted, parties frequently enter into confidentiality stipulations to provide protection for confidential business, financial and personal information. Often in the past these proposed orders were signed by the court. However, orders of this kind, even though proposed on consent of all parties, may not always survive judicial scrutiny.[79] A protective order may be issued not to prevent production to the other side but to limit distribution of documents to purposes directly related to the litigation.[80]

4. Protection with Regard to Discovery by Subpoena

When the deposition noticed is that of a nonparty or a demand is made that a nonparty produce documents, a subpoena is required to command a person to attend and give testimony at deposition, to produce documents or both.[81] The level of protection that FRCP 45 affords a person, including a nonparty, subpoenaed during discovery corresponds to that provided generally by FRCP 26(c).[82] The court has broad discretion in ruling on subpoenas.[83]

The party who causes a subpoena to be issued must "take reasonable steps to avoid imposing undue burden or expense on a person subject to that subpoena."[84] The court on behalf of which the subpoena was issued "shall enforce this duty and impose upon the party or attorney in breach of this duty an appropriate sanction, which may include, but is not limited to, lost earnings and a reasonable attorney's fee."[85] A person who is subpoenaed to produce books and records need not appear in person unless he or she is also to be deposed or to testify.[86]

---

79 District judges today are looking more carefully at protective orders that call for the sealing of documents, etc., even when presented on consent. Commercial cases tend to involve less difficulty, but tort and other cases concerned with product safety may require more than a pro forma showing to obtain judicial approval. *See, e.g., Sprinturf v. Southwest Recreational Indus.*, 216 F.R.D. 320, 323 (E.D. Pa. 2003).

80 *Sprinturf*, 216 F.R.D. at 324.

81 FRCP 45(a)(1); see Appendix, "Subpoena" and "Subpoena *Duces Tecum*" (federal forms).

82 *Mannington Mills v. Armstrong World Indus.*, 206 F.R.D. 525, 529 (D. Del. 2002) (provisions are "overlapping and interrelated"); *Concord Boat Corp. v. Brunswick Corp.*, 169 F.R.D. 44, 48 (S.D.N.Y. 1996).

83 *Linder v. Nat'l Sec. Agency*, 94 F.3d 693, 695 (D.C. Cir. 1996); *Tiberi v. Cigna Ins. Co.*, 40 F.3d 110, 112 (5th Cir. 1994).

84 FRCP 45(c)(1).

85 *Id.*

86 FRCP 45(c)(2)(A).

When a subpoena calls for the production of documents, the person subpoenaed may, within 14 days after service or prior to the deadline if less than 14 days, serve written objection. The recipient of the subpoena must raise all objections at one time, in a timely fashion "so that discovery does not become a 'game.'"[87] If objection is made, inspection cannot occur except by court order. The party seeking the documents may move to compel their production.[88] Any order to compel "shall protect any person who is not a party or an officer of a party from significant expense resulting from the inspection and copying commanded."[89]

On a motion to quash or modify, the burden is on the movant.[90] The motion should be made by the person to whom the subpoena is directed unless the challenger has a personal right or privilege regarding the subject matter at issue in the subpoena.[91] As discussed earlier in this chapter with regard to party witnesses, it is rare that a deposition subpoena will be quashed (as opposed to one commanding production of documents) since there is usually no basis for doing so until the witness testifies.[92]

Whether a subpoena for documents imposes an "undue burden" depends upon a variety of factors, such as relevance, the party's need for the information, the breadth of the request, the time period covered by it, the specificity with which documents are described, and the burden involved.[93] The

---

87   *In re DG Acquisition Corp.*, 151 F.3d 75, 81 (2d Cir. 1998); *see Tuite v. Henry*, 98 F.3d 1411, 1416 (D.C. Cir. 1996).

88   FRCP 45(c)(2)(B).

89   *Id.*

90   *Flatow v. Islamic Republic of Iran*, 196 F.R.D. 203, 207 (D.D.C. 2000), *vacated on other grounds*, 305 F.3d 1249 (D.C. Cir. 2002); *Linder v. Calero-Portocarrero*, 180 F.R.D. 168, 171–72 (D.D.C. 1998); *Williams v. City of Dallas*, 178 F.R.D. 103, 109 (N.D. Tex. 1998), *aff'd*, 200 F.3d 814 (5th Cir. 1999); *Concord Boat Corp. v. Brunswick Corp.*, 169 F.R.D. 44, 48 (S.D.N.Y. 1996).

91   *Smith v. Midland Brake, Inc.*, 162 F.R.D. 683, 685 (D. Kan. 1995).

92   9 James W. Moore, Federal Practice § 45.04[3][b], at 45-38 (3d ed. 2003) (hereinafter "Moore"). The person seeking to quash "cannot rely on a mere assertion that compliance would be burdensome and onerous without showing the manner and extent of the burden and the injurious consequences of insisting upon compliance." 9 Wright, *supra* note 44, at 46 (footnote omitted). *See Nat'l Paint & Coatings Ass'n v. City of Chicago*, 147 F.R.D. 184 (N.D. Ill. 1993) (subpoena quashed where depositions would not be relevant to issues that remained after prior court ruling).

93   *Cytodyne Techs. v. Biogenic Techs.*, 216 F.R.D. 533, 535 (M.D. Fla. 2003); *Flatow*, 196 F.R.D. at 206–207; *Am. Elec. Power Co. v. United States*, 191 F.R.D. 132, 136 (S.D. Ohio 1999); *Nova Biomed. Corp. v. i-Stat Corp.*, 182 F.R.D. 419, 422–23 (S.D.N.Y. 1998); *Williams*, 178 F.R.D. at 109 (a facially overbroad subpoena constitutes undue burden); *Concord Boat Corp.*, 169 F.R.D. at 49 (subpoena quashed due to undue burden); *United States v. IBM*, 83 F.R.D. 97, 104 (S.D.N.Y. 1979); *see Calero-Portocarrero*, 180 F.R.D. at 174 (undue burden shown).

showing required is a specific one.[94] Generally, modification of a subpoena is considered preferable to quashing it.[95]

A motion to quash or modify a subpoena must be "timely."[96] The court shall grant the motion if the subpoena does not allow reasonable time for compliance, requires a person who was not a party or an officer of a party to travel more than 100 miles from the place where that person resides or works, requires disclosure of privilege or other protected matter or subjects a person to "undue burden."[97] The court may quash or modify a subpoena that requires disclosure of a trade secret or other confidential research, development or commercial information. Or, the court may order production on conditions if the party seeking production shows a substantial need that cannot otherwise be met without undue hardship, and the subpoenaed person is compensated reasonably.[98]

If information is withheld as privileged or work product, the claim must be made expressly and must be supported by a privilege log.[99] Precise reasons for the objection must be stated; blanket claims of privilege do not suffice.[100] If it is not practical to provide the log together with

---

94   *Misc. Docket Matter 1 v. Misc. Docket Matter 2*, 197 F.3d 922, 926–27 (8th Cir. 1999); *Flatow*, 196 F.R.D. at 207; 9 Moore, *supra* note 92, § 45.04[3][b], at 45-44. If the motion seeks to quash because the documents demanded contain confidential commercial information, the movant needs to demonstrate that clearly defined and serious harm will flow from production. *Composition Roofers Union Local 30 Welfare Trust Fund v. Graveley Roofing Enters.*, 160 F.R.D. 70 (E.D. Pa. 1995) (burden not met).

95   *Linder v. Nat'l Sec. Agency*, 94 F.3d 693, 695 (D.C. Cir. 1996); *Calero-Portocarrero*, 180 F.R.D. at 176.

96   FRCP 45(c)(3)(A).

97   *Id.*

98   FRCP 45(c)(3)(B). Further, a subpoena may be quashed or modified if it requires disclosure of an unretained expert's opinion or certain information "resulting from the expert's study made not at the request of a party." *Id.*

99   FRCP 45(d)(2); *In re Grand Jury Subpoena*, 274 F.3d 563, 575–76 (1st Cir. 2001); *Goodyear Tire & Rubber Co. v. Kirk's Tire & Auto*, 211 F.R.D. 658, 660–61 (D. Kan. 2003); *Avery Dennison Corp. v. Four Pillars*, 190 F.R.D. 1, 2 (D.D.C. 1999) (failure to submit a log may be deemed waiver); *Mass. Sch. of Law v. Am. Bar Ass'n*, 914 F. Supp. 1172, 1178 (E.D. Pa. 1996) (noncompliance may be deemed waiver; attorney cannot ignore discovery obligations and later seek to justify that action with an objection not previously raised; "[d]iscovery is not poker where the cards are turned up one at a time").

100   *Goodyear Tire & Rubber Co.*, 211 F.R.D. at 660–61; *Avery Dennison Corp.*, 190 F.R.D. at 1–2 (a privilege log is "the universally accepted means of asserting privileges in discovery in the federal courts"); *Mass. Sch. of Law*, 914 F. Supp. at 1178.

objections, then at least the latter must be made on time, with the log to follow within a reasonable time thereafter.[101]

Failure to object to a subpoena to produce documents within the time set forth in FRCP 45(c)(2)(B) usually constitutes a waiver of the objection, including a privilege objection.[102] Failure to produce a privilege log will constitute a waiver.[103] Under unusual circumstances and for good cause, the failure to object in a timely manner will nevertheless not bar consideration of the objections.[104] Courts have found such unusual circumstances when the subpoena is overly broad on its face and exceeds the bounds of fair discovery, the person subpoenaed is a nonparty acting in good faith, and counsel for the witness and the party seeking the discovery were in contact about compliance prior to the time the challenge was raised.[105]

In regard to relevance, the scope of discovery under FRCP 45 is the same as under FRCP 26(b) and 34—it is very broad.[106] When a request seems relevant on its face, it has been said, the person resisting production must show a lack of relevance. The court need not pass on the admissibil-

---

101 *In re DG Acquisition Corp.*, 151 F.3d 75, 81 (2d Cir. 1998); *Tuite v. Henry*, 98 F.3d 1411, 1416 (D.C. Cir. 1996) (both things must be done to avoid a waiver).

102 *In re Grand Jury Subpoena*, 274 F.3d at 575–76; *In re DG Acquisition Corp.*, 151 F.3d at 83–84; *McCoy v. Southwest Airlines*, 211 F.R.D. 381, 385 (C.D. Cal. 2002); *Am. Elec. Power Co. v. United States*, 191 F.R.D. 132, 136–37 (S.D. Ohio 1999); *In re Motorsports Merch. Antitrust Litig.*, 186 F.R.D. 344, 349 (W.D. Va. 1999); *Williams v. City of Dallas*, 178 F.R.D. 103, 115 (N.D. Tex. 1998), *aff'd*, 200 F.3d 814 (5th Cir. 1999); *Concord Boat Corp. v. Brunswick Corp.*, 169 F.R.D. 44, 48 (S.D.N.Y. 1996).

103 *Avery Dennison Corp.*, 190 F.R.D. at 3.

104 *McCoy*, 211 F.R.D. at 385; *Am. Elec. Power Co.*, 191 F.R.D. at 136–37; *Williams*, 178 F.R.D. at 115; *Concord Boat Corp.*, 169 F.R.D. at 48.

105 *McCoy*, 211 F.R.D. at 385 (exceptions not found); *Am. Elec. Power Co.*, 191 F.R.D. at 136–37 (no waiver found); *In re Motorsports Merch. Antitrust Litig.*, 186 F.R.D. at 349; *Williams*, 178 F.R.D. at 115 (no waiver; subpoena facially overbroad); *Concord Boat Corp.*, 169 F.R.D. at 48 (waiver not found where these conditions were present); *see In re DG Acquisition Corp.*, 151 F.3d at 81 (assertion of Fifth Amendment privilege).

106 *Micro Motion, Inc. v. Kane Steel Co.*, 894 F.2d 1318 (Fed. Cir. 1990); *Goodyear Tire & Rubber Co. v. Kirk's Tire & Auto*, 211 F.R.D. 658, 660–61 (D. Kan. 2003); *Avery Dennison Corp.*, 190 F.R.D. at 3; *Williams*, 178 F.R.D. at 110–11; *Int'l Bhd. of Teamsters v. E. Conference of Teamsters*, 162 F.R.D. 25, 29 (S.D.N.Y. 1995); *Jackson v. Brinker*, 147 F.R.D. 189, 194 (S.D. Ind. 1993); 9 Wright, *supra* note 44, at 45–46 (there is no reason to apply a different test of relevancy when the subpoena is directed to a nonparty, as the language of the rule does not so provide).

ity of the documents at trial. Again, the test is whether the matter sought is reasonably calculated to lead to the discovery of admissible evidence.[107] If the request seems on its face to seek irrelevant documents, the person seeking the documents must show their relevance.

Need must be balanced against the burden involved in production of the documents. The status of the person subpoenaed as a nonparty is a factor entitled to weight.[108] As noted above, the party demanding production has a duty to avoid imposing an excessive burden on the subpoenaed person.[109]

Even if information sought is relevant, discovery will not be allowed if no need is shown, compliance is unduly burdensome or the potential harm outweighs the benefit.[110] The sound discretion of the court is required.[111]

As indicated with regard to parties, a confidentiality order can be used to protect sensitive, confidential, financial and other information sought from a nonparty.[112]

B. Protective Orders during Depositions

The discussion thus far in this section has addressed protective orders in advance of depositions of parties or nonparties under FRCP 26(c) and 45. Once the deposition begins, the deponent is afforded the right to seek relief from improper questioning, as follows.

A court may terminate the deposition or limit the scope and manner of its taking as provided in FRCP 26(c) "on motion of a party or of the deponent and upon a showing that the examination is being conducted in bad

---

107   *Echostar Communications Corp. v. News Corp.*, 180 F.R.D. 391, 394–95 (D. Colo. 1998); *Mass. Mut. Life Ins. Co. v. Cerf*, 177 F.R.D. 472, 476 (N.D. Cal. 1998); *Int'l Bhd. of Teamsters*, 162 F.R.D. at 29; 9 Wright, *supra* note 44, at 42–45.

108   *Misc. Docket Matter 1 v. Misc. Docket Matter 2*, 197 F.3d 922, 926–27 (8th Cir. 1999); *Cytodyne Techs. v. Biogenic Techs.*, 216 F.R.D. 533, 535 (M.D. Fla. 2003); *Goodyear Tire & Rubber Co.*, 211 F.R.D. at 662–63; *Am. Elec. Power Co.*, 191 F.R.D. at 136; *Nova Biomed. Corp. v. i-Stat Corp.*, 182 F.R.D. 419, 422–23 (S.D.N.Y. 1998); *Williams*, 178 F.R.D. at 109.

109   *Misc. Docket Matter 1*, 197 F.3d at 926–27.

110   *Mannington Mills v. Armstrong World Indus.*, 206 F.R.D. 525, 529 (D. Del. 2002).

111   *Cytodyne Techs.*, 216 F.R.D. at 536. Disclosure of confidential information to a competitor is presumed to be more harmful than to a noncompetitor. *Id.*

112   *Micro Motion, Inc. v. Kane Steel Co.*, 894 F.2d 1318 (Fed. Cir. 1990); *Flatow v. Islamic Republic of Iran*, 196 F.R.D. 203, 205 (D.D.C. 2000), *vacated on other grounds*, 305 F.3d 1249 (D.C. Cir. 2002); *In re Motorsports Merch. Antitrust Litig.*, 186 F.R.D. 344, 350 (W.D. Va. 1999).

faith or in such manner as unreasonably to annoy, embarrass, or oppress the deponent or party."[113] Any party or the deponent may make a motion for a protective order under this provision. On demand of the objecting party or the deponent, the officer who is conducting the deposition must suspend the deposition to accommodate the making of the motion.

Counsel for the deponent who objects to the proceedings may direct his or her client not to answer a question only in order to preserve a privilege, to enforce a limitation directed by the court or to present a motion for a protective order under FRCP 30(d)(4).[114]

A motion pursuant to FRCP 30(d)(4) may be sought from the court where the action is pending or from the court for the district in which the deposition is being taken. The movant on a motion under FRCP 30(d)(4) has the burden of showing that the interrogation is being conducted in bad faith or in such a manner as unreasonably to harass, embarrass or oppress the deponent or a party.[115] If the movant makes an insufficient showing, the motion will be denied.[116] The grounds upon which a motion under FRCP 30(d)(4) may be made are varied.[117] The failings upon which such a motion is based may result in a protective order pursuant to FRCP 30(d)(4) restricting the questioning or, if grave enough, causing it to end.

The rule authorizes the court to issue an order to terminate the deposition altogether or to limit the scope and manner of the deposition pursuant to FRCP 26(c). Here again, the court has broad discretion to ensure that fair disclosure takes place while protecting the rights of those providing it. Although the court clearly has the power to terminate a deposition, that power is employed cautiously.[118]

The court may issue an order finding that certain questioning is not relevant, that it seeks to intrude upon a valid privilege or the work product protection or that it is excessively protracted. The court may limit areas of questioning, rule on privilege or work product objections or issue direc-

---

113   FRCP 30(d)(4); see Appendix, "Notice of Motion to Terminate Deposition" (federal form).

114   FRCP 30(d)(1).

115   *Oleson v. Kmart Corp.*, 175 F.R.D. 568 (D. Kan. 1997); *Caplan v. Fellheimer Eichen Braverman & Kaskey*, 161 F.R.D. 29, 31 (E.D. Pa. 1995); *Smith v. Logansport Cmty. Sch. Corp.*, 139 F.R.D. 637, 640 (N.D. Ind. 1991).

116   8A Wright, *supra* note 44, § 2116, at 122.

117   See chapter 5 for a discussion of many of these grounds.

118   *Smith*, 139 F.R.D. at 640; 7 Moore, *supra* note 92, § 30.51, at 30-76 (power "sparingly used").

tives regarding the extent of further questioning. This may be done upon formal motion or, as noted *supra* in I.B., by informal ruling. Of course, the more significant the perceived problem, the more likely a formal motion will be required.

The court shall award reasonable expenses, including attorneys' fees, to the movant or to the examiner, whichever party prevails, unless the court determines that the losing party was "substantially justified" in taking the action it did or if "other circumstances make an award of expenses unjust."[119]

The earlier analysis of deposition conduct[120] considered the obligation of the attorney for the deponent to make a motion under FRCP 30(d)(4) rather than simply issue a direction not to answer and provide a defense on a motion to compel.[121] The attorney for the deponent should not abuse the power afforded by FRCP 30(d)(1) to direct the deponent not to answer by relying on the last portion of this provision to make objections. For example, an attorney should not object to an odd irrelevant question when the grounds therefor are not serious enough to meet the 30(d)(4) standard. Presumably, the provision will not be misused because a motion is required, which entails some effort and expense. Beyond that, a meritless motion likely will generate an award of reasonable expenses, including attorneys' fees, under FRCP 37(a)(4) against the obstructive defending counsel.

---

119   FRCP 37(a)(4).

120   See *supra* I.B.

121   *Vopak USA, Inc. v. Hallett Dock Co.*, 210 F.R.D. 660 (D. Minn. 2002).

CHAPTER SEVEN

MOTIONS TO COMPEL
AND FOR SANCTIONS

The previous chapter addressed obtaining protection against depositions or document demands in connection with depositions thought to be unjustified and prejudicial. This chapter discusses remedial action when deposition notices or document demands in connection with depositions are not responded to satisfactorily.

I. STATE PRACTICE

A. In General

An attorney seeking discovery or conducting a deposition may move to compel testimony pursuant to CPLR 3124 if (1) the attorney seeks documents for use in preparation for or in connection with a deposition or seeks a deposition itself and the party or person noticed fails or refuses to produce all or some of the documents or fails or refuses to appear for a deposition, or (2) the witness appears at a deposition but refuses to testify or, directly or through counsel, engages in misconduct obstructive of the discovery process.[1] The attorney seeking information may also move for penalties pursuant to CPLR 3126.[2]

The motion to compel must be accompanied by an affirmation or affidavit that the movant has made an unsuccessful good faith effort to resolve the dispute informally (such effort usually takes the form of a letter that follows and memorializes efforts made at obtaining the discovery).[3] Any formal motion with regard to problems at a deposition would most efficiently be an omnibus one. In this connection, Professor Siegel states:

> [T]he hope of CPLR 3124 is that the deposition will turn to other things until everything susceptible of resolution between the parties is covered. Its preference is that all unanswered questions be gathered up afterwards in one batch and made the subject of a single, formal, written motion for a disclosure order in which the court can all at

---

1   *Jamaica Pub. Serv. Co. v. La Interamericana Compania de Seguros Generales*, 293 A.D.2d 336, 740 N.Y.S.2d 319 (1st Dep't 2002); see Appendix, "Motion to Compel," "Motion to Dismiss (CPLR 3126)" and "Motion for Sanctions (CPLR 3126)" (state forms).

2   Generally, the person seeking not to answer questions at a deposition proceeds under CPLR 3113(b) and 3103, while the one seeking to compel answers proceeds under CPLR 3124 or 3126.

3   Uniform Rule 202.7; *see Dennis v. City of New York*, 304 A.D.2d 611, 758 N.Y.S.2d 661 (2d Dep't 2003) (motion to strike pleadings properly denied for lack of affirmation). See Appendix, "Affirmation on Motion to Compel," "Affirmation on Motion to Dismiss (CPLR 3126)" and "Affirmation on Motion for Sanctions (CPLR 3126)" (state forms). A certification pursuant to 22 N.Y.C.R.R. § 130-1.1a is required as well.

once pass on the validity of, and hence the need to respond
to, each question.[4]

Whenever a motion is filed regarding alleged misconduct at a deposition, the movant should include with the motion papers either excerpts from the deposition or the entire transcript. If the former, the excerpts must be selected with utmost accuracy and fairness. If an attorney makes a tendentious presentation, he or she likely will endanger critical credibility with the court and risk an ethical violation. If the entire transcript is submitted, counsel should identify for the court all the instances of alleged misconduct at issue in a manner that is convenient for the court, such as by including a list or chart of relevant page numbers. The burden of locating alleged problems in a transcript should never be placed on the court.[5]

With regard to documents, if objections to a CPLR 3120 document demand are made pursuant to CPLR 3122 or if there is a failure to respond to the demand, the party seeking disclosure may move under CPLR 3124 for an order to compel.[6]

The attorney who encounters difficulty in obtaining production of a witness for deposition or an interrogator at a deposition whose examination is frustrated by baseless directions not to answer, speaking objections, improper consultations during pending questions or other misconduct likely will prefer CPLR 3126 to CPLR 3124. The former is a more potent weapon, as it permits the imposition of penalties, while CPLR 3124 contemplates a disclosure order without a penalty.[7] However, CPLR 3126 can be used only against a party or an officer, director, member, employee or agent of a party or person otherwise under a party's control, whereas CPLR 3124 can be used against a party or nonparty.[8]

Pursuant to CPLR 3126, a court may enter an order penalizing the conduct of the offending party or attorney. The court may make "such orders

---

4　　David D. Siegel, New York Practice § 366, at 576 (3d ed. 1999) (footnote omitted) (hereinafter "Siegel").

5　　*See Am. Reliance Ins. Co. v. Nat'l Gen. Ins. Co.*, 174 A.D.2d 591, 571 N.Y.S.2d 493 (2d Dep't 1991).

6　　CPLR 3122(a).

7　　Siegel, *supra* note 4, § 366, at 576. For a nonparty who refuses to provide discovery, the weapon is a motion for contempt pursuant to CPLR 2308.

8　　Siegel, *supra* note 4, § 367.

. . . as are just."[9] Such orders include those that (1) resolve issues related to the disputed information in accordance with the claims of the party obtaining the order; (2) prohibit the offending party from supporting or opposing designated claims or defenses, producing designated evidence or using certain witnesses; and (3) strike pleadings or parts thereof, dismiss the action or a part thereof or render a default judgment.

Under CPLR 3124, the court may issue an order compelling discovery when a person fails to respond to or comply with a request, notice, question or discovery order. With CPLR 3126, however, the penalties set forth may be imposed only when a party or an officer, director, member, employee or agent of a party or person under a party's control "refuses to obey an order for disclosure or wilfully fails to disclose information which the court finds ought to have been disclosed." In other words, there must be *a refusal to obey a discovery order* or *a willful failure to disclose* information that should have been disclosed.[10]

B. Striking Pleadings and Other Severe Sanctions

Courts are reluctant to issue orders that directly or effectively bring a party's case to an end, especially because of misconduct by the party's lawyer. An order dismissing a complaint or striking an answer, of course, ends the case for the party affected. However, an order precluding a party from opposing certain claims or defenses can, depending on the facts, have an equivalent effect, or one close thereto.[11] Likewise, an order prohibiting the introduction of specified testimony can have a case-terminating effect. The state courts often observe in the discovery context that the policy of the state is to decide cases on their merits.[12]

---

9   CPLR 3126.

10   This formulation means that the party seeking discovery need not move to compel before resorting to CPLR 3126. Siegel, *supra* note 4, § 367, at 578.

11   *Patterson v. New York City Health & Hosps. Corp.*, 284 A.D.2d 516, 726 N.Y.S.2d 715 (2d Dep't 2001) (preclusion drastic remedy, which effectively results in striking of pleading; violation of court order must be willful, deliberate and contumacious); *Cianciolo v. Trism Specialized Carriers*, 274 A.D.2d 369, 711 N.Y.S.2d 441 (2d Dep't 2000) (same); *Goodman, Rackower & Agiato v. Lieberman*, 260 A.D.2d 599, 688 N.Y.S.2d 662 (2d Dep't 1999) (same).

12   *Mendez v. City of New York*, 7 A.D.3d 766, 778 N.Y.S.2d 501, 502 (2d Dep't 2004) ("actions should be resolved on the merits wherever possible"); *Marks v. Vigo*, 303 A.D.2d 306, 756 N.Y.S.2d 568 (1st Dep't 2003) (strong preference*); Byrne v. City of New York*, 301 A.D.2d 489, 753 N.Y.S.2d 132 (2d Dep't 2003); *Catarine v. Beth Israel Med. Ctr.*, 290 A.D.2d 213, 735 N.Y.S.2d 520 (1st Dep't 2002) (strong preference); *Corsini v. U-Haul Int'l*, 212 A.D.2d 288, 630 N.Y.S.2d 45 (1st Dep't 1995) (however, the court dismissed the complaint because of the extreme and abusive conduct of the pro se plaintiff, an attorney).

The courts have broad discretion over the discovery process, including the nature and extent of sanctions under CPLR 3126.[13] In a noteworthy case, the N.Y. Court of Appeals observed:

> If the credibility of court orders and the integrity of our judicial system are to be maintained, a litigant cannot ignore court orders with impunity. Indeed, the Legislature, recognizing the need for courts to be able to command compliance with their disclosure directives, has specifically provided that a "court may make such orders * * * as are just," including dismissal of an action (CPLR 3126). Finally, we underscore that compliance with a disclosure order requires both a timely response and one that evinces a good-faith effort to address the requests meaningfully.[14]

The court can strike a pleading or issue a broad preclusion order that has the same effect, but these are extreme sanctions that should be used only on a clear showing that the failure to provide discovery is willful, deliberate or contumacious.[15] The burden of proof rests upon the party

---

13 *Byrne*, 301 A.D.2d 489; *Jaffe v. Hubbard*, 299 A.D.2d 395, 751 N.Y.S.2d 491 (2d Dep't 2002); *Emanuel v. Broadway Mall Props.*, 293 A.D.2d 708, 741 N.Y.S.2d 278 (2d Dep't 2002); *Rocco v. Advantage Sec. & Prot. Inc.*, 283 A.D.2d 317, 724 N.Y.S.2d 419 (1st Dep't 2001); *Nowak v. Veira*, 289 A.D.2d 383, 737 N.Y.S.2d 372 (2d Dep't 2001); *Patterson*, 284 A.D.2d 516; *Bodine v. Ladjevardi*, 284 A.D.2d 351, 726 N.Y.S.2d 129 (2d Dep't 2001).

14 *Kihl v. Pfeffer*, 94 N.Y.2d 118, 123, 700 N.Y.S.2d 87, 722 N.E.2d 55 (1999) (Kaye, Ch. J.).

15 *Appler v. Riverview Ob. & Gyn., P.C.*, ___ A.D.3d ___, 780 N.Y.S.2d 188 (3d Dep't 2004) (order striking answer upheld where defendant engaged in dilatory tactics and repeatedly refused to provide discovery, including a deposition; refusal continued even after two motions brought); *Mendez*, 7 A.D.3d 766; *Longo v. Armor Elevator Co.*, 307 A.D.2d 848, 763 N.Y.S.2d 597 (1st Dep't 2003) (resolving order on notice issue proper for defendants' repeated and contumacious failure to produce documents as required by court order without adequate explanation); *Sloniger v. Niagara Mohawk Power Corp.*, 306 A.D.2d 842, 761 N.Y.S.2d 757 (4th Dep't 2003) (to strike answer, it must be conclusively shown that the discovery failure was deliberate or contumacious); *Dennis v. City of New York*, 304 A.D.2d 611, 758 N.Y.S.2d 661 (2d Dep't 2003); *Marks*, 303 A.D.2d 306; *Byrne*, 301 A.D.2d 489; *Diane v. Ricale Taxi, Inc.*, 291 A.D.2d 320, 739 N.Y.S.2d 8 (1st Dep't 2002); *Emanuel*, 293 A.D.2d 708; *Balla v. Jones*, 300 A.D.2d 1076, 752 N.Y.S.2d 486 (4th Dep't 2002) (error to grant conditional order striking answer if defendant failed to appear for deposition absent clear showing of willful, contumacious or bad faith conduct; defendant not likely to provide information beyond that provided by property manager and, being elderly and ill, should not be deposed); *Catarine*, 290 A.D.2d 213; *Nowak*, 289 A.D.2d 383; *Telles v. Mohamoud*, 288 A.D.2d 78, 733 N.Y.S.2d 145 (1st Dep't 2001); *Patterson*, 284 A.D.2d 516; *Rocco*, 283 A.D.2d 317; *Bodine*, 284 A.D.2d 351; *Cianciolo*, 274 A.D.2d 369 (error to preclude defendants from offering any testimony at trial; proper remedy is to preclude testimony of defendant if not produced for deposition prior to trial); *Rivers v. Embassy Club*, 207 A.D.2d 876, 616 N.Y.S.2d 988 (2d Dep't 1994).

seeking the sanction.[16] Willful, deliberate and contumacious conduct may be inferred from the actions or inactions of the offending party.[17] The courts look to such things as (1) whether prior orders were violated and, if so, how many; (2) the length of time the discovery went unprovided; (3) whether discovery notices were also ignored; (4) the extent of the failure to provide discovery; (5) whether the offending party received and reacted

---

16   *Goodman, Rackower & Agiato v. Lieberman*, 260 A.D.2d 599, 688 N.Y.S.2d 662 (2d Dep't 1999).

17   *Mendez*, 7 A.D.3d 766 (inferred from repeated failure to comply with disclosure orders, including failure to produce witness for deposition; inadequate excuses; error to have denied motions to strike answer of city and board of education); *Emanuel*, 293 A.D.2d 708 (inferred from failure to comply with two court orders and protracted delay in providing partial response to discovery demands, not adequately explained); *Kopin v. Wal-Mart Stores, Inc.*, 299 A.D.2d 937, 750 N.Y.S.2d 379 (4th Dep't 2002) (inferred from failure to comply with two court orders and protracted delay in providing partial response to demands; no adequate explanation); *Nowak*, 289 A.D.2d 383 (inferred from repeated failure to comply with court-ordered discovery schedule and failure to appear at depositions and medical exam as scheduled over two years; error not to have dismissed complaint unconditionally); *Bodine*, 284 A.D.2d 351 (inferred from numerous adjournments of scheduled depositions, failure to produce documents, failure to comply with court orders without adequate excuse; dismissal proper).

to inquiries or complaints from the other side; and (6) whether any reasonable excuse is offered for the conduct involved.[18]

If the allegedly offending party can show a reasonable excuse, such as
that the information sought was not produced because of an inability to do
so or confusion as to the meaning of an order, rather than lack of industry
or contemptuousness, an ultimate sanction ought not be granted.[19] The
inability of an attorney to find his or her client is not an excuse for failure

18   *Baez v. Arrow Linen Supply Co.*, 10 A.D.3d 408, 781 N.Y.S.2d 143 (2d Dep't 2004) (improvi-
     dent exercise of discretion to preclude defendant from testifying at trial without affording him
     another opportunity to be deposed); *Wilson v. Galicia Contracting & Restoration Corp.*, ___
     A.D.3d ___, 779 N.Y.S.2d 527 (2d Dep't 2004) (answer properly stricken when conditional order
     became absolute; two-year pattern of failure to respond to demands, court orders and condi-
     tional order; no reasonable excuse); *Longo*, 307 A.D.2d 848 (resolving order on notice issue
     proper for defendants' repeated and contumacious failure to produce documents as required by
     court order without adequate explanation); *Sloniger*, 306 A.D.2d 842 (to strike answer, it must
     be conclusively shown that the discovery failure was deliberate or contumacious); *Dennis*, 304
     A.D.2d 611; *Marks*, 303 A.D.2d 306; *Byrne*, 301 A.D.2d 489 (diligent search for records by
     defendant, substantial compliance with demand and reasonable excuse for inability to provide
     further information; motion to strike answer improvidently granted); *Healy v. ARP Cable, Inc.*,
     299 A.D.2d 152, 753 N.Y.S.2d 38 (1st Dep't 2002) (failure by company in violation of discov-
     ery orders to produce witness with knowledge of critical issue of work procedures; proper to
     preclude it from offering its own witnesses at trial but excessive to bar it from offering proof of
     any kind); *Jaffe v. Hubbard*, 299 A.D.2d 395, 751 N.Y.S.2d 491 (2d Dep't 2002) (two orders
     directing plaintiff to produce documents and appear for deposition by date certain violated; pre-
     clusion properly ordered); *Penafiel v. Puretz*, 298 A.D.2d 446, 748 N.Y.S.2d 767 (2d Dep't 2002)
     (failure to comply with at least three orders over extended period without excuse; improvident
     to deny motion to dismiss complaint); *Emanuel*, 293 A.D.2d 708 (failure to comply with two
     court orders and protracted delay in providing partial response to discovery demands, not ade-
     quately explained); *Abouzeid v. Cadogan*, 291 A.D.2d 423, 737 N.Y.S.2d 634 (2d Dep't 2002)
     (failure to comply with four court orders, including conditional order striking complaint; no
     excuse offered; order to show cause to extend time properly denied and complaint dismissed);
     Nicoletti v. Ozram Transp., Inc., 286 A.D.2d 719, 730 N.Y.S.2d 165 (2d Dep't 2001) (repeated
     failure to comply with discovery demands, to respond to inquiries, to comply with conditional
     order; inadequate excuse); *Rocco*, 283 A.D.2d 317 (failure of crucial party witness to appear for
     deposition repeatedly adjourned and rescheduled at his request was willful and contumacious;
     conditional order to strike proper).

19   *Riley v. ISS Int'l Serv. Sys., Inc.*, 304 A.D.2d 637, 757 N.Y.S.2d 593 (2d Dep't 2003); *Byrne*, 301
     A.D.2d 489; *Balla*, 300 A.D.2d 1076; *EIFS, Inc. v. Morie Co.*, 298 A.D.2d 548, 749 N.Y.S.2d
     43, 45 (2d Dep't 2002) (error to preclude expert testimony at trial regarding lost business claim
     for failure to provide documents reviewed by expert where there was ambiguity regarding oral
     conditional order of preclusion); *Schrader v. Sunnyside Corp.*, 297 A.D.2d 369, 747 N.Y.S.2d
     26 (2d Dep't 2002) (defendant unable to obtain file in another law firm's office in another state;
     conduct not willful and contumacious); *Telles*, 288 A.D.2d 78 (failure to serve correctly condi-
     tional order striking answer; failure to attend deposition not willful and contumacious; error to
     have stricken answer).

to provide discovery.[20] Normally, if an order striking a pleading is granted, it should apply only to those parts of the pleading having to do with the suppressed information.[21] A pleading should not be stricken when doing so would adversely affect the rights of an innocent party.[22]

Absent a showing of willful or contumacious conduct, a court ought not to dismiss a complaint for failure to comply with a scheduling order issued as a result of a preliminary conference. This is especially so when the order was not a conditional order of preclusion or the like and the opposing party was not prejudiced.[23] A preliminary conference order normally would not set forth penalties for failure to provide specific discovery as a contingency. A lesser sanction for violation of a scheduling order would be appropriate.[24]

These cases indicate that an ultimate sanction requires notice to the offending party that noncompliance will have the stated result. Probably, though, violation of a series of orders directing specific discovery will result in a severe sanction even if none of those orders contains a conditional imposition of that sanction. An example might be if a court in four different orders directed a party to produce a named person for deposition on stated dates and the party failed to do so without adequate excuse. In such a case, preclusion or the striking of a pleading might occur even

---

20 *Robinson v. Rollins Leasing Corp.*, 288 A.D.2d 367, 734 N.Y.S.2d 83 (2d Dep't 2001) (not error to order striking of answer unless defendant submits to deposition within set deadline); *Rocco*, 283 A.D.2d 317 (same); *Cianciolo v. Trism Specialized Carriers*, 274 A.D.2d 369, 711 N.Y.S.2d 441 (2d Dep't 2000) (if defense counsel cannot locate client, proper remedy is not to bar all testimony, but to preclude the missing defendant's testimony if defendant not located and deposed before trial).

21 *Diane v. Ricale Taxi, Inc.*, 291 A.D.2d 320, 739 N.Y.S.2d 8, 10 (1st Dep't 2002) (witness not produced would have testified regarding liability only, so striking should be limited to liability).

22 *Quintanilla v. Harchak*, 259 A.D.2d 681, 686 N.Y.S.2d 854 (2d Dep't 1999) (intoxicated driver failed to appear for deposition despite five court orders; court properly declined to preclude testimony of this defendant but allowed plaintiff to pursue him for contempt; plaintiff needed his testimony on dram-shop claim against movants, defendant tavern owners).

23 *Thomas v. Benedictine Hosp.*, 296 A.D.2d 781, 745 N.Y.S.2d 606 (3d Dep't 2002) (no showing of prejudice; violation of scheduling order willful but based on genuine, though erroneous, belief that the plaintiff was entitled to demand further depositions of defendant prior to deposing others, not evasive and uncooperative strategy of delay; dismissal inappropriate, but plaintiff should have been barred from deposing defendant as penalty for disregard of order); *SDR Holdings Inc. v. Town of Fort Edward*, 290 A.D.2d 696, 735 N.Y.S.2d 656 (3d Dep't 2002) (case dismissed for failure to comply with scheduling order on motion made four months after issuance of order; error to impose drastic sanction of dismissal, though other penalty justified; delay not willful, no direct prejudice and scheduling order did not contain conditional imposition of dismissal or preclusion).

24 *Thomas*, 296 A.D.2d 781; *SDR Holdings Inc.*, 290 A.D.2d 696.

though none of the orders conditionally imposed that penalty. Repeated violations without justification would amount to contumacious conduct.[25]

C. Spoliation of Evidence

The destruction or spoliation of evidence may provide grounds for a severe sanction against the wrongdoer, as it can deprive the adversary of key evidence.[26] If the evidence is not central to the case nor its loss prejudicial, then a lesser sanction, if any, may be more appropriate.[27] If a party destroys evidence and the party seeking it is thereby deprived of appropriate means to present or confront a claim, the pleading of the first party may be stricken as a matter of fundamental fairness, despite the general reluctance of courts to impose a dispositive sanction. Such a sanction may even be imposed when spoliation occurs through negligence rather than willfulness or bad faith if the consequence is sufficiently prejudicial.[28]

D. Lesser Sanctions for Discovery Violations

When there is a clear, unexcused violation of a preliminary conference or court scheduling order, some penalty may well be in order. The failure of courts to impose penalties in such circumstances would be unfair to the parties who are adversely affected by the failure—even if there is no substantial, irrevocable prejudice from the violation—and would tend to encourage disrespect for court orders.

A key prospective deponent not produced on time might die before the rescheduled date. Even absent such grave prejudice, the opposing party is adversely affected by violation of a scheduling order to the extent that disposition of the case is delayed; in addition, that party must go to some trouble and perhaps expense to obtain compliance with an order that ought to have been adhered to without further action. Indeed, under the

---

25 *Longo v. Armor Elevator Co.*, 307 A.D.2d 848, 763 N.Y.S.2d 597 (1st Dep't 2003); *Kutner v. Feiden, Dweck & Sladkus*, 223 A.D.2d 488, 637 N.Y.S.2d 15 (1st Dep't), *appeal denied*, 88 N.Y.2d 802, 644 N.Y.S.2d 689 (1996).

26 *See Piazza v. Great Atl. & Pac. Tea Co.*, 300 A.D.2d 381, 753 N.Y.S.2d 86 (2d Dep't 2002); *Sage Realty Corp. v. Proskauer Rose LLP*, 275 A.D.2d 11, 713 N.Y.S.2d 155 (1st Dep't 2000).

27 *Riley v. ISS Int'l Serv. Sys., Inc.*, 304 A.D.2d 637, 757 N.Y.S.2d 593 (2d Dep't 2003); *Klein v. Ford Motor Co.*, 303 A.D.2d 376, 756 N.Y.S.2d 271 (2d Dep't 2003) (design defect case; inadvertent loss of vehicle and defendant had previously inspected it and taken photos; dismissal not warranted). Professor Siegel offers a maxim on this point: "Spoliation without prejudice is no spoliation at all." Siegel, McKinney's Practice Commentary, CPLR 3126, at 269 (Supp. 2004).

28 *Madison Ave. Caviarteria v. Hartford Steam Boiler Inspection & Ins. Co.*, 306 A.D.2d 324, 761 N.Y.S.2d 271 (2d Dep't), *vacated on reargument*, 2 A.D.3d 793, 770 N.Y.S.2d 724 (2d Dep't 2003); *Mylonas v. Town of Brookhaven*, 305 A.D.2d 561, 759 N.Y.S.2d 752 (2d Dep't 2003).

CPLR a mere deposition notice is supposed to suffice by itself to secure production of a witness. When the notice or an order does not work, remedies are available.

As the N.Y. Court of Appeals noted in *Kihl v. Pfeffer*,[29] lack of enforcement of court orders undermines their credibility and increases the likelihood that they will be violated or ignored in the future. It is important for other cases and for the system of justice that orders have teeth. Thus, when a scheduling order is violated without excuse, some sort of sanction would be in order.

The following scenario illustrates what may and does occur. A party is directed in a scheduling order to produce a witness for deposition by a set date. The party fails to do so. The party's defense of its conduct is that the other side did not respond adequately to communications about discovery issues and did not produce documents which, under the order, were due prior to the deposition dates. At a conference, the court discovers these difficulties and resolves them by issuing a new order—a compliance conference order—to reschedule the uncompleted discovery. The party again fails to produce the witness. The adversary moves to strike the pleading. The party defends against the motion by complaining about the movant. If the party's excuses lack weight, the court might well set a new date for the deposition, perhaps penalize the offending attorney for violating two scheduling orders by imposing a monetary sanction (discussed below), and perhaps conditionally preclude the party (i.e., if the witness is not produced) from offering testimony at trial on an issue about which the witness would be questioned if produced at deposition.

The foregoing example illustrates the common reality. Courts, in recognition of the law discussed thus far, tend to issue a severe sanction only by way of a conditional order, which gives the offending party and attorney clear notice of the danger they run and an opportunity—at least a second chance—to avoid it.[30] Conditional orders have the advantage of achieving enforcement of court directives on discovery but doing so in a way that promotes the disposition of matters on their merits.

If, however, only a conditional order is issued in situations such as that just posed, the result may not do full justice. In the example, the offending

---

29   94 N.Y.2d 118, 123, 700 N.Y.S.2d 87, 722 N.E.2d 55 (1999).

30   *See, e.g., Mines v. Am. Honda Motors Co.*, 305 A.D.2d 271, 761 N.Y.S.2d 24 (1st Dep't 2003); *Ferraro v. New York Tel. Co.*, 94 A.D.2d 784, 463 N.Y.S.2d 31 (2d Dep't 1983); Siegel, *supra* note 4, § 367.

party and attorney would have failed on two occasions to comply with directives of the court regarding the production of the witness. If there is no adequate excuse, such as illness on the witness's part, it would seem that the imposition at that point of only a conditional order would not be enough. This conditional order would not seem fair to the movant, who will have suffered at least somewhat from the delay and who, in the hypothetical, was obliged to go to the trouble and expense of a motion to strike to obtain information to which the movant had a clear right by notice alone. Nor would such indulgence tend to promote the credibility of court orders.[31]

One lesser sanction that may be used in proper circumstances in the case of a party that fails to take a deposition as scheduled without good excuse is to find that the party has waived the right to take that deposition. The party's right to present evidence and challenge claims or defenses is not limited by such a ruling—the penalty is not severe. However, there is an impact since there will be no record regarding that witness to assist the party in preparing for trial, nor will the party be able to impeach directly the trial testimony of the witness by means of this prior testimony.

Another lesser sanction is a monetary one. An order pursuant to CPLR 3126 may include monetary sanctions. Section 3126 does not authorize this penalty in so many words, but it is well settled that the court, empowered thereby to issue such orders as are just, may, in the exercise of its discretion, issue such an order if the circumstances warrant. Because this sanction is a lesser penalty, the court need not find before imposing it that the offending party acted willfully, deliberately and contumaciously in violation of a prior order. It suffices if the party or attorney upon whom the penalty is imposed was at fault, which includes an attorney treating a court's scheduling order negligently or casually.

The monetary sanction will usually consist of the costs imposed on the adversary by the misconduct, such as attorneys' fees and the costs of a motion for sanctions based upon violation of a preliminary conference order or opposition to a motion for a protective order.[32] (If the party is truly being offensive, the motion that brings the matter before the court

---

31   *See, e.g., Agron v. Response Vehicle, Inc.*, 251 A.D.2d 234, 674 N.Y.S.2d 677 (1st Dep't 1998) (city inexcusably failed to appear for deposition rescheduled at its request; a flagrant violation of court order, as well as "indefensibly rude"; order to strike answer unless city paid costs of $1,500 to third-party plaintiff); *see also* Harold Baer, Jr. & Robert C. Meade, Jr., *Some Reflections on Pre-Trial Delay in State Court*, N.Y. St. B.J., Vol. 65, No. 1, at 30 (Jan. 1993).

32   Although CPLR 3126 resembles FRCP 37(b), the two provisions differ considerably relative to the imposition of expenses. See *infra* II.D. for further discussion.

more likely will be a CPLR 3126 motion, rather than one under CPLR 3103, although the offending party may cross-move for that relief on the theory that tactical boldness might obscure the absence of an excuse.) If the misconduct consists of obstructive and baseless objections and directions not to answer at a deposition, the court might also impose some portion of the reporter's fee as a cost (the portion attributed to the wasted parts of the deposition).[33]

If the misconduct is that of the lawyer, the order is likely to punish the offending attorney only by requiring that he or she personally compensate the moving party for the expense to which that party was put by the need to take legal action to counter the misconduct. Discovery violations may well occur without the client being aware of them. In the case of misconduct at depositions by the defending attorney, the transcript may readily reveal that the attorney, and not the client, was at fault.

No appeal lies as of right from an order denying a motion to direct a witness to answer questions posed at a deposition. The court can deem the notice of appeal an application for leave to appeal and hear the case by that route.[34]

A guiding rule with regard to sanctions in connection with the production of witnesses for depositions, the production of documents in preparation for or in connection with depositions or the conduct of counsel at depositions is that, as Gilbert and Sullivan put it, the punishment should fit the crime. A lesser offense warrants less severe sanctions; grave obstruction of the discovery process and violation of court orders may call for severe penalties.

Notwithstanding this general principle, Professor Siegel has expressed some concern about the adequacy of the penalties used by the courts when discovery violations occur:

> Judicial reluctance to make free use of severe sanctions such as those presently listed in CPLR 3126, which trepidation accounts for the evolution of the conditional order with an attorney's fee as an alternative, is a residuum of the common law hostility to open pretrial disclosure. Some judges may still feel that keeping one's cards close to the

---

33 *Lewis v. Brunswick Hosp.*, 2001 N.Y. Misc. LEXIS 407, at **13 (Sup. Ct., Queens Co. May 10, 2001).

34 *Kinkela v. Inc. Vill. of Mineola*, 306 A.D.2d 382, 761 N.Y.S.2d 284 (2d Dep't 2003).

vest is part of the game, or at least that the player should not be too gravely punished for trying. This attitude is at war with the CPLR, however, and it as much as anything else accounts for the high number of disclosure applications on the motion calendars.[35]

II. FEDERAL PRACTICE

A. Motions to Compel in General

A motion to compel disclosure[36] in federal practice shall be made on "reasonable notice" to the court where the action is pending if the order sought would be directed at a party and, in the case of nonparties, to the court in the district where the discovery is being, or will be, taken.[37] Grounds for a motion to compel include failure to answer a deposition question, to make a FRCP 30(b)(6) designation or to respond positively to a FRCP 34 document demand.[38] A certification that a good faith effort was made to resolve the dispute must accompany the motion. The examiner who will make a motion regarding improper conduct at a deposition is authorized to complete or adjourn the deposition. An evasive or incomplete answer or response is considered a failure to answer or respond.

If the motion is granted or if the discovery is provided after the motion is made, the court, after affording an opportunity to be heard, must require the noncomplying party or deponent or the attorney or both to pay to the movant the "reasonable expenses incurred in making the motion, including attorney's fees" unless the movant failed to make a good faith effort to obtain the discovery directly, the failure to provide discovery was "substantially justified" or other circumstances make an award of expenses unjust.[39]

The court may enter a protective order under FRCP 26(c) if the motion is denied. In such case, the court, after affording an opportunity to be heard, must require the movant, the moving attorney or both to pay to the opposing party or person "the reasonable expenses incurred in opposing the motion, including attorney's fees," unless the motion was "substan-

---

35   Siegel, *supra* note 4, § 367, at 581. Elsewhere, Professor Siegel laments what he calls "the court's . . . propensity, upon its first involvement in disclosure resistance, to give the resister a second chance." Siegel, McKinney's Practice Commentary, CPLR 3126, at 270 (Supp. 2004).

36   See Appendix, "Motion to Compel" and "Affidavit on Motion to Compel" (federal forms).

37   FRCP 37(a).

38   FRCP 37(a)(2)(B).

39   FRCP 37(a)(4).

tially justified" or other circumstances make an award of expenses unjust.[40] If the motion is granted in part and denied in part, an appropriate protective order may be issued, and the court may apportion the reasonable expenses incurred in a just manner.[41]

B. Motions for Sanctions in General

If an impediment, delay or other conduct frustrates the fair examination of a deponent, the court may impose an appropriate sanction upon the person responsible, including reasonable costs and attorneys' fees.[42] If the deponent or party moves pursuant to FRCP 30(d)(4) for protection because the deposition is being conducted in bad faith or so as to annoy, embarrass or oppress the deponent or party, the provisions of FRCP 37(a)(4) shall apply to the award of expenses incurred in relation to the motion.[43]

If the examiner fails to attend the deposition and proceed, the court may order the party to pay to another party that did attend as noticed the reasonable expenses of the party and counsel, including attorneys' fees.[44] A similar provision[45] applies if the examiner fails to serve a subpoena on a nonparty witness and that witness does not attend.

A deponent who fails to proceed or answer a question at a deposition when directed to do so by the court where the deposition is being taken may be considered in contempt.[46] If a party or an officer, director or managing agent of the party or a FRCP 30(b)(6) designee fails to obey an order to provide discovery, the court where the action is pending may make such order as is just.[47] The court may order, inter alia, that

1. the matters about which the order was made or other designated facts be deemed established in accordance with the claim of the party who obtained the order;[48]

---

40   FRCP 37(a)(4)(B).

41   FRCP 37(a)(4)(C).

42   FRCP 30(d)(3).

43   FRCP 30(d)(4).

44   FRCP 30(g)(1).

45   *See* FRCP 30(g)(2).

46   FRCP 37(b)(1).

47   FRCP 37(b)(2).

48   FRCP 37(b)(2)(A).

2. the disobedient party be precluded from supporting or opposing designated claims or defenses or that the party be barred from introducing evidence on designated matters;[49]

3. pleadings be struck in whole or in part, the matter be dismissed or that a default judgment be rendered;[50] and

4. in place of or in addition to the above, the person be held in contempt.[51]

In lieu of or in addition to the above, the court "shall require" the disobedient party or counsel or both to pay the reasonable expenses, including attorneys' fees, caused by that failure unless the failure was "substantially justified" or other circumstances make an award of expenses unjust.[52]

Sanctions under FRCP 37 serve three purposes: (1) to prevent a party from benefiting from the party's own failure to comply; (2) as a specific deterrent and to obtain compliance with the particular order issued; and (3) as a general deterrent in the case at hand and in other litigation, provided the party against whom the sanction is issued was in some sense at fault.[53] For the most part, the *in terrorem* effect of this rule has, from a practical standpoint, deterred all but the most egregious violations.

C. Motions to Compel in Detail

As noted, when a party fails to answer a question at a deposition, a motion to compel an answer is authorized.[54] The examiner is permitted to adjourn the deposition immediately for this purpose or to complete such of it as is thought appropriate. At times, a refusal to answer a question or a group of questions may interfere with the remainder of the deposition so that adjournment at that point may be necessary. As noted in chapter 6, it may well be possible to obtain a ruling from the court quickly by telephone or an in-person conference. Generally, though, the questioner will

---

49   FRCP 37(b)(2)(B).

50   FRCP 37(b)(2)(C).

51   FRCP 37(b)(2)(D).

52   FRCP 37(b)(2)(E).

53   *Update Art, Inc. v. Modiin Pub., Ltd.*, 843 F.2d 67, 71 (2d Cir. 1988); *Shamis v. Ambassador Factors Corp.*, 34 F. Supp. 2d 879, 887 (S.D.N.Y. 1999); *Williams v. Nat'l Hous. Exch.*, 165 F.R.D. 405, 408 (S.D.N.Y. 1996) (Baer, J.).

54   FRCP 37(a)(2)(B).

probably want to and be able to complete questioning on other matters before making the motion or seeking the ruling.

When problems with the scheduling or conduct of depositions or the production of documents in connection with depositions arise, a court may request or direct that the parties address the issues in letter briefs rather than formal motions in order to minimize expense and expedite progress in the case. Parties should familiarize themselves with relevant court rules or judges' rules.

If the adversary fails to produce documents called for by a FRCP 34 demand and these are needed, as they often are, to prepare for depositions, a motion to compel under FRCP 37(a)(2)(B) should be made promptly so that the depositions may proceed. A failure to designate a FRCP 30(b)(6) witness similarly should lead to a motion to compel. When there is a failure to appear for a deposition or to produce documents in compliance with a court order, a motion for sanctions under FRCP 37(b) would be in order. The failure of a nonparty witness without adequate excuse to produce documents or appear for a deposition pursuant to subpoena may be deemed a contempt of the court from which the subpoena issued.[55]

The Federal Rules of Civil Procedure regarding motions to compel and sanctions are directed at unjustified failure or refusal to produce witnesses for depositions, failure or refusal to allow the witnesses to testify at the depositions, failure or refusal to produce documents necessary for proper depositions and other discovery malfeasance. Some failures and refusals are the result of error, misjudgment or misunderstanding of the law. Others, however, are the product of bad faith, an intentional misuse of the discovery process to interfere with the rights of the adversary and to obstruct the case. Sometimes this sort of conduct is thought of as no more than aggressive litigation tactics, but it remains improper all the same.

In one case, for example, a party failed to respond to written discovery on time and used that failure as an excuse to delay production of two witnesses for deposition. The party then postponed the depositions. The party responded to the written discovery only after the discovery deadline and then refused to produce the two witnesses for deposition because the discovery period was over. This behavior is pure gamesmanship, which has no place in the litigation process.[56]

---

55   FRCP 45(e); *PaineWebber Inc. v. Acstar Ins. Co.*, 211 F.R.D. 247 (S.D.N.Y. 2002).

56   *Johnson v. J.B. Hunt Transport, Inc.*, 280 F.3d 1125 (7th Cir. 2002) (court barred defendant from producing two witnesses at trial).

Although FRCP 37(a) does not set forth a precise deadline for the making of a motion to compel, the tenor of the rules is that such motion should be made promptly. The cases so indicate. The moving party should have a good reason if a motion is not made shortly after the failure occurs. If the moving party could have made the motion long before and waits for a significant period of time after the close of discovery, the court may be disinclined to consider the motion on the merits. The motion may be judged untimely and denied on that ground alone.[57]

As noted earlier, a motion to compel must be supported by a certification that the movant has conferred, or attempted to confer, with the adversary in an effort to resolve the dispute without need for court intervention.[58] The drafters surely did not intend that this requirement be treated as an exercise or a mere formality. The movant should therefore certainly confer with the adversary or attempt seriously to do so and make a genuine, good faith effort to resolve the dispute.[59] Further, the certification should contain some detail about the efforts made to resolve the dispute without involving the court; it should not consist of conclusory formulae (e.g., "I attempted to confer with my adversary but without success").[60]

D. Motions for Sanctions in Detail

A party served with a proper notice of deposition is not entitled to refuse to attend without a court order excusing such appearance. Sanctions may befall the party who so acts.[61] Sanctions can be awarded for such failure under FRCP 37(b)(2) when a prior order has been violated;

---

57   *Rossetto v. Pabst Brewing Co.*, 217 F.3d 539, 542 (7th Cir. 2000) (Posner, J.), *cert. denied*, 531 U.S. 1192 (2001) (filed two months after discovery completion date; no excuse offered; untimely as court was commendably trying to spare the parties "the expense of protracted discovery, the bane of modern litigation"); *Ayala-Gerena v. Bristol Myers-Squibb Co.*, 95 F.3d 86, 94 (1st Cir. 1996) (motion to compel untimely; made more than a month after end of second extended discovery period; prejudice); *Shamis*, 34 F. Supp. 2d at 886; *see Freeman v. Allstate Life Ins. Co.*, 253 F.3d 533, 537 (9th Cir. 2001).

58   FRCP 37(a)(2)(B).

59   *Murphy v. Barberino Bros.*, 208 F.R.D. 483 (D. Conn. 2001) (improper to move to compel and for sanctions without an effort to confer); *Tri-Star Pictures, Inc. v. Unger*, 171 F.R.D. 94, 99–100 (S.D.N.Y. 1997) (conferring should be meaningful and genuine); *Reidy v. Runyon*, 169 F.R.D. 486, 490–91 (E.D.N.Y. 1997). If at a deposition objections are raised for certain reasons, the examiner explains why those reasons are not valid, and the points are discussed but no resolution reached, that interchange may constitute adequate consultation. *Bristol-Myers Squibb Co. v. Rhone-Poulenc Rorer, Inc.*, 1998 U.S. Dist. LEXIS 12 (S.D.N.Y. Jan. 6, 1998) (Patterson, J.).

60   *Tri-Star Pictures, Inc.*, 171 F.R.D. at 99–100.

61   *Hoffman v. UPS*, 206 F.R.D. 506, 508 (D. Kan. 2002); *Keller v. Edwards*, 206 F.R.D. 412, 416 (D. Md. 2002); see Appendix, "Motion for Sanctions" (federal form).

like sanctions may be awarded under FRCP 37(d) for a failure to appear in response to a proper notice even without a court order.[62]

When a party appears for a deposition but refuses to cooperate by testifying, or answers some questions but declines to answer others on the basis of articulated objections or otherwise, a proper procedure, as noted, is to obtain a court order pursuant to a FRCP 37(a) motion to compel.[63] The order may include an award of the expenses on the motion to compensate the moving party,[64] as well as additional costs incurred by the need to take a second deposition. If the party then refuses to obey that order, a significant sanction may be imposed.[65]

The failure to appear for a deposition or to produce documents in violation of a court order may even result in dismissal of the action or the striking of a defendant's answer.[66] The court may also issue an order precluding the offender from offering proof to support or defend claims or defenses or in regard to certain issues.[67] Compliance with discovery orders "is necessary to the integrity of our judicial process. A party who flouts such orders does so at his peril."[68]

As noted above, the sanctions listed in FRCP 37(b)(2), including the ultimate ones of dismissing a case or striking an answer and awarding a default judgment, may be imposed only when a court order has been vio-

---

62   *Haraway v. NASCAR*, 213 F.R.D. 161, 165 (D. Del. 2003).

63   *Dawes v. Coughlin*, 210 F.R.D. 38, 42–43 (W.D.N.Y. 2002) (refusal to answer certain questions); *EEOC v. Exel, Inc.*, 190 F. Supp. 2d 1179 (E.D. Mo. 2002); *Frazier v. S.E. Pa. Transp. Auth.*, 161 F.R.D. 309, 317 (E.D. Pa. 1995) (repeated interruptions and objections at deposition, including objections suggesting answers and directions not to answer; attorney sanctioned personally for costs and attorneys' fees on motion to compel per FRCP 37(a)(4)(A)).

64   *See, e.g., Hearst/ABC-Viacom Entm't Servs. v. Goodway Mktg., Inc.*, 145 F.R.D. 59 (E.D. Pa. 1992).

65   *Dawes*, 210 F.R.D. at 42–43; *see Eaves v. K-Mart Corp.*, 193 F. Supp. 2d 887 (S.D. Miss. 2001) (plaintiff failed to comply with discovery and magistrate judge's directives; magistrate judge directed plaintiff to answer questions regarding prior employment; plaintiff gave incomplete and evasive answers; case dismissed under inherent power).

66   *Sterling Promotional Corp. v. Gen. Accident Ins. Co.*, 212 F.R.D. 464 (S.D.N.Y. 2003) (failure to appear, despite court order and without an application or court approval, for long-delayed deposition; conduct amounted to willful flouting of court order; case dismissed; attorneys' fees also awarded to defendant against plaintiff and its counsel).

67   *Am. Int'l Tel., Inc. v. Mony Travel Servs., Inc.*, 203 F.R.D. 153 (S.D.N.Y. 2001) (defendant refused to appear for deposition as ordered; service issue resolved against defendant; defendant in default; default judgment to be granted unless answer within ten days; costs of motion to plaintiff).

68   *Update Art, Inc. v. Modiin Pub., Ltd.*, 843 F.2d 67, 73 (2d Cir. 1988).

lated.[69] There is some disagreement in the cases as to whether the order in question is limited to one on a motion to compel under FRCP 37(a). Some courts hold that the order need not be one on a motion to compel; it is enough if there is a clear order from the court directing the deposition or other discovery.[70] Others indicate that FRCP 37(b)(2) contemplates that an order to compel must have been violated, at least in the usual case.[71] In any event, courts emphasize that there should have been an order issued that provided clear notice of the action to be taken by the offending party.[72]

Dismissal or the striking of an answer should not be resorted to readily. Such a serious weapon is one of last resort.[73] Dismissal or a default judgment should only be awarded when the court finds willful violation, bad faith or fault.[74] Such a remedy must be available, however, not only to punish the wrongdoer, but also to deter others.[75]

---

69   *Genentech, Inc. v. U.S. Int'l Trade Comm'n*, 122 F.3d 1409, 1422–23 (Fed. Cir. 1997) (violation of court order required for dismissal); *Dawes*, 210 F.R.D. at 42–43 (dismissal pursuant to FRCP 37(b) requires court order; as no order here, case not dismissed now but will be later if refusal to testify continues).

70   *Daval Steel Prods. Div. of Francosteel Corp. v. M/V Fakredine*, 951 F.2d 1357 (2d Cir. 1991); *Metro. Opera Ass'n v. Local 100 Hotel Employees & Rest. Employees Int'l Union*, 212 F.R.D. 178, 225 (S.D.N.Y. 2003); *Buffalo Carpenters Pension Fund v. CKG Ceiling & Partition Co.*, 192 F.R.D. 95, 98 (W.D.N.Y. 2000) (striking answer would be premature as no order yet to provide discovery).

71   *McMullen v. Bay Ship Mgmt.*, 335 F.3d 215, 217 (3d Cir. 2003).

72   *Genentech, Inc.*, 122 F.3d at 1422–23 (general discovery order that does not provide "specific notice" cannot be basis for dismissal); *Daval Steel Prods.*, 951 F.2d 1357 ("a clearly articulated order of the court requiring specified discovery" is necessary).

73   *Golant v. Levy*, 239 F.3d 931, 937 (7th Cir. 2001) (deliberate defiance of various court orders to produce documents justifies default judgment); *Simmons v. Abruzzo*, 49 F.3d 83 (2d Cir. 1995); *Update Art, Inc. v. Modiin Pub., Ltd.*, 843 F.2d 67, 71 (2d Cir. 1988).; *T & W Funding Co. XII, L.L.C. v. Pennant Rent-A-Car Midwest, Inc.*, 210 F.R.D. 730, 734 (D. Kan. 2002); *Shamis v. Ambassador Factors Corp.*, 34 F. Supp. 2d 879, 887 (S.D.N.Y. 1999).

74   *Golant*, 239 F.3d at 936; *Keefer v. Provident Life & Accident Ins. Co.*, 238 F.3d 937, 941 (8th Cir. 2000) (dismissal requires that there have been an order compelling discovery, willful violation and prejudice to other side); *Sieck v. Russo*, 869 F.2d 131 (2d Cir. 1989); *Sterling Promotional Corp. v. Gen. Accident Ins. Co.*, 212 F.R.D. 464 (S.D.N.Y. 2003) (deposition aborted on several occasions; failure to appear on court-ordered date without approval of court or application; willful flouting of court orders justifies dismissal, plus expenses); *In re Sumitomo Copper Litig.*, 204 F.R.D. 58 (S.D.N.Y. 2001) (Pollack, J.) (default judgment granted against defendant who violated a court order to submit to deposition by telephone; defendant informed counsel he would not appear for a deposition at all); *Shamis*, 34 F. Supp. 2d at 887; *Williams v. Nat'l Hous. Exch. Inc.*, 165 F.R.D. 405, 409 (S.D.N.Y. 1996) (Baer, J.).

75   *Valentine v. Museum of Modern Art*, 29 F.3d 47, 49–50 (2d Cir. 1994); *Update Art, Inc.*, 843 F.2d at 71; *Williams*, 165 F.R.D. at 408 (quoting *Nat'l Hockey League v. Metro. Hockey Club, Inc.*, 427 U.S. 639, 643 (1976)).

Before imposing severe sanctions, the court should consider lesser ones, as well as the need for deterrence.[76] Although the least severe sanction possible need not be chosen, the court will exercise care to ensure that the penalty imposed is proportionate to the offense committed.[77] Distinguished commentators state:

> [I]t is clear that any failure to disclose, regardless of the reason for it, brings the sanctions of Rule 37 into play, although the reason for the failure is an important consideration in determining what sanction to impose. If the failure is because of inability to comply, rather than because of willfulness, bad faith, or any fault of the party, the action should not be dismissed, nor a default judgment given, and less severe sanctions are the most that should be invoked.[78]

"Traditionally, the courts have administered justice with mercy. They have allowed a party a second opportunity to comply with the discovery rules and orders made under them."[79] Before imposing an ultimate sanction, courts often warn the offending party of the imminence of sanctions if the misconduct is not corrected.[80] Before dismissal is allowed, the offender must have had notice of the alleged misconduct and been given an opportunity to comply.[81]

---

76   *Keefer*, 238 F.3d at 941 (fairness requires lesser sanction be considered); *Shamis*, 34 F. Supp. 2d at 887 (lesser sanctions must not be adequate); *Satcorp Int'l Group v. China Nat'l Import & Export Corp.*, 917 F. Supp. 271, 277 (S.D.N.Y.), *vacated on other grounds*, 101 F.3d 3 (2d Cir. 1996).

77   *Everyday Learning Corp. v. Larson*, 242 F.3d 815 (8th Cir. 2001) (default judgment upheld for repeated willful violations of orders (delays in producing documents and repeated refusal to produce defendant for deposition)); *Golant*, 239 F.3d at 937; *Keefer*, 238 F.3d at 941.

78   8A Charles Alan Wright et al., Federal Practice and Procedure § 2284, at 620–22 (2d ed. 1994) (footnotes omitted) (hereinafter "Wright").

79   *Id.* § 2284, at 633 (footnote omitted).

80   *Id.* § 2284, at 636–37. The warning may be accompanied by a "soft" sanction. *Sieck v. Russo*, 869 F.2d 131 (2d Cir. 1989); *In re Sumitomo Copper Litig.*, 204 F.R.D. 58 (S.D.N.Y. 2001) (Pollack, J.)

81   *Genentech, Inc. v. U.S. Int'l Trade Comm'n*, 122 F.3d 1409, 1422–23 (Fed. Cir. 1997); *Simmons v. Abruzzo*, 49 F.3d 83 (2d Cir. 1995); *Daval Steel Prods. Div. of Francosteel Corp. v. M/V Fakredine*, 951 F.2d 1357 (2d Cir. 1991) (clear order to produce an appropriate witness for deposition; violation justified FRCP 37(b)(2) sanction (preclusion on an issue)); *Davidson v. Dean*, 204 F.R.D. 251, 255 (S.D.N.Y. 2001) (ultimate sanction may be issued considering willfulness, reason offered for noncompliance, efficacy of lesser sanctions, duration of noncompliance and prior warning).

A number of factors may be considered before an ultimate sanction is imposed, including willfulness or bad faith on the part of the offending party, a history of noncompliance, the effectiveness of lesser sanctions, whether a warning had been issued and prejudice to the movant.[82] When an ultimate sanction is proper, it may fall on the client even for actions taken by the attorney, of which the client claims to have been ignorant.[83] In any event, resolution of a case on its merits is preferable to a default judgment.[84]

The failure to provide complete answers to questions at a deposition and the resort to evasion may justify the imposition of sanctions.[85] Also, various courts have considered the failure to produce a knowledgeable witness as required by FRCP 30(b)(6) tantamount to a failure to appear at a deposition pursuant to FRCP 37(d).[86] Such failure may warrant the imposition of a penalty.[87] The penalties available include a new deposition of a knowledgeable person or persons at the plaintiff's expense, together with the costs of the motion.[88]

If the entity finds the deposition notice confusing or vague, it should take appropriate action. Such action may include a motion for a protective order, if necessary, to clarify the situation in advance of the deposition.

---

82   *In re Sumitomo Copper Litig.*, 204 F.R.D. 58; *Yucyco, Ltd. v. Ljubljanska Banka d.d.*, 2001 U.S. Dist. LEXIS 8120, at *11 (S.D.N.Y. June 19, 2001).

83   *Everyday Learning Corp. v. Larson*, 242 F.3d 815, 817 (8th Cir. 2001).

84   *Williams v. Nat'l Hous. Exch. Inc.*, 165 F.R.D. 405, 409 (S.D.N.Y. 1996) (Baer, J.); *see In re Sumitomo Copper Litig.*, 204 F.R.D. 58; *Yucyco, Ltd.*, 2001 U.S. Dist. LEXIS 8120, at *11.

85   *Eaves v. K-Mart Corp.*, 193 F. Supp. 2d 887 (S.D. Miss. 2001).

86   *Black Horse Lane Assocs., L.P. v. Dow Chem. Corp.*, 228 F.3d 275, 304 (3d Cir. 2000) ("if a Rule 30(b)(6) witness is unable to give useful information he is no more present for the deposition than would be a deponent who physically appears for the deposition but sleeps through it"); *Resolution Trust Corp. v. S. Union Co.*, 985 F.2d 196 (5th Cir. 1993); *In re Vitamins Antitrust Litig.*, 216 F.R.D. 168, 174 (D.D.C. 2003); *Starlight Int'l, Inc. v. Herlihy*, 186 F.R.D. 626, 639 (D. Kan. 1999); *Bank of New York v. Meridien Biao Bank Tanz.*, 171 F.R.D. 135, 151 (S.D.N.Y. 1997); *United States v. Taylor*, 166 F.R.D. 356, 363 (M.D.N.C.), *aff'd, motion denied*, 166 F.R.D. 367 (1996).

87   *Reilly v. NatWest Mkts. Group*, 181 F.3d 253, 268 (2d Cir. 1999), *cert. denied*, 528 U.S. 1119 (2000) (preclusion for failure to produce two witnesses); *In re Vitamins Antitrust Litig.*, 216 F.R.D. at 174 (witness authenticated documents but asserted ignorance as to facts; found to be a failure to educate a witness as to noticed topics); *T & W Funding Co. XII, L.L.C. v. Pennant Rent-A-Car Midwest*, 210 F.R.D. 730 (D. Kan. 2002) (unprepared witness produced; new deposition ordered at plaintiff's expense; expenses awarded); *Paul Revere Life Ins. Co. v. Jafari*, 206 F.R.D. 126 (D. Md. 2002) (witness "woefully unprepared").

88   *In re Vitamins Antitrust Litig.*, 216 F.R.D. at 174; *T & W Funding Co. XII*, 210 F.R.D. 730; *Paul Revere Life Ins. Co.*, 206 F.R.D. 126.

The need for clarification of the deposition notice is not an acceptable excuse if raised for the first time in response to a FRCP 37 motion.[89]

E. Awarding Expenses

The court is required to award reasonable expenses on the motion to compel, including attorneys' fees, unless stated exceptions apply, including that the adversary's position was "substantially justified."[90] Similarly, the reasonable expenses, including attorneys' fees, of opposition to a motion to compel that is denied shall be awarded unless the motion was "substantially justified" or an award would be unjust.[91] A similar procedure applies in lieu of or in addition to other sanctions authorized by FRCP 37(b)(2) for failure to comply with a court order.

"[T]he rule [regarding payment of expenses] is mandatory unless one of the conditions for not making an award is found to exist."[92] Thus, "[t]he great operative principle of [the rule] is that the loser pays."[93] The award may be made against the offending party or deponent or his or her counsel or both, depending upon who is at fault.[94] Clearly, the drafters hoped that the fact that the expenses of a motion to compel or for sanctions *will* presumptively be imposed on the offending party or on counsel or both would operate to discourage obstructionist tactics and reduce discovery disputes largely to those in which genuine and reasonable disagreements exist.

---

89 *See Arctic Cat, Inc. v. Injection Research Specialists, Inc.*, 210 F.R.D. 680, 683 (D. Minn. 2002).

90 FRCP 37(a)(4)(A); *Cobell v. Norton*, 213 F.R.D. 16, 28 (D.D.C. 2003) (further deposition ordered; reasonable expenses, including attorneys' fees, to plaintiffs on motion to compel per FRCP 37(a)(4)(A); award against counsel personally); *see Harp v. Citty*, 161 F.R.D. 398 (E.D. Ark. 1995). The costs of the motion may be recovered under FRCP 37 but not those incurred in preparing the underlying discovery requests. *Tollett v. City of Kemah*, 285 F.3d 357, 367–68 (5th Cir.), *cert. denied*, 537 U.S. 883 (2002); *see Hoffman v. UPS*, 206 F.R.D. 506, 508 (D. Kan. 2002) (cost of preparatory work for deposition not awarded). However, the added costs of a second deposition may also be imposed on the obstructive counsel for the witness. *Auscape Int'l v. Nat'l Geographic Soc'y*, 2002 U.S. Dist. LEXIS 16675 (S.D.N.Y. Sept. 6, 2002).

91 FRCP 37(a)(4)(B).

92 8A Wright, *supra* note 78, § 2288, at 664 (footnotes omitted); *see Interactive Prods. Corp. v. a2z Mobile Office Solutions Inc.*, 326 F.3d 687, 700 (6th Cir. 2003); *Cobell*, 213 F.R.D. at 28; *Hoffman*, 206 F.R.D. at 507 (award of expenses mandatory unless exceptions apply).

93 8A Wright, *supra* note 78, § 2288, at 657–58 (footnote omitted).

94 *See, e.g.*, *Hoffman*, 206 F.R.D. at 507 (sanctions should not be imposed on party unless party responsible; court will hold attorney responsible); *Starlight Int'l, Inc. v. Herlihy*, 190 F.R.D. 587, 593 (D. Kan. 1999).

Although expenses are presumptively to be awarded, the conditions that would outweigh the presumption "are themselves broad enough that the court retains some discretion in the matter."[95] What is "substantially justified" is shown by whether there was a genuine dispute or whether reasonable persons could differ about the matter.[96] In order for an award of expenses to be made, it is not necessary to establish that the unsuccessful person was acting in bad faith.[97] The burden of showing substantial justification is on the unsuccessful person.[98]

As noted, when the movant establishes that there has been "any impediment, delay, or other conduct [that] has frustrated the fair examination of the deponent" at a deposition, the court is also authorized by FRCP 30(d)(3) to impose upon the person or persons at fault "an appropriate sanction, including the reasonable costs and attorney's fees incurred by any parties as a result thereof."[99]

If the attorney for the deponent directs a witness not to answer a question at a deposition on a ground other than privilege or prior court limita-

---

95 8A Wright, *supra* note 78, § 2288, at 664.

96 *Pierce v. Underwood*, 487 U.S. 552, 565 (1988); *Maddow v. Procter & Gamble Co.*, 107 F.3d 846, 853 (11th Cir. 1997) (substantial justification in relying upon Supreme Court dictum and out-of-circuit case law); *Mitchell v. Nat'l R.R. Passenger Corp.*, 217 F.R.D. 53, 55 (D.D.C. 2003); *Cobell*, 213 F.R.D. at 28 (reasonable persons could not differ regarding privilege asserted at deposition (communications between attorney and client regarding scheduling are not privileged, especially when disclosed in open court); sanctions awarded per FRCP 37(a)(4)(A)); *Cobell*, 213 F.R.D. at 14–15 (no sanctions because reasonable persons could differ about application of privilege and work product doctrine to testimony and documents); *Bowne of New York City, Inc. v. AmBase Corp.*, 161 F.R.D. 258, 265 (S.D.N.Y. 1995) ("Courts must be careful not to chill the imaginative use of advocacy in pursuit of changing the law."); 8A Wright, *supra* note 78, § 2288, at 665–66.

97 *Telluride Mgmt. Solutions v. Telluride Inv. Group*, 55 F.3d 463, 466 (9th Cir. 1995), *overruled on other grounds by Cunningham v. Hamilton County*, 527 U.S. 198 (1999); *Cobell*, 213 F.R.D. at 29.

98 *Telluride Mgmt. Solutions*, 55 F.3d at 466.

99 *Antonino-Garcia v. Shadrin*, 208 F.R.D. 298 (D. Or. 2002) (witness refused to answer questions and her "supporter" interfered with process; plaintiffs could move per FRCP 30(d)(3), as well as FRCP 37(a)(2)(B); further deposition ordered; costs to plaintiffs for attorneys' and court reporter fees); *Morales v. Zondo, Inc.*, 204 F.R.D. 50, 53, 57–58 (S.D.N.Y. 2001) (improper directions not to answer, consultations, coaching, etc.; offending counsel ordered to reimburse plaintiff for transcript cost and to pay plaintiff's attorneys' fees; defendant ordered to produce witness if plaintiff wished to depose him again); *Bristol-Myers Squibb Co. v. Rhone-Poulenc Rorer, Inc.*, 1998 U.S. Dist. LEXIS 12 (S.D.N.Y. Jan. 6, 1998) (Patterson, J.) (directions not to answer invalid; depositions to be resumed, with witnesses to be made available at defendant's expense; costs of the motion to plaintiff); *Riddell Sports, Inc. v. Brooks*, 158 F.R.D. 555, 558 (S.D.N.Y. 1994) (wasted time at depositions because of questioning on irrelevant issues does not justify protective order against harassment sufficient to stop depositions; questions primarily concerned relevant topics; FRCP 30(d)(3) and 45)).

tion, he or she should move pursuant to FRCP 30(d)(4),[100] under which the provisions of FRCP 37(a)(4) apply to the award of expenses incurred in relation to the motion. As a result, the court "must award sanctions if the objection was not substantially justified."[101] The objecting party takes that action "at its own peril if it is wrong on the merits of its objection."[102]

Thus, for conduct that interferes with a fair examination, such as speaking objections, coaching, unauthorized consultations during pending questions and improper directions not to answer, the court has tools to penalize the misconduct and prevent it in the future.

F. Discretion under FRCP 37

The court has broad discretion when it comes to the imposition of sanctions pursuant to FRCP 37 and the nature of any to be awarded.[103]

> The appropriateness of a given sanction is not guided by any firmly defined rules or doctrines. Clearly a sanction should be "just," in accordance with the terms of Rule 37(d), and should also serve the three general purposes [of preventing benefit to a wrongdoer, serving as a specific deterrent and serving as a general deterrent in the case at hand and other cases]. Within those general guidelines, the Second Circuit has chosen to allow the district courts to exercise their sound discretion in determining which sanctions are appropriate in a specific case.[104]

G. Other Bases for Sanctions

Sanctions are also authorized by 28 U.S.C. section 1927 when an attorney engages in misconduct at a deposition in a federal case. Sanctions are

---

100   FRCP 30(d)(1).

101   *Miller v. Waseca Med. Ctr.*, 205 F.R.D. 537, 539 (D. Minn. 2002).

102   *Id.*; *see Boyd v. Univ. of Md. Med. Sys.*, 173 F.R.D. 143, 146 (D. Md. 1997). The court in *Boyd* set forth factors it would consider as to whether sanctions should be imposed under FRCP 37 when an attorney directs a witness not to answer a question. *Id.* at 147.

103   *Reilly v. NatWest Mkts. Group*, 181 F.3d 253, 267 (2d Cir. 1999), *cert. denied*, 528 U.S. 1119 (2000) (discretion to sanction a party for discovery abuses, whether pursuant to FRCP 37 or inherent power); *Valentine v. Museum of Modern Art*, 29 F.3d 47, 49 (2d Cir. 1994); *Daval Steel Prods. Div. of Francosteel Corp. v. M/V Fakredine*, 951 F.2d 1357, 1365 (2d Cir. 1991); *Update Art, Inc. v. Modiin Pub., Ltd.*, 843 F.2d 67, 71 (2d Cir. 1988); *Cobell v. Norton*, 213 F.R.D. 16, 28 (D.D.C. 2003); *Davidson v. Dean*, 204 F.R.D. 251, 255 (S.D.N.Y. 2001).

104   *Williams v. Nat'l Hous. Exch. Inc.*, 165 F.R.D. 405, 408 (S.D.N.Y. 1996) (Baer, J.).

awarded under this provision only when the conduct demonstrates intentional or reckless disregard of counsel's duties to the court. Sanctions also may be awarded under the federal court's inherent powers if an attorney acts in bad faith. However, the court must exercise restraint since the power is significant and unconstrained by legislative action.[105]

H. What Not to Do

The fact that one attorney at a deposition engages in misconduct does not provide an excuse for the other attorney to respond in kind.[106] The victimized attorney should instead seek a ruling or resort as appropriate to a motion to compel or for sanctions.

---

105   *Carroll v. Jaques Admiralty Law Firm P.C.*, 110 F.3d 290 (5th Cir. 1997); *Morales v. Zondo, Inc.*, 204 F.R.D. 50 (S.D.N.Y. 2001); *Higginbotham v. KCS Int'l, Inc.*, 202 F.R.D. 444 (D. Md. 2001).

106   *See Higginbotham*, 202 F.R.D. 444; *McDonough v. Keniston*, 188 F.R.D. 22 (D.N.H. 1998); *Ethicon Endo-Surgery v. U.S. Surgical Corp.*, 160 F.R.D. 98, 100 (S.D. Ohio 1995).

CHAPTER EIGHT

CORRECTIONS TO THE DEPOSITION

Once the deposition is concluded, the transcript will be prepared and certified by the court reporter and submitted to the witness for review and signature. This chapter discusses a number of important aspects to the process of making corrections.

I. STATE PRACTICE

Upon completion of the deposition, the transcript must be given to the witness to read and make "any changes in form or substance which the witness desires to make."[1] The witness should not edit or alter the body of the transcript. Rather, these changes, along with a statement of the witness's reasons for making them, are to be entered at the end of the transcript on an errata sheet. The witness must not list the corrections without the reasons therefor.[2] This requirement is important. If the witness does not provide reasons for the corrections being made, the court may reject the proffered corrections.

Changes may be made because the transcript inaccurately records what the witness said, or because the witness better understands the question or remembers now facts she could not recall at the deposition, or simply because she made a mistake at the deposition. The more noteworthy the changes being made, the greater the need for a detailed and thorough explanation of why the same answer was not or could not have been given at the deposition.[3] The original answer, the corrections and the reasons therefor may be used at trial to challenge the witness's credibility.

The witness must sign the transcript before an officer authorized to administer an oath. Some witnesses fail to sign the deposition, and some refuse to do so. Nonparty witnesses particularly can be, let us say, independent-minded. Absent the signature, the deposition would at least present a problem at trial, and its weight might be weakened in the minds of the jurors. Therefore, if the transcript is not signed and returned within 60 days, it can be used just as if it had been signed.[4] Further, the witness may

---

1   CPLR 3116(a); *see Boyce v. Vazquez,* 249 A.D.2d 724, 671 N.Y.S.2d 815 (3d Dep't 1998); *In re Will of Mancuso,* 196 Misc. 2d 897, 764 N.Y.S.2d 800 (Surr. Ct., Kings Co. 2003).

2   *See Principale v. Lewner,* 187 Misc. 2d 878, 724 N.Y.S.2d 575 (Sup. Ct., Kings Co. 2001).

3   Manifest transcription errors or the like require little explanation. An important alteration in the substance of the testimony requires a different approach. *See Zamir v. Hilton Hotels Corp.,* 304 A.D.2d 493, 758 N.Y.S.2d 645 (1st Dep't 2003).

4   CPLR 3116(a); *Chisholm v. Mahoney,* 302 A.D.2d 792, 756 N.Y.S.2d 314 (3d Dep't 2003); *Morchik v. Trinity Sch.,* 257 A.D.2d 534, 684 N.Y.S.2d 534 (1st Dep't 1999); *Thomas v. Hampton Express, Inc.,* 208 A.D.2d 824, 617 N.Y.S.2d 831 (2d Dep't 1994).

not make any changes more than 60 days after submission of the transcript to him or her.[5]

If corrections are made after the 60-day deadline, the untimeliness may not necessarily be fatal. The deadline is presumably subject to extension pursuant to CPLR 2004.[6] However, such an extension requires a showing of good cause.[7] "[C]ourts should be circumspect about extending the 60-day period inasmuch as 'any indication from the courts that an extension will be allowed without a strong showing of justification will quickly evolve a dilatory attitude that can undermine the purpose of CPLR 3116(a)'s time limit altogether.'"[8] The deponent who is unable to justify a delay is perhaps best left to deal with cross-examination at trial if her testimony there should depart in some significant respect from the deposition transcript.[9]

If the deponent presents an errata sheet in a timely manner and it attempts to explain why the changes were necessary and justified, there may be little limit upon how dramatic the changes can be. This issue is an important one, both to the deponent, who should have it well in mind when considering or making corrections to a transcript, and to all parties.[10]

The officer before whom the deposition was taken must certify that the witness was duly sworn by him or her and that the deposition is a true record of the testimony given.[11] Although the rule provides for filing of the transcript with the clerk of the court,[12] the parties customarily will

---

5   CPLR 3116(a).

6   *See Zamir*, 304 A.D.2d 493 (citing Siegel, McKinney's Practice Commentary, CPLR 3116 (1991)).

7   *See id.* at 493 (no showing of good cause made).

8   *Id.* at 494; *see Sheikh v. Sinha*, 272 A.D.2d 465, 707 N.Y.S.2d 241 (2d Dep't 2000) (attempt to change deposition answers 18 months after they were due rejected); *cf. Binh v. Bagland USA, Inc.*, 286 A.D.2d 613, 730 N.Y.S.2d 317 (1st Dep't 2001) (errata sheet prepared three months after deposition and seven months before summary judgment motion by adversaries acceptable; correction "[did] not appear to be patently untrue or tailored to avoid the consequences of [plaintiff's] earlier testimony, made as it was before defendants moved for summary judgment"); *Rodriguez v. OD&P Constr.*, 194 Misc. 2d 284, 752 N.Y.S.2d 799 (Sup. Ct., Bronx Co. 2002) (errata sheet allowed 47 days late on motion for extension of time); *compare Zamir*, 304 A.D.2d 493, *with Chisholm*, 302 A.D.2d 792 (discussed in David D. Siegel, *Siegel's Practice Review*, No. 139, at 2 (Sept. 2003)).

9   *See Binh*, 286 A.D.2d 613; *Rodriguez*, 194 Misc. 2d 284.

10   As this issue may arise in the context of a motion for summary judgment, it is discussed in chapter 10, which addresses that subject.

11   CPLR 3116(b).

12   *Id.*

stipulate to waive the filing of the transcript. The officer should annex to the transcript any exhibits marked at the deposition or, upon request, return them to the party who produced them if an opportunity to copy or inspect was provided.[13]

The expenses of the deposition, principally the cost of transcription or, perhaps more significant, of videotaping, are normally borne by the party who took it.[14] Usually included is the cost of providing copies to the other parties, absent agreement otherwise.[15] Deposition costs may be taxed at the end of the case.[16]

A deponent may make a motion to suppress the deposition, in whole or in part, because of errors of the officer or problems with the transcript.[17] Such a motion must be made with reasonable promptness after the difficulties are, or should have been, noted.[18] Of course, because the deponent is afforded ample opportunity to correct errors in the transcript, there will often be little need to use the option of suppression. Moreover, such a motion has the disadvantage from the point of view of the witness's attorney of possibly reopening the deposition for the adversary.[19] Errors must be prejudicial for suppression to be ordered.[20]

II. FEDERAL PRACTICE

Upon request of the deponent or a party prior to the conclusion of the deposition and after notification by the officer that the transcript, video-

---

13   CPLR 3116(c).

14   CPLR 3116(d). The court may order otherwise.

15   *Kamp v. Miller*, 175 Misc. 2d 516, 670 N.Y.S.2d 670 (App. Term 2d Dep't 1997); *Brown v. Univ. of Rochester Strong Mem'l Hosp.*, 77 Misc. 2d 221, 353 N.Y.S.2d 666 (Sup. Ct., Monroe Co.), *aff'd*, 46 A.D.2d 1016, 363 N.Y.S.2d 321 (4th Dep't 1974); 6 J. Weinstein, H. Korn & A. Miller, New York Civil Practice ¶ 3116.12 (2004). CPLR 3116(d) authorizes the court to order a different arrangement when justified. *See Brown*, 77 Misc. 2d at 223.

16   CPLR 8301(a)(9). The statute allows for the inclusion in taxable disbursements of the reasonable expense of taking and making two transcripts of a deposition. However, this aspect of taxable disbursements may not exceed $250, which will usually be well below the actual expense incurred.

17   CPLR 3116(e).

18   *Id.*; *see Cox v. Jeffers*, 222 A.D.2d 395, 634 N.Y.S.2d 519 (2d Dep't 1995) (certification by court reporter who had not been present improper; transcripts suppressed).

19   *See Principale v. Lewner*, 187 Misc. 2d 878, 724 N.Y.S.2d 575 (Sup. Ct., Kings Co. 2001).

20   *See id.*; *In re Will of Mancuso*, 196 Misc. 2d 897, 901, 764 N.Y.S.2d 800 (Surr. Ct., Kings Co. 2003) ("[s]uppression under CPLR 3116(e) . . . is a drastic remedy").

tape or other record is available, the deponent has 30 days within which to review the transcript and make corrections.[21] The witness shall sign a statement setting forth the changes, which can be "changes in form or substance," and the reasons for making them.[22] The officer is to indicate in his or her certification whether review was requested and, if so, to attach any changes made during the period allowed. The deponent must not alter the original transcript.

The requirements that the deponent request, prior to completion of the deposition, an opportunity to make corrections and that the officer certify as much are absent in state practice. If there is no certification reflecting such a request, later changes will be untimely; even if there is a certification, changes must be made within 30 days or they will be untimely.[23]

The courts have required strict adherence to the mandate that reasons be given for the changes made.[24] The reasons must not be set out in a conclusory manner.[25] The changes ordinarily should be made by identifying the page and line of the transcript affected by each change.[26]

The cases disagree as to whether there are any restrictions on the kind of changes that can be made to the transcript. As noted, FRCP 30(e) speaks of "changes in form or substance." It does not qualify these terms, which would seem to indicate that the changes can go so far as to be contradictory and unconvincing. However, some courts have rejected such a read-

---

21   FRCP 30(e).

22   *Id.*; see Appendix, "Changes to Deposition (FRCP 30(e))" (federal form).

23   *Griswold v. Fresenius USA, Inc.*, 978 F. Supp. 718, 722 (N.D. Ohio 1997) (untimely changes to a deposition were unacceptable as mere supplementation of discovery responses under FRCP 26(e)); *Blackthorne v. Posner*, 883 F. Supp. 1443, 1454 n.16 (D. Or. 1995).

24   *DeLoach v. Philip Morris Cos.*, 206 F.R.D. 568, 570 (M.D.N.C. 2002); *Holland v. Cedar Creek Mining, Inc.*, 198 F.R.D. 651, 653 (S.D. W.Va. 2001) (motion to exclude changes granted for lack of reasons); *Duff v. Lobdell-Enery Mfg. Co.*, 926 F. Supp. 799, 804 (N.D. Ind. 1996) (changes stricken for lack of reasons).

25   *Summerhouse v. HCA Health Servs.*, 216 F.R.D. 502, 509–11 (D. Kan. 2003) (some reasons clear and allowed; some not understandable and conclusory and disallowed); *Tingley Sys., Inc. v. CSC Consulting, Inc.*, 152 F. Supp. 2d 95, 120 (D. Mass. 2001); *Hawthorne Partners v. AT&T Techs.*, 831 F. Supp. 1398, 1406–1407 (N.D. Ill. 1993).

26   *Summerhouse*, 216 F.R.D. at 510.

ing as permitting deponents to undermine the deposition process.[27] In *Greenway v. International Paper Co.*,[28] the court stated that the obvious purpose of the rule was to permit correction of typographical errors, not all other changes, including changes of substance:

> The Rule cannot be interpreted to allow one to alter what was said under oath. If that were the case, one could merely answer the questions with no thought at all then return home and plan artful responses. Depositions differ from interrogatories in that regard. A deposition is not a take home examination.[29]

Some cases suggest that *Greenway* and the like represent the "modern trend,"[30] but that proposition is debatable. In any event, the *Greenway* view is not universal. Other courts, including the Second Circuit, take a more relaxed approach to the process.[31] In this approach, as long as the mechanics set forth in FRCP 30(e) are complied with, contradictory or unconvincing changes can be made, because the rule does not limit the nature of the changes, permitting "changes in form *or substance*,"[32] and does not assign the court any role in evaluating proposed changes.[33]

---

27 *Burns v. Bd. of County Comm'rs*, 330 F.3d 1275 (10th Cir. 2003); *Garcia v. Pueblo Country Club*, 299 F.3d 1233, 1242 n.5 (10th Cir. 2002); *Wigg v. Sioux Falls Sch. Dist.*, 274 F. Supp. 2d 1084, 1090–1093 (D.S.D. 2003), *aff'd in part, rev'd in part on other grounds*, 382 F.3d 807 (8th Cir. 2004); *Rios v. Welch*, 856 F. Supp. 1499, 1502 (D. Kan. 1994), *aff'd sub nom. Rios v. Bigler*, 67 F.3d 1543 (10th Cir. 1995); *Greenway v. Int'l Paper Co.*, 144 F.R.D. 322 (W.D. La. 1992); *see Thorn v. Sundstrand Aerospace Corp.*, 207 F.3d 383, 389 (7th Cir. 2000) (Posner, C.J.). In *Summerhouse*, 216 F.R.D. 502, the court, after an extensive analysis, concluded that FRCP 30(e) permits all changes to be made to a deposition except for certain material ones. Material changes that should be barred would be determined by application of a series of factors. *Id.* at 507 (following *Burns*, 330 F.3d 1275).

28 144 F.R.D. 322.

29 *Id.* at 325.

30 *SEC v. Parkersburg Wireless, LLC*, 156 F.R.D. 529, 535 (D.D.C. 1994).

31 *See, e.g., Podell v. Citicorp Diners Club*, 112 F.3d 98, 103 (2d Cir. 1997); *Foutz v. Town of Vinton*, 211 F.R.D. 293, 294–95 (W.D. Va. 2002); *DeLoach v. Philip Morris Cos.*, 206 F.R.D. 568, 572 (M.D.N.C. 2002) (citing numerous cases); *Tingley Sys., Inc. v. CSC Consulting, Inc.*, 152 F. Supp. 2d 95, 118–21 (D. Mass. 2001); *Holland v. Cedar Creek Mining, Inc.*, 198 F.R.D. 651, 653 (S.D. W.Va. 2001); *Elwell v. Conair, Inc.*, 145 F. Supp. 2d 79, 84–87 (D. Me. 2001); *Innovative Mktg. & Tech., L.L.C. v. Norm Thompson Outfitters*, 171 F.R.D. 203 (W.D. Tex. 1997); *United States ex rel. Burch v. Piqua Eng'g, Inc.*, 152 F.R.D. 565, 566–67 (S.D. Ohio), *aff'd*, 1993 U.S. Dist. LEXIS 17118 (S.D. Ohio Apr. 1, 1993).

32 FRCP 30(e) (emphasis added).

33 *Podell*, 112 F.3d at 103.

The witness's original testimony must and will remain unaltered[34] and can be used against the deponent at trial to challenge his or her credibility. Further, as noted, the deponent must explain why the changes are being made, and the explanation can also be used, probed and tested at trial.[35] These facts create a disincentive for the witness to prevaricate. If the witness constructs "artful responses" as convenience and self-interest suggest, "jurors should be able to discern the artful nature of the changes."[36]

The unscrupulous witness is further constrained by the fact that the court may allow the deposition to be reopened if the changes made are so extensive and significant as to render the deposition incomplete or useless.[37] In the reopened deposition, the adversary will be allowed to inquire into the changes, the reasons therefor and the facts at issue. The prevaricating witness would seem to have little chance to accomplish much by "editing" the transcript to "improve" it if, in the process of doing so, he renders it at least incomplete in regard to the issues addressed and opens himself to further questioning.[38]

Beyond these considerations arising out of FRCP 30(e), the problem can also surface in the context of summary judgment. As to whether a deponent is constrained in any respect from making or using alterations to the deposition in that context, see the discussion in chapter 10 regarding depositions and motions for summary judgment.

A big risk at this point is a client who only glances at the deposition, makes no changes and then at trial finds his or her credibility attacked because of an error that could have been, but was not, corrected when he or she reviewed, or was supposed to review, the transcript. This, of course, is an area in which the lawyer too might be negligent, so counsel should be sure to impress upon the client the importance of reading the transcript and, if need be, discussing with counsel the changes to be made.

---

34   *Id.*; *Innovative Mktg. & Tech., L.L.C.*, 171 F.R.D. at 205.

35   *LaMarche v. Metro. Life Ins. Co.*, 236 F. Supp. 2d 34, 40–41 (D. Me. 2002) (change of substance made in errata sheet; fatigue and confusion, stated reasons, legitimate bases for correcting deposition); *Innovative Mktg. & Tech., L.L.C.*, 171 F.R.D. at 205; *United States ex rel. Burch*, 152 F.R.D. at 566–67.

36   *Elwell v. Conair, Inc.*, 145 F. Supp. 2d 79, 87 (D. Me. 2001).

37   *Foutz v. Town of Vinton*, 211 F.R.D. 293, 294–95 (W.D. Va. 2002) (substance of prior testimony changed in 19 pages of errata sheets; deposition reopened); *Tingley Sys., Inc. v. CSC Consulting, Inc.*, 152 F. Supp. 2d 95, 121 (D. Mass. 2001) (depositions reopened); *Innovative Mktg. & Tech., L.L.C.*, 171 F.R.D. at 205.

38   *Holland v. Cedar Creek Mining, Inc.*, 198 F.R.D. 651, 653 (S.D. W.Va. 2001).

The officer must certify that the witness was sworn and that the transcript is an accurate record.[39] The officer will then send it to the attorney who arranged for it.[40]

Documents or things produced for inspection during the deposition shall, upon request of a party, be marked for identification and annexed to the transcript. They may be inspected and copied by any party. The person who produced the materials may retain them while affording parties an opportunity to copy them or to compare copies to the originals.[41]

The basic notion is that each party normally bears its own costs on depositions.[42] The expenses of depositions, including the cost of the transcript, may, however, be awarded as costs to the victorious party.[43] Where depositions in foreign countries are required and the party that needs the deposition is far less able to fund the trip, application to the court for a modification can, on occasion, be fruitful.

---

39   FRCP 30(f).

40   *See* FRCP 5(d) (depositions are not to be filed until used in the proceeding or the court otherwise orders).

41   *See* FRCP 30(f).

42   *See* FRCP 30(f)(2).

43   *See* FRCP 54(d)(1).

CHAPTER NINE

USE OF THE DEPOSITION

I. STATE PRACTICE

The use of depositions at trial, on a motion[1] or in an interlocutory proceeding is governed by CPLR 3117.[2] Any part or all of a deposition may be used to the extent admissible under the rules of evidence. The deposition may be used as follows:

1. A deposition may be used by a party to impeach the deponent's testimony as a witness.[3]

2. The deposition of a party or party representative when the testimony was taken (i.e., officer, director, member, employee or managing or authorized agent) can be used for any purpose by an adverse party.[4]

3. The deposition of a person may be used by a party for any purpose against any other party who was present or represented at the deposition or had the required notice thereof[5] (1) when the court determines that the witness is dead, more than 100 miles away or out-of-state (such absence must not have been procured) or unable to testify because of age, illness, infirmity or imprisonment; (2) where the party offering the deposition has been unable to procure the witness's attendance despite diligent efforts; or (3) on motion or notice, in exceptional circumstances in the interest of justice and with due regard to the importance of live testimony.[6]

4. The deposition of a medical witness may be used by a party without the need to show unavailability or special circumstances (subject to protective orders as needed).[7]

---

1   *See, e.g., R.M. Newell Co. v. Rice*, 236 A.D.2d 843, 653 N.Y.S.2d 1004 (4th Dep't 1997).

2   CPLR 3117 parallels, and its language is based on, FRCP 32(a). CPLR 3117(c) is based on FRCP 32(a)(4). CPLR 3117(d) parallels FRCP 32(c).

3   CPLR 3117(a)(1).

4   CPLR 3117(a)(2); *Gonzalez v. Medina*, 69 A.D.2d 14, 417 N.Y.S.2d 953 (1st Dep't 1979). The party must have been adversely interested when the deposition was given or be adversely interested when the deposition is offered in evidence.

5   *Loschiavo v. DeBruyn*, 6 A.D.3d 1113, 776 N.Y.S.2d 416 (4th Dep't), *reh'g denied*, 779 N.Y.S.2d 798 (2004); *Bigelow v. Acands, Inc.*, 196 A.D.2d 436, 601 N.Y.S.2d 478 (1st Dep't 1993).

6   CPLR 3117(a)(3); *Goldblatt v. Avis Rent A Car Sys.*, 223 A.D.2d 670, 637 N.Y.S.2d 188 (2d Dep't 1996).

7   CPLR 3117(a)(4).

If a party reads part of a deposition, another party may read any other part which in fairness ought to be considered in connection therewith.[8] It is preferable, for all concerned, especially jurors, if the passages are read so that they follow contextually. Or, one lawyer may read all passages after an explanation by the lawyer or the court of precisely what is happening and why.

The substitution of parties does not affect the right to use previous depositions.[9] Depositions from any prior state or federal case may be used in a later action just as if taken therein when the same subject matter is involved and the parties or their representatives are the same.[10]

What is the consequence for a party of using a deposition? First, taking a deposition of a person does not automatically make him or her the witness of the questioning party.[11] Second, if a party uses all or part of a deposition for a purpose other than impeachment and other than pursuant to CPLR 3117(a)(2),[12] the result is to make the deponent the party's witness.[13]

The rule makes clear that depositions, to the extent admissible, may be used on motions.[14] It is, of course, common for depositions or excerpts therefrom to be used on motions for summary judgment. Under this rule, the testimony relied on for a motion must be admissible and used in accordance with CPLR 3117(a). Depositions and motions for summary judgment are discussed in the next chapter.

Importantly, the deposition can be used only to impeach, not as substantive evidence.[15] This practice contrasts with that concerning the deposition of an adverse party under CPLR 3117(a)(2), in which the deposition

---

8   CPLR 3117(b); *McGowan v. Kornos Taxi, Inc.*, 251 A.D.2d 466, 674 N.Y.S.2d 708 (2d Dep't 1998); *Bigelow*, 196 A.D.2d 436; *Gonzalez*, 69 A.D.2d 14.

9   CPLR 3117(c).

10   *Id.; see In re Eighth Judicial Dist. Asbestos Litig.*, 190 A.D.2d 1008, 595 N.Y.S.2d 574 (4th Dep't 1993); *Chin v. Ademaj*, 188 A.D.2d 579, 591 N.Y.S.2d 71 (2d Dep't 1992).

11   CPLR 3117(d).

12   CPLR 3117(a)(2) states that the deposition of a party or party representative may be used for any purpose by an adverse party.

13   *Id.* At trial, any party may rebut any relevant evidence in the deposition regardless of who introduced it.

14   CPLR 3117(a).

15   CPLR 3117(a)(1).

can be used for any purpose.[16] Further, the deposition of any person may be used only upon a showing of the person's unavailability,[17] whereas the deposition of an adverse party can be used for any purpose regardless of the availability of the deponent.

The deposition of a nonparty witness may be used for any purpose when diligent but unsuccessful efforts have been made to present that person at trial.[18] It apparently is insufficient merely to serve a subpoena upon the witness if the witness is within the jurisdiction of the court but refuses to appear. The party seeking to offer the deposition must attempt to enforce the subpoena by applying for an order of contempt.[19]

II. FEDERAL PRACTICE

The use of depositions in federal practice is governed by FRCP 32. Generally, of course, testimony at trial is to be offered live.[20] A deposition, in whole or part, may be used at trial, on a motion[21] or in an interlocutory proceeding to the extent admissible under the rules of evidence applied as though the witness were then testifying, against any party present or represented at the deposition or who had reasonable notice of it,[22] in accordance with a number of standards. The standards permit use of the deposition as follows:

1. A deposition may be used by a party to contradict or impeach the testimony of the deponent or for any other purpose allowed by the Federal

---

16   *Fanek v. City of Yonkers*, 287 A.D.2d 683, 732 N.Y.S.2d 99 (2d Dep't 2001); *State v. Markowitz*, 273 A.D.2d 637, 710 N.Y.S.2d 407 (3d Dep't 2000).

17   CPLR 3117(a)(3).

18   *Id.*; *Ramkison v. New York City Hous. Auth.*, 269 A.D.2d 256, 702 N.Y.S.2d 825 (1st Dep't 2000); *Daughtery v. City of New York*, 137 A.D.2d 441, 524 N.Y.S.2d 703 (1st Dep't 1988); *Iheme v. Simmons*, 148 Misc. 2d 223, 560 N.Y.S.2d 167 (Civ. Ct., Richmond Co. 1990).

19   *Miller v. Daub*, 128 Misc. 2d 1060, 492 N.Y.S.2d 703 (Civ. Ct., N.Y. Co. 1985).

20   *Hillman v. U.S. Postal Serv.*, 171 F. Supp. 2d 1174 (D. Kan. 2001); *Banks v. Yokemick*, 144 F. Supp. 2d 272, 288 (S.D.N.Y. 2001); *Bobrosky v. Vickers*, 170 F.R.D. 411, 413 (W.D. Va. 1997).

21   *See, e.g., Nippon Credit Bank, Ltd. v. Matthews*, 291 F.3d 738, 750–51 (11th Cir. 2002); *Dorn v. Potter*, 191 F. Supp. 2d 612 (W.D. Pa. 2002); *see* FRCP 43(e), 56(c).

22   *Hub v. Sun Valley Co.*, 682 F.2d 776, 778 (9th Cir. 1982); *Acme Printing Ink Co. v. Menard Inc.*, 812 F. Supp. 1498, 1523 (E.D. Wis. 1992). Courts have held that depositions also may be used against a party who was not present, represented or noticed when another party having the same motive to question the witness was present or represented. *See, e.g., Ikerd v. Lapworth*, 435 F.2d 197, 205–206 (7th Cir. 1970); *Mid-West Nat'l Life Ins. Co. v. Breton*, 199 F.R.D. 369, 371 (N.D. Fla. 2001); *Acme Printing Ink Co.*, 812 F. Supp. at 1523.

Rules of Evidence.[23] In federal court, impeachment is the most frequent use of deposition testimony (for which counsel must be sure there is something inconsistent in the testimony before reading it or else the jury will think ill of the effort).

2. An adverse party may use for any purpose the deposition of a party or of any person who, when the deposition was taken, was an officer, director or managing agent[24] of a party or a person designated pursuant to FRCP 30(b)(6) or FRCP 31(a) to testify on behalf of certain party entities (public or private corporation, partnership, association or governmental entity).[25]

3. The deposition of a party or nonparty witness may be used by a party for any purpose if (1) the witness is dead, more than 100 miles away or is abroad (unless the absence was procured)[26] or cannot testify because of age, sickness, infirmity or imprisonment; (2) the party offering the deposition was unable to procure attendance of the witness by subpoena; or (3) on application and notice, exceptional circumstances justify it, in the interest of justice and with due regard to the importance of live testimony.[27]

Substitution of parties does not affect the right to use prior depositions. Depositions properly taken in a previous state or federal case involving the same subject matter and the same parties or their representatives may be used.[28] A deposition previously taken may also be used as permitted by the Federal Rules of Evidence.[29] A deposition taken in the same or a different matter is admissible if the party against whom it is offered or a pre-

---

23 FRCP 32(a)(1).

24 *Reed Paper Co. v. Procter & Gamble Distrib. Co.*, 144 F.R.D. 2 (D. Me. 1992).

25 FRCP 32(a)(2).

26 *Daigle v. Maine Med. Ctr., Inc.*, 14 F.3d 684, 691 (1st Cir. 1994); *Fairchild 274–278 Clarendon Trust v. Dwek*, 970 F.2d 990, 994–95 (1st Cir. 1992).

27 FRCP 32(a)(3); *Banks v. Yokemick*, 144 F. Supp. 2d 272, 288 (S.D.N.Y. 2001); *First Sav. Bank, F.S.B. v. U.S. Bancorp*, 196 F.R.D. 608 (D. Kan. 2000); *Bobrosky v. Vickers*, 170 F.R.D. 411, 413 (W.D. Va. 1997). However, a deposition cannot be used against a party who receives less than 11 days' notice of it and promptly files a motion for a protective order seeking to bar, postpone or relocate the deposition, which motion is pending when the deposition is held. FRCP 32(a)(3). See the same rule with regard to a party who could not obtain counsel.

28 FRCP 32(a)(4); *Miwon, U.S.A., Inc. v. Crawford*, 629 F. Supp. 153, 154 n.3 (S.D.N.Y. 1985).

29 *Angelo v. Armstrong World Indus.*, 11 F.3d 957, 962–63 (10th Cir. 1993); *Clay v. Buzas*, 208 F.R.D. 636 (D. Utah 2002); *see, e.g.*, FRE 801, 804.

decessor in interest was provided with an opportunity and had a similar motive to question the deponent.[30]

If a party offers only part of a deposition in evidence, an adverse party may require the offering party to introduce any other part which in fairness ought to be considered with the former part. Any party may introduce any other parts.[31]

Federal Rule of Civil Procedure 32 does not draw a distinction between depositions taken for use at trial and those taken for discovery purposes.[32] Because FRCP 32(a)(3)(D) refers to a situation in which the party offering a deposition at trial has been "unable" to obtain the presence of a witness by means of a subpoena, it implies that reasonable diligence must have been used.[33]

Federal Rule of Civil Procedure 32(a)(3) does not support use of a deposition at trial unless the witness is unavailable.[34] When a party claims that a witness is sick, aged or otherwise unable to attend the trial, a showing is necessary that such disability in fact exists and precludes attendance.[35]

It is not only a party's need for the evidence in a deposition that determines whether it can be used pursuant to FRCP 32(a)(3)(E). Even serious prejudice is not alone decisive. The nature of the circumstances that led to the unavailability must be taken into account.[36] Courts in the United States

---

30　FRE 804(b)(1); *Nippon Credit Bank, Ltd. v. Matthews*, 291 F.3d 738, 751 (11th Cir. 2002); *McKnight v. Johnson Controls, Inc.*, 36 F.3d 1396, 1410 (8th Cir. 1994); *Rodriguez v. Pacificare of Texas, Inc.*, 980 F.2d 1014, 1020 (5th Cir. 1993); *Jean v. Dugan*, 814 F. Supp. 1401, 1405 (N.D. Ind. 1993), *aff'd*, 20 F.3d 255 (7th Cir. 1994); *see GAVCO, Inc. v. Chem-Trend Inc.*, 81 F. Supp. 2d 633, 638 (W.D.N.C. 1999).

31　FRCP 32(a)(4); *Mid-West Nat'l Life Ins. Co. v. Breton*, 199 F.R.D. 369, 371 (N.D. Fla. 2001). Unless otherwise ordered, a party presenting testimony may offer it in stenographic or other form, but, if it is the latter, the party must also provide the court with a transcript. FRCP 32(c).

32　*Chrysler Int'l Corp. v. Chemaly*, 280 F.3d 1358, 1362 n.8 (11th Cir. 2002); *Tatman v. Collins*, 938 F.2d 509, 510–11 (4th Cir. 1991); *Integra Lifesciences I, Ltd. v. Merck KgaA*, 190 F.R.D. 556, 558–59 (S.D. Cal. 1999); *United States v. IBM Corp.*, 90 F.R.D. 377, 381 (S.D.N.Y. 1981).

33　*Griman v. Makousky*, 76 F.3d 151, 154 (7th Cir. 1996); *In re Ashley*, 903 F.2d 599, 603 (9th Cir. 1990).

34　*Schwartz v. Sys. Software Assocs., Inc.*, 32 F.3d 284, 289 (7th Cir. 1994).

35　*Walling v. Holman*, 858 F.2d 79, 82 (2d Cir. 1988); *Boca Investerings P'ship v. United States*, 197 F.R.D. 18 (D.D.C. 2000).

36　*Griman*, 76 F.3d 151; *Angelo v. Armstrong World Indus.*, 11 F.3d 957, 963–64 (10th Cir. 1993); *Allgeier v. United States*, 909 F.2d 869, 876 (6th Cir. 1990).

have a strong preference for live testimony, especially when credibility is at issue.[37]

A party may use a deposition of an adverse party in compliance with FRCP 32(a)(2) for any purpose, including as substantive evidence, even if the deponent is available to testify. There is no need to demonstrate the unavailability of the witness.[38] However, courts have discretion and accordingly may limit the use of the deposition if it is repetitious or immaterial.[39]

As to whether a deposition should be available for use at trial because of "exceptional circumstances," the court should consider whether doing so is desirable in the interests of justice. But the court is also called upon to give due regard to "the importance of presenting the testimony of witnesses orally in open court."[40] Courts have looked to whether a particular set of circumstances can fairly be analogized to the exceptions set forth in FRCP 32(a)(3), which can provide guidance.[41]

Illustrative of possible claims of exceptional circumstances are cases in which a party seeks to use at trial a deposition of a physician whose schedule is extremely full with important medical commitments.[42] The party opposing an application on a claim of exceptional circumstances may argue that when the deposition was taken it was assumed that the witness would be available so that cross-examination had been forgone, curtailed or modified as a result and admission of the testimony would therefore be unfair.[43]

It was noted earlier that the rules of evidence have a basic role to play here. Federal Rule of Civil Procedure 32 creates an exception to the hear-

---

37   *Griman*, 76 F.3d 151; *Nash v. Heckler*, 108 F.R.D. 376 (W.D.N.Y. 1985).

38   *Coletti v. Cudd Pressure Control*, 165 F.3d 767, 773 (10th Cir. 1999); *King & King Enters. v. Champlin Petroleum Co.*, 657 F.2d 1147, 1163–64 (10th Cir. 1981), *cert. denied*, 454 U.S. 1164 (1982).

39   *Coletti*, 165 F.3d at 773; *King & King Enters.*, 657 F.2d at 1163–64.

40   FRCP 32(a)(3)(E); *see Bobrosky v. Vickers*, 170 F.R.D. 411, 414 (W.D. Va. 1997).

41   *Griman*, 76 F.3d at 153; *Bobrosky*, 170 F.R.D. at 413.

42   *Allgeier v. United States*, 909 F.2d 869 (6th Cir. 1990); *Bobrosky*, 170 F.R.D. 411 (showing based on fact of depositions and potential hostility of physicians if called was not sufficient); *Rubel v. Eli Lilly & Co.*, 160 F.R.D. 28 (S.D.N.Y. 1995) (Kaplan, J.) (court found adequate showing of unavailability (physician was handling a four-doctor practice alone); however, plaintiffs allowed to take additional deposition with defendants to have a right to cross-examine).

43   *Rubel*, 160 F.R.D. 28.

say rule for depositions.[44] Evidence authorized by FRCP 32(a) cannot be excluded on the grounds of hearsay unless it would be inadmissible even if delivered in the courtroom.[45]

Counsel must keep in mind FRE 804(b)(1). This rule creates a hearsay exception for former testimony if the declarant is unavailable[46] as a witness. Testimony is not excluded if given by a witness

> in a deposition taken in compliance with law in the course of the same or another proceeding, if the party against whom the testimony is now offered, or, in a civil action or proceeding, a predecessor in interest, had an opportunity and similar motive to develop the testimony by direct, cross, or redirect examination.[47]

This rule may provide a basis for the use of a deposition independent of FRCP 32.[48]

Federal Rule of Civil Procedure 32 may permit a deposition to be used at trial, but satisfaction of the rule's various specific criteria, discussed above, does not suffice to ensure its use. Such use also must be permitted by the rules of evidence.[49]

---

44 *Ueland v. United States*, 291 F.3d 993, 995–96 (7th Cir. 2002); *Angelo v. Armstrong World Indus.*, 11 F.3d 957 (10th Cir. 1993); *S. Ind. Broad., Ltd. v. Fed. Communications Comm'n*, 935 F.2d 1340, 1342 (D.C. Cir. 1991); *Clay v. Buzas*, 208 F.R.D. 636, 638 (D. Utah 2002); 5 Jack B. Weinstein & Margaret Berger, Weinstein's Federal Evidence § 804.04[1][a] (2d ed. 2004).

45 *Ueland*, 291 F.3d at 996; *see Moss v. Ole S. Real Estate, Inc.*, 933 F.2d 1300, 1311–12 (5th Cir. 1991).

46 FRE 804(a) defines *unavailability*.

47 FRE 804(b)(1); *see United States v. Salerno*, 505 U.S. 317 (1992); *McKnight v. Johnson Controls, Inc.*, 36 F.3d 1396, 1410 (8th Cir. 1994).

48 *Angelo*, 11 F.3d at 963; *Clay*, 208 F.R.D. at 638.

49 8A Charles A. Wright et al., Federal Practice and Procedure § 2142, at 159, § 2143 (2d ed. 1994).

CHAPTER TEN

DEPOSITIONS AND MOTIONS FOR SUMMARY JUDGMENT

Depositions are commonly used in support of, and in opposition to, motions for summary judgment. They are, indeed, vital tools on such motions. Therefore, an understanding of the key principles that apply to such motions, where and how depositions fit into summary judgment practice and the rules that apply to depositions in this context is important.

I. STATE PRACTICE

A. Summary Judgment in General

Summary judgment is the functional equivalent of a trial.[1] The movant on a motion for summary judgment has an obligation to produce evidence in support of the motion, and the party opposing it has the same duty. Depositions are expressly recognized as proof that may be used on such motions—the rule states that the motion must be supported by affidavit, a copy of the pleadings and "other available proof, such as depositions and written admissions."[2]

Any party may move for summary judgment after issue has been joined.[3] However, the court may set a deadline for the making of such a motion, which can be no earlier than 30 days after the filing of the note of issue. If no deadline is set, then a motion can be made no later than 120 days after filing of the note of issue, except with leave of court for good cause.[4]

---

1   *S.J. Capelin Assocs., Inc. v. Globe Mfg. Corp.*, 34 N.Y.2d 338, 341, 357 N.Y.S.2d 478, 313 N.E.2d 776 (1974).

2   CPLR 3212(b).

3   CPLR 3212(a).

4   *See Gonzalez v. 98 Mag Leasing Corp.*, 95 N.Y.2d 124, 711 N.Y.S.2d 131, 733 N.E.2d 203 (2000); *Slate v. State*, 284 A.D.2d 767, 728 N.Y.S.2d 523 (3d Dep't 2001) (failure to make summary judgment motion on time excusable where party was unable to obtain deposition on time under court-ordered schedule); *Di Rosario v. Williams*, 276 A.D.2d 583, 714 N.Y.S.2d 310 (2d Dep't 2000); *Andaloro v. Hidden Ponds Dev. Corp.*, 273 A.D.2d 185, 709 N.Y.S.2d 432 (2d Dep't 2000). The purpose of the deadline, established by the legislature at the urging of the chief administrative judge, is to eliminate or at least reduce the practice of filing CPLR 3212 motions on the eve of trial in order to delay the case or secure a transfer to another judge, which practice interfered with court calendars and case management and penalized the adversary, who may well have spent time and money preparing for trial. *John v. Bastien*, 178 Misc. 2d 664, 681 N.Y.S.2d 456 (Civ. Ct., Kings Co. 1998).

The proponent of the motion must demonstrate entitlement to judgment as a matter of law;[5] failure to do so will defeat the motion irrespective of the sufficiency of the papers submitted in opposition.[6] The movant must affirmatively show the merit of its claim or defense.[7] The affidavits submitted in support of the motion cannot be composed of conclusory assertions or allegations, speculation or mere hope, nor may the movant rely only upon the pleadings.[8] The movant must present evidentiary facts,[9] in admissible form.[10] The affiants must have personal knowledge of the facts.[11] The motion must be denied if any party shows facts sufficient to require a trial.[12]

> [T]he standard of "evidentiary proof in admissible form" is a term of art. Affidavits—written statements under oath—are almost never admissible as evidentiary proof at trial, yet they are one of the principal forms of permissible evidence on a motion for summary judgment. What is meant by "admissible form" in this context is that the statements made in the affidavit would be admissible were the affiant called to testify as a witness at trial.[13]

5   *Gonzalez*, 95 N.Y.2d 124; *Zuckerman v. City of New York*, 49 N.Y.2d 557, 562, 427 N.Y.S.2d 595, 404 N.E.2d 718 (1980); *Friends of Animals, Inc. v. Associated Fur Mfrs., Inc.*, 46 N.Y.2d 1065, 416 N.Y.S.2d 790, 390 N.E.2d 298 (1979); *Santanastasio v. Doe*, 301 A.D.2d 511, 753 N.Y.S.2d 122 (2d Dep't 2003); *Fillippo v. Russo*, 296 A.D.2d 374, 744 N.Y.S.2d 500 (2d Dep't 2002); *Borchardt v. N.Y. Life Ins. Co.*, 102 A.D.2d 465, 477 N.Y.S.2d 167 (1st Dep't), *aff'd*, 63 N.Y.2d 1000, 483 N.Y.S.2d 1012 (1984).

6   *Greenidge v. HRH Constr. Corp.*, 279 A.D.2d 400, 720 N.Y.S.2d 46 (1st Dep't 2001); *Pappalardo v. N.Y. Health & Racquet Club*, 279 A.D.2d 134, 718 N.Y.S.2d 287 (1st Dep't 2000).

7   *Peskin v. New York City Transit Auth.*, 304 A.D.2d 634, 757 N.Y.S.2d 594 (2d Dep't 2003).

8   *Kremer v. Buffalo Gen. Hosp.*, 269 A.D.2d 744, 703 N.Y.S.2d 622 (4th Dep't 2000).

9   *Zuckerman*, 49 N.Y.2d at 562; *Friends of Animals, Inc.*, 46 N.Y.2d 1065; *Indig v. Finkelstein*, 23 N.Y.2d 728, 296 N.Y.S.2d 370, 244 N.E.2d 61 (1968).

10   *Friends of Animals, Inc.*, 46 N.Y.2d 1065; *Santanastasio*, 301 A.D.2d 511; *Baez v. Sugrue*, 300 A.D.2d 519, 752 N.Y.S.2d 385 (2d Dep't 2002) (unsworn physicians' reports); *Fillippo*, 296 A.D.2d 374; *Republic W. Ins. Co. v. RCR Builders, Inc.*, 268 A.D.2d 574, 702 N.Y.S.2d 609 (2d Dep't 2000); *Desola v. Mads, Inc.*, 213 A.D.2d 445, 623 N.Y.S.2d 889 (2d Dep't 1995); *Borchardt*, 102 A.D.2d 465; *Allstate Ins. Co. v. Loester*, 177 Misc. 2d 372, 675 N.Y.S.2d 832 (Sup. Ct., Queens Co. 1998); *see Davis v. Golub Corp.*, 286 A.D.2d 821, 730 N.Y.S.2d 370 (3d Dep't 2001) (deposition testimony establishing prima facie lack of notice).

11   *Deronde Prods., Inc. v. Steve Gen. Contractor, Inc.*, 302 A.D.2d 989, 755 N.Y.S.2d 152 (4th Dep't 2003) (affidavit of attorney without personal knowledge of the facts of no probative value).

12   CPLR 3212(b). Under defined circumstances, an immediate trial may be ordered. CPLR 3212(c).

13   Vincent C. Alexander, *New York Practice: Opposing Summary Judgment with Hearsay*, N.Y.L.J., at 3 (Mar. 15, 2004) (hereinafter "Alexander").

If the movant makes out a prima facie case by means of a proper submission, it then falls to the party opposing the motion to rebut that showing and establish the existence of a genuine issue of material fact requiring a trial.[14] The opponent likewise cannot rest upon a repetition of allegations set forth in the pleadings or bills of particulars. Rather, the opponent must come forward with a demonstration, by way of evidentiary facts in admissible form, contesting the demonstration made by the movant and establishing the existence of triable issues of material fact.[15]

The party opposing a motion for summary judgment that sets out a prima facie case in proper form may not rely upon speculation, conjecture, conclusory assertions, self-serving statements or the mere hope that something may eventually come to light.[16] Witnesses must have personal knowledge of the facts.[17] An affidavit from an attorney lacking personal knowledge of the facts may be used as a vehicle to submit a deposition transcript or excerpts therefrom or to marshal proof presented in proper form elsewhere, and this is often done both in support of and in opposition to motions for summary judgment.[18]

However, an affidavit by an attorney who lacks personal knowledge of the facts is otherwise of no probative value. Speculation on the attorney's part as to what the facts are or will be shown to be at trial does not give

---

14 *Gonzalez v. 98 Mag Leasing Corp.*, 95 N.Y.2d 124, 129, 711 N.Y.S.2d 131, 733 N.E.2d 203 (2000).

15 *Id.*; *Zuckerman v. City of New York*, 49 N.Y.2d 557, 562, 427 N.Y.S.2d 595, 404 N.E.2d 718 (1980); *Friends of Animals, Inc. v. Associated Fur Mfrs., Inc.*, 46 N.Y.2d 1065, 416 N.Y.S.2d 790, 390 N.E.2d 298 (1979); *Indig v. Finkelstein*, 23 N.Y.2d 728, 296 N.Y.S.2d 370, 244 N.E.2d 61 (1968) (affidavits that referred to persons named in bill of particulars as witnesses but devoid of facts as to what their testimony would be, how that was known or where the witnesses were during the events held insufficient to defeat motion); *Borchardt v. N.Y. Life Ins. Co.*, 102 A.D.2d 465, 477 N.Y.S.2d 167 (1st Dep't 1984); *Ratut v. Singh*, 186 Misc. 2d 350, 718 N.Y.S.2d 135, 137 (Civ. Ct., Kings Co. 2000); *see, e.g., Chisholm v. Mahoney*, 302 A.D.2d 792, 756 N.Y.S.2d 314 (3d Dep't 2003) (deposition transcripts submitted describing a different version of the accident).

16 *Banco Popular N.A. v. Victory Taxi Mgm't, Inc.*, 1 N.Y.3d 381, 383–84, 774 N.Y.S.2d 480, 806 N.E.2d 488 (2004); *Gonzalez*, 95 N.Y.2d at 129; *Zuckerman*, 49 N.Y.2d at 562; *Friends of Animals, Inc.*, 46 N.Y.2d 1065; *Ehrlich v. Am. Moninger Greenhouse Mfg. Corp.*, 26 N.Y.2d 255, 309 N.Y.S.2d 341, 257 N.E.2d 890 (1970); *Leggio v. Gearhart*, 294 A.D.2d 543, 743 N.Y.S.2d 135 (2d Dep't 2002) (speculation by expert cannot defeat summary judgment); *Thomas v. Our Lady of Mercy Med. Ctr.*, 289 A.D.2d 37, 734 N.Y.S.2d 33 (1st Dep't 2001); *Ratut*, 186 Misc. 2d 350; *see Bockelmann v. New Paltz Golf Course*, 284 A.D.2d 783, 726 N.Y.S.2d 782 (3d Dep't 2001).

17 *Patti v. New York City Transit Auth.*, 296 A.D.2d 484, 745 N.Y.S.2d 558 (2d Dep't 2002).

18 *See, e.g., Blazer v. Tri-County Ambulette Serv.*, 285 A.D.2d 575, 728 N.Y.S.2d 742 (2d Dep't 2001) (submitted in support of motion).

rise to an issue of fact.[19] The requirement that evidentiary proof be submitted in admissible form means that, for example, hearsay statements cannot be relied upon on such a motion.[20] These requirements apply both with regard to fact witnesses and expert witnesses.[21]

The requirement for the submission of evidentiary proof in admissible form may be relaxed with regard to the party opposing the motion when that party presents an acceptable excuse for the failure to tender such proof in admissible form.[22] Provided there is an acceptable excuse for the failure to tender the evidence in proper, admissible form, hearsay can be used in opposition to a motion for summary judgment when the opponent of the motion properly identifies the witnesses, the substance of their testimony, how it is known what the testimony will be and how the witnesses acquired their knowledge.[23] "An underlying factor in a substantial proportion of the cases appears to be the fact that the defects in the opposition to

---

19 *Zuckerman*, 49 N.Y.2d at 563; *Karakostas v. Avis Rent A Car Sys.*, 301 A.D.2d 632, 756 N.Y.S.2d 61 (2d Dep't 2003); *Desola v. Mads, Inc.*, 213 A.D.2d 445, 623 N.Y.S.2d 889 (2d Dep't 1995); 7 Jack B. Weinstein et al., New York Civil Practice ¶ 3212.09 (2004).

20 *Goberdhan v. Waldbaum's Supermarket*, 295 A.D.2d 564, 745 N.Y.S.2d 46 (2d Dep't 2002); *Davis v. Golub Corp.*, 286 A.D.2d 821, 730 N.Y.S.2d 370 (3d Dep't 2001); *Siegel v. Terrusa*, 222 A.D.2d 428, 635 N.Y.S.2d 52 (2d Dep't 1995).

21 *Banco Popular N.A. v. Victory Taxi Mgm't, Inc.*, 1 N.Y.3d 381, 384, 774 N.Y.S.2d 480, 806 N.E.2d 488 (2004) (expert opinion must be in admissible form and be set forth with reasonable professional certainty; authenticity of signature); *Diaz v. N.Y. Downtown Hosp.*, 99 N.Y.2d 542, 754 N.Y.S.2d 195, 784 N.E.2d 68 (2002); *Fields v. S&W Realty Assocs.*, 301 A.D.2d 625, 754 N.Y.S.2d 348 (2d Dep't 2003); *Youthkins v. Cascio*, 298 A.D.2d 386, 751 N.Y.S.2d 216 (2d Dep't 2002); *Pollack v. Fitzgerald's Driving Sch., Inc.*, 272 A.D.2d 595, 708 N.Y.S.2d 165 (2d Dep't 2000). Bare conclusory allegations and assumed material facts in an expert affidavit would not be enough to defeat summary judgment. *Arias v. Flushing Hosp. Med. Ctr.*, 300 A.D.2d 610, 753 N.Y.S.2d 518 (2d Dep't 2002); *Merritt v. Saratoga Hosp.*, 298 A.D.2d 802, 750 N.Y.S.2d 140 (3d Dep't 2002); *Avella v. Jack LaLanne Fitness Ctrs.*, 272 A.D.2d 423, 707 N.Y.S.2d 678 (2d Dep't 2000) (affidavit of expert based on unauthenticated photos taken well after the accident; expert never visited site).

22 *Zuckerman*, 49 N.Y.2d at 562; *Friends of Animals, Inc. v. Associated Fur Mfrs., Inc.*, 46 N.Y.2d 1065, 416 N.Y.S.2d 790, 390 N.E.2d 298 (1979); *Fields*, 301 A.D.2d 625; *Barbour v. Knecht*, 296 A.D.2d 218, 743 N.Y.S.2d 483 (1st Dep't 2002); *Davis*, 286 A.D.2d 821 (hearsay); *Shapiro v. Butler*, 273 A.D.2d 657, 709 N.Y.S.2d 687 (3d Dep't 2000) (hearsay); *Arnold Herstand & Co. v. Gallery: Gertrude Stein, Inc.*, 211 A.D.2d 77, 626 N.Y.S.2d 74 (1st Dep't 1995); *State v. Metz*, 171 Misc. 2d 525, 654 N.Y.S.2d 989 (Sup. Ct., N.Y. Co. 1997), *modified, aff'd, remanded*, 241 A.D.2d 192, 671 N.Y.S.2d 79 (1st Dep't 1998); *see Phillips v. Joseph Kantor & Co.*, 31 N.Y.2d 307, 338 N.Y.S.2d 882, 291 N.E.2d 129 (1972) (testimony barred by the dead person's statute).

23 *Maniscalco v. Liro Eng'g Constr. Mgmt., P.C.*, 305 A.D.2d 378, 759 N.Y.S.2d 163 (2d Dep't 2003) (plaintiff did not offer excuse for failure to submit evidence in admissible form (hearsay)); *Gizzi v. Hall*, 300 A.D.2d 879, 754 N.Y.S.2d 373 (3d Dep't 2002); *Ratut v. Singh*, 186 Misc. 2d 350, 718 N.Y.S.2d 135 (Civ. Ct., Kings Co. 2000).

the motion are curable upon the trial of the action."[24] Whether an excuse will be acceptable depends upon the circumstances of the particular case.[25]

In one case, the affidavit of defendant driver was submitted in opposition to a motion for summary judgment. That affidavit ordinarily would have given rise to an issue of fact. The defendant, however, was precluded from testifying at the trial for failure to appear at a deposition. The defendant failed to show the existence of other admissible proof not then produced but that could be produced at trial, nor did defendant offer any excuse for the failure to appear at the deposition. Plaintiff's motion was granted.[26]

Courts have also ruled that proof in inadmissible form may be used in opposition to summary judgment as long as it is not the only proof submitted.[27] A third situation is one in which a statement is likely to be admissible pursuant to a hearsay exception.[28] The requirement for the submission of proof in admissible form will not be relaxed for the movant.[29]

As noted, the party opposing a motion for summary judgment must assemble and lay bare affirmative proof. Failure of the opponent of a proper motion for summary judgment to submit adequate opposition in proper

---

24   *Ratut*, 186 Misc. 2d at 353. Professor Alexander refers to these and similar cases as establishing the need for "hearsay plus." Alexander, *supra* note 13, at 6.

25   *Friends of Animals, Inc.*, 46 N.Y.2d 1065.

26   *Ratut*, 186 Misc. 2d 350.

27   *Thomas v. Our Lady of Mercy Med. Ctr.*, 289 A.D.2d 37, 734 N.Y.S.2d 33 (1st Dep't 2001) (hearsay only evidence regarding notice and causation; motion granted); *Wilbur v. Wilbur*, 266 A.D.2d 535, 699 N.Y.S.2d 103 (2d Dep't 1999) (deposition testimony relied on in opposition to motion was inadmissible hearsay insufficient to defeat motion); *Guzman v. L.M.P. Realty Corp.*, 262 A.D.2d 99, 691 N.Y.S.2d 483 (1st Dep't 1999) (hearsay evidence plus photographs sufficient to defeat summary judgment); *Sunfirst Fed. Credit Union v. Empire Ins. Co.*, 239 A.D.2d 894, 659 N.Y.S.2d 656 (4th Dep't 1997) (plaintiff failed to submit anything beyond hearsay in opposition to motion and offered no excuse for failing to do so; thus, no issue of fact presented); *Callari v. Pellitieri*, 130 A.D.2d 935, 516 N.Y.S.2d 371 (4th Dep't 1987).

28   Alexander, *supra* note 13, at 6 (citing, e.g., *Levbarg v. City of New York*, 282 A.D.2d 239, 723 N.Y.S.2d 445 (1st Dep't 2001)).

29   *Phillips v. Joseph Kantor & Co.*, 31 N.Y.2d 307, 338 N.Y.S.2d 882, 291 N.E.2d 129 (1972).

form establishing the existence of triable issues of material fact will result in the granting of the motion.[30]

If moving and opposition papers are presented in proper form, the role of the court is to look for material issues of fact that require a trial. It is not the court's function to weigh the proof and decide who is likely to prevail or to resolve disputes or determine credibility.[31] A jury must resolve those issues after an opportunity to consider all the proof, including the testimony of the witnesses, presented live or by deposition.

In looking for material issues of fact, the judge will examine the record in the light most favorable to the nonmoving party—the party opposing summary judgment.[32] Summary judgment is a drastic remedy. It will not be granted unless it is free from doubt.[33]

B. Affidavits and Depositions on Summary Judgment

Situations often arise in which one party to a case submits a deposition or excerpts therefrom in support of its motion for summary judgment. The

---

30   This is qualified by the possibility that, under FRCP 3212(f), the court may deny the motion or direct a continuance if it appears from the opposition affidavits that facts essential to the opposition exist but cannot then be stated. *Int'l Rescue Comm. v. Reliance Ins. Co.*, 230 A.D.2d 641, 646 N.Y.S.2d 112 (1st Dep't 1996). However, the opponent cannot successfully invoke this provision by vague assertions or by expressions of mere hope that something will eventually turn up. *See Karakostas v. Avis Rent A Car Sys.*, 301 A.D.2d 632, 756 N.Y.S.2d 61 (2d Dep't 2003); *Firth v. State*, 287 A.D.2d 771, 731 N.Y.S.2d 244 (3d Dep't 2001), *aff'd*, 98 N.Y.2d 365, 747 N.Y.S.2d 69, 775 N.E.2d 463 (2002); *Jones v. Surrey Coop. Apartments, Inc.*, 263 A.D.2d 33, 700 N.Y.S.2d 118 (1st Dep't 1999); *Steinberg v. Abdul*, 230 A.D.2d 633, 646 N.Y.S.2d 672 (1st Dep't 1996); *Lavin & Kleiman v. J.M. Heinike Assocs., Inc.*, 221 A.D.2d 919, 633 N.Y.S.2d 901 (4th Dep't 1995); *Wood v. Otherson*, 210 A.D.2d 473, 620 N.Y.S.2d 481 (2d Dep't 1994) (plaintiff had testified at deposition that her injuries had occurred during an assault by defendant; the argument that discovery might show that the injuries had been due to defendant's negligence was an expression of mere hope); *see Keeley v. Tracy*, 301 A.D.2d 502, 753 N.Y.S.2d 519 (2d Dep't 2003); *Hernandez v. Yonkers Contracting Co.*, 292 A.D.2d 422, 739 N.Y.S.2d 723 (2d Dep't 2002). A party seeking to invoke FRCP 3212(f) will fail if the absence of the discovery claimed to be necessary is the result of the party's failure to pursue disclosure with reasonable diligence. *Liberman v. Gelstein*, 80 N.Y.2d 429, 439, 590 N.Y.S.2d 857, 605 N.E.2d 344 (1992); *Karakostas*, 301 A.D.2d 632; *Firth*, 287 A.D.2d 771; *Cooper v. 6 W. 20th St. Tenants Corp.*, 258 A.D.2d 362, 685 N.Y.S.2d 245 (1st Dep't 1999).

31   *Mason v. Dupont Direct Fin. Holdings, Inc.*, 302 A.D.2d 260, 756 N.Y.S.2d 153 (1st Dep't 2003); *Herrin v. Airborne Freight Corp.*, 301 A.D.2d 500, 753 N.Y.S.2d 140 (2d Dep't 2003); *Schaufler v. Mengel, Metzger, Barr & Co., LLP*, 296 A.D.2d 742, 745 N.Y.S.2d 291 (3d Dep't 2002); *State v. Int'l Fid. Ins. Co.*, 272 A.D.2d 726, 708 N.Y.S.2d 504 (3d Dep't 2000); *Forman v. Fed. Express Corp.*, 194 Misc. 2d 441, 753 N.Y.S.2d 348 (Civ. Ct., N.Y. Co. 2003).

32   *Chisholm v. Mahoney*, 302 A.D.2d 792, 756 N.Y.S.2d 314 (3d Dep't 2003).

33   *Mason*, 302 A.D.2d 260; *Herrin*, 301 A.D.2d 500; *Grossman v. Amalgamated Hous. Corp.*, 298 A.D.2d 224, 750 N.Y.S.2d 1 (1st Dep't 2002); *Forman*, 194 Misc. 2d 441.

adversary, in an effort to stave off defeat, may be tempted to respond with an affidavit from the deponent "improving upon" the deposition transcript, "correcting" the weaknesses in it that the movant has fixed upon. One of the objectives of the deposition is to get a witness to commit to a position on the facts, to tie a witness down. This context is one in which the ties bind. If a witness testifies to certain facts at a deposition and the transcript or portions thereof are used by the adversary in support of a motion for summary judgment, the witness does not and should not have freedom to untie the knots in whatever manner is convenient at the time of the motion.

Generally, of course, as indicated, the court will not resolve issues of fact or credibility on a summary judgment motion. However, "[w]here a party submits an affidavit in opposition to a motion for summary judgment which is directly contrary to his or her deposition testimony, the affidavit will be rejected as a feigned attempt to avoid the consequences of the earlier admission."[34] An unexplained reversal of deposition testimony is inherently suspect as a basis for opposing summary judgment.[35]

Is there any comparable limitation on the right of a person to make corrections to his or her deposition pursuant to CPLR 3116(a)? When a court considers whether an affidavit contradicts a deposition in important respects, what is the "deposition" for this purpose? Are the corrections to be automatically included if made in compliance with the CPLR?

Corrections must be made in temporal proximity to the deposition session, and the errata sheet is an adjunct to the transcript.[36] However, some cases suggest that the court may evaluate corrections and might ignore

---

34   *Gadonniex v. Lombardi*, 277 A.D.2d 281, 282, 715 N.Y.S.2d 738 (2d Dep't 2000) (citations omitted) (affidavit as to conditions on sidewalk directly contrary to deposition testimony; rejected).

35   *Rodriguez v. New York City Hous. Auth.*, 304 A.D.2d 468, 758 N.Y.S.2d 53 (1st Dep't 2003); *see Sosna v. Am. Home Prods.*, 298 A.D.2d 158, 748 N.Y.S.2d 548 (1st Dep't 2002); *Harty v. Lenci*, 294 A.D.2d 296, 743 N.Y.S.2d 97 (1st Dep't 2002); *Krakowska v. Niksa*, 298 A.D.2d 561, 749 N.Y.S.2d 55 (2d Dep't 2002); *Goberdhan v. Waldbaum's Supermarket*, 295 A.D.2d 564, 745 N.Y.S.2d 46 (2d Dep't 2002); *Reed v. New York City Transit Auth.*, 299 A.D.2d 330, 749 N.Y.S.2d 91 (2d Dep't 2002); *Schiavone v. Brinewood Rod & Gun Club*, 283 A.D.2d 234, 726 N.Y.S.2d 615 (1st Dep't 2001) (constructive notice issue). *Accord Barretta v. Trump Plaza Hotel & Casino*, 278 A.D.2d 262, 717 N.Y.S.2d 333 (2d Dep't 2000); *Phillips v. Bronx Lebanon Hosp.*, 268 A.D.2d 318, 701 N.Y.S.2d 403 (1st Dep't 2000) (notice issue); *Prunty v. Keltie's Bum Steer*, 163 A.D.2d 595, 559 N.Y.S.2d 354 (2d Dep't 1990). *Cf. Bosshart v. Pryce*, 276 A.D.2d 314, 714 N.Y.S.2d 40 (1st Dep't 2000) (plaintiff's affidavit did not contradict her deposition, but rather raised questions of fact).

36   CPLR 3116(a). *See Sheikh v. Sinha*, 272 A.D.2d 465, 707 N.Y.S.2d 241 (2d Dep't 2000) (untimely attempt to amend transcript).

contradictory ones on the ground that they constitute a sham on a motion for summary judgment.

In *Boyce v. Vazquez*,[37] for example, a party argued that corrections should be ignored on a motion for summary judgment. The court rejected the argument because it is not the court's role on a motion for summary judgment to assess credibility "unless untruths are clearly apparent."[38] On the record before it, the court concluded that "plaintiff's corrections do not appear to be patently untrue as they conform to [defendant's] version of the accident," so that the credibility question should have been left to the jury.

In *Binh v. Bagland USA, Inc.*,[39] the court reached a similar result. The correction made there, the court stated, "[did] not appear to be patently untrue or tailored to avoid the consequences of [the witness's] earlier testimony, made as it was before defendants moved for summary judgment."[40]

Timely compliance with CPLR 3116(a) will be relevant and so will the timing of the motion for summary judgment. Under certain circumstances, these cases suggest, a court, notwithstanding its role as a finder of issues and not as an evaluator of credibility, may determine that the errata sheet is patently untrue or tailored to avoid the consequences of prior testimony.

II. FEDERAL PRACTICE

A. Summary Judgment in General

A claimant or a party against whom a claim, counterclaim or cross-claim is asserted may, with or without supporting affidavits, move for summary judgment or partial summary judgment.[41] Judgment shall be rendered "if the pleadings, depositions, answers to interrogatories, and admissions on file, together with the affidavits, if any, show that there is no

---

37 249 A.D.2d 724, 671 N.Y.S.2d 815 (3d Dep't 1998).

38 *Id*. at 726 (citations omitted).

39 286 A.D.2d 613, 730 N.Y.S.2d 317 (1st Dep't 2001).

40 *Id*. at 614; *see Prunty v. Keltie's Bum Steer*, 163 A.D.2d 595, 559 N.Y.S.2d 354 (2d Dep't 1990). In *Hazelhurst v. Brita Prods. Co.*, No. 603367/98 (Sup. Ct., N.Y. Co. Mar. 31, 2003) (Cahn, J.), *available at* www.nycourts.gov/comdiv/law_report_-_May_2003.html, the court disregarded errata sheets, as well as affidavits, on a motion for summary judgment because they conflicted with deposition testimony and were tailored to avoid the consequences thereof.

41 FRCP 56. FRCP 56(a) authorizes the claimant to move at any time after the expiration of 20 days from commencement of the action. FRCP 56(b) authorizes the defending party to move at any time.

genuine issue as to any material fact and that the moving party is entitled to a judgment as a matter of law."[42]

Affidavits on the motion shall be made on personal knowledge, set forth facts that would be admissible in evidence and show affirmatively that the affiant is competent to testify about the subjects contained in the affidavit.[43] Affidavits can be supplemented by depositions, as well as interrogatory answers or other affidavits. "Because a deposition is taken under oath and the deponent's responses are relatively spontaneous, it is one of the best forms of evidence for supporting or opposing a summary-judgment motion."[44]

The party moving for summary judgment bears the initial burden of informing the court of the grounds for the motion and indicating what parts of the pleadings, depositions, interrogatory answers and admissions on file, and affidavits, if any, support the motion. The movant also must establish that no trial is required and that judgment should be granted to the movant as a matter of law because no genuine issue of material fact exists.[45] The movant can meet this initial burden by presenting evidence showing that there is no dispute of material fact or that the other party has failed to present evidence in support of an element of its case on which it bears the ultimate burden of proof.[46]

If a motion is properly made and supported, the opposing party cannot simply cite to allegations or denials in its pleading.[47] Rather, to prevail and defeat the motion, the nonmoving party must make an active and serious response that grapples with the movant's position—that is, it must set forth "specific facts showing that there is a genuine issue for trial."[48]

---

42   FRCP 56(c).

43   FRCP 56(e). Sworn or certified copies of papers referred to in an affidavit shall be attached to or served with the affidavits. *Id.*

44   10A C. Wright, et al., Federal Practice and Procedure § 2722, at 373 (1998) (footnote omitted) (hereinafter "Wright").

45   *Celotex Corp. v. Catrett*, 477 U.S. 317, 323 (1986); *Anderson v. Liberty Lobby, Inc.*, 477 U.S. 242, 247–48 (1986); *Fed. Deposit Ins. Corp. v. Giammettei*, 34 F.3d 51, 54 (2d Cir. 1994); *Hunter-Reed v. City of Houston*, 244 F. Supp. 2d 733, 737–38 (S.D. Tex. 2003); *Kephart v. Data Sys. Int'l, Inc.*, 243 F. Supp. 2d 1205, 1208 (D. Kan. 2003); *Ashley v. S. Tool Inc.*, 201 F. Supp. 2d 1158, 1163 (N.D. Ala. 2002), *aff'd*, 62 Fed. Appx. 318 (11th Cir. 2003).

46   *Celotex Corp.*, 477 U.S. at 322–23.

47   FRCP 56(e); *Celotex Corp.*, 477 U.S. at 322–23.

48   FRCP 56(e); *Celotex Corp.*, 477 U.S. at 322–23.

It will not suffice to set out a factual smokescreen of immaterial or irrelevant facts. The facts must be specific and they must go to the relevant point of showing that at least one genuine issue exists for trial.[49] Speculation, conclusory assertions or allegations, rumor, conjecture, ignorance of facts, hope or unfounded or improbable inferences, whether in an affidavit or a deposition,[50] are not enough to defeat a well-founded motion for summary judgment.[51] Self-serving affidavits lacking a factual basis in the record are likewise of little use.[52] This is true for ordinary fact witnesses and for experts as well.[53] "When the moving party has carried its burden under Rule 56(c), its opponent must do more than simply show that there is some metaphysical doubt as to the material facts."[54] The opponent must present specific facts.

If the movant fails to meet the initial burden described above, summary judgment must be denied. The motion will be denied regardless of the quality or lack thereof of the opposing party's papers.[55]

---

49   *See Behrens v. Pelletier*, 516 U.S. 299, 309 (1996); *Anderson*, 477 U.S. at 248–50; *Crown Operations Int'l, Ltd. v. Solutia Inc.*, 289 F.3d 1367, 1375 (Fed. Cir. 2002); *Information Sys. & Networks Corp. v. City of Atlanta*, 281 F.3d 1220, 1224 (11th Cir. 2002); *Walker v. City of Lakewood*, 272 F.3d 1114, 1123 (9th Cir. 2001); *Albiero v. City of Kankakee*, 246 F.3d 927, 932 (7th Cir. 2001); *Santos v. Murdock*, 243 F.3d 681, 683 (2d Cir. 2001); *Herring v. Canada Life Assurance Co.*, 207 F.3d 1026, 1030 (8th Cir. 2000); *Hargett v. Valley Fed. Sav. Bank*, 60 F.3d 754, 763 (11th Cir. 1995); *Hunter-Reed*, 244 F. Supp. 2d at 738; *Kephart*, 243 F. Supp. 2d at 1208; *Ashley*, 201 F. Supp. 2d at 1163.

50   *Markel v. Bd. of Regents of Univ. of Wis. Sys.*, 276 F.3d 906 (7th Cir. 2002).

51   *Magarian v. Hawkins*, 321 F.3d 235, 240 (1st Cir. 2003); *Crown Operations Int'l, Ltd.*, 289 F.3d at 1375; *Markel*, 276 F.3d at 912; *Harrison v. Wahatoyas, L.L.C.*, 253 F.3d 552, 557 (10th Cir. 2001); *Mullins v. Crowell*, 228 F.3d 1305, 1313–14 (11th Cir. 2000); *Wood v. City of Lakeland*, 203 F.3d 1288, 1292 (11th Cir. 2000); *Patel v. Allstate Ins. Co.*, 105 F.3d 365, 370 (7th Cir. 1997); *Guerin v. Pointe Coupee Parish Nursing Home*, 246 F. Supp. 2d 488, 494 (M.D. La. 2003); *Kephart*, 243 F. Supp. 2d at 1209; *Robinson v. Regions Fin. Corp.*, 242 F. Supp. 2d 1070, 1084–85 (M.D. Ala. 2003); *Paukstis v. Kenwood Golf & Country Club, Inc.*, 241 F. Supp. 2d 551, 561–62 (D. Md. 2003); *Evans v. Siegel-Robert, Inc.*, 139 F. Supp. 2d 1120, 1124 (E.D. Mo.), *aff'd*, 22 Fed. Appx. 688 (8th Cir. 2001); *see Jeseritz v. Potter*, 282 F.3d 542, 546–47 (8th Cir. 2002).

52   *Albiero*, 246 F.3d at 933 (specific, concrete facts must be presented instead); *Kephart*, 243 F. Supp. 2d at 1209.

53   *Magarian*, 321 F.3d at 240.

54   *Matsushita Elec. Indus. Co. v. Zenith Radio Corp.*, 475 U.S. 574, 586 (1986) (footnote omitted).

55   *Giannullo v. City of New York*, 322 F.3d 139, 140–41 (2d Cir. 2003) (opponent not required to rebut insufficient showing); *Mullins*, 228 F.3d at 1313–14; *Patel*, 105 F.3d at 370; *Guerin*, 246 F. Supp. 2d at 494; *Evans*, 139 F. Supp. 2d at 1124.

Substantive law makes clear which facts are material and which are irrelevant.[56] A dispute over issues of fact does not matter if the facts in contention are immaterial.[57] The dispute must be a genuine one.[58] The test is one of reasonableness. If a reasonable jury could return a verdict for the party opposing the motion, the motion will fail.[59]

The court on summary judgment views the proof presented through the prism of the substantive evidentiary burden at trial.[60] The court will consider the facts in the light most favorable to the nonmoving party[61] and will draw all reasonable inferences in that party's favor. The judge's job is not to weigh and evaluate the evidence and determine the truth of things; it is merely to decide whether there is a genuine issue for trial.[62] The court will not make determinations of credibility. If the evidence submitted in opposition to the motion is merely colorable or not significantly probative, summary judgment may be granted.[63]

The parties need not present proof in a form that would be admissible at trial. However, the substance or content of the proof must be admissi-

---

56   *Anderson v. Liberty Lobby, Inc.*, 477 U.S. 242, 248 (1986); *Ashley v. S. Tool, Inc.*, 201 F. Supp. 2d 1158, 1163 (N.D. Ala. 2002), *aff'd*, 62 Fed. Appx. 318 (11th Cir. 2003).

57   *Anderson*, 477 U.S. at 248.

58   *Id.*

59   *Id.* at 248–49; *see Reeves v. Sanderson Plumbing Prods., Inc.*, 530 U.S. 133, 150 (2000); *Jackson v. Ark. Dep't of Educ.*, 272 F.3d 1020, 1025 (8th Cir. 2001); *Sowell v. Alumina Ceramics, Inc.*, 251 F.3d 678, 682 (8th Cir. 2001).

60   *Nebraska v. Wyoming*, 507 U.S. 584, 590 (1993); *Anderson*, 477 U.S. at 248; *Monarch Knitting Mach. Corp. v. Sulzer Morat GmbH*, 139 F.3d 877, 880–81 (Fed. Cir. 1998).

61   *Giannullo v. City of New York*, 322 F.3d 139, 140 (2d Cir. 2003); *Crown Operations Int'l, Ltd. v. Solutia Inc.*, 289 F.3d 1367, 1375 (Fed. Cir. 2002); *Information Sys. & Networks Corp. v. City of Atlanta*, 281 F.3d 1220, 1224 (11th Cir. 2002); *Herring v. Canada Life Assurance Co.*, 207 F.3d 1026, 1029 (8th Cir. 2000); *Williams v. Kelso*, 201 F.3d 1060, 1064 (8th Cir. 2000); *Wood v. City of Lakeland*, 203 F.3d 1288, 1292 (11th Cir. 2000); *Monarch Knitting Mach. Corp.*, 139 F.3d at 880; *Hargett v. Valley Fed. Sav. Bank*, 60 F.3d 754, 760 (11th Cir. 1995); *Kephart v. Data Sys. Int'l, Inc.*, 243 F. Supp. 2d 1205 (D. Kan. 2003); *Guerin v. Pointe Coupee Parish Nursing Home*, 246 F. Supp. 2d 488, 494 (M.D. La. 2003); *Ashley*, 201 F. Supp. 2d at 1163.

62   *Anderson v. Liberty Lobby, Inc.*, 477 U.S. 242, 249 (1986).

63   *Id.*

ble.[64] "Only that portion of a deposition that would be admissible in evidence at trial may be introduced on a summary-judgment motion."[65] Statements that are merely conclusory will be disregarded, as will those not based on personal knowledge.[66] Hearsay is another example of proof that would be inadmissible at trial and that would not be relied upon on summary judgment.[67]

Parties cannot succeed on summary judgment by relying upon documents unless the admissibility of the documents has been stipulated to or they have been properly authenticated.[68] "Authentication is a 'condition precedent to admissibility.' . . . [U]nauthenticated documents cannot be considered in a motion for summary judgment."[69] An extract from a deposition lacking certification[70] is unauthenticated and thus inadmissible.[71]

64　*Collier v. Budd Co.*, 66 F.3d 886, 892 (7th Cir. 1995); *Wells Dairy, Inc. v. Travelers Indem. Co.*, 241 F. Supp. 2d 945, 956 (N.D. Iowa 2003); *Kephart*, 243 F. Supp. 2d at 1209; *Ashley*, 201 F. Supp. 2d at 1164 (depositions); *Conoco Inc. v. J.M. Huber Corp.*, 148 F. Supp. 2d 1157, 1166 (D. Kan. 2001), *aff'd*, 289 F.3d 819 (Fed. Cir. 2002); *Pas Communications, Inc. v. Sprint Corp.*, 139 F. Supp. 2d 1149, 1179 (D. Kan. 2001); 10B Wright, *supra* note 44, § 2738, at 330 ("the first requisite is that the information [the affidavits] contain (as opposed to the affidavits themselves) would be admissible at trial") (footnote omitted).

65　10A Wright, *supra* note 44, § 2722, at 371–72.

66　*Santos v. Murdock*, 243 F.3d 681, 683 (2d Cir. 2001); *Wells Dairy, Inc.*, 241 F. Supp. 2d at 956; *Ashley*, 201 F. Supp. 2d at 1164 (depositions); *Conoco Inc.*, 148 F. Supp. 2d at 1166; *Pas Communications, Inc.*, 139 F. Supp. 2d at 1179.

67　*Club Car, Inc. v. Club Car (Quebec) Import, Inc.*, 362 F.3d 775, 783 (11th Cir. 2004); *Hillstrom v. Best Western TLC Hotel*, 354 F.3d 27, 32 (1st Cir. 2003); *Patel v. Allstate Ins. Co.*, 105 F.3d 365, 370 (7th Cir. 1997); *Griffin v. City of Milwaukee*, 74 F.3d 824 (7th Cir. 1996); *King v. Town of Wallkill*, 302 F. Supp. 2d 279, 299 (S.D.N.Y. 2004); *Dawson v. Bumble & Bumble*, 246 F. Supp. 2d 301, 325 (S.D.N.Y. 2003); *Davis v. G N Mortgage Corp.*, 244 F. Supp. 2d 950, 958 (N.D. Ill. 2003); *Hunter-Reed v. City of Houston*, 244 F. Supp. 2d 733, 745–46 (S.D. Tex. 2003); *Wells Dairy, Inc.*, 241 F. Supp. 2d at 956; *Betts v. Advance Am.*, 213 F.R.D. 466, 476 (M.D. Fla. 2003); *Ashley*, 201 F. Supp. 2d at 1164 (depositions); *Conoco Inc.*, 148 F. Supp. 2d at 1166; *Pas Communications, Inc.*, 139 F. Supp. 2d at 1179; *Gaston v. Home Depot USA Inc.*, 129 F. Supp. 2d 1355, 1361 (S.D. Fla.), *aff'd without opinion*, 265 F.3d 1066 (11th Cir. 2001); *Smith v. Bd. of County Comm'rs*, 96 F. Supp. 2d 1177, 1182 n.2 (D. Kan. 2000) (hearsay in depositions).

68　*Hunter-Reed*, 244 F. Supp. 2d at 745–46 (unsworn, unauthenticated note and postal service document); *Conoco Inc.*, 148 F. Supp. 2d at 1166.

69　*Orr v. Bank of Am.*, 285 F.3d 764, 773 (9th Cir. 2002) (citations omitted). Unauthenticated documents might be considered if they can clearly be reduced to admissible authenticated form at trial. *U.S. Aviation Underwriters v. Yellow Freight Sys.*, 296 F. Supp. 2d 1322, 1327 n.2, 1334 (S.D. Ala. 2003).

70　The officer taking the deposition must certify in a writing accompanying the deposition transcript that the witness was duly sworn and that the deposition is a true record of the testimony. FRCP 30(f)(1).

71　*Orr*, 285 F.3d at 774.

Finally, a party should not submit an entire deposition transcript without any specific citations to relevant portions.[72]

Thus, as in other areas of law, there are parallels between New York State and federal rules. But there are differences too, and it is wise for a primarily state practitioner to review carefully the federal rules and the interpretations of those rules set forth in the cases before diving headlong into this or other dispositive motions.

B. Affidavits and Depositions on Summary Judgment

The same problem obtains in federal practice as it does in state practice when parties are disappointed by the adverse use of a deposition previously taken in the case and feel the need to respond by submitting an affidavit from the deponent—one that perhaps endeavors to challenge the previous deposition. To what extent may history be rewritten in this way? That is, can the party opposing a motion for summary judgment attempt to create a material issue of fact by "correcting" the deposition through the submission of a contradictory affidavit from the deponent?

As explained earlier, once a deposition transcript has been corrected or the opportunity to do so foregone, the transcript becomes final. In general, a party may not endeavor to repair damage at the deposition through submission of an affidavit that contradicts his or her earlier deposition testimony. When such a conflict arises, the deposition testimony will prevail over the affidavit.[73] The reason for such a resolution is that

---

72   *Id.* at 775 ("The efficient management of judicial business mandates that parties submit evidence responsibly. . . . [W]hen a party relies on deposition testimony in a summary judgment motion without citing to page and line numbers, the trial court may in its discretion exclude the evidence" (footnote omitted)); *Jeseritz v. Potter*, 282 F.3d 542, 547 (8th Cir. 2002); *Poss v. Morris*, 260 F.3d 654, 665 (6th Cir. 2001); *Joseph P. Caulfield & Assocs. v. Litho Prods., Inc.*, 155 F.3d 883, 888–89 (7th Cir. 1998); *Little v. Cox's Supermarkets*, 71 F.3d 637, 641 (7th Cir. 1995).

73   *Maxwell v. City of New York*, 380 F.3d 106, 109 (2d Cir. 2004) (citing *Hayes v. New York City Dep't of Corrections*, 84 F.3d 614, 619 (2d Cir. 1996)); *Sea-Land Serv., Inc. v. Lozen Int'l, LLC*, 285 F.3d 808, 820 (9th Cir. 2002); *Copeland v. Wasserstein, Perella & Co.*, 278 F.3d 472, 482–83 (5th Cir. 2002); *Ralston v. Smith & Nephew Richards, Inc.*, 275 F.3d 965, 973 (10th Cir. 2001); *Commercial Underwriters Ins. Co. v. Aires Envtl. Servs.*, 259 F.3d 792, 799 (7th Cir. 2001); *Dotson v. Delta Consol. Indus., Inc.*, 251 F.3d 780, 781 (8th Cir. 2001); *Selenke v. Med. Imaging of Colo.*, 248 F.3d 1249, 1258 (10th Cir. 2001); *Herring v. Canada Life Assurance Co.*, 207 F.3d 1026, 1030–31 (8th Cir. 2000); *Piscione v. Ernst & Young, L.L.P.*, 171 F.3d 527, 532–33 (7th Cir. 1999); *Thomas v. Roach*, 165 F.3d 137, 144 (2d Cir. 1999); *BDT Prods., Inc. v. Lexmark Int'l, Inc.*, 274 F. Supp. 2d 880, 897–98 (E.D. Ky. 2003); *Betts v. Advance Am.*, 213 F.R.D. 466, 476 (M.D. Fla. 2003); *Dawson v. Bumble & Bumble*, 246 F. Supp. 2d 301, 307 n.1 (S.D.N.Y. 2003); *Evans v. Siegel-Robert, Inc.*, 139 F. Supp. 2d 1120, 1126 n.5 (E.D. Mo. 2001), *aff'd*, 22 Fed. Appx. 688 (8th Cir. 2001); *First Nat'l Bank v. Colonial Bank*, 898 F. Supp. 1220, 1232 n.13 (N.D. Ill. 1995).

> [a]ffidavits are normally . . . written by lawyers, and if such documents were allowed to be used to "correct" unguarded statements that had been made in the more spontaneous setting of oral questioning, the value of pretrial discovery as a tool for eliciting truth and heading off trials based on fabrications would be seriously impaired. . . . Recollecting in tranquility the admissions blurted out under the pressure of a hostile interrogation, the witness and his lawyer can easily cobble together a plausible denial.[74]

Such easy denials cannot be allowed to eliminate the benefits that flow to litigants and the system of justice from the existence of a sound summary judgment procedure.[75]

There are, however, some limits that need to be carefully noted here. There actually must be a contradiction between the deposition and the affidavit, not merely an effort to supplement and explain the previous testimony.[76] The court may accept an affidavit if its purpose is to clarify ambiguous portions of a deposition.[77] Also, if there is a contradiction but the party can offer a suitable explanation, the court may accept the affidavit.[78] The court may accept an affidavit when the witness adequately explains that he or she was confused when the deposition testimony was given.[79] Mistake or a lapse in memory, if adequately explained, might suffice;[80] so, too, might newly discovered evidence.[81]

---

74   *Sullivan v. Conway*, 157 F.3d 1092, 1096–97 (7th Cir. 1998).

75   *Palazzo ex rel. Delmage v. Corio*, 232 F.3d 38, 43 (2d Cir. 2000).

76   *Sea-Land Serv., Inc.*, 285 F.3d at 820; *Palazzo ex rel. Delmage*, 232 F.3d at 43; *Beasley v. Conopco, Inc.*, 273 F. Supp. 2d 1239, 1248–49 (M.D. Ala. 2003) (affidavit contradictory in part).

77   *Maxwell*, 380 F.3d at 109; *Selenke*, 248 F.3d 1249; *Palazzo ex rel. Delmage*, 232 F.3d at 43; *Shepherd v. Slater Steels Corp.*, 168 F.3d 998, 1007 (7th Cir. 1999).

78   *Maxwell*, 380 F.3d at 109; *Copeland*, 278 F.3d at 482–83; *Commercial Underwriters Ins. Co.*, 259 F.3d at 799; *Herring*, 207 F.3d at 1030–31; *Betts*, 213 F.R.D. at 476; *Hyde v. Stanley Tools*, 107 F. Supp. 2d 992, 993 (E.D. La. 2000).

79   *Commercial Underwriters Ins. Co.*, 259 F.3d at 799; *Herring*, 207 F.3d at 1030–31.

80   *Commercial Underwriters Ins. Co.*, 259 F.3d at 799 (deponent not responsible for and did not deal with insurance matters and thus was not prepared to answer insurance-related questions); *Piscione v. Ernst & Young, L.L.P.*, 171 F.3d 527, 532–33 (7th Cir. 1999).

81   *Sullivan v. Conway*, 157 F.3d 1092, 1096 (7th Cir. 1998); *Bank of Ill. v. Allied Signal Safety Restraint Sys.*, 75 F.3d 1162, 1172 (7th Cir. 1996).

In evaluating whether an affidavit creates a sham or feigned issue, some courts inquire as to whether the affiant was cross-examined during the deposition, the affiant had access to the relevant evidence at the time of the deposition or the deposition reflects confusion that the affiant seeks to explain.[82] If the affiant was asked about certain documents during the deposition but did not have access to them at the time the answers were given and has been able to study them since and, based upon that study, noted that some statements in the deposition were in error, a court might find the affidavit acceptable if this explanation is set forth in a candid and detailed way.[83] (This example suggests the importance of advising witnesses not to give answers when they do not actually recall the facts.[84])

When an affidavit flatly contradicts an earlier deposition by the affiant and there is the possibility that a court may nevertheless accept the affidavit when an explanation is offered for the deponent's error during the deposition, some deponents may attempt to skirt the bounds of strict propriety. Courts are, we trust, aware of this possibility and weigh the affidavit and its post-facto explanations and excuses with appropriate care.

On the other hand, some courts have pointed to the need to exercise caution in the application of the general rule against contradicting depositions by later affidavits. A distinction, it is suggested, should be drawn between discrepancies that create transparent shams and those that create an issue of credibility or go to the weight of the evidence, which are matters for the trier of fact that should not be foreclosed on summary judgment.[85] One court stated:

> The purpose of summary judgment is to separate real, genuine issues from those which are formal or pretended. To allow every failure of memory or variation in a witness's testimony to be disregarded as a sham would require far

---

82   *Ralston v. Smith & Nephew Richards, Inc.*, 275 F.3d 965, 973 (10th Cir. 2001).

83   The possibility of being able to explain in an affidavit a seemingly contradictory statement made at a prior deposition might increase if the transcript showed that the witness had indicated some doubt about the subject during the deposition (there might be a seemingly categorical statement at one place in the transcript but perhaps less categorical statements in other places), or if the transcript contained several different and inconsistent items of testimony about the subject, reflecting the possibility of confusion on the witness's part. *See, e.g.*, *Pries v. Honda Motor Co.*, 31 F.3d 543 (7th Cir. 1994). The manner in which the relevant questions were formulated may have a bearing on this evaluation.

84   See chapter 1 in the second part of this book for further discussion.

85   *Bank of Ill.*, 75 F.3d at 1169–71; *Pries*, 31 F.3d 543; *Tippens v. Celotex Corp.*, 805 F.2d 949 (5th Cir. 1986).

too much from lay witnesses and would deprive the trier of fact of the traditional opportunity to determine which point in time and with which words the witness (in this case, the affiant) was stating the truth. Variations in a witness's testimony and any failure of memory throughout the course of discovery create an issue of credibility as to which part of the testimony should be given the greatest weight if credited at all. Issues concerning the credibility of witnesses and weight of the evidence are questions of fact which require resolution by the trier of fact.[86]

A particular problem, not present in state practice, can arise when a party opposes a motion for summary judgment that is premised on facts set forth in that party's FRCP 30(b)(6) deposition. As noted earlier, the deponent is obliged in advance of such a deposition to gather the facts and prepare for the deposition on behalf of the corporation or other entity. A subsequent contradictory affidavit should not contain explanations or excuses that ignore that unique duty. A court cannot allow a party to "wing it" in the FRCP 30(b)(6) deposition and later "correct" the record by submitting a contradictory affidavit in opposition to a motion for summary judgment. To exercise such indulgence would undermine FRCP 30(b)(6) and weaken the duty of the deponent under that rule.[87]

Chapter 8 discusses the correction of deposition transcripts and possible limits on the use of errata sheets in general under FRCP 30(e). It has been held in the context of summary judgment that the court can disregard an errata sheet prepared by a deponent after conclusion of the deposition.

> There is no reason to distinguish . . . between an attempt to conjure up a triable issue of fact through the proffer of a late affidavit and an attempt to achieve the same end through the submission of delayed errata sheets or supplemental answers to interrogatories. None will defeat a motion for summary judgment.[88]

---

86   *Tippens*, 805 F.2d at 953, *quoted in Bank of Ill.*, 75 F.3d at 1170.

87   *Hyde v. Stanley Tools*, 107 F. Supp. 2d 992, 993 (E.D. La. 2000) (affidavit of expert submitted on motion stated that defendant had not manufactured the hammer in issue; but at its FRCP 30(b)(6) deposition, defendant through its witness had testified that he had conducted a close inspection of the hammer and had determined that defendant had manufactured it during a particular three-year period; defendant unsuccessfully attempted to defend the contradictory affidavit on the ground that the expert's analysis had been more extensive).

88   *Margo v. Weiss*, 213 F.3d 55, 61 (2d Cir. 2000).

Another court wrote:

> If a party were allowed to create material factual disputes by altering one's deposition testimony via an errata sheet, summary judgment would rarely, if ever, be granted. Parties should not be able to evade an answer given under oath during a deposition when it is later used against them by simply stating the opposite in the errata sheet.[89]

With regard to summary judgment on a 42 U.S.C. section 1983 claim, a court disregarded an errata sheet that substantially contradicted plaintiff's deposition testimony as to the reason for his termination.[90] The court concluded that plaintiff had clearly attempted to furnish "artful answers" in the sheet. The original testimony gave no hint of confusion about the questions, and plaintiff did not rely upon the discovery of new evidence as justification for the corrections. Furthermore, the court observed, the questions were ones on which plaintiff's attorney could have cross-examined him at the time. Therefore, the corrections were disregarded.[91]

This might be argued: FRCP 30(e) governs the correction of depositions during the discovery process. Thus, as the rule imposes no limitation on the extent of substantive changes, none should be imposed by the court; the deadline in FRCP 30(e) is intended to produce a final transcript within a short time after the deposition; if significant changes are made during the correction process, the court may reopen the deposition on the point to ensure fairness.

In this view, the transcript as corrected in compliance with the rule, including in a timely manner, is the final transcript, and an affidavit that is in accord with the corrections made but not with the original testimony is not contradictory. Whereas some courts would rule that neither the corrections (or at least certain material ones) nor the affidavit could be considered,[92] others would allow the corrections if made in compliance with the

---

89   *Wigg v. Sioux Falls Sch. Dist.*, 274 F. Supp. 2d 1084, 1091 (D.S.D. 2003), *aff'd in part, rev'd in part on other grounds*, 382 F.3d 807 (8th Cir. 2004).

90   *Burns v. Bd. of Comm'rs*, 197 F. Supp. 2d 1278, 1292 (D. Kan. 2002), *aff'd*, 330 F.3d 1275 (10th Cir. 2003).

91   *Id.*; *see Xiangyuan Zhu v. Countrywide Realty Co.*, 165 F. Supp. 2d 1181, 1195 (D. Kan. 2001); *see also Thorn v. Sundstrand Aerospace Corp.*, 207 F.3d 383, 389 (7th Cir. 2000).

92   *See, e.g., Burns v. Bd. of County Comm'rs*, 330 F.3d 1275 (10th Cir. 2003); *Wigg*, 274 F. Supp. 2d at 1090–92.

rule and would permit consideration of an affidavit consistent with those changes.[93]

If, on the other hand, corrections are submitted after the deadline set forth in FRCP 30(e) and in connection with a motion for summary judgment, the court could treat the corrections as it would a contradictory affidavit on summary judgment.[94] In *Summerhouse v. HCA Health Services*,[95] however, the court considered but rejected this approach. "[T]here is nothing in the language of Rule 30(e) that suggests a different application of the rule based on the pendency of particular types of motions. Accordingly, whatever changes Rule 30(e) permits, they are permitted without regard to the pendency of a summary judgment motion."[96]

Finally, as always, local court rules must be consulted. Some federal court judges require that the parties exchange motion papers before submitting them to the court in an effort to promote a resolution without court intervention. When questions of apparent fact arise based on the use of depositions or affidavits, perhaps the papers should not be submitted to the court after all.

---

93   *LaMarche v. Metro. Life Ins. Co.*, 236 F. Supp. 2d 34, 41 (D. Me. 2002) (timely errata sheet revealed changed view on facts; subsequent affidavit on summary judgment consistent with changed view found not contradictory); *see Podell v. Citicorp Diners Club*, 914 F. Supp. 1025, 1034–35 (S.D.N.Y. 1996), *aff'd*, 112 F.3d 98 (2d Cir. 1997) (Judge Haight allowed corrections to stand although the reasons given were "unconvincing in the extreme." The "changed answers [became] part of the record generated during discovery." The court considered the answers "a scintilla of evidence," but that was outweighed by the rest of the record so that summary judgment was granted against the plaintiff deponent).

94   *See Margo v. Weiss*, 213 F.3d 55, 61 (2d Cir. 2000).

95   216 F.R.D. 502 (D. Kan. 2003).

96   *Id.* at 507 (relying on, inter alia, *Burns*, 330 F.3d 1275).

CHAPTER ELEVEN

DEPOSITION ON
WRITTEN QUESTIONS

It is appropriate to save for the last chapter in this first part of the book a brief discussion of depositions on written questions, because depositions on written questions rank last, or almost so, in the affections and the arsenals of litigators, both state and federal.

There are several reasons for the uncertain repute of this device. Although it can be, comparatively speaking, inexpensive (which can be an important consideration in a case involving modest damages) and it can be helpful if taken as the first step to ascertain whether a person has sufficient knowledge to be questioned further orally, the deposition on written questions is cumbersome to effectuate.

It has other disadvantages as well. The questioner cannot observe the demeanor of the witness and gauge his or her credibility, which could be important if the person may or will testify at trial. Questioning the witness about documents is difficult. The principal weakness, which is readily apparent, flows from the very nature of the device. Because the interrogation is confined to questions written in advance, the inquiring party's ability to pursue a topic thoroughly is necessarily constrained. There is no opportunity to adjust questioning based upon the answers given or the witness's demeanor while giving them. The witness can be vague, confused, confusing or evasive, but the questioner cannot follow up with clarifying inquiries. A witness with an ax to grind or a plan to make life difficult can more easily achieve that objective by means of this device than with an oral deposition.

Magistrate Judge Francis made the following observations about depositions on written questions:

> In certain limited circumstances, depositions by written questions are appropriate. For example, where the issues to be addressed by the witness are narrow and straightforward and the hardships of taking an oral deposition would be substantial, written questions may be an adequate substitute, at least in the first instance.

> But there are several reasons why oral depositions should not be routinely replaced by written questions. First, the interrogatory format does not permit the probing follow-up questions necessary in all but the simplest litigation. Second, without oral deposition, counsel are unable to observe the demeanor of the witness and evaluate his

credibility in anticipation of trial. Finally, written questions provide an opportunity for counsel to assist the witness in providing answers so carefully tailored that they are likely to generate additional discovery disputes.[1]

I. STATE PRACTICE

Depositions on written questions can be taken when the examining party and the deponent so stipulate or when the testimony is to be taken outside the state.[2] Although a commission or letters rogatory may be issued if necessary or convenient for the taking of the deposition outside the state, they are not required.[3]

Rule 3109 of the CPLR sets forth the procedures that must be followed for taking depositions on written questions. It is here that the word *cumbersome* comes to mind. The person seeking the deposition shall serve each party with a notice stating the name and address of the deponent if known or, if the name is unknown, a sufficient description. The notice must include the name or descriptive title and address of the officer before whom the deposition is to be taken.[4] Accompanying the notice shall be the written questions to be asked.[5] Within 15 days thereafter, a party served may serve written cross-questions upon each party. Within seven days after that, the original party may serve written redirect questions upon each party. Within five days after service of same, a party may serve written re-cross questions upon each party.

The party taking the deposition must deliver copies of all the questions and the notice to the officer designated in the notice. No precise time is fixed for the conduct of the deposition, but the officer is required to act

---

1   *Mill-Run Tours, Inc. v. Khashoggi*, 124 F.R.D. 547, 549 (S.D.N.Y. 1989) (citations omitted). Professor Siegel agrees:

> The oral examination is a more effectual device. The give and take of the session in which the attorneys are present and the witness is being directly questioned probes the facts deeper and enables at least superficial objections to be overcome immediately . . . . For depositions to be taken of the witness (whether a party or not) within the state the oral deposition is the commonly used device.

Siegel, McKinney's Practice Commentary, CPLR 3108, at 458–59 (1991) (hereinafter "Siegel").

2   CPLR 3108.

3   *Id.*; *Gorie v. Gorie*, 48 Misc. 2d 411, 265 N.Y.S.2d 19 (Sup. Ct., N.Y. Co. 1965).

4   CPLR 3113(a) defines who may serve as the officer for the deposition.

5   Any errors or irregularities in the notice will be waived unless written objection is served on the noticing party at least three days before the taking of the deposition. CPLR 3112.

"promptly." It will be up to the officer to arrange a convenient time and location. At the deposition, the officer will read the various groups of questions to the witness, and the witness will give oral answers and these answers will be recorded. (The oral answers and the layers of questioning distinguish this deposition from interrogatories.) The officer will then prepare the deposition transcript.

Although the examining party and deponent must stipulate to depositions on written questions within the state,[6] in the case of a deposition noticed as an oral examination, any party served with the notice may transmit written questions to the officer.[7] Normally, this would be an even less hospitable environment for written questions than a deposition based solely on written questions because the attorneys present will be able to pursue thorough, probing oral questioning with suitable follow-up, but the party who submits written questions obviously will not.

When a party objects to the form of written questions, the objections will be waived unless served in writing upon the party who served the questions, within the time allowed for serving succeeding questions or within three days after service of the questions. Thus, there can be a flurry of written questions dispatched through the mails by various parties and a flurry of objections thereto as well.

Another disadvantage to a deposition on written questions is the possibility that the witness will be able to review the questions, cross-questions and other questions in advance. There is "ancient commentary to the effect that, in order to preserve the spontaneity of the answers to written questions it is improper practice to show a prospective deponent either the direct interrogatories or the cross-questions."[8] How much force this principle still has in the real world of practice is unclear.[9]

The party who takes a deposition out of state may do so on oral questions but can choose to proceed on written questions. In the latter event, the other party, if so advised, may conduct an oral cross-examination, at his or her own expense. The examining party may then choose to convert

---

6   CPLR 3108.

7   CPLR 3113(b).

8   6 Jack B. Weinstein et al., New York Civil Practice ¶ 3109.07, at 31-331 (2004) (footnote omitted).

9   *Id.* (suggesting that the Court of Appeals' decision in *Tai Tran v. New Rochelle Hosp. Med. Ctr.*, 99 N.Y.2d 383, 756 N.Y.S.2d 509, 786 N.E.2d 444 (2003) regarding surveillance tapes may have tacitly undermined this principle).

the written examination into an oral one as well, again at that party's own expense.[10]

A deposition outside the state will often be that of a nonparty witness who resides in another state or foreign jurisdiction. As noted in chapter 6, however, although depositions of parties in state practice will generally take place in the state,[11] the court may order, under appropriate circumstances, that the party deponent be saved the trouble of coming to New York for a deposition, at least during the discovery phase of the case. The party deponent would have to show, by way of a protective order application under CPLR 3103 absent stipulation, that coming to New York would work a hardship. Upon a sufficient showing, the court could allow a deposition on oral examination where the party resides.

If, however, there was some reason for limiting the questioner's inquiry or to avoid travel expenses for counsel, the court could instead direct that the deposition proceed out-of-state on written questions. If the party's role in the case is clearly nominal or technical or the party is elderly or ill, the court might choose to direct a deposition on written questions.[12] In order to accommodate the inquiring party's need for a more thorough and probing interrogation, the court might, in addition, require that the party deponent appear in New York for a deposition on oral questions a short time before trial, when the party will normally be present.[13]

---

10   *Lane Bryant, Inc. v. Cohen*, 86 A.D.2d 805, 452 N.Y.S.2d 573 (1st Dep't 1982); *Corona Hair Net Corp. v. Chemaco, Ltd.*, 33 A.D.2d 1001, 307 N.Y.S.2d 264 (1st Dep't 1970); *Walborsky v. Wolf*, 28 A.D.2d 1120, 285 N.Y.S.2d 176 (1st Dep't 1967); Siegel, *supra* note 1, at 459.

11   CPLR 3110.

12   *Rosenstock v. Weberman*, 98 A.D.2d 921, 471 N.Y.S.2d 32 (3d Dep't 1983) (elderly person with title to but little involvement with property who was sole caregiver of invalid spouse); *Fielding v. S. Klein Dep't Stores, Inc.*, 44 A.D.2d 668, 354 N.Y.S.2d 438 (1st Dep't 1974) (elderly retiree).

13   *See Fielding*, 44 A.D.2d 668 (permitting plaintiff's deposition to be on written questions and by oral examination in New York at least ten days before trial or, at defendants' election, by open commission, in which event parties would pay their respective expenses, to be taxed as costs); Siegel, *supra* note 1, at 460; *see also Fusfeld v. Novogroder*, 97 A.D.2d 729, 468 N.Y.S.2d 636 (1st Dep't 1983) (allowing plaintiff, who sought to depose two nonresident physician defendants, to depose them on written questions or, in the alternative, orally in New York at least 20 days prior to trial; the Appellate Division added the option of an oral deposition at defendants' residences); *Zilken v. Leader*, 23 A.D.2d 644, 257 N.Y.S.2d 185 (1st Dep't 1965) (allowing plaintiff, a resident of West Germany, in action arising out of services there to take his own deposition on written questions; denying defendants' cross-motion for an oral deposition of plaintiff in New York County without prejudice to renewal if written process unsatisfactory; further requiring plaintiff to notify defendants if he would be coming to the United States and to make himself available for oral deposition in New York County).

With the advance of technology, depositions by video conference may come to displace depositions on written questions in some circumstances.[14]

The parties ought normally be able to resolve disagreements about written questions on their own. Objections to form have been mentioned. Although CPLR 3115(e) speaks only of objections to form, other objections can be raised if necessary.[15]

II. FEDERAL PRACTICE

The deposition of any person can be taken by written questions.[16] A nonparty witness can be compelled to appear under FRCP 45. This device can be used without leave of court unless the deponent is in prison or, absent a stipulation, the deposition would exceed the ten-deposition maximum, the deponent has already been deposed or the deposition would occur before the time set forth in FRCP 26(d). Court approval is to be granted consistent with FRCP 26(b)(2). A deposition on written questions may be taken of a corporation, partnership, association or government agency in accordance with FRCP 30(b)(6).

As in state court, the questioning party must serve the questions on the other parties with a notice identifying the deponent or, if unknown, describing him or her and identifying the officer by name, title and address. Within 14 days of service, cross-questions may be served, followed (within seven days) by redirect questions and (within seven additional days) re-cross questions. The questioning party shall deliver all questions and the notice to the officer, who shall conduct the deposition promptly pursuant to FRCP 30(c), (e) and (f). Incorporation of these subdivisions means that the review, correction, signature and certification procedures applicable to depositions on oral questions apply. The officer must supply a copy of the deposition to any party or the witness on payment of reasonable charges.

---

14   *See Rogovin v. Rogovin*, 3 A.D.3d 352, 770 N.Y.S.2d 342 (1st Dep't 2004) (defendant to be deposed by live video conferencing in view of hardship that would be caused by travel to New York; defendant sole caregiver of elderly ailing relative and young child with special needs).

15   *Gorie v. Gorie*, 48 Misc. 2d 411, 411, 265 N.Y.S.2d 19 (Sup. Ct., N.Y. Co. 1965); Siegel, *supra* note 1, at 474.

16   FRCP 31.

When circumstances warrant limitation of the burden that a deposition would otherwise impose, the court, upon an application for a protective order, may direct that the deposition proceed by written questions.[17]

---

17 *Boutte v. Blood Sys., Inc.*, 127 F.R.D. 122 (W.D. La. 1989) (granting protective order limiting plaintiff's deposition of blood donor to a deposition on written questions, with donor's identity to remain confidential in an action involving allegedly negligent screening of blood); *McGoldrick v. Koch*, 110 F.R.D. 153 (S.D.N.Y. 1986) (granting protective order against depositions of police officials and an assistant district attorney involved in police department's trial process to extent of allowing depositions on written questions only and prescribing plaintiff's right to apply for oral deposition later if justified by answers to written questions); *Gatoil, Inc. v. Forest Hill State Bank*, 104 F.R.D. 580, 582 (D. Md. 1985) (ordering deposition of witness in Houston to proceed on written questions where all counsel were in Baltimore and few substantive questions would be answered, as witness would invoke privilege against self-incrimination). *But see Mill-Run Tours, Inc. v. Khashoggi*, 124 F.R.D. 547, 549–50 (S.D.N.Y 1989) (denying motion for protective order, as plaintiff needed oral examination of defendants to explore all aspects of the issues presented).

PART TWO

STRATEGIC AND PRACTICAL
CONSIDERATIONS

INTRODUCTION

This part of the book discusses strategic and practical or tactical considerations regarding depositions. There may not necessarily be one "right answer" in all the situations addressed. Differences in the facts among cases matter. Personality can play a role—both that of the witness and that of counsel. So, too, the sums at stake and the relative cost of depositions come into play. The availability and likely utility of other discovery will have an important impact upon the approach to depositions in a particular case. In some instances, the manner in which an attorney undertakes certain aspects of deposition practice may be a question of personal preference. Therefore, the text herein presents not fixed rules, but considerations that might usefully be taken into account when planning and conducting depositions.

CHAPTER ONE

BEFORE THE DEPOSITION

I. PURPOSES OF DEPOSITIONS

In preparing for and taking depositions, an attorney must have a clear objective, not just for the depositions as a whole, but for each deposition. Depositions can be taken for a number of reasons, and many are taken for several at once.

A deposition can be taken to *preserve testimony.* If an attorney needs the testimony of a witness who will not, or may not, be present at trial, such as someone who is in ill health or who resides in another state far away, a deposition may be needed. Life is full of uncertainties, and even a young person in perfect health who plans on testifying at trial may be prevented by accident or circumstance from doing so. Sometimes an attorney has to assume such risks, depending on the size and significance of the case and the importance of the witness's testimony to it. But in other situations, the testimony of a witness may be too important for an attorney to run any such risk.

Parties and nonparties are deposed *to force them formally, on the record, to commit to a position regarding the case.* This is, in many ways, analogous to the reason a prosecutor puts witnesses in front of the grand jury. Memories fade as time passes. The accounts of relevant events offered by nonparty witnesses and particularly by parties, who by definition are interested, may change over the life of the case. This change may happen because the investigation in preparation of the case and the discovery process may lead a witness to a better understanding of the facts and a clearer recollection.

Recollections can be and are refreshed in litigation every day. Exposure to documents not seen perhaps for months or years is a common way for this to occur. Other depositions shed light. Beyond this, some witnesses with a stake in the case may, if left unchecked, try to color their position on the facts in accordance with their own self-interest as it is perceived at any particular point in the life of the case. Stories may change over time as the needs of the case seem to require. More scrupulous witnesses may nevertheless see things through a not disinterested lens, perhaps without even realizing what is occurring. Therefore, it is vital to cause a witness to commit to an account of events under oath.

Once so committed, subject to an opportunity to correct errors, the witness cannot alter his or her version of what happened without opening himself or herself to possible impeachment. On a motion for summary judgment, the witness will be unable to recast his or her version of what happened to suit the convenience of the moment; absent some sort of reasonable explanation (e.g., that the questions were unclear and confused the witness), an affidavit that contradicts deposition testimony of the witness may well be ignored. At trial (assuming the case is not lost on summary judgment), the witness can present the contradictory account, but the trier of fact may in fact disregard it because the witness's credibility has been undermined by the conflict with the deposition testimony. Thus, an aim of the deposition is to "lock in" testimony that can then, if suitable, be used on summary judgment or at trial.

Committing witnesses to positions on the record also helps all parties to pursue discovery effectively. An issue that has been raised by the pleadings may fall away as a result of a deposition, or the issue may be narrowed, or it may appear in a different light. The effect may be to close some avenues for discovery or to open others, or even both.

Closely related to this objective is the purpose of *developing material for possible use at trial or on a motion to impeach the credibility of a party or nonparty witness*. It has been a long time since the rack was used to ensure or at least promote the truth. Now we rely upon cross-examination. Cross-examination is the great leveler. It is the way lawyers challenge dubious, unreliable, inaccurate or dishonest testimony. Nothing is quite as effective a tool on cross-examination as, or resounds more effectively on a motion for summary judgment than, a demonstration that, on an important subject about which the witness just testified, he or she said something completely contradictory at a prior deposition.

With regard to opposing parties and key witnesses who might testify at trial in an unfriendly vein, it is important or even vital to develop material for impeachment. Documents may be helpful, but prior inconsistent deposition testimony is usually more powerful. A witness might find a way around the document, but he or she cannot so easily sidestep a clearly phrased and straightforward question (that the question should be in such form is a point worth emphasizing) and a direct answer from the witness's own mouth that contradicts what the witness just said on the stand. Not only may a contradiction undermine the witness's statement on the subject, but it may even cast doubt on all important aspects of the witness's testimony.

Another basic purpose of the deposition is *as a tool to gather facts*. Interrogatories can be important, particularly as a preliminary, definitional device in commercial cases, but the answers thereto are carefully crafted at the hands of the opposing lawyer. Production of documents is fundamental in many cases. But the documents alone may not tell the full story, and sometimes the documents are confusing or misleading and require an explanation. The deposition provides a unique means to find out the full story (at least as it is perceived and understood by the witness) since the questioning attorney can pursue any fact in any direction at the deposition (with the relatively narrow exceptions discussed in chapter 5 in the first part of this book).

The inquiring attorney will want to explore at deposition not just the events at issue, but also the identities of other persons with knowledge, perhaps for depositions in their turn, as well as the nature and location of relevant documents to be made the subject of a document demand. Some depositions are taken of persons who lack knowledge about the transactions at issue but who are familiar with the location of documents and document retention policies or with the structure of an organization. These depositions open the pathways to relevant documents and witnesses with knowledge of the facts.

A deposition is also a mechanism for *the authentication of documents.* The deposition can be used to find documents and to identify those that are important to the issues or upon which the case may turn, but it can also provide an opportunity to authenticate documents and lay the basis for their use at trial. This can be quite significant.

The deposition presents an opportunity to examine the testimonial skills of persons who are likely to testify at trial and to evaluate the kind of impression they might make upon a jury or judge. Often, there will be witnesses central to the case whose success or lack thereof as witnesses will have an important impact on the ultimate outcome of the matter. The attorney for the deponent and the adversaries from their varying perspectives can benefit greatly and plan for future action in the case most effectively if they can see how well the witness copes with the challenges of responding to questions and dealing with the pressures of what is, for most, a high-pressure and unfamiliar setting.

Was the witness overly loquacious? Was she perhaps evasive, "forgetting" things she must have known? Did she seem calculating or too well rehearsed? Did the experience unsettle the witness unduly? Did the questioning cause her to become confused? Were the answers given difficult to understand? What impression will the witness be likely to make on a jury of laypersons? Obtaining some sense of these and similar things influences the calculations of the parties about trial and about settlement as well.

II. ANALYZING THE CASE

Before instituting the lawsuit, the attorney for the plaintiff must ana-
lyze the legal theories to be relied upon and the causes of action to be
asserted. There must, of course, be a good faith basis for making the
claims. Beyond that, even though trial may be far in the future, the plaintiff must also consider how the claims can be proven—what documents
support them, what facts the defendant will or should agree upon, what
witnesses are available to testify at trial or by deposition in support of the
claims and so forth. The plaintiff will also try to gain some sense as to the
witnesses who may be available to assist the defendant.

As the case begins for the defendant, the attorney for the defendant will
undertake a comparable analysis from the opposing perspective, examining the elements of the claims and defenses and the proof available, or
likely to be so, to support or oppose them. Preparation and more preparation is the key to a trial lawyer's success, and the process of preparation
commences at the outset of the case.

III. FRAMING A DISCOVERY PLAN

Before discovery begins, motions to dismiss or other motions may be
made. Depending on the court and the circumstances, discovery may or
may not be stayed. In federal court, the attorneys will have to prepare for a
FRCP 26(f) conference at an early point. In a state court case, the discovery process may not commence in quite as structured a way, nor, for that
matter, as soon. It may begin with a preliminary conference or without
one, and in the latter circumstance, perhaps without judicial intervention
even having taken place.

As discovery nears its initiation, the attorneys will have to carry forward and expand upon their initial analysis of the case, now looking
toward the development of a concrete and realistic discovery plan for the
case. This is the specific mandate of FRCP 26(f), but it also is the purpose
of counsel in a state case, though less formalized.

In developing the plan, plaintiff's counsel will need to focus not on the
causes of action in general, but upon each element of each cause of action.
What exactly must plaintiff prove? Counsel should also examine the affirmative defenses and other defenses or counterclaims defendant will, or
likely will, present. What elements will defendant have to prove? What will
defendant want to show to explain the conduct plaintiff challenges? As to
all these points, what proof will plaintiff wish to rely upon, what proof

will plaintiff need to acquire and what proof will defendant use? Counsel for defendant will undertake a similar process from its side of the case.

The nature of the case, the pleadings and information from the client will assist an attorney in determining what facts may not be in dispute. The attorney will need to examine existing relevant documents and to consider what other documents there may be, where they may be and how they can be located.

The attorney will need to consider whether interrogatories might be useful. Interrogatories will be less productive than document production and depositions because the answers are prepared by an attorney. But interrogatories can help by providing a first layer or broad sweep of facts which, even though edited by counsel, can contribute to orienting the interrogating side or providing direction and focus for the detailed and thorough inquiries to follow. In some cases, interrogatories can be useful in clarifying a corporate structure and identifying documents, persons with knowledge of the facts and document custodians or others with knowledge of relevant documents or document retention procedures, thus setting the stage for document demands and depositions.

A. Discovery and ADR

In preparation for the establishment of a discovery plan, if not before, the attorney might want to consider whether the case might be a good one for alternative dispute resolution (ADR). If the case does not turn on a question of law, if a precedent is not essential, if personal emotions are not involved to a large degree, if discovery will be extensive in relation to the value of the case, if there is a relationship that might continue to the benefit of both sides if the present dispute can be overcome—these are just some of the relevant considerations—the parties might find ADR, particularly mediation, advantageous.

If the parties do wish to go to mediation, that may affect what discovery should be taken and in what order. Sometimes, much discovery can be put off, which will result in substantial savings if the case is settled. In other cases, some discovery may be needed—say, a deposition of a key witness or two; physical and medical reports are almost essential in personal injury cases—in order for ADR to be practical. Even so, this minimal discovery may be much less expensive than what will be required if the case goes ahead full steam on the merits.

B. Whether to Take Depositions

Should any depositions be taken? This is a threshold question. Depositions are expensive. Computer and telecommunications technologies are improving daily. Before long, video communications between business-persons and in ordinary life may become daily occurrences, taken entirely for granted, just as telephone conversations, once regarded as technological miracles, have long since been. The prospects are good that future technological progress will reduce the cost of depositions. That reduction has already happened in part with regard to depositions out-of-state. However, we have not yet reached the point where the cost of depositions can be ignored or taken lightly. Therefore, in some cases, it is appropriate to ask the question whether any depositions should be taken.

In some cases, depositions may be unnecessary. In all cases, the attorneys, in preparing a discovery plan, will consider other available sources of information, such as informal disclosure, mandatory discovery in federal cases, interrogatories and document requests. What needs to be done by way of deposition and when it should be done will be influenced by the availability of information from other sources.

Some cases can be resolved on stipulated facts.[1] Some cases may present questions of law only, such as a dispute over contract interpretation in which parol evidence is usually not admissible, which can be resolved on motion. In other cases, the question is a closer one.

The amount of damages at issue should be taken into account. In a case in which the damages sought are modest, the expense of depositions may be excessive and disproportionate. Of course, if the case is one in which attorneys' fees may be awarded to the prevailing attorney, damages may play a lesser role in the decision about whether to take depositions and, if so, the number to be taken.

If in a particular case the disputes of fact are few, if a party can rely on its own witness and perhaps a nonparty witness located nearby who is willing to appear at trial, if documents are available to narrow and clarify the issues, incurring the expense of depositions may be unnecessary.

---

1   Although New York State procedure contains a mechanism for the submission of cases on stipulated facts, *see* CPLR 3222, this mechanism is rarely used. New York also has a simplified procedure for court determination of disputes, likewise infrequently employed. *See* CPLR 3031–3037.

In most cases in federal court and in state supreme court, at least a few depositions will be taken or in any event scheduled. In state supreme court, depositions are routinely scheduled in personal injury litigation: a deposition of the plaintiff, a deposition of the defendant who allegedly caused the accident and perhaps a deposition of a notice witness. The federal court practitioner seems to take more and more depositions, perhaps because the cases have become larger and larger.

C. Type and Number of Depositions to Take

If depositions are to be taken, what kind of deposition and how many should be taken? Again, the complexity, size and financial value of the case will have to be taken into account in answering this question. Because depositions are costly, counsel should not be profligate in seeking them. The attorney needs to prepare her case as required by the ethical obligation of zealousness. But more now than in prior decades, counsel also must keep in mind the costs being incurred in the process. Failing to do so can produce a Pyrrhic victory for the client. Can a client be content with a full recovery of $100,000 if it cost $50,000 to achieve it?

Further, attention should be given to the nature of the case: Is this primarily a "law case" rather than a "fact case"? Is this a case in which documents are important? Who are the possible witnesses needed to support the elements of one's case? The adversary's case? Can nonparty witnesses be called voluntarily at trial? The less one must impose on nonparty witnesses, perhaps the more benevolently they will look upon one's requests.

Counsel will also want to consider the purposes of depositions listed above and their possible application to the particular case at hand. This sort of analysis should go into the planning process and not be left to chance. Is it especially important given the nature of the specific case to pin down various witnesses to stories in order to prepare the case adequately?

Sometimes the case is such that there may be reason to think that some witnesses might be tempted to be less than candid. This is more likely to happen when personal relationships and human emotions are involved in a case than in other kinds of matters. In a case in which, say, the controversy has to do with whether 100 of the 1000 items delivered to plaintiff were damaged, the parties may view the dispute as a business problem in which no one's emotions or personal integrity are implicated. The tendency to shade the truth may be less in such a case than in others. Careful attention should be given to how to develop material for impeachment at trial.

Will it be helpful to size up certain persons as potential trial witnesses? Will the chances for settlement be affected by doing so, or not doing so? Because the great majority of cases settle, this is an important question, even though thinking of depositions as part of preparation for trial comes far more naturally to the litigator than thinking of them as preparation for settlement.

What other discovery devices may be used, and how productive are they likely to be? Can document production and interrogatories produce much, given the nature of the case? If one does use other devices, what will be left to prove, and what witnesses are available to use in this regard? Is it possible that relevant documents and witnesses exist and the identification of them requires depositions? If there are documents in the case, how will they be admitted at trial?

How helpful will depositions be in uncovering facts? How will the depositions be used at trial? What necessary testimony will be or should be presented live? How might the rules limit what can come in by deposition (e.g., distance, absence, illness, etc.)? How will key documents and other evidence get admitted at trial? Are certain depositions essential to getting certain evidence before the jury if no one is available to offer it live? Counsel should plan and pursue discovery with the needs and realities of trial in mind and not leave things to chance or wait until the eve of trial to organize the case.

The discussion thus far in this part has addressed oral examinations. But the deposition on written questions is also a tool that may be useful under some circumstances, although it is generally much less flexible, thorough, penetrating and effective than the oral variety.[2] In a state case, there must be a stipulation or out-of-state witness involved. A deposition on written questions may be appropriate if the case is one of modest dimensions and expenses are a special concern. One is more likely to use the device if the deposition will be simple and narrow in scope. One would not want to limit oneself to written questions if the witness is a key one.

With most witnesses, the interrogator will wish to observe the witness's demeanor and manner of responding, to weigh the content of the answers and to frame and modify questions accordingly during the course of the deposition. With a witness whose credibility will be important at trial, an attorney will also want to evaluate how well the witness testifies in order

---

2   Part One, chapter 11 discusses in detail depositions on written questions.

to be better able to prepare for the trial or to effectuate a settlement. These sorts of witnesses will not be suitable ones to depose by written questions.

Use of the deposition on written questions might also be influenced by the fact that the witness may be able to read every question before the session such that the possibility of spontaneity is limited, if not entirely remote. Thus, a witness who has no stake in the outcome of the litigation and who is not tempted to assume a tactical posture during the deposition is perhaps a candidate for a deposition on written questions.

The deposition on written questions might be used to present a modest number of narrow inquiries about documents, but not for extensive, detailed probing about many documents. If there is a dispute as to whether a person should be deposed orally, a deposition on written questions might be employed as a threshold mechanism to clarify that person's knowledge about relevant subjects, which could then be explored in an oral deposition if it turned out that the witness in fact had sufficient relevant information.

As to the number of depositions that should be taken, the federal rules presume that there should generally be no more than ten depositions and that each deposition will take no more than seven hours.[3] Stipulations between the parties are highly touted by FRCP 26(f) and other aspects of the rules. Counsel should calculate their own needs and those of their adversaries and attempt to reach agreement about the number and length of depositions. An attorney may need to compromise a bit to get what he or she needs from the adversary, but agreement is encouraged by the rules, is less expensive and time-consuming than disputation and is usually achievable.

Although there are no rules on the number and length of depositions in state court, justices also expect that counsel will seriously endeavor to reach agreement on such issues without having to trouble the court about them. Should a motion regarding discovery be made, an affirmation of good faith under Uniform Rule 202.7 is required.

At the FRCP 26(f) discovery conference, the parties must arrange for the mandatory disclosures under FRCP 26(a)(1), which include the identification of witnesses, and then present any changes needed in regard to such disclosures. Federal Rule of Civil Procedure 26(f)(3) requires consideration of changes to any limitations on discovery imposed by the

---

3   FRCP 30(d)(1), (a)(2)(A).

rules. The parties thus should prepare for the conference by giving attention to the number of depositions needed. The post-conference discovery plan mandated by FRCP 26(f) should address the number of depositions needed by the parties.

If a party is considering taking a deposition on written questions in a federal case, that deposition will be included in the calculation of the ten-deposition maximum. In a case in which the maximum will be exceeded, stipulation or court approval is required. A litigant may not wish to be barred from taking oral depositions because he or she took some on written questions, all other things being equal.

D. Who Should Be Deposed?

Together with the calculations as to the number of depositions to be taken, counsel must focus on the identity of the prospective deponents. The two questions obviously are interrelated.

When it comes to nonparties, a side may be able to achieve voluntary production of a particular person at trial. Sometimes the sole objective of a nonparty deposition is the production of documents. The state rules in this regard are intended to facilitate document production and authentication of documents without the need to produce the witness to testify.

With regard to parties, the adversary, of course, is generally deposed (unless, perhaps, the case involves very small sums).

E. Depositions of Corporations and Other Entities

If the adversary is a corporation, the situation is a bit complicated, as discussed in chapter 2 of the first part of this book. In a state court case, the organization has the right in the first instance to select the person to produce on behalf of the organization. There is no formal mechanism in place to prevent organizations from seeking to misuse the process by producing an uninformed person and then claiming that the adversary has had her opportunity to depose the entity. Courts, however, are alert to the potential for abuse. Good faith on the part of the organization and its attorney is expected. Manipulation of the process is unlikely to be successful. The court will simply order someone else produced if there is an indication that the witness was ignorant. The effect will merely be to waste everyone's time and increase expenses, including for the organization, an eventuality about which virtually every organization nowadays is quite concerned. As noted, sanctions can also be imposed upon an attorney who abuses the rules.

In federal court, counsel who seeks to gather facts about and to build a record regarding the conduct of a corporate party or other entity initially must consider whether to proceed under FRCP 30(b)(6). As noted,[4] that provision does not preclude an attorney from naming specific individuals who carried out the corporation's actions in the matter and deposing them directly. If only one or two individuals were involved and their identities are known (usually because they are known to the attorney's client), there may be no utility to proceeding by FRCP 30(b)(6).

Counsel must be confident that he or she knows the basic facts of the case and the identity of the persons involved. Documents may also influence this calculus. If there are few documents in the case, it may be relatively easy to obtain testimony about them and to authenticate them. When masses of documents are produced, the challenge can be greater. If the one or two deponents will likely be familiar with a modest number of documents, depositions of them may suffice.

If the party does not know the individuals at the entity who took part in the events at issue and does not know whom to ask about documents, then a FRCP 30(b)(6) deposition may well be in order.[5] If there will be fairly tight limits upon the number of persons to be deposed, one would not want to use up many of the allowable number "searching" for the correct deponent.

When a FRCP 30(b)(6) deposition is used, the examining party may learn at the deposition or otherwise the identities of individuals not produced by the entity for the 30(b)(6) deposition who must nevertheless be deposed. Here, too, the interrogating party must consider the limit on the number of depositions. If the 30(b)(6) deposition yields the names of persons whose depositions are truly needed and whose existence was previously unknown, counsel, if necessary, may have a basis for asking the court to adjust the limit on the number of depositions.

In federal court, the party seeking to depose the entity pursuant to FRCP 30(b)(6) should pay close attention to the deposition notice, which must identify the topics about which the entity is to be deposed "with rea-

---

4   *See* Part One, chapter 2.

5   Sidney I. Schenkier, *Deposing Corporations and Other Fictive Persons: Some Thoughts on Rule 30(b)(6)*, Litig., Vol. 29, No. 2, at 20, 21–22 (2003) (hereinafter "Schenkier")

sonable particularity."[6] The notice should be clear; the noticing party should eschew prolix, vague descriptions filled with jargon. The notice must be particular enough so that the corporation can, in a reasonable manner, determine whose presence is needed at the entity's deposition to testify on its behalf and be able to work with that person or those persons to prepare for the deposition. If the notice is overly broad and vague, it prevents the entity from carrying out its basic duties under FRCP 30(b)(6) and defeats the objective of the rule. Further, an overly broad and vague notice may elicit an objection and perhaps a motion for a protective order, which can lead to delay and expense. Thus, it should be in the interest of the examiner to avoid obscurity in the notice.

On the other hand, the notice should not be framed so narrowly as to create an unfair advantage at the deposition. Counsel should keep in mind the jurisprudence discussed in chapter 2 of the first part of this book, concerning the notice as a possible limitation on the scope of discovery. The notice ought not constitute such a limit. Nor should the inquiring party attempt to seek an unfair advantage by trickery, framing the notice in a narrow way with a view toward "sandbagging" the entity by springing new topics upon a witness quite reasonably not prepared for them. Discovery is not a game of trickery, and attorneys have ethical obligations to fulfill. The witness faced with questions for which he or she is unprepared for this reason—because they are plainly outside the scope of the notice—should not be expected simply to guess. Another person may have to be produced by the entity to answer these questions.

The notice also should not be unduly voluminous. Discovery, of course, despite the best efforts of the drafters of the rules and the courts, does occasionally go overboard. In the past, for example, courts used to witness from time to time service of exceptionally voluminous interrogatories, replete with parts and subparts, and answers just as voluminous, though perhaps filled with not particularly enlightening stock phrases, some repeated over and over again. The absence in FRCP 30(b)(6) of any express restriction on the number of subjects to be included in the deposition notice does not mean there are no limits whatsoever. The approach of the deposing party should be a reasonable one. If too many subjects are listed, the entity may seek judicial intervention by means of a motion for a protective order on the ground that the notice imposes an undue burden, which, again, will delay progress and increase expenses.

---

6   See Appendix, "Notice of Deposition (FRCP 30(b)(6))" (federal form).

The interrogating party should be able to list a reasonable number of subjects and do so in reasonable detail to achieve its goal of obtaining a meaningful deposition while avoiding imposition of an excessive burden upon the entity.[7]

For its part, the entity served with a FRCP 30(b)(6) notice needs to take its obligations just as seriously. Federal Rule of Civil Procedure 30(b)(6) was intended in part to prevent entities from producing ignorant persons in an effort to trick the adversary—the so-called bandying problem. The rule was also designed to assist entities by protecting them from repetitious productions. Thus, compliance with the rule serves the interests of the responding entity.

The entity has a clear and definite obligation—the case law is unmistakable about this—to prepare for the deposition by gathering relevant facts and producing a knowledgeable witness. If one is not readily available, then one must be educated. If several persons need to be produced to give a full picture, then so be it—they must be produced. The inquiring party has a right to a deposition of the entity that is not an empty formality. The entity should be careful about adhering to this requirement because the penalty for abuse can be severe—if persuaded that the rule has been abused, the court can find there has been the equivalent of a failure to appear altogether, which, in a proper case, can result in a significant sanction. An entity that does not fulfill its obligations to produce a knowledgeable witness or witnesses may only achieve a direction from the court to produce someone else, along with an imposition of costs on a motion.

At times, the FRCP 30(b)(6) notice may create difficulties for the responding entity. Some of the potential defects in such a notice have been alluded to. The entity faced with a defective notice should not make an inadequate effort to prepare and then hope later to blame it all on the notice. If the notice truly is seriously flawed, such flaws should promptly be brought to the attention of the adversary, and an effort should be undertaken to remedy the situation. If that does not work, the court should be alerted. Here, as in so many other areas of discovery, it is important that issues be addressed immediately so that discovery can proceed expeditiously. It is particularly important to avoid the all-too-common situation in which a dispute about a specific item of discovery throws a wrench into a schedule of discovery covering other items.

---

7   Schenkier, *supra* note 5, at 22. As noted in chapter 2 of the first part of this book, the deposing party cannot properly demand the production of the most knowledgeable person at the entity, only the one(s) called for by the rule. *Id.*

F. Testifying Experts

In a case in state court, setting aside depositions of parties who are experts (e.g., a doctor in a medical malpractice case) or experts who are testifying as witnesses to events (e.g., a key treating physician), an opportunity to depose a testifying expert (barring a stipulation between the parties[8]) will arise as a practical matter only when it is demanded by the adversary and only when the circumstances of the case fall within the narrow confines of *special circumstances* as interpreted by the cases under CPLR 3101(d)(1)(iii).[9]

Thus, almost by definition, if it is possible under governing law to obtain a deposition of a testifying expert, one will want to take that deposition. The expert will have knowledge of tests or scenes or conditions that can no longer be duplicated, and the attorney will want to find those facts on the record and to gain information that will be needed by the inquiring attorney's own expert. The witness's opinions will be excluded.

In a federal case, in which one can obtain an expert deposition much more readily and where its scope will be much broader, a question might arise as to whether a deposition should be taken. One commentator reports that the overwhelming majority of lawyers take expert depositions and do so in part because, since most cases are settled, it is advisable to confront the opposing expert at deposition and see whether the outcome may affect settlement value in a favorable way.[10]

For the small minority of practitioners, foregoing the deposition can be risky and should be considered only when the expert report is thorough and clear, the potential examining attorney is comfortable with the subject matter and will be well and adequately prepared at trial and a trial is highly likely.[11] Alternatively, the attorney may take only a brief deposition of the expert in order to evaluate the expert as a witness, which also avoids

---

8   A stipulation might be entered into in a commercial case.

9   It is theoretically possible in a medical, dental or podiatric malpractice case for a party to offer a trial expert for deposition and, if the other side accepts, to take the deposition of that side's expert. CPLR 3101(d)(1)(ii). However, because a party is eager to take the deposition of the adversary's expert but is never eager to offer up his or her own, this provision is not often used. Each side prefers the CPLR 3101(d)(1)(i) disclosure, even with all its weaknesses.

10   Laurin H. Mills, *Taking Chances at Depositions*, Litig., Vol. 28, No. 1, at 30, 36 (2001) (hereinafter "Mills").

11   *Id.* at 36.

disclosing to the adversary the attorney's view of the case.[12] As noted in chapter 4 of the first part of this book, the drafters of amendments to FRCP 26 hoped that a detailed expert report might obviate the need for a deposition of the testifying expert.

Gregory Joseph sounds a cautionary note about the advisability of expert depositions.[13] He reminds the attorney who considers deposing the adversary's testifying expert that the expert report, the elements of which are enforced in federal court, itself provides a significant means to "lock in" the expert's testimony. If there is a failure to disclose prior to trial all required information—which includes "all opinions to be expressed and the basis and reasons therefor"—the information will be excluded at trial if its admission would be harmful.

Furthermore, taking the deposition will help to educate the expert and opposing counsel as to the examiner's theories and what may come on cross-examination and can allow an expert to broaden the subjects upon which the expert will be able to testify beyond those set forth in the report, since discovery by deposition supplements the expert report. It should also be remembered that the potential examiner can demand production of the notes, drafts and other documents of the expert pertaining to the case, which may provide enough additional information beyond the report itself to obviate the need for a deposition.[14]

In any event, counsel should keep in mind the time for the exchange of expert reports when working out a discovery schedule.

G. Where Should Depositions Be Taken?

Generally, a deposition is taken in the office of the attorney who noticed it. This customary practice usually suffices. In some instances, however, an attorney may anticipate difficulties at a particular deposition because of the expected hostility of the witness, the aggressive temperament of opposing counsel or the likelihood that significant objections, perhaps on privilege or other grounds, might be raised. The attorney may therefore provide in the notice of deposition that the situs will be the courthouse if it is possible to get a ruling from the court should the need arise.

---

12 *Id.*

13 Gregory P. Joseph, *Expert Approaches*, Litig., Vol. 28, No. 4, at 20 (2002) (hereinafter "Joseph").

14 *Id.* at 20–22. "[T]he answer to the question whether you really want to depose that expert is often no." *Id.* at 21.

It is expected that the plaintiff, having commenced the action in the district or county, will generally appear there for deposition. Defendant will also generally be deposed in the state in a state case. Parties planning a discovery schedule should consider whether any other parties are nonresidents who may seek to avoid deposition here due to considerations of age, ill health and the like.

A nonparty generally will be deposed in the county or state or country where he or she resides. This may necessitate a commission in a state case, which should be sought well in advance, preferably by stipulation but by motion if needed. Discovery abroad is likely to be even more time-consuming to obtain in either a state or federal case. Unless this discovery is pursued in timely fashion and energetically, the attorney seeking the deposition or documents may find that too much time has gone by without the deposition having occurred or the documents having appeared, with the result that a waiver may be threatened. Care, diligence and early planning and action are very important when foreign discovery is anticipated.

As noted, provisions in the CPLR may avoid the need for deposition in order to collect and authenticate documents. If a deposition is necessary and it must take place far from New York, the parties will have to incur, in addition to the normal expenses, the cost of travel and accommodations. In some cases, it may be worthwhile, as alluded to earlier, to use some technological assistance and avoid actually having to travel to the witness's location. Or, with some witnesses under some circumstances, it may be wise to plan for a deposition on written questions.

H. When in Relation to Other Devices Should Depositions Be Taken?

The discovery plan must, of course, include other discovery devices as required by the case. This requirement means that the attorneys at the outset should decide what other devices should be employed and when depositions should be taken in relation to the other devices. In some kinds of cases, this matter of timing is simple and almost self-evident. In others, careful thought is required. In a federal case, mandatory discovery will be available from the outset.

Many personal injury cases in state court involve a standardized order of staged discovery, which may be embodied in a preliminary conference order issued after a bill of particulars has been supplied. The defendant will need, first, authorizations for the plaintiff's medical records and employment records if lost wages are claimed. These authorizations will be sought at the outset because some months are usually required before the records are produced by those who maintain them. The plaintiff may seek records of defendant bearing on the issue of notice, records regarding the design of a product or changes to a site and so forth.

Depositions generally will be scheduled for a date later than the time by which the various records are to be produced. In light of defendant's priority, the plaintiff will likely be produced first and will be questioned about the events of the incident, the injury and any consequences thereof for plaintiff, in which respects the records produced from the authorizations will be fundamental.

The defendant or defendants will be deposed next, perhaps beginning on the same day as the plaintiff's deposition. There generally will be no provision for expert depositions. The plaintiff's physical will be scheduled to take place after the depositions, followed by a date for the service of medical reports and a note of issue deadline. The plaintiff will also have to produce a CPLR 3101(d) statement. The statement may arrive comparatively late in the day, and discovery should be planned for and pursued accordingly.

A similar schedule might be established in a federal court case involving alleged personal injury. As noted, however, experts may be deposed in federal cases. Such depositions usually will occur in the later part of the discovery period, after other information has been produced.

In a commercial case in either court, the order in which discovery should take place and the devices that will be used may be clear and require little study. Interrogatories may be used first in order to generate information clarifying further the facts at issue, setting a general framework for the case and identifying potential witnesses and the nature and location of documents. If a corporation or other entity is a party, interrogatories can be used to elucidate the structure of the entity and the portions of it that may have had a role in the contract or other transaction at issue and thus may be in a position to produce relevant evidence. The interrogatories will often be followed by a demand for the production of documents.

As explained in chapter 3 of the first part of this book, a party may demand that documents be produced at a deposition. Generally, however, it is much preferable to have documents produced in advance of, rather than at, the deposition. Put another way, it will be a rare case in which an attorney can benefit from having documents he or she demanded produced at the deposition rather than in advance.

It is better to have the documents in hand in advance of the deposition so that one can study them with care before asking questions at the deposition. It is much harder to make effective use of documents when they are produced at the session itself. There is barely time to read the documents, let alone think through what they mean in the context of the case as a whole and develop questions based upon them. Often documents are collected from various sources, and the attorney will need to review documents produced and compare them carefully to others collected from elsewhere. There is also the fact, noted in Part One, that some questioning may need to touch on the documents during the deposition before the documents are actually produced.

A party may demand documents by category in advance of the deposition, and the demand must identify the documents sought by item or by category with "reasonable particularity." Counsel should be very alert to this requirement, as it may prove key to being able to use CPLR 3120 rather than the less helpful CPLR 3111. In a commercial case, interrogatories can be useful in achieving the necessary identification.

Even if documents are produced in advance of the deposition, questioning during the deposition should touch on the possibility of other documents of relevance and their possible locations. Such information can be used to support additional document demands.

If a case does not fit into the personal injury or commercial paradigms, some variations to the above scenarios may be necessary. The critical point is that counsel weigh all aspects of the case that could bear upon the question and make appropriate decisions in advance about the order in which to proceed with the various discovery devices that are useful in that case.

A schedule ought to be embodied in a stipulation or court order. Sometimes in federal court, the pretrial scheduling order[15] will set out a rough schedule and a closing date. If more is necessary, the court will likely be receptive to a proposed order and counter order. In state court, the preliminary conference order will fulfill this role.

If an adversary violates the order or stipulation by failing to produce discovery in the order scheduled, the victimized counsel should consider seeking relief, by motion if necessary. The victimized counsel should certainly not violate the court order because the adversary has done so. But doing nothing at all is neither necessary nor advisable. An adversary should

---

15   See Appendix, "Pretrial Scheduling Order" (federal form).

not be able to eliminate the efficiencies gained from a staged, orderly discovery process by violating an aspect of the discovery plan and then insisting that the other side proceed in accordance with the original schedule anyway.

I. In What Order Should Depositions Proceed?

In framing a discovery plan, counsel should consider as well the order in which the various depositions should proceed. Some of this procedure already may be determined—in state court cases, as noted, the defendant generally has priority. To the extent possible, it may be beneficial to an attorney's case to proceed with depositions in a particular order. Would it be helpful to the plaintiff's case, for example, to depose one defendant— say, one less involved—before others? Might the stories of witnesses align themselves if a particular one were allowed to be deposed before another? Would it be better to have the accounts of the parties on the record before those of nonparty witnesses—persons with no particular interest or stake in the outcome?

The attorneys might be assisted if some depositions were to be taken before others simply as a matter of logic and efficiency. In a complex commercial case in which many depositions will be taken, there may be benefit to taking depositions in stages according to some logical subject matter order. There may also be reason to take some depositions in a particular order, perhaps in stages, in accordance with a plan for motion practice, such as a motion on jurisdictional grounds, ADR proceedings or the like.

The circumstances of individual cases will affect how the order is developed. The point is that counsel will wish to focus on this question in drawing up a discovery plan for the particular case at hand.

J. Using Technology When Taking a Deposition

Technology can aid attorneys taking depositions. It will be helpful for counsel to give thought to the possibility when making a discovery plan.

A witness can be deposed by telephone. In state court, as pointed out earlier, a telephonic deposition requires a stipulation. Generally, of course, not being able to see the witness as he or she is questioned poses a considerable disadvantage. The questioning attorney will normally want to be able to watch the witness as questions are posed to gauge whether the witness is being candid or evasive. The witness's demeanor during questioning bears on credibility (as noted in the discussion of videotaped depositions in chapter 5 of the first part of this book), and that is something the questioning lawyer will usually want to evaluate, together with the witness's likely impact upon the jury. The witness's reaction to questions can suggest avenues to pursue or points to emphasize during the questioning.

Moreover, questioning about documents, photographs and the like is cumbersome when done by telephone. Some attorneys might well decline ever to take a deposition by phone for these reasons. There may, however, be witnesses who can be deposed in this way effectively and efficiently. Probably such a witness will be a nonparty whose involvement in events is narrow and who has no stake in the outcome so that the deposition will be simple, brief and free of contention.

Video conferencing clearly allows for a more convenient deposition. The attorneys can see the witness and one another so that everyone knows who is present and can observe the demeanor of the witness and the actions of the questioning and defending attorneys. Video conferencing is relatively expensive, and the facilities needed may not be available in every community. However, it can be a considerable convenience and conserve resources if an attorney can avoid travel to a distant location for the purpose of taking a deposition, and the cost of video conferencing is likely to decline.

It may be helpful to record some depositions by videotape rather than traditional stenographic means (or with the latter used in addition). Video is more expensive than stenographic means, but it can be worthwhile in certain circumstances. A video deposition may be beneficial, for example, if one expects that an important witness will not be available at trial. A seriously ill plaintiff may wish to have his or her deposition so recorded. There may be an important nonparty witness who resides out-of-state and will not testify at trial. These may be situations in which a videotaped deposition would be useful.

Further, the attorney needs to consider whether the witness will appear to better advantage on tape than in a cold record. Some witnesses will do better on tape than others, just as some persons make better witnesses at trial than others. If a party expects special difficulty in a deposition, it may be useful to proceed by video. If, for instance, one can anticipate that another party or a nonparty witness may be quite hostile and that the testimony may be highly evasive, it may assist one's case at trial if one can demonstrate this dramatically by video. The video displaying such flaws can have a far greater impact than can a transcript.

Impeachment can be more effective on video (though one must have an effective operator at trial). If an attorney is worried that the adversary may be extremely obstructive during the deposition, the use of video can serve as an incentive against misbehavior. Misconduct at a deposition by a defending attorney will seem more stark and dramatic on video than it will on a cold record. Since the defending attorney will likely realize that, he will probably be on better behavior on camera than he would be when the camera is unplugged.

When preparing a discovery plan, an attorney should reflect, with regard to depositions, not just on how to achieve the various basic objectives of the party in collecting and recording necessary evidence and testimony bearing on the claims, counterclaims and defenses, but also more generally on how to contribute to a presentation at trial that will be powerful and effective. This is a call for acute and sophisticated foresight, employed well before and during the discovery process. Lawyers, of course, pay close attention to how they present themselves before the jury, the preparation of their witnesses, the opening, cross-examination, closing and so forth. Attorneys should also consider *before depositions are taken* how the depositions can contribute to a powerful trial presentation, and counsel should prepare to take the depositions accordingly.

Video can help. Jurors are accustomed to seeing things on television screens and video monitors. Many are attuned to getting information in this way. For many, information comes across more powerfully and is better understood and absorbed through video. This advantage can apply to the deposition as well. In addition, counsel might employ documents and exhibits to render the deposition particularly clear and might conduct the interrogation generally in such a way that the presentation will be strong and effective so that the deposition, if used at length at trial, will favorably impress the jury.

When the usual stenographic record is used, an impeaching attorney may quote snippets to a witness by simply reading them. If extended portions of a deposition are to be included in the record, the attorney offering the testimony may read the questions and answers, perhaps with the assistance of an associate playing the role of the witness (but being instructed by counsel or the court to maintain a flat affect when responding to the questions so as to avoid tendentiousness). If the circumstances warrant, such as if the testimony is very important and needs to be especially persuasive from the presenting attorney's point of view, it may be advisable to think in advance about taking by video a deposition of this sort.

There are rules about how video depositions may be taken, as noted in chapter 5 in the first part of this book. One concern about video is the opportunity it presents for distortion. A video deposition should be a neutral recording of the testimony and should not be manipulated; anyone who harbors a private ambition to be a director or producer should give in to it on another occasion. The attorney for the deponent will want to be sure that the setup in the room is such that the witness is not made to appear shifty or unreliable.

A videotaped deposition obviously is not convenient on a motion for summary judgment. Counsel will want to have a transcript of the videotaped session that can be used in that context. Counsel also should keep in mind that editing may occur in response to objections, and editing can give rise to complications.

IV. PREPARING TO TAKE THE DEPOSITION

When a deposition is to take place, it should hardly need be said, the interrogating attorney must engage in preparation that is careful and thorough. In this process, there will be an investigatory phase and a phase in which questions are prepared. These phases will be different depending upon whether the witness is an expert or a lay witness and, if the latter, whether a party or a nonparty.

A. Investigatory Phase—Expert Depositions

When deposing a testifying expert in a federal case, counsel will need to carefully consider the kind of deposition he or she wishes to take. One can, as noted earlier, sometimes plan for and take a brief and relatively simple deposition. However, if, as is more likely, the examiner is inclined to pursue a detailed and thorough interrogation, he or she may wish to consider the ultimate objective at which aim is taken.

One choice is a straightforward discovery deposition, in which the examiner's only purpose is to gather facts about the expert's analysis and theories in order to prepare to face the witness at trial with as much knowledge as possible about what the witness will say and to provide ammunition for the examiner's own expert.

Another, certainly more aggressive and probably more risky, approach is, in addition to gathering information, to set one's sights on the goal of challenging and undermining to some degree the witness's opinions.[16] The intent of the latter approach is to attack and, ideally, thereby weaken the witness's confidence in her theory. By doing this, one could seek to shake the other side, to rattle their nerves, perhaps helping to render the atmosphere for settlement more sunny. By attacking, the examiner might force the witness to back off assertions in the expert report, committing her on the record to a position less favorable to the expert's side from which it will be difficult to depart at trial.

One might create contradictions to be exploited at trial. Or the examiner could even elicit concessions or admissions that will tie the other side's hand somewhat at trial. Or perhaps the examiner may hope to gain support for a motion for summary judgment. If the witness is confident, she may not be expecting an aggressive approach and may be thrown off balance by it, possibly leading to some helpful answers or concessions.

Which approach to take—perhaps there are really three, the third being a blend of the two—will vary with the case. Some cases are more difficult than others. In some there may be problematic and complex science, as a result of which the challenge of undermining the witness would be great and the risk of confusing the jury great too. Some experts are more forceful and formidable than others. Lawyers vary too, of course, and so will their level of comfort with the field of expertise involved.

Challenging the expert is difficult in any case. It surely requires more study and preparation than a more or less pure information-gathering approach. Because one is attacking on the expert's home ground, in her field of expertise, in which the attorney is only an amateur and autodidact, the battle will be uneven and success uncertain. Beyond the difficulty of the thing itself, there is the disadvantage that, at least in some instances, a confrontational approach will assist the other side in understanding the theory of the examiner and expert and in preparing all the better for trial.[17] One commentator writes:

> Once you have elicited at the deposition all information
> that is in the expert's brain, you should resist the urge to
> cross-examine and "destroy" the expert. All you are doing
> is educating him, and his counsel, as to the flaws in the
> analysis. At trial, you will face a better-prepared foe who

---

16 Steven C. Day, *Playing Hardball in Expert Witness Depositions*, Litig., Vol. 26, No. 4, at 19 (2000). This commentator refers to the second approach as that of the "hardball deposition."

17 *Id.*

will be grateful that you exposed his weaknesses before-
hand, while he still had time to make corrections.[18]

Instead, this commentator states, the "paramount goal should be to lock
the expert into his testimony and seal off all means of escape."[19]

In other cases, perhaps, the facts may be such that the tack the interrogator will take at trial will already be fairly obvious to the adversary simply because of the paucity of plausible alternatives.

Clearly, the examiner contemplating possible use of an aggressive
approach needs to carefully assess the circumstances. Much, if not all, of
the work described above will have to be undertaken at some point in any
case in which the adversary will present an expert at trial who will be
deposed. However, some of the preparatory work may be postponed until
the time of trial preparation if the examiner decides not to pursue an
aggressive deposition of the expert.

In a federal case, the examiner will want to consider in advance of the
expert deposition whether *Daubert v. Merrell Dow Pharmaceuticals, Inc.*[20]
may be involved. If it is, the deposition will need to explore, and ideally
pin down, the witness's work and opinions with the potential for a hearing
in mind.[21]

In order to prepare for an expert deposition, an examiner will, of course,
begin with the expert report. The report should provide all the information
required by FRCP 26(a)(2) and be signed by the witness. The examiner
will want to be sure the report complies with the rule. If it is in proper
form, the report will provide the key elements on which to focus. If it is
not in proper form, a conference with the adversary or the court or a
motion may be necessary to achieve that. This additional clarification is
not something about which counsel can afford to be casual. In addition,
the interrogator needs to collect everything available about the expert's
background and professional activities. He or she also must gather testimony given by the witness in other cases and everything the expert has
written about the subject at issue.

---

18   Peter L. Winik, *Strategies in Expert Depositions*, Litig., Vol. 24, No. 3, at 14, 17 (1998) (herein-
      after "Winik"); *see* Joseph, *supra* note 13, at 20.

19   Winik, *supra* note 18, at 18.

20   509 U.S. 579 (1993); *see Kumho Tire Co. v. Carmichael*, 526 U.S. 137 (1999).

21   Winik, *supra* note 18, at 14, 18, 73–74.

The attorney also must thoroughly immerse himself in the subject about which the expert will testify, whether it be medicine, accounting or investing in currency swaps. The attorney cannot hope to compete with the scope of the expert's knowledge. However, it might be possible through intensive study, and with the assistance of the examiner's expert, to acquire enough knowledge about the narrow sector of the expert's field that is at issue in the case to be able to ask productive follow-up questions at the deposition or, perhaps, to challenge the expert's opinions and conclusions.

One should prepare to explore at the deposition in detail the expert's education, academic career, positions of employment, research efforts, government assignments, publications and the like. The inquisitor should prepare to ask all about the witness's prior activities as an expert and explore all previous cases in which the witness served as an expert.[22]

Obviously, the examiner will explore with the witness in detail her analyses and the conclusions or opinions to which they have led. The expert report must contain "a complete statement of all opinions to be expressed and the basis and reasons therefor."[23] The examiner will want to elicit firm statements as to what the expert's conclusions or theories are and the reasons for those conclusions and theories so that no new conclusions, theories and supporting reasons can be offered at trial without giving rise to the possibility of impeachment. The examiner will want to box the expert in.

Further, the expert's report must state the "information considered by the witness in forming the opinions."[24] The examiner should explore in detail what that information is. What tests or studies were performed? What calculations made? What sources were considered? The examiner will want to review with the witness the reports or documents he or she considered during work on the case.

In addition to understanding how the expert arrived at his or her conclusions, the examiner will want to learn in full how the witness prepared the report and what the expert did to get ready for the deposition. The examiner should be alert to the chance that documents considered by the expert were not disclosed in the report, or that other documents were used in preparation for the deposition. If any documents were used by the wit-

---

22   *Id.* at 21.

23   FRCP 26(a)(2)(B).

24   *Id.*

ness but not produced, the questioner will want to seek them, through motion practice if necessary.

Part One, chapter 4 addresses the issue of production of work product, including core work product, if furnished to and considered by a testifying expert, a subject on which there is a diversity of opinion. The examiner will want to inquire to gather a factual basis for seeking any work product that the expert may have used that was not produced by the other side.

Depending on the case, the examiner may wish to inquire why certain tests or calculations that might have been performed were not. This inquiry can help to set up a clash at trial by clarifying what facts were assumed by the expert in coming to conclusions. It might be possible to establish at trial that the assumptions were incorrect, or that, although correct so far as they went, they were incomplete or inapplicable to the case at hand.

It will be important for the interrogator to elicit from the witness information about other reliable sources in the field—articles, textbooks, official standards, research studies, leading experts. Armed with this information, the attorney can prepare to deal with the expert on cross at trial. It is a great help if the questioner knows well in advance of trial that the expert believes, for example, that a particular text is authoritative—a position the witness can hardly change her mind about at trial, having already committed herself on the record. The attorney and his expert can study that text with care to see if it provides any fodder for an attack on the witness's opinions at trial.[25]

Even if the questioner decides to use an aggressive approach at the deposition of the expert, it may not be wise for the attorney to fire all her rounds. Some things may usefully be saved for trial in the hope of undercutting the expert's testimony then, when the witness may not be prepared to deal with them.

B. Investigatory Phase—Witnesses in General

When preparing to take a deposition, the interrogating attorney must be fully aware of the claims and defenses in the case and the elements thereof. The initial analysis of the case may remain unaltered at this point. But, depending upon when in the life of the case the deposition is to take place, the analysis may be different as a result of motion practice, the addition of parties, amendments, stipulations or discontinuances. The discovery to that

---

25   Winik, *supra* note 18, at 21.

date also may have an impact upon the legal posture or framework of the case. In light of this, the attorney should bring the analysis up-to-date and confirm the purpose(s) the deposition is intended to achieve under the circumstances then existing.

The attorney must make a thorough investigation of the facts relevant to the deposition. If the deposition is of a document custodian and record retention official, the investigation may be simple and brief. As just discussed, it will, at the other end of the spectrum, have to be elaborate if the deponent is a testifying expert witness.

If the deponent is a key fact witness or party, the focus will be upon the principal facts rather than technical concepts or expert analyses. Thorough preparation will still be required. The attorney may need to spend extended time with the client, with corporate officers or employees or with cooperative nonparty witnesses going over all facts that may be relevant and all contacts with or transactions involving the deponent.

Part of the investigation may also focus on the background and personality of the witness. It would be helpful to know whether the witness has been involved in other lawsuits and whether she or he has testified before. It may be useful to know about the witness's professional background. If the deponent is a corporation or other entity, these kinds of questions should be inquired into with regard to the entity. If the lawsuit has to do with a certain kind of transaction, it may be relevant to know whether the entity has been a party to similar transactions.

The attorney will want to integrate information gleaned from contacts with relevant persons with information gathered from documents produced by the deponent or by others in the case or used in other depositions. The attorney will also want to review other documents that may be encountered during the preparatory investigation, including the client's documents. All this information must be put together with the facts as revealed in the discovery and other depositions taken up to that point, as well as perhaps testimony from related litigation. This investigation should provide a solid understanding of the events at issue, in particular, the role of the witness therein, the documents the witness wrote or received and those about which she is otherwise likely to be aware.

It is hard to overstate the importance of thorough preparation. It is the key to building a case through discovery, especially depositions.

At the end of the investigation, the attorney should be in a position to develop some specific objectives for the deposition—not the general goals discussed earlier, but specific things he wishes to accomplish from the questioning of this particular witness.

What specific admissions does the attorney hope to obtain? What conflicts in testimony or with documents can be developed? What are the areas of the case as to which one hopes for enlightenment from this witness? Is there a particular account of events the attorney could reasonably hope the deponent would give? What important documents can the witness ideally illuminate? Do particular documents need to be authenticated for use on motion or at trial, and would the deponent be a good person to use for that purpose?

Does the examining attorney anticipate using the testimony primarily for impeachment? Does the attorney expect the witness not to testify at trial and to be able, under the applicable rule on use of depositions at trial, to use the testimony generally? What facts does the attorney hope to establish thereby? The attorney may wish to ask himself whether the deponent may know about other documents or other potential witnesses.

C. Preparing Questions

With these concrete sorts of things in mind, the attorney will turn to the preparation of questions for the deposition. This process may be somewhat looser than the attorney might use when preparing to question a witness at trial, since the ground rules of the deposition are more relaxed than those that prevail at trial. Nevertheless, this process cannot be treated casually. Cases can be won or lost at deposition.

There are perhaps three approaches: (1) the extremely elaborate, scripted one, consisting of numerous detailed questions; (2) an outline composed of subjects to be covered rather than individual questions; and (3) one that combines the latter with some aspects of the former. Documents to be included as exhibits need to be worked into the questions or outline.

In addition to preparing to ask questions to achieve the very concrete objectives developed through the investigation, the attorney also must strive, as suggested above, to produce a transcript, videotape or other presentation that will be coherent, powerful and persuasive to a jury in the event it is used at trial. The examiner needs to get the information and, ideally, get it in such a way that, if the transcript or other record is used at trial, it will be understandable and, moreover, have a significant impact favorable to the examiner's position.

A detailed script affords the questioner certain advantages. One can create on paper a presentation that follows a desired, presumably logical order that may at least be better understood by the jury as a result. One can be sure to cover all points of interest this way and to avoid, for example, failing to ask questions about a certain subject or failing to ask questions necessary to the identification or authentication of specific documents. One also can work out the list of exhibits to be used during the questioning and incorporate them into the questioning with ease and efficiency.

The disadvantage to any highly scripted approach, however, is substantial: The questioner may find himself or herself tethered too tightly to the script, lacking the flexibility to respond to the surprises that may arise or the unanticipated avenues that may open. Answers may surprise the questioner, may require prompt follow-up and thorough exploration. Or, the subject matter of certain responses, though not surprising, may be a detour from the path laid out in the outline. Sometimes answers bounce around even though the questions may not. At times the questioner might be able to make a note, literal or at least mental, and return to the new subject at another point in the script. But at other times, it may be more suitable, beneficial and effective not to let the opportunity pass, but rather to explore the new subject in detail then and there.

The witness may have made an admission or presented an account that is helpful to the questioner. Then, the questioner may want to explore the details and "nail it all down" before the witness, for example, during an overnight break, has an opportunity to reformulate the answer to better suit his or her own interest. That reformulation, of course, still can be attempted by the witness, but it is less easy to do when it appears not to be a correction of an isolated misstatement, but a change in an answer already thoroughly explored and affirmed and reiterated by the witness. There is, in short, a danger that the questioner may become a prisoner of a detailed script and may have difficulty departing from it when it would be wise to do so, as it often will be.

There may also be a tendency for a questioner using a detailed script to become overly comfortable with and reliant upon it and, as a result, to fail to master the facts with the ideal detail. The script may seem to provide such protection that it becomes unnecessary, the questioner may feel, to achieve easy command of the facts. If this phenomenon occurs, the examiner may find it difficult to adapt to the flow of the answers and to depart from the script and pursue a line of inquiry with adequate understanding when that course is needed to achieve the best outcome.

Departures from the script can wreak havoc with it. Thus, if the examiner were to decide to use one, it would almost surely require a good deal of editing during breaks. The questioner may find that the script very soon loses some of the clarity and orderliness he or she originally intended.

The questioning attorney may avoid the disadvantages that can arise from a detailed script by creating an outline consisting of topics to be covered, set out in a logical and effective order. Such an approach is much more flexible than a detailed script. It requires complete command of all relevant facts.

With an outline, there are two risks. First, of course, the attorney using this approach may forget to ask important questions. As only the topics are written down, it is certainly possible to leave something out. One can take stock overnight (or if necessary at the lunch break) if the deposition is to continue (in a federal case, it will be recalled, depositions are presumed to last for one day of seven hours), but one will not have any transcript to review for gaps or oversights (barring simultaneous transcription, an expensive proposition).

Second, one may ask the necessary questions in a general way but formulate them improperly under the stress of the questioning and find oneself with a problem later, on summary judgment or at trial. If the interrogator poses a compound question, for instance, and fails to correct it upon an objection as to form, the error may come back to haunt. Errors of this sort will occur less frequently when important questions are written down.

Some attorneys may find a middle approach beneficial—using a topical outline but incorporating specific questions that have important technical aspects or that are of special importance and carefully formulating them in a sound manner.

Some examiners prefer to bounce around from subject to subject during a deposition, rather than pursue a chronological or narrowly topical approach to the events at issue. The examiner may inquire about a particular meeting, go on to three or four other subjects, return to the meeting for some further questioning, proceed to an entirely new topic, return to one of the three or four and so on. The feeling is that the witness is less comfortable when open to any question about any subject at any time, less likely to recite a well-prepared account. If the examiner's style of questioning involves this sort of bouncing about, he must be very careful that all topics of interest and all events of importance are covered by the time the deposition concludes. There certainly is a risk in this manner of inquiry that something will be omitted through inadvertence.

Furthermore, the examiner must give some thought to the impression the record will make on a jury. If, in presenting testimony from the deposition transcript or using it to impeach a witness at trial, the examiner must bounce all over, reading a snippet from here and one from there, the impact is likely to be less than if the presentation is more organized. This diminished result especially will be the case with videotaped depositions. A choppy presentation of numerous little video bites will dilute a benefit that video offers.

Whatever approach is adopted, the interrogating counsel will want to be careful that documents are integrated into the questioning as needed. One can do this readily with a detailed script, but if in the actual questioning departures therefrom are required, questions based on documents can become confused. With a topical outline, one can collate a group of documents with the relevant topic.

The questioning attorney may wish to focus upon how clear and understandable the interrogation regarding documents may appear to a future jury. This appearance may be worth considering from the vantage point of whether the questioning proceeds in the orderly and logical way originally outlined. But it is also worth thinking about in light of the fact that there may be multiple documents by the same author on the same subject written at or about the same time, and copies of the same document may be used in a number of different depositions. The potential is there for confusion of the jury. The inadvisability of walking into a deposition without having received and analyzed the important documents cannot be emphasized too strongly.

Whether the examiner uses a script or a topical outline, he or she may wish to include therein some questions about what the witness, whether an expert or not, did to prepare for the deposition, apart from privileged consultations with the attorney and the client only. Such questions could reveal the existence of documents of which the questioner was unaware, the names of individuals of interest or possible waiver of a protection or of a privilege (e.g., waiver of a privilege because of the presence of a third person).

Also, the examiner should ask what documents the witness studied to prepare for the deposition. Mention was made above in connection with expert depositions about the possibility of waiver of work product with respect to materials furnished to the expert. As noted in chapter 3 of the first part of this book, documents used by a witness to refresh his or her recollection prior to a deposition may be discoverable. These should be produced if the examiner does not have them already.

V. PREPARING TO DEFEND A DEPOSITION

A. Facts and Documents

The attorney who is scheduled to defend the deposition will also need to pursue a careful analysis of the case and a thorough investigation of the facts. Once the deposition is impending, unless the witness being deposed is a noncontroversial nonparty or a person with very limited knowledge (say, a person who is to testify only about document retention policies or corporate structure), a thorough factual inquiry must be pursued with the witness and with other relevant persons, and this inquiry must be focused upon the deposition and what is likely to unfold there.

The investigation should include all relevant documents in the possession, custody or control of the client and those previously turned over to the attorney by the client. It should also embrace relevant documents produced in the case, other deposition testimony, related trial testimony and documents previously marked as exhibits. The investigation should be a mirror image of that conducted by the inquiring attorney—the same facts and issues should be looked at, but from the perspective of the other side.

For a FRCP 30(b)(6) deposition, counsel will want to be meticulous about compliance. The entity should identify potential persons to appear. If a number of such persons are available, the attorney will want to choose one who will meet the production obligations under the rule but who will also be an effective witness from the entity's viewpoint. A candid assessment may indicate that more than one person must be produced in order to provide the information called for in the notice. If so, that should be done and the necessary preparation of each undertaken.

When different persons are to testify about different areas, each should understand his or her assignment as such and should prepare accordingly. The attorney will want to undertake a thorough preparation and review of the subjects set forth in the deposition notice, working with the person(s) being produced. Good faith compliance with the production obligations is essential. The attorney will want to consider and address with the person(s) to be produced the possibility that the questioning might expand beyond the areas set forth in the notice and how that will be handled.

Although there is no analogue to the FRCP 30(b)(6) deposition in state practice, defending counsel may need to offer to produce, and to prepare, more than one person on behalf of the entity.

The defending attorney must give careful attention to the attorney-client privilege and work product protection, as well as any other privileges that may apply, and must provide comprehensive advice to the client about the deposition process and how best to testify at one.

With regard to privilege and work product, the attorney, of course, should not conduct the preparation in the presence of third persons. The attorney must also be cautious about documents used by the witness. If the witness is a testifying expert, as discussed in chapter 4 of Part One, materials prepared by the lawyer that would otherwise be protected by the work product doctrine may lose that protection if furnished to the expert and used by her in preparing for deposition.

Documents that an ordinary witness uses to refresh her recollection may have to be produced to the interrogating counsel because that use constitutes a waiver. Documents that have been produced in the case and may become exhibits at the deposition should of course be reviewed in detail. But as to other protected documents, the attorney will want to consider whether disclosure and production of the documents at the deposition will be undesirable, in which case the attorney may want to avoid providing the documents to the witness during the review process.

The attorney will want to review with the witness the facts which the witness has knowledge of and about which she may be called on to testify. These facts should include documents the witness wrote or received or on which she was copied. Counsel should also consider whether the witness saw or heard about a key document that does not bear her name, or had any involvement with the discussions or transactions referred to therein.

The defending attorney should know from his or her legal analysis and previous investigation the likely weak points of the case from the defense perspective. The attorney will want to pay close attention to these areas while preparing the witness. On the one hand, the witness will need to be well prepared to report the facts concerning these topics. On the other hand, counsel should be careful when framing the discussion of the case's weaknesses, lest the witness inadvertently conclude that she should manipulate or modify the truth in these areas.

With the usual witness, preparation concerns his or her role in the transactions. The witness needs to review those incidents so he or she can deal with them if questions are asked, to the extent memory and refreshing recollection permit. Preparation should not encompass educating a witness about transactions, events or communications with which she had no involvement.

The FRCP 30(b)(6) witness is different. Some such witnesses may testify about things in which they were involved and nothing else. But others may have a broader role: to state the position of the corporation or entity on the noticed topics. It may be that no one is still available to testify about topics from direct personal knowledge. Many a 30(b)(6) witness will need to undergo a process of education.

All this preparation must be careful, meticulous and thorough with respect to every document, event and fact that could conceivably arise at the deposition. The importance of this preparation cannot be overemphasized. Slapdash, half-hearted or cursory preparation is most dangerous for the attorney—and that attorney's client. One commentator forcefully sounded the following warning:

> I . . . am stunned by how few practitioners adequately prepare their witnesses, or themselves, for depositions. That is the chanciest proposition of all. Whether this failure is the result of ignorance, sloth, concern for fees, the refusal of witnesses to be prepared, the attorney's schedule, or some combination thereof, any attorney who does not adequately prepare his witnesses and himself is taking a big risk. Adequate preparation involves reviewing every non-privileged document in the case that the witness might have seen or written, and questioning the witness about every issue. Witnesses are obligated to tell the truth. But the truth always comes out better when your witness has heard a question, and thought about the answer, before he hears it at the deposition.[26]

The attorney will want to size up the witness in an effort to estimate how well she will perform under the stress of the deposition. If personal

---

26   Mills, *supra* note 10, at 36.

animosity, anger or other emotions are likely to surface at the deposition, the defending attorney should go over the issues with the witness during the preparation process and help her to conquer these emotions. Answering questions at a deposition while in the grip of powerful emotions will most likely fail to advance the deponent's cause.

The attorney may want to be cautious when it comes to witnesses who have testified before or personalities who might tend to be overly confident and to take the deposition too casually. Past experience as a witness can, of course, be very helpful, but it can also produce complacency. Overconfidence is dangerous whatever its origin. It can lead the witness to prepare insufficiently and to see the deposition as a contest with the interrogating attorney. It is important that the witness not be diverted by such emotions from a calm but serious approach to the deposition. If the attorney detects possible overconfidence on the part of the witness, he may need to address the problem with the witness directly and candidly. Even if the witness is a very senior official at the corporate client, the attorney may have to confront her if she seems to be hurrying through the preparation sessions, concentrating insufficiently and so forth.

Whoever the witness is, whether a high-level corporate official or individual client, the attorney will want to review with her the procedures that will be followed in the deposition and to provide advice about the attitudes with which to approach the questioning and the techniques useful to answering. It is wise as well to underscore that the witness will have to take an oath to tell the truth and, if necessary, explain the ramifications that might follow if the witness does not do so.

Every deponent who has not testified before should be given a description of the setting he or she will encounter and the mechanics that will be followed: the role of the reporter, questioning, answers, objections, the possibility of court rulings and so forth. In this regard, a novice witness would probably benefit to a considerable degree from viewing a video enactment of a deposition. Such a video would probably also be quite useful in getting across to the witness ideas on how to answer questions and how not to do so.

Some attorneys may find it useful to conduct role-play exercises with the client. The attorney may run through mock questioning to familiarize the client with the process. The personal experience may be enlightening in a way that watching a video, reading written material or listening to counsel may not. It is one thing for a witness to be advised, for instance, to answer the question asked without resort to narrative responses; it is another for the witness to become accustomed to giving answers in this way by actually practicing doing so.

The attorney can play the role of the defending counsel while an associate plays that of the examiner (assuming, from a practical point of view, that such an expenditure of time and effort would be reasonable given the sums at stake in the case).[27] The attorney could even tape-record a mock session for the witness, which would surely be of great assistance to the witness in understanding how to answer questions well. There can never be too much preparation, whether it be for deposition testimony or for trial.

B. Words of Caution and Advice

With regard to the manner in which a witness should answer questions, the defending attorney will want to impress a number of guidelines upon the witness, as discussed below.

1. Tell the Truth

Telling the truth is clearly the first and most important rule. No matter how significant the case to the person testifying or to the entity on behalf of which the person is appearing, the witness must always tell the truth. That practice is the only honorable and morally correct course. It is the course the attorney is ethically obligated to pursue. And, it is the course best suited to enhance the ultimate tactical posture of the case (again, although the reference is to the party witness, this injunction and the guidelines are applicable to nonparty witnesses too). If a witness is dishonest, that shortcoming is likely to emerge and redound to his or her detriment or that of the employer later on.

This obligation is broad. It does not mean the witness should avoid only flat-out lies; it also rules out half-truths, distortions, obfuscations and willful and insupportable misunderstandings of questions asked. The witness cannot adopt a private, unsupportable definition or interpretation of a question and answer based on that interpretation when all the world would interpret the question differently.

---

27   One commentator suggests that counsel be careful that role-playing not degenerate into a form of witness coaching. The witness should not be made to feel that the process is an act and that one's job is to come off well at any cost. Janeen Kerper, *Preparing a Witness for Deposition*, Litig., Vol. 24, No. 4, at 11 (1998).

2. Answer the Question Asked

A witness should always concentrate closely upon the questions, paying attention to the precise wording. The necessary level of concentration may be tiring and the witness may require breaks from time to time. If so, so be it; that occasional recess is the witness's right. The important thing is that the witness answer the exact question asked. The answer should be precisely responsive to the question. The witness should not make assumptions about what the questioner "really" seeks, or what the next question might be, or what the questioner must have meant. If one starts down that road, it can lead to many problems.

If, for example, the interrogating attorney asks, "Did you attend a meeting with your supervisor on July 14?," the witness should not assume that, because there was no such meeting on that date but there was one on the 13th, the questioner is concerned with the latter date and answer accordingly. The answer should be no. If there was a meeting on the 14th but it had to do with the company's annual softball game, not any issue in the suit, the witness should not mentally edit the question and answer in the negative. Since the question asked about "a meeting" and there was one on that date, however irrelevant, the answer should be yes. Further questioning will bring out the details.

The witness should assume, as is frequently the case, that the ultimate product of the deposition will be a transcript read by a judge on a summary judgment motion or heard or seen by jurors at trial. Private interpretations of the witness about the meaning of particular questions, of course, will not be apparent later on to the judge or jury. The result very likely will be confusion. A yes answer to a question about attendance at a meeting on the 14th that is premised upon the witness's interpretation that the questioner was really thinking of, or ought to have been thinking of, the 13th can lead attorneys, the judge and the jury to understand that there were two meetings when there was only one or, at a minimum, complicate and confuse the discovery process for a time.

The witness may find the questioning process difficult and ponderous and may want to "cut to the chase." It may be especially hard if the examiner seems ill-prepared, disorganized or not very skillful. The witness must resist the temptation to help move things along. It may be that the examiner's air of befuddlement is an affectation designed to induce just this reaction in the witness. Even if it reflects true weakness, the witness should follow the advice of counsel and answer just the question posed because doing otherwise puts the witness on terrain that is perilous to negotiate.

The witness should be wary of leading questions or questions that contain assumptions. Although the question may call for a yes or no answer, the witness may be called upon by that question to adopt factual statements or premises. The witness must be careful that these premises are accurately stated. If they are not, the witness may need to answer no to a question that almost calls for a yes. Similarly, the witness must be careful about a question that begins "You testified earlier about thus and so"; a mischaracterization, perhaps inadvertent, may easily be slipped into such a question, and, although it may call forth an objection from the attorney for the deponent, the witness must still be careful about an answer that might later be interpreted as endorsing what is in fact an inaccuracy.

Practice during preparation can be very helpful to a witness in developing the habit of listening closely to the questions and responding precisely to the questions as framed.

3. Do Not Volunteer Information

This guideline is related to the one that precedes it. The witness should not volunteer information for which the question does not call; he or she should simply respond to the question as framed, in a way that is complete but succinct. If there is more to it all, the questioning attorney will ask more questions. The witness's job is to provide answers; it is the interrogating counsel's job to ask the questions, and it is the job of the lawyer for the witness to prepare her for the deposition. If a witness is not advised to, and does not, curtail an inclination to volunteer information, the deposition will be prolonged. Moreover, if no firm constraints bind the witness, she may wander far afield. If the witness is a party, volunteering of information is certainly tactically unhelpful.

The personality of the interrogating counsel, or at least that presented during the deposition, has the potential to affect how the witness answers questions. Some attorneys are extremely aggressive and tough. Others believe that honey works better and affect a friendly, informal manner. Faced with a questioner of the latter variety, an uncounseled witness might succumb to an inclination to "help out" the personable interrogator.

The witness should be made to realize that, whatever the examiner's manner, he is not the witness's friend. Friendly feeling should not be allowed to influence how the witness responds; she simply should not volunteer information. Nor, on the other hand, should the witness feel pressured by an aggressive manner on the interrogator's part. The principle remains the same. If the interrogator goes too far and begins bullying and harassing the witness, defense counsel is present to protect the witness, if need be by an application for a ruling.

4. Do Not Guess

The deposition is a search for facts. The defending attorney will want to strongly emphasize during preparation that the witness should not guess what an accurate answer might be, whether because intimidated by the questioning attorney or influenced by a desire to "be helpful" to the friendly opposing counsel. The deposition is not analogous to a test in college in which the objective is to be right as often as possible and to make a good impression by doing so. Nor, in contrast with some tests in the educational setting, is there any benefit from an "educated guess." The witness should not be afraid to admit that she does not know an answer. Indeed, *afraid to admit* is not the best way to put it; better to say that the witness should not hesitate to provide as an answer that she does not know whenever that is the case.

The examiner might be unhappy with the answer and view the witness as someone not very good at his or her job if unable to recall what to the examiner seems important information. The witness should recognize that the good opinion of the questioning attorney in this context is not worth anything; it is irrelevant. What will matter is the opinion of the trier of fact, and the witness should prepare well and then follow the advice of counsel if she wishes to have an impact for the good on the audience that counts.

Similarly, if the witness once knew a certain fact but can recall it no longer, she should say "I do not recall" or the like; the fact that she once did know should not induce the witness to guess out of embarrassment or a similar emotion at having forgotten.

But, this guideline, like others, equally should not be abused. A witness who testifies over and over that she "does not know" or "does not recall" with regard to questions for which she must know the answers is acting improperly and risks imposition of a sanction. The witness must act in good faith. This tactic is, furthermore, unlikely to succeed. On any questions of significance, the examiner will not be satisfied with evasions, will seek a ruling and will probably prevail.

If the questioner inquires into an area in which there are or may be relevant documents extant, the witness, rather than guessing, may, if appropriate and if accurate, qualify an answer along the lines of the following:

"I cannot recall as I sit here now. However, if there is a document bearing on this, I might be able to remember upon seeing it."

If the examiner refers to a document, the witness can and should by all means request an opportunity to read it before answering questions about it. The witness should then read it in its entirety.

A guess should be distinguished from a reasonable estimate. If a foundation is established to show that a witness observed certain facts and an ordinary person could make a reasonable estimate with regard to the matter, such as distance with respect to an auto accident, then something other than a guess is sought by questions along these lines. Questions of this sort should be further distinguished from expert opinion, which is the province of experts to the extent the rules permit inquiry of them by deposition.

5.   Avoid Arguments with Counsel

The defending attorney will want to urge the witness to avoid being drawn into arguments with the interrogating attorney. That attorney has the right to ask about the facts. Arguing with the witness, however, is improper and will no doubt elicit an objection from the defending lawyer. The witness may be exasperated at, or angry with, the inquiring lawyer, but nothing is served if the witness gives in to the inclination to be drawn into argument.

There is also no point in a witness's venting anger at the examiner about the existence of the lawsuit, even if the witness is a defendant in what he or she believes is a meritless case. That behavior will not deter the questioner and may well distract the witness from the job of testifying well. If the examiner's conduct descends to the realm of harassment, defending counsel, if need be, can seek a ruling.

6.   Do Not Answer Until the Question Is Completed

In daily life, we often engage in conversations in which a listener anticipates the completion of a statement and provides an early response. In that context, informality is acceptable (even then, only within the bounds of decorum). Although a deposition occurs in an informal environment—in a conference room with no judge and no jury—and even though the rules that govern the questioning are considerably more relaxed than those that apply at trial, the asking of questions and the provision of answers are significant. The answers given can resonate on summary judgment and in the jury room and sometimes may be decisive of the case. Therefore, the witness would be well advised to approach the questioning with considerably more formality and care than might be appropriate in daily life.

The witness needs to hear the question in full to be sure what it seeks. Failing to do so can lead to a confusing record. It also can become a variety of the inadvisable practice of volunteering.

7. If the Question Is Confusing, Say So

The question may confuse the witness. The witness, out of fear of admitting to being confused, might attempt to provide an answer of a sort anyway. It will help the witness to hear from counsel that she should feel no reluctance when confused by a question to answer, "I do not understand the question. Will you please repeat it or restate it." If one tries to answer a question one does not understand, the answer is a sort of guess, which can confuse the record, mislead the attorneys and prolong the deposition.

8. Ask for a Question to Be Read Back if Necessary

The witness should feel free, and is within his or her rights, to ask for a question to be read back when repetition would help to elicit a sound response.

9. Correct Errors

If the witness answers a question and later realizes the answer was inaccurate, she can correct it at a suitable point in the deposition. The attorney should explain to the deponent in preparation that the transcript will be sworn to and that before the sign-off occurs there will be an opportunity to make corrections. But that does not mean a witness cannot offer a correction during the deposition if she realizes that an answer given a few minutes before was incorrect in some respect, and it may be advisable to make a correction quickly. Of course, the witness should be prepared to expect inquiry from the examiner designed to fully clarify the information.

10. Ask for Breaks as Needed

If the witness concentrates properly, the deposition is apt to be tiring. The more tired the witness is, the more likely she will provide inaccurate answers. So, the witness should understand that she may request breaks as needed. A break should not, however, be requested while a question is pending except to discuss a possible privilege.

11. Understand the Place of Objections in the Deposition

The defending attorney should explain to the witness what objections are and how they may be raised at the deposition. Counsel and the witness will want to review potential areas of inquiry that may be objectionable on some ground. The witness needs to understand objections so that she does not provide a rapid answer to a question before defending counsel has a chance to assert an objection. The witness should listen carefully to the objection and follow the directions of her attorney. The deponent should realize that, on occasion, the deposition may be interrupted in order to obtain a ruling from the judge.

Of special importance, of course, is the attorney-client privilege. It will be helpful if the witness understands the basic aspects of the privilege. The defending attorney will want to review with the deponent in advance of the deposition any communications the deponent had with counsel during the events that will be at issue in the deposition. Counsel will reach conclusions as to whether any such communications are privileged. The deponent should know which communications are privileged and should be aware that any questions seeking privileged matter will be objected to and the deponent will be instructed not to answer the questions. The same process should be followed with any other privilege that may be involved.

With thorough preparation, counsel and the witness should be able to review together all communications that might be privileged and that may be raised at the deposition, whether subject to the attorney-client privilege or any other privilege. However, a surprise may occur even then. The witness should be made aware that if a question asks for a communication between counsel and the deponent about legal matters or seeks to invade another privilege, the communication may be privileged and the deponent may consult with her attorney in private about the possibly privileged nature of the communication.

CHAPTER TWO

AT THE DEPOSITION

I. AGREEING UPON ADDITIONAL GROUND RULES

The basic rules governing depositions are set forth in the Federal Rules of Civil Procedure and the N.Y. Civil Practice Law and Rules, as discussed in detail in Part One. The parties often reach agreement upon other ground rules by consent at the outset of the deposition. An attorney will customarily seek such consent by asking the opposing counsel whether he agrees to the "usual stips" or the "standard stips." Before agreeing, counsel ought to be sure she is aware of the exact terms being proposed.[1] What is standard in one part of the state might differ considerably from what is standard elsewhere. Even greater diversity exists across the country in the federal system.

Counsel commonly will agree that all objections except those as to form are preserved for trial. Absent such stipulation, however, the rules impose a greater burden on the defending attorney—all objections are preserved for trial, except those as to form *or anything else that could have been cured by a timely objection.*[2] Because the examiner naturally would prefer to know about curable problems at the time when they can be easily cured, it would seem advantageous from the examiner's perspective to use the rules rather than the "standard stipulations."

II. ROLE OF EXAMINING ATTORNEY

Chapter 5 in the first part of this book discussed at length the law governing conduct of the deposition. That discussion is not repeated here. Counsel should be fully familiar with it. An attorney in a deposition should adhere to those rules even if the adversary conspicuously fails to do so.

At the outset of the deposition, the examining attorney should ask the witness whether she has been deposed before and explain briefly the procedures that will be followed. The interrogator might wish to inform the witness that if she does not understand a question, she should so advise the attorney, in which event the question will be rephrased. It is not in the interest of any party for confusion or misunderstanding to intrude.

A. Take Charge

The examiner will want to set a tone and a pace that establish that he is in control in the sense that he has a firm command of the material at issue

---

1   Professor McElhaney believes that most lawyers agree to the usual stipulations without knowing what they are. James McElhaney, *Deposition Notebook* 21 (2003) (ABA course materials).

2   See Part One, chapter 5.

and the questions to be covered, which will tend to inhibit the witness from trying to evade questions, offer unresponsive answers or overwhelm the questioner with the witness's greater knowledge and experience in the matters involved in the case. The interrogator's tone should be professional but determined. There is no need for anger, quarreling or harsh words. At the same time, the examiner has a right to the information being sought (unless it lies within the narrow confines of protected information) and therefore can and should pursue it doggedly and vigorously.

If the witness tries to be evasive, the questioner will need to bear down and to pursue information with rigorous follow-up questions. Generally, this approach will succeed, perhaps even tying up a hostile and elusive witness in verbal knots or eliciting answers that undercut those initially given. If, however, the witness attempts to make a mockery of the process by feigning ignorance, it may be necessary to seek judicial intervention. A judge's rejection of such efforts by the witness can go a long way toward preventing further outbreaks of convenient memory lapses.

The questioner must be respectful and professional toward the defending attorney while simultaneously being determined and dogged. In the early part of the deposition, a defending attorney of a certain stripe may try to test what he can "get away with" in the form of obstructive tactics. An interrogator who is a novice may well experience challenging, testing behavior from an adversary who hopes to intimidate and divert the questioner, or at least cause him to be less thorough. The interrogator who is asking proper questions will need to fend off all such behavior by proceeding to require answers.[3] As thoroughly discussed in chapter 5 of the first part of this book, the defending attorney may object but can direct the witness not to answer only in limited circumstances. Absent those circumstances, the examining attorney is entitled to an answer.

The attorneys at the deposition are obliged to try to work out any problems on their own. Discussion for this purpose is encouraged. However, some defending attorneys might wish to engage the examiner in frequent colloquy. The examiner will want to avoid these exchanges, as they can distract the witness, interrupt the progress of the deposition and suggest answers to the witness. To avoid being drawn into frequent discussions with the adversary on the record, the examiner can allow the adversary to state an objection, forgo any inclination to debate it but request an answer from the witness.

---

3   See *infra* II.E. for further discussion about handling obstructive behavior.

When the defending attorney objects to the form of a question or asserts another curable defect, the interrogator should consider whether responsive action is needed. In some instances, the problem with the question will be obvious. If the objection has merit, the interrogator should rephrase the question right away, again without debate, and continue with the deposition.

Some objections may be groundless. In some instances, it may not be clear what the basis of the objection is, in which event the interrogator may wish to seek a brief explanation from the defending attorney. If the defending attorney has been complying with the rules and is not being obstructive, it usually would make sense for the examiner unsure of a ground for an objection to ask for clarification. If the examiner is unaware of the basis for an objection and fails to correct a problem, the question may be ruled out of bounds later on, which, depending on its importance, could be quite harmful to the examiner's position.

If the defending attorney objects that a question is repetitive, the question should nevertheless be answered.[4] If defending counsel is not being obstructive, it may be well for the examiner to discuss the alleged problem with counsel. If the questions are important and the adversary is contemplating an application for a ruling, the examiner may wish to see if the reporter can, perhaps during a break, find and read back prior questions that are claimed to duplicate the latest ones. Disputes of this sort often arise because of differences of recollection, of course highly fallible, about earlier questions that may have been, or seemingly were, slightly different. Likewise, the questioner must stand on defensible ground if other nonformal objections are raised.

An examiner may encounter a verbose witness who ignores the advice undoubtedly given by his or her counsel and offers lengthy answers to questions. Such witnesses, who often ramble in a confusing way, may answer a question in part, perhaps a small part, but then bury the rest of the question under a pile of irrelevant words. With such a witness, clarifying follow-up questions likely will be needed. The questioner must eliminate any confusion and pursue the threads of the question left unanswered. Such witnesses often wander far afield in their answers; the examiner may need to come back to points to focus the witness's attention and to obtain a responsive answer. With such a witness in the chair, examining counsel also must continually keep in mind the shape of the record that is emerg-

---

4   See Part One, chapter 5.

ing. Although those present in the room may understand what is being said, the record must be comprehensible, especially, of course, in regard to key points.

If the interrogator has prepared well, he or she should be able to keep the deposition flowing. The interrogator can help to maintain an atmosphere of control by avoiding frequently lengthy pauses to think of what to ask next, to find his or her place in the outline, to figure out which document to inquire about next and so forth. Here again, preparation is vital and pays off.

Taking a deposition is hard work because it requires so much preparation and so much effort during the questioning itself. The questioner must concentrate intensely in order to frame questions that simultaneously are proper in form and will not lead to technical difficulties later on, effectuate the strategy the questioner developed for the deposition and pursue all the information sought. On critical issues, the examiner must be sure to pin the witness down to a complete and unambiguous account. The examiner will not want to leave gaps or ambiguities that the witness can use on summary judgment or at trial to avoid defeat or impeachment.

Although the examiner can and should be persistent, he or she must not abuse the process. The questioner should not argue with the witness or make discourteous remarks, nor ask plainly improper questions to harass, intimidate or oppress the witness. The questioner should particularly avoid highly personal and embarrassing questions not relevant to the issues in the case. It is unprofessional to press such questions. If that is not reason enough to eschew such questions, the examiner should wish to avoid damaging his or her standing with the court by the use of such tactics, and in perhaps more than just this one case. It is not worth it.

B. Listen Closely to the Testimony

The questioner should listen closely to everything the witness says. This directive may seem simple enough, but it can often prove difficult. The questioner, having posed one question, may begin to formulate in his or her mind the next question in proper form while the answer is being given; but the formulation process should not distract the attorney from hearing fully, understanding and absorbing the witness's answer. The answer might be unexpected, helpful, unhelpful, a diversion, productive of leads to other areas of inquiry, contain a small equivocation and so forth. Close listening to the answers and modification of the inquiry based on those answers is necessary.

If the questioner uses a detailed outline, there may be less need for concern about the formulation of the next question, but there may instead be potentially distracting instances in which the answers have departed from the order in the outline, requiring the attorney to find the proper place in the outline from which to launch the next question.

C. Avoid Irrelevant Questions

Relevancy is an area about which there is often disagreement at depositions. The interrogator should not ask irrelevant questions. As explained in chapter 5 of Part One, relevancy is broadly defined under state and federal law and should leave the interrogator with plenty of scope to proceed.

Objections on the ground of relevancy can and usually will be addressed at trial. However, the defending attorney may contend that a line of questioning would be palpably irrelevant, or both irrelevant and prejudicial. If an objection is raised, the examiner needs to be confident that the questioning can be satisfactorily defended if the adversary demands a ruling from the court.

D. Use of Documents

Especially with regard to testimony in critical areas, the examiner must develop an adequate foundation for the testimony. It is likewise important to authenticate documents fully. The examiner may assume that the witness will be available for trial, but fate may intervene, forcing the examiner to use the transcript. Admissibility may also come to matter on summary judgment.

In state practice, any documents demanded under a CPLR 3111 notice[5] need not actually be produced until the deposition touches on them. Therefore, the examiner will probably want to ask broad, open questions about the areas listed in the CPLR 3111 notice so that the deposition turns to the documents and they can be produced for inspection. The examiner will want to review with the witness, with reference to each item in the demand, what was done to search for the documents. The examiner must be able to develop an understanding as to whether the production is complete or not.

If, prior to the deposition, documents were produced by the witness or the entity for which he or she works, the examiner may want to review

---

5   See Appendix, "Notice of Deposition—CPLR 3111 Document Request" (state form).

with the witness what was done to ensure that there has been a full response to each item in the demand.

If necessary to the case, the examiner may wish to explore document retention policies with a witness. If the witness is not the correct person to testify about those policies (or, indeed, about other particular subjects), the questioner should find out who is.

E. Handling Obstructive Behavior

Defending counsel may not use speaking objections—a common problem in the past. This is particularly clear in federal cases, but it should not be attempted in state cases either. The defending attorney may not issue a direction not to answer except in quite limited circumstances. If the defending attorney abuses this authority, makes speaking objections or in any other way seeks to obstruct the deposition, the interrogator will have to take action.

First, the examining attorney should alert the adversary to the error of his or her ways. If that does not work, the attorney should seek judicial intervention. Conduct of this sort will surely prolong the deposition and make it more difficult than it needs to be and may even defeat it altogether. The interrogator should not have to accept such a situation.

It will often be most efficient for the examiner to postpone an application for a ruling or a motion to compel or for sanctions until the deposition is concluded with respect to other matters. That way, the court can address all issues at once. Sometimes, however, it may not be possible to wait. An immediate answer may be needed for questioning to continue in a whole area related to the questions(s) objected to. If the defending attorney is engaged in a seriously disruptive course of conduct, immediate intervention may be required for any progress to be made. Or action may be necessary if the defending counsel in a state case objects on relevancy grounds to a line of questioning that will be substantial and prolonged and directs the witness not to answer the claimed palpably irrelevant questions.

The best way to obtain a prompt and inexpensive resolution is to seek a ruling, perhaps even by phone. This is the preferred course. Only if difficult legal issues are involved would it ordinarily be advisable to proceed by formal motion.

III. ROLE OF DEFENDING ATTORNEY

It may be helpful for the attorney for the witness to inform the adversary at the outset of the deposition that he or she has no desire to obstruct the inquiry, will object only when necessary and will adhere to the rules. The attorney might also inquire whether the interrogator would be amenable to going off the record if a special problem arises so that the attorney may explain it to the interrogator without seeming to make suggestions to the witness. Discussions along these lines at the outset may set a tone of mutual respect and professional courtesy, which may advance the prospects for a smooth deposition.

A. Listen Closely to Testimony

Although the defending attorney's role by definition is much less active than that of the interrogator, the defending attorney has important functions to fulfill, which might be described (with some overlap) as protecting the witness and protecting the record. The defending attorney needs to concentrate intensely upon the questions and the answers. Although a deposition can be more relaxed than trial testimony for the defending attorney since many objections are preserved until the time of trial, the attorney (absent stipulation) must be alert to assert all objections—as to form but also as to all other curable matters—that will be waived if not raised.

The defending attorney must particularly listen for questions that (1) mischaracterize prior testimony in the deposition then taking place or in earlier depositions, (2) misstate other evidence, (3) misstate the allegations, (4) are ambiguous, (5) are unclear or confusing, (6) assume facts not in the record, (7) are compound, (8) lack a proper foundation, (9) are leading (where that may matter) or (10) are otherwise defective (even though the defects are curable).

In view of the comparative informality of the deposition process, and because the examiner may be searching for facts or leads to relevant evidence, he or she will be more prone during the deposition to ask questions that are defective in form or contain a curable defect than would be asked at trial. The defending counsel cannot afford to allow the informality of the setting to weaken his or her attention.

The attorney must also pay close attention in order to raise in a timely manner all objections based on the attorney-client privilege and other privileges. In light of the nature of the case and the pre-deposition preparation, counsel should be aware of and prepared to deal with areas of inquiry that could possibly intrude upon a privilege. However, counsel must remain continuously attentive because questioning might touch upon a privilege in a context beyond those the client and the attorney may have identified during pre-deposition preparation.

B. Consulting with the Client

Part One, chapter 5 discusses in detail the issue of consultation with a client-deponent during depositions. This discussion makes clear that the matter is a sensitive one, perhaps more so than many practitioners may recognize. There is disagreement in the cases and among commentators and bar groups. The Second Circuit seemingly has not yet settled on a clear rule, and there is almost no authority on the subject in state court cases or commentary.

On the one hand is the imperative of ensuring an honest and fair deposition, which means one that is not the product of coaching from counsel as the deposition proceeds. The client should be testifying, not conveying the ideas and words the attorney whispers into his or her ear. A deposition should proceed basically as does testimony in court, which of course cannot be coached. On the other hand, the client has a right to the advice of counsel. Where to draw the line?

The authorities clearly agree on one principle: When a question is pending, the witness and the attorney cannot consult unless it is to discuss the possible assertion of the attorney-client or other privilege. The witness should be instructed about this in preparation for the deposition. To assure the examiner, before such consultation occurs, the defending attorney should state on the record that the purpose of the consultation is consideration of the privilege. The defending attorney should clearly not confer with the proponent while a question is pending in other circumstances.

Defending counsel may wish to discuss with the examiner how any inadvertent errors by the witness might be addressed. The attorneys may be able to agree that if defending counsel believes the witness misspoke in response to a question, he or she can raise the issue with the examiner. With regard to some errors or confusion in the record, defending counsel may need to take up the question on cross-examination. The attorney for the witness should not, various cases suggest, call breaks during the deposition in order to coach the witness on how to answer questions being posed by the examiner.

As Part One, chapter 5 points out, the question of what is allowable during regularly scheduled breaks, overnight breaks and any extended hiatus between sessions of the deposition is difficult, and there are differences of opinion about it, at least in federal court. Defending counsel must be aware of this issue and be sensitive to it. Counsel should strive to avoid accusations that he or she is distorting the testimony by conferring with the deponent at length during such breaks about the content of the testimony.

C. Protecting the Witness

The defending attorney must protect the witness. If the questioning attorney appears to be harassing, intimidating or abusing the deponent rather than trying to elicit information, defending counsel should object and request that the misconduct cease. If the interrogator cannot be persuaded to cease and desist, counsel might have no choice but to seek a ruling from the court or to make a motion for a protective order. Counsel should make a solid record on the issue before seeing a judge. If the abuse seemingly will continue, the defending attorney may have no choice but to seek a remedy immediately rather than wait until other questioning is concluded.

An openness on the part of the attorney for the witness to seek rulings rather than to engage in self-help tends to demonstrate to opposing counsel and the court that the attorney's aim is an efficient resolution to a real issue, not obstruction of the deposition. That sort of attitude on the part of the attorney for the witness helps to keep the atmosphere in the deposition room professional and devoid of acrimony. The attorney for the witness can further contribute to that atmosphere by cooperating whenever possible with the interrogator's requests as to when the rulings should be sought or motion made.

D. Guidelines for Making Objections

If the questioning will yield confusion in the record, the attorney should object. One cannot be completely certain that confusion will not redound to the disadvantage of the deposing party (if the witness is a nonparty, she may have no interest in the outcome), whether on summary judgment or at trial, so the attorney will want to object. Often confusion can arise from questions that are formally defective in some respect. If a question is compound or assumes facts not in evidence, for example, the judge or jury later may not be able to ascertain with certainty the actual answer or, more perilously, may misunderstand it.

At the same time, defending counsel will not want to appear in the record as being hypertechnical and abusive. Objections to problems that cannot possibly matter—such as trivial instances of leading questions—may well be ignored. One needs to strike a balance, which will be influenced by the interrogator's skill, between preserving objections to form and other curable defects and so cluttering the record as to create a possible problem for the court should the examiner complain about interference.

In offering objections, the defending attorney who is not abusing his or her role ought to state briefly the basis of the objection. If this is done in good faith and briefly and does not amount to a speaking objection, the examining counsel normally will be glad to have the basis stated. If there is any validity to that basis, the attorney can rephrase the question and thereby avoid problems later on. If the objection is invalid or if the examiner does not care about admissibility so much as gathering information, the objection can be ignored. The parties should be able to arrive at a modus vivendi with regard to stating the bases for objection.

A problem arises if many hypertechnical objections are raised, even when the answer must be harmless to the client, particularly if these objections are stated in a verbose manner that has the effect of telegraphing answers to the witness. If the defending attorney avoids this tactic, the deposition should proceed smoothly.

E. Relevancy of Questions

As noted, relevancy is one of the principal sources of contention between attorneys during depositions. As explained in Part One, the scope of discovery, including depositions, is quite liberal and is much broader than the bounds of admissibility at trial. The test to be applied: Can the questions lead to the discovery of admissible evidence?

Furthermore, irrelevancy is an objection that is preserved for trial since the alleged irrelevancy of the information sought cannot be cured by a rephrasing of the question. The problem lies in the information sought, not in how it is requested. Thus, it is not necessary to object on relevancy grounds, and such objections normally should not be made. If a challenge is brought before the judge, the defending attorney may lose credibility by pursuing unnecessary objections. Further, such use of objections by the defending attorney may be turned against him or her when the chairs are shifted.

Some attorneys, when representing party witnesses, may tend to judge relevancy by an overly strict standard: whether the claim has facial or factual validity. A defamation claim may be defectively pled, or a cause of action alleging breach of contract may not be able to survive a motion for summary judgment. Nevertheless, such defects are not a basis for the assertion of irrelevancy.

Absent a successful motion to dismiss for failure to state a claim or cause of action or a successful motion for summary judgment, the claim is in the case and the defending attorney will have to accept that discovery thereon will be sought. If the attorney wishes to avoid a waste of time and resources resulting from discovery into the defective or baseless claim, he or she should aggressively pursue dismissal or summary judgment.

The foregoing is qualified by the reality that if the examination descends into a pursuit of the palpably irrelevant in state court, a direction not to answer may be justified. An individual question or two may be clearly irrelevant, but an answer may be harmless. In such circumstances, the defending attorney may wish to consider whether a direction not to answer is really needed. Usually, it would not be.

However, when the question is clearly irrelevant and an answer would be prejudicial, or when the examining attorney seemingly intends to pursue a detailed and time-consuming inquiry into a palpably irrelevant area, the defending attorney may be authorized to block the questioning in state court. The same may be said with regard to clearly irrelevant questioning that seeks to elicit personal, confidential or embarrassing information.

The defending attorney should not, however, decide these questions on his or her own—"unilaterally," to borrow from some of the cases. Rather, counsel should seek a ruling from the court at the time or make a motion for a protective order. This is the sound course, even though the courts in some cases have upheld objections on motions to compel.

The federal courts are stricter than the state courts concerning objections based on irrelevancy and will rarely grant a motion for a protective order prohibiting a deposition on those grounds. However, the defending attorney in a federal case may occasionally want to seek a ruling or bring a motion under FRCP 30(d)(4) if the inquiry truly is sufficiently oppressive to justify it.

If the court has already ruled that an area is no longer relevant to the case on a motion to dismiss or for summary judgment or otherwise, an application would seemingly be well justified. Also, a prior directive of the court can be a basis for a direction not to answer. The defending attorney should seek a ruling or make a FRCP 30(d)(4) motion, rather than rest on the objection until a motion to compel is made.

F. Cross-Examination

When the questioning of the deponent concludes, the defending attorney will have an opportunity to cross-examine. Merely because an opportunity for questioning exists does not mean it should be exploited. If the testimony is accurate, the defending attorney may do better to remain silent. Sometimes the testimony may have been accurately given but, because of the direction of the questioning, present an incomplete picture of what occurred, overemphasizing aspects of the case unhelpful to the party deponent and underemphasizing the positive ones. This problem is quite common.

If it is simply a matter of putting in one's proverbial two cents, silence may be preferable for the defending attorney. One will have a chance on summary judgment and at trial to do that, as well as to depose the examiner's client and perhaps cast him or her in the same sort of light. If one tries to present a more balanced view, one may only incite the examiner to ask yet more questions to restore the imbalance. Questioning that is not truly necessary may also educate the adversary.

If, on the other hand, the defending attorney is aware of some important errors the deponent made, it will usually be advisable to correct them then and there. If the testimony is accurate so far as it goes but presents a seriously distorted picture that might prejudice the deponent if not supplemented, some questioning may be necessary. Prejudice can occur, for example, on a motion for summary judgment if the deponent is precluded from clarifying important facts and placing them in a more favorable light, pursuant to the doctrine that a party opposing a motion for summary judgment cannot contradict deposition testimony.[6]

It should be remembered that when courts evaluate contradictory affidavits and the excuse that the witness was confused and made an error during the deposition, they may look to whether counsel for the witness made use of the opportunity for cross-examination to correct the error. If such an error is recognized at the time, the defending attorney should correct it. Again, questioning of the client-witness may well generate more

---

6   See Part One, chapter 10.

interrogation from the examiner, but, depending upon the nature of the corrections or supplementation, this may not be a problem or may be unavoidable.

G. Requesting the Transcript

Because the opportunity to read and correct the transcript or tape is very important, the defending attorney should always request on the record that the transcript promptly be sent to him for this purpose. In federal cases, this step is a necessity.

CHAPTER THREE

CORRECTING THE TRANSCRIPT

Once the transcript or tape of the deposition is delivered for correction pursuant to the witness's request, the defending attorney and the deponent should confer about the correction process. The client needs to understand how the correction process works.

I. REVIEWING THE TRANSCRIPT

The witness must review the record with care, despite what may be a natural inclination to think of the deposition as having concluded. The deposition is not over until the correction process is completed. It is vital that any errors in the record be located and corrected at this time because of the serious difficulty that might ensue if the party deponent tries to "correct" the record of the deposition later in an affidavit in opposition to a motion for summary judgment in both state and federal court. Even if no such motion were to be made, the witness naturally will want to minimize the possibility of impeachment at trial based upon errors or inaccuracies that could have been, but were not, corrected when the transcript was produced.

Coping with the weaknesses inherent in most cases is normally a challenge; it is hardly useful to compound the task by the addition of errors that could have been corrected. Here again, the attorney for the client-witness needs to be thinking ahead to trial. The attorney should assist in the process by carefully reviewing the transcript or record as well. The worst-case scenario for an attorney is to fail to correct an error and then at trial have to sit and watch the client try to wriggle out from under what is now a prior inconsistent statement.

The process of review and correction should be undertaken expeditiously. As discussed in chapter 8 of the first part of this book, corrections must be made in timely fashion or else they may be rejected.[1] The defending attorney cannot allow this to occur.

Counsel and client will want to confer about any questions that need to be corrected. Counsel should explore completely with the deponent all changes of significance. Counsel cannot afford to allow any equivocations or mistakes to remain, especially with respect to matters that could harm the client's position at trial.

---

1   *See Sheikh v. Sinha*, 272 A.D.2d 465, 707 N.Y.S.2d 241 (2d Dep't 2000) (denying plaintiff's attempt to amend responses in a deposition transcript because plaintiff waited 18 months to do so, and 18 months is "untimely").

II. HOW TO MAKE CORRECTIONS

The original answers must be left unchanged. The errors are listed on an errata sheet designated by page and line number.[2] It is critical that the reasons for all the changes are set forth on the errata sheet in adequate detail. Absent reasons, the corrections may be rejected.

The more significant the change, the more care must be devoted to framing the explanation. This is particularly true if the answers were given unequivocally, free from apparent doubt or difficulty in recollection. In such instances, defending counsel should be wary of the deponent's being overly economical with explanatory words. The client needs to be persuasive when making major changes about which the adversary may be or is likely to be suspicious and which perhaps involve areas in which a reasonable examiner would expect the deponent to make no errors of importance.

Counsel for the deponent must ensure that all errors are corrected completely and in a timely manner and that the explanations for them are both truthful and persuasive. This is critical because counsel can be sure that any change of significance will be used against the witness at trial, if it is at all possible to do so. If possible, the adversary will surely try to undermine the witness's credibility at trial with the original answers, the corrections and the reasons given therefor. (Even so, the witness is in a better position if, at trial, he or she faces this challenge rather than the more difficult one of attempting to explain why what is now claimed to be an error was never corrected before the trial.)

III. MINIMIZING THE NEED FOR CORRECTIONS

As noted in Part One, chapter 8, some cases apply to the process of correcting a transcript the standards used with regard to affidavits in opposition to summary judgment that conflict with the affiant's prior deposition testimony. Clearly, it is far better to avoid this danger, as well as the risk of impeachment at trial, by taking the right action at the proper time— engaging in careful and thorough preparation *in advance of the deposition*.

The attorney should be fully familiar with the legal principles involved in the case and should thoroughly investigate all the facts prior to the deposition. The witness should be well prepared, and there should not be errors in the testimony, especially on critical issues. If errors do occur in the testimony, the attorney should note them at the time and see to it that they are

---

2   CPLR 3116(a); *see* Siegel, McKinney's Practice Commentary, CPLR 3116 (1991).

corrected at least upon cross-examination. There really should be no occasion for the witness to make a significant error in the deposition (as opposed to one of transcription), especially one that could be decisive of the case on summary judgment or significantly undermine the witness at trial. If counsel prepares for a deposition with care and thoroughness, the correction process should not prove traumatic for the case.

IV. TIMELINESS

Once any corrections are made, they should be timely circulated. When the deposition is concluded and the transcript delivered, the work of the examining attorney is not done, even if that work will now be confined to reaction. If the witness's counsel fails to ensure that corrections are timely made, the examining counsel can assume that there are no corrections to be made. In the past, the failure to sign the transcript gave rise to difficulties in state court. Now, however, the transcript, if not signed and returned within 60 days, can be used as though it had been signed. In federal court, the deponent who has requested an opportunity to review the transcript has 30 days after notice of its availability within which to make corrections.

Even after the 60-day period, the examining counsel must remain alert to attempts to modify the transcript. If an untimely attempt is made to correct the transcript, the examining attorney may well want to challenge that effort by a motion to strike if, of course, the corrections are significant. An untimely errata sheet might be submitted at the time of and in connection with a motion for summary judgment, in a gambit designed either to create an issue of fact or to avoid one. Again, the challenge should be met by the examiner.

The examining counsel also needs to be vigilant about efforts to "correct" a transcript in an untimely manner through the affidavit on summary judgment that contradicts prior deposition testimony. Although some cases allow affidavits that vary from the deposition testimony when, for example, there seems in the record to be some confusion on the witness's part, post-facto "corrections" are generally disallowed, and examining counsel should be on the watch for them. If the affidavit is submitted after the time for correction of the transcript has concluded, the examining attorney should be concerned about, and may want to make use of, the fact that the error being corrected by the affidavit could have been but was not corrected in the normal course.

V. REVIEW OF CORRECTIONS BY EXAMINING COUNSEL

If corrections are made to the transcript in a timely manner, the examining attorney should promptly review what has been done. Are the corrections of any moment? If so, the questioning counsel should study very closely whether reasons are presented for the changes made and the nature of those reasons. If the opponent and defending counsel did not prepare adequately before the testimony, corrections may be presented that matter and that are not adequately explained. For the witness with a problem, there may well be a temptation to try to slide corrections by behind vague or cryptic "explanations" or boilerplate.

The examining attorney who is confronted with corrections of this variety must be careful. Counsel for the witness may be trying to undo damage done at the deposition in such a way as to mask the significance of what is taking place. The examining attorney must insist that the rules of the correction process be observed—in other words, that the changes be explained. Counsel may wish to do this as soon as the change occurs by way of a motion to strike. One could wait until trial. However, if the change is significant, one may wish to confront the problem at the time so that it will be clear before trial what examining counsel is dealing with. Furthermore, how the matter is resolved could have ramifications for a motion for summary judgment, or a defense against one.

If the corrections set forth in the errata sheet flatly contradict the original deposition testimony, one might wish to consider an application to bar the changes on that ground, which position is supported by some case law.

If the corrections are significant enough, the examining counsel might seek from the court a directive, as a condition to allowing changes to be made, to reopen the deposition for the examining counsel on the subjects involved. If the change is significant enough and if counsel for the witness persuades the court that the explanation is specific enough, the examining counsel may be able to persuade the court in turn that a fair process of discovery requires allowing the examiner to ask additional questions of the deponent about the subject. Otherwise, confusion of the witness during the deposition can lead to a corrected transcript but an insufficient chance for the examiner to discover the facts about a particular topic or to nail down testimony about all aspects of it.

CHAPTER FOUR

USE OF DEPOSITIONS

I. SUMMARY JUDGMENT MOTIONS

As contemplated by the rules, depositions are commonly submitted to the court in support of and in opposition to motions for summary judgment. Because they are occasions for thorough and searching inquiry and the other side was present and had an opportunity to cross-examine, depositions can be powerful proof for and against such motions.

A. Guidelines for Excerpting Depositions

The parties should never submit a deposition on a summary judgment motion without identifying the portions being relied upon; the court will decline to read an entire deposition searching for the facts relied on by the submitting party in its brief. It is discourteous to the court and the adversary and a breach of basic procedural propriety to do this.

On the other hand, the submitting attorney must be scrupulous when submitting excerpts. These excerpts must not be challenged or undermined by the other portions of the transcript that are not submitted. It can be particularly damaging to the submitting attorney's cause to present excerpts that the adversary establishes were unfairly selected and misleading; indeed, this is another example of conduct that can damage the credibility of the attorney with a court even in other cases.

One recommended procedure is to submit a complete transcript together with page and line citations for each proposition for which the deposition is supposed to provide support. In some complicated, multi-deposition cases, this procedure may be difficult to follow. If a party submits and cites to excerpts from a dozen depositions, it may be too cumbersome to submit each deposition in its entirety.

The record must support the assertions made by the advocate in affidavits or briefs about the topic. In depositions, witnesses may face questions perhaps framed without the precision that can be used in an affidavit or brief, and the answers inevitably will lack such precision, as well as perhaps syntactical purity and verbal accuracy. An attorney should not cite a passage in a deposition when, as a result of the words chosen or the manner in which they were put together, there is any doubt that the statements made say just what the attorney purports they say. Perhaps the attorney was present and is sure from the intonation and the facial expressions used by the witness that she meant thus and so; however, if the attorney is now relying upon a cold transcript, the attorney must be sure that thus and so is unmistakably there on the page, in the absence of indications of intonation and expression.

Furthermore, during the course of a deposition, a witness may testify about a subject numerous times. The subject may come up in a number of contexts, from a number of angles. The examiner might opt to bounce around from topic to topic to keep the witness off-guard. Also, the witness may be questioned by a number of attorneys. All citations to and summaries of the testimony must accurately reflect what the witness testified to on all the occasions on which the subject arose.

B. Mining for Inconsistencies and Ambiguities

Counsel opposing summary judgment will rejoice to find in the moving papers an inaccurate citation to a transcript page on some point of note or unfair selection of portions of the transcript. These things may help to raise an issue of fact. Of course, one can, regardless of the quality of the moving papers, seek to mine the transcript oneself when preparing opposition papers by looking for inconsistencies in the witness's testimony—either internal inconsistencies (that is, differences in the witness's deposition testimony at various points about the same subject) or external inconsistencies with the testimony of others or with affidavits or other proof on the motion.

One can also hope to find ambiguities in the witness's answers. If, for example, the movant states that the witness testified to thus and so but the passages cited are something short of or other than that, an issue of fact might be established or at least the attorney may thereby advance toward that goal.

Of course, an attorney will want to vigorously and aggressively advocate his or her client's position. But it will be unproductive, or even counterproductive, for an attorney to try to squeeze out of a deposition more than is actually there. An aggressive and vigorous approach must also be a realistic and accurate one.

The imprecision of spoken speech compared to writing and the reality that the atmosphere in a deposition room cannot be reflected on a page of transcript remind one that videotape may be useful. Beyond that, these factors underscore the importance of preparing for a deposition by analyzing the key areas and issues, as well as points that may later surface on a motion or at trial, so that counsel can be alert at the deposition to the way in which questions and answers on any such areas or issues are framed.

Imprecision and ambiguity can be cleared up then or, at least, during the correction process. Otherwise, the attorney may face problems on a motion.

C. Limitations on Deposition Corrections

If an attorney opposing a summary judgment motion attempts to submit an affidavit that contradicts the affiant's deposition, he will need a strong reason for the change of position—some change in circumstance or some confusion in the deposition. If the latter, the confusion ought to be demonstrable in the record itself so that the court can clearly see that it is not dealing with a post-facto rationalization. The attorney will also need to address why the error was not corrected earlier on the errata sheet. Otherwise, the court may conclude that the affidavit is no more than an attempt to create a feigned issue of fact.

D. Admissibility of Deposition Testimony

When depositions are cited on a motion for summary judgment, close attention should be paid to the admissibility of the testimony. It is, of course, natural and fundamental for a trial attorney to do this in preparation for trial, but it may be less a matter of second nature on a motion. The testimony relied on by the movant must be admissible. Generally, it should also be admissible when offered by a party opposing summary judgment, but there are some exceptions, discussed at length in chapter 10 of the first part of this book.

When presenting or opposing a motion for summary judgment, an attorney should always evaluate deposition testimony from the standpoint of admissibility. One would not want to submit such testimony in support of a motion only to have the adversary point out in responsive papers that the testimony is inadmissible. Furthermore, one would not want to neglect through oversight the opportunity to draw the court's attention to such a problem in the adversary's presentation.

II. AT TRIAL

Regarding the use of depositions at trial,[1] attorneys can benefit greatly if the deposition was recorded by the reporter with software that permits sophisticated searches through the transcript. Such software is widely available now and can be quite helpful to the attorney preparing for and trying

---

1   *See* John P. Di Blasi, *Lawyers Need Detailed Knowledge of Rules for Using Depositions at Trial*, N.Y. St. B.J., Vol. 73, No. 8, at 27 (Oct. 2001).

a case involving depositions. At trial, it can be especially useful in locating deposition testimony that may be fuel for impeachment.

Depositions can be broadly used as permitted by the rules discussed in Part One. For example, a deposition of a party may be used for any purpose by an adverse party, as may a deposition of a witness located at a distance from the point of trial. In trial preparation, building upon past analyses and one's discovery plan, the attorney will decide what can be proven at trial by deposition and what requires live testimony. Live testimony may be required by the rules or by a sound assessment of the practicalities of the case. A witness may be too important to testify by means of a deposition record. Or, more often, the witness may be too effective not to be used in person—witnesses who can be helpful should be put on the stand when possible.

A. Guidelines

If an attorney is going to offer deposition testimony at trial for a purpose other than impeachment, court rules may require the disclosure of the relevant portions prior to trial, as well as the identification of portions to be challenged. Thus, each side will know what the other intends to do by this means. One can then prepare carefully and fully to use depositions at trial and to counter what may come in opposition to them.

The attorney should supply the court with copies of transcripts to be used at trial as required by any relevant court rules. If the court has not previously been supplied with a copy of a deposition from which counsel intends to read at trial, that should be done at the time of the reading. The trial lawyer should be sure the deposition transcript was supplied to the witness as required by the rules so that the witness could review and correct it.

If any objections have been raised by a party to the proposed use of a deposition at trial as required by court rules, the trial lawyer should seek a resolution in advance of trial so that everyone can be well prepared.

B. Evidentiary Rulings on Objections Made during Deposition

If the court's procedures permit, this is an opportunity for evidentiary rulings on all those objections that, as Part One, chapter 5 discusses, are preserved for trial, along with objections to the form or other curable matters that were raised on the record of the deposition and remain viable (that is, the problems were not corrected when the objection was made). If not all, perhaps at least the more serious objections can be considered and ruled on initially.

If serious issues are raised and the court permits an *in limine* motion, one might seek leave to present argument and papers to the court on the point. Even when rules do not require it, courts are often eager to entertain difficult evidentiary problems in advance of trial and to receive relevant argument and citation. Sometimes objections with grounds (if not made clear in the transcript) must be provided, in advance, as to passages the adversary plans to read, to be ruled on during argument of the motion *in limine*.

C. Use of Deposition Testimony in Lieu of Witness

A party may seek to use a deposition because a witness is too ill to appear, or resides at a distance from the court, and so forth. Here, there is the potential for disputes as to whether the basis for the use of the deposition has been established. The attorney may wish to seek a stipulation from the adversary on the point. If agreement cannot be reached, the attorney may wish to raise the matter with the court at a pretrial conference. Otherwise, the attorney may have to produce a witness to testify as to the witness's health, residence, etc.

D. Impeachment Based on Inconsistent Statements

Because impeachment—particularly the testing of credibility—is one of the fundamental uses for depositions, the attorney getting ready for trial will want to prepare the ground for impeachment well. One can, of course, use testimony of an adverse party against the party for any purpose. That is, however, a different matter.

The use of prior testimony to impeach occurs when the attorney is cross-examining the deponent witness. The adversary will have elicited certain testimony on direct examination. Or the cross-examining attorney will elicit it on cross. If the examining attorney wishes to attack that testimony, he or she will need to use a statement in the deposition *that is inconsistent with that just given at trial.*

If the testimony is not inconsistent, there is no basis for impeachment. If the testimony varies somewhat or uses a different formulation or is unclear but is not actually inconsistent, it cannot be used for this purpose.[2]

---

2   *Fowler v. Parks*, 222 A.D.2d 239, 635 N.Y.S.2d 579 (1st Dep't 1995).

If for any reason counsel believes the testimony is not inconsistent but is concerned about what the jury might think, counsel can ask the court for a limiting instruction. The court will generally oblige, the attorney will look good and the jury will realize that it is their decision whether the statement is inconsistent with the trial testimony and, if deemed so, what the statement can be used for.

If one seeks to use testimony to refresh the witness's recollection, the proper method is to show the testimony to the witness, not to read it, allow him or her to refresh recollection from it, and ask whether that has occurred. The examining attorney would then proceed with the inquiry with the witness having, it is hoped, changed direction somewhat in light of the refreshed recollection.

Impeachment takes place in the following manner. The cross-examiner elicits the statement on the subject at issue, or confirms a statement elicited on direct. The cross-examiner then asks whether the witness recalls having appeared at a deposition and having given answers to questions under oath. This may be done in the following manner, although the best practice is to give the witness and the adversary a copy of the transcript if they do not have one, and, in any event, a citation to the page and line:

Q: Do you recall being asked questions in this case and giving answers at a deposition?

A: Yes.

Q: Do you recall that this deposition was taken under oath?

A: Yes.

Q: Do you recall that your attorney was present at the deposition?

A: Yes.

Q: Do you recall meeting with your attorney in advance of the deposition?

A: Yes.

Q: Do you recall that at the deposition you took an oath and swore to tell the truth in the deposition?

A: Yes.

Q: Do you recall that after the deposition, the questions and the answers were typed up into a booklet and that was given to you for review?

A: Yes.

Q: Do you recall that you signed the deposition?

A: Yes.

Q: Do you recall that in signing the deposition you again swore to the truth and accuracy of your answers after having had the opportunity to review and correct them?[3]

A: Yes.

Q: I now read the following questions and answers from the deposition beginning at p. X, line X.

Q: Do you recall being asked those questions and giving those answers at your deposition?

A: Yes.

The witness usually will not directly challenge the transcript since it is so difficult to do so in a credible manner in view of the questions about the procedure that led up to the notation of the inconsistency. If the witness were to pin his or her testimony on the assertion that the cited portions of the deposition had been transcribed inaccurately by the reporter, the jury will naturally wonder why the errors were not corrected when the deponent had a chance to do so. Instead, the witness in all likelihood will try to offer an excuse, a sort of "yes, but."

However, the question is clear: Did the witness give the key answer? It is a yes-or-no question, with "no" being very difficult to assert. So if the witness starts off on an excuse, the cross-examining counsel is within her rights to, and certainly should, ask the court to strike the answer as nonresponsive. If the witness tries again to give another answer that is also off point, the attorney should again move to strike. It is vital that the attorney control this part of the interrogation in particular and not let the witness off the hook created by her own inconsistent statements.

---

3   For a federal case, see FRCP 30(e) regarding signing.

If the same inconsistency appears in a number of places in the deposition, the cross-examining attorney might wish to use all of them to suggest that the statements were given carefully and with deliberation, in addition to having remained unchanged despite there having been an opportunity for correction. On the other hand, the attorney needs to consider the risk of boring the jury with repetition, perhaps even robbing the inconsistency of some of its force.

Likewise, if the witness testified inconsistently at trial about a number of different subjects, the adversary will likely want to impeach the witness with regard to each to establish a cumulative effect in the jurors' minds— that this witness cannot be believed about anything that matters. Again, if the subjects, though different, are similar, the adversary needs not only to exercise his skills at cross-examination as a good and aggressive trial lawyer, but also to consider whether at a certain point the length of the demonstration will undermine in the jury's mind the effectiveness of the point being made.

If the witness testified one way at the deposition but changed the testimony during the correction process, the change, as noted, is valid if made in a timely manner and if a reason was given (subject to possible application of the jurisprudence that may restrict some corrections if flatly contradictory to unambiguous deposition testimony). A change is invalid if untimely or if no reason was given, and counsel should seek to bar citation to the change if use is sought to be made of the modified testimony.

Even if the correction was properly made, the original answer is not to be expunged, and the cross-examiner is free to note for the jury the original answer and to explore the reasons offered for the change.[4] The more one can do to show that the change was a calculated move rather than the correction of an inadvertent slip, the better for one's cause. Thus, if the original answer was given at several different points in the transcript, this fact may assist in bringing the idea of calculation home to the jury. Also, if the deposition was videotaped and the witness shows no sign of any doubt about the original answers when giving them, not much more may be required to cast a cloud over the witness's later explanation.

E. Use of Deposition on Case in Chief

With regard to the use of a deposition on one's case in chief, if the case is before a judge only, the judge likely will require the attorney to submit

---

4   See Part One, chapter 8.

the transcript with designations instead of entertaining a reading of the transcript in court. In a jury case, the attorney can read the relevant portions. The trial lawyer will need to think about when in her case to present this proof. Since it is apt to be inherently more boring than other portions, there may be utility in making the presentation at a particular, very logical place in the case in chief. Or, the attorney might wish to present it just before conclusion of her case in the hope of having a greater impact.

Again, the attorney should consider how lengthy the presentation might be. One wants to do what is needed to make the point as forcefully as possible. On the other hand, repetition at a certain juncture may become unproductive or counterproductive. When presenting such proof, it is usually advisable to have a colleague play the role of the witness and read the answers in response to the examiner's reading of the questions but, again, with a flat affect, not with enthusiasm to help the cause. This will lend some vitality and interest to a procedure that may otherwise seem quite boring to the jurors.

If the excerpts are from a videotaped deposition, that problem is eliminated. The attorney must ensure, however, that the video presentation will flow smoothly and quickly, particularly if passages or snippets are being used. The jurors will inevitably judge the presentation in comparison with those they see on television every day, and a choppy, prolonged, gap-filled presentation will not pass ready muster.

F. Fairness Considerations

Federal and state rules provide for fairness in the use of depositions. When a party reads some excerpts, another party may read any portions that in fairness ought to be read also. With regard to portions being used on the case in chief and identified in advance, an attorney can prepare and select any appropriate additional portions. When the response is to material used to impeach and not designated in advance, the attorney will have to respond more quickly and thus will need to have firm command of the material.

Sometimes courts will allow an attorney to read the additional portions needed for fairness after the initial portions are quoted. Others may require that the responsive excerpts be read on the responding attorney's case.

APPENDIX

FEDERAL AND STATE FORMS
FOR DEPOSITION PRACTICE

FEDERAL FORMS

STATE FORMS

FEDERAL FORMS

FORM 1—NOTICE OF DEPOSITION

UNITED STATES DISTRICT COURT
SOUTHERN DISTRICT OF NEW YORK

---x

                              :

        Plaintiff(s),   :   ___ Civ. ___ (Judge's Initials)

                              :

           - against -   :   **NOTICE OF DEPOSITION**

                              :

        Defendant(s).   :

---x

PLEASE TAKE NOTICE that, pursuant to Rule 30 of the Federal Rules of Civil Procedure, the defendant will take the deposition upon oral examination of the plaintiff, _____, who resides at _____, New York, New York, at the offices of the undersigned counsel for the defendant, _____, New York, New York on _____, at 9:30 A.M. The deposition shall be recorded by stenographic means.

Dated: _____

                                _____[Firm]

                                By: _____[Signature]

                                [Name, Initials, Attorney Number
                                   of Signatory]
                                [Address]
                                [Phone]

                                Attorneys for _____

To: _____
         _____
         _____

FORM 2—NOTICE OF DEPOSITION (FRCP 30(b)(6))

UNITED STATES DISTRICT COURT
SOUTHERN DISTRICT OF NEW YORK

```
----------------------------------------------x
                                              :
          Plaintiff(s),           :   ___ Civ. ___ (Judge's Initials)
                                              :
              - against -         :   NOTICE OF DEPOSITION
                                              :
          Defendant(s).           :
----------------------------------------------x
```

PLEASE TAKE NOTICE that, pursuant to Rule 30(b)(6) of the Federal Rules of Civil Procedure, the defendant will take the deposition upon oral examination of the plaintiff, _____ Corporation, the principal office of which is located at _____, New York, New York, at the offices of the undersigned counsel for the defendant, _____, New York, New York on _____, at 9:30 A.M. Pursuant to said Rule, the said corporate plaintiff shall designate an individual or individuals to appear at said location at the indicated time to testify as to matters known or reasonably available to the plaintiff regarding the subjects set forth below. The deposition shall be recorded by stenographic means.

Dated: _____

_____[Firm]

By: _____[Signature]

[Name, Initials, Attorney Number
     of Signatory]
[Address]
[Phone]

Attorneys for _____

To: _____
       _____
       _____

SUBJECTS OF EXAMINATION

(1) The negotiations that occurred on or about _____ between plaintiff and defendant concerning a proposed arrangement for an investment by defendant in plaintiff's planned commercial development to be built along the riverside at 50th–53rd Streets, New York, New York.

(2) Financial projections prepared by plaintiff for any investors in said project prior to _____.

(3) Financial projections prepared by plaintiff for any investors in said project subsequent to _____.

(4) The meeting between representatives of plaintiff and representatives of defendant held on or about _____ concerning the said project.

(5) Meetings or communications subsequent to _____ between plaintiff and persons or entities other than defendant concerning a prospective investment by said persons or entities in the development referred to above.

FORM 3—NOTICE OF DEPOSITION BY VIDEO

UNITED STATES DISTRICT COURT
SOUTHERN DISTRICT OF NEW YORK

---x
                               :

       Plaintiff(s),   :   ___ Civ. ___ (Judge's Initials)

                               :

            - against -   :   **NOTICE OF DEPOSITION**

                               :

       Defendant(s).   :
---x

PLEASE TAKE NOTICE that, pursuant to Rule 30 of the Federal Rules of Civil Procedure, the defendant will take the deposition upon oral examination of the plaintiff, _____, who resides at _____, New York, New York, at the offices of the undersigned counsel for the defendant, _____, New York, New York on _____, at 9:30 A.M. The deposition shall be recorded by video.

Dated: _____

                         _____[Firm]

                         By: _____[Signature]

                         [Name, Initials, Attorney Number
                           of Signatory]
                         [Address]
                         [Phone]

                         Attorneys for _____

To: _____
          _____
          _____

FORM 4—NOTICE OF DEPOSITION
AND DOCUMENT REQUEST

UNITED STATES DISTRICT COURT
SOUTHERN DISTRICT OF NEW YORK

```
----------------------------------------------x
                                              :
          Plaintiff(s),          :     ___ Civ. ___ (Judge's Initials)
                                              :
                 - against -     :     NOTICE OF DEPOSITION
                                              :
          Defendant(s).          :
----------------------------------------------x
```

PLEASE TAKE NOTICE that, pursuant to Rule 30 of the Federal Rules of Civil Procedure, the defendant will take the deposition upon oral examination of the plaintiff, _____, who resides at _____, New York, New York, at the offices of the undersigned counsel for the defendant, _____, New York, New York on _____, at 9:30 A.M. The deposition shall be recorded by stenographic means.

PLEASE TAKE FURTHER NOTICE that, pursuant to Rule 30(b)(5), plaintiff is requested to produce at the examination the documents set forth in the notice annexed hereto.

Dated: _____

                                           _____[Firm]

                                     By: _____[Signature]

                                     [Name, Initials, Attorney Number
                                        of Signatory]
                                     [Address]
                                     [Phone]

                                     Attorneys for _____

To: _____
        _____
        _____

NOTICE OF DOCUMENTS TO BE PRODUCED
AT EXAMINATION

(1) Drafts of the extension agreement with respect to the loan extended to plaintiff by defendant in _____ that were prepared by or on behalf of plaintiff.

(2) Written communications between plaintiff and representatives of defendant regarding the loan extension agreement proposed by plaintiff in _____.

(3) Written communications between plaintiff and representatives of defendant regarding the defendant's decision to call the loan in _____.

FORM 5—DOCUMENT REQUEST (FRCP 34)

UNITED STATES DISTRICT COURT
SOUTHERN DISTRICT OF NEW YORK

--x
                                                :
      Plaintiff(s),   :   ___ Civ. ___ (Judge's Initials)
                                                :
                                                :   **NOTICE FOR THE**
      - against -   :   **PRODUCTION OF**
                                                    DOCUMENTS (RULE 34)
                                                :
      Defendant(s).   :
--x

PLEASE TAKE NOTICE that, pursuant to Rule 34 of the Federal Rules of Civil Procedure, plaintiff is requested to produce and permit inspection and copying of the documents identified below, at the office of the undersigned counsel for defendant _____, at _____, New York, New York, on _____, at 9:30 A.M. Pursuant to Rule 34(b), a response to this request shall be served within 30 days after service hereof.

DEFINITIONS

With respect to this demand, the following definitions shall apply:

"Documents" shall mean: All records, whether written, typed, copied, transcribed, or otherwise reproduced or maintained, of writing, printing, drawing, images or other forms of communication, including, but not limited to, letters, memoranda, notes, computer files, charts, tables, books, telegrams, statements, bills, messages transmitted by fax or electronic mail, notices, demands, or proposals, together with any drafts or revisions thereof.

"Communications" shall mean: Any and all transmissions of information from one person to another, including correspondence, faxes, electronic mail messages, whether written, printed or transcribed or otherwise reproduced or recorded.

DOCUMENTS TO BE PRODUCED

(1) Correspondence or other communications between plaintiff and any representative of defendant regarding plaintiff's request made in or about _____ for an extension of the term of a loan made by defendant to plaintiff in _____.

(2) Correspondence or other records reflecting communications between plaintiff and any third party regarding plaintiff's request made in or about _____ for an extension of the term of a loan made by defendant to plaintiff in _____.

(3) Notes or other writings relating to a meeting between plaintiff and representatives of defendant held at the offices of defendant on or about _____ concerning said request by plaintiff.

(4) Documents embodying or reflecting commitments allegedly made by representatives of defendant in or about _____ regarding extension of the term of a loan made by defendant to plaintiff in _____.

Dated: _____

_____[Firm]

By: _____[Signature]

[Name, Initials, Attorney Number
    of Signatory]
[Address]
[Phone]
Attorneys for _____

To: _____

        _____

        _____

FORM 6—SUBPOENA

UNITED STATES DISTRICT COURT
SOUTHERN DISTRICT OF NEW YORK

```
--------------------------------------------x
                                            :
         Plaintiff(s),                      :    ___ Civ. ___ (Judge's Initials)
                                            :
              - against -                   :    SUBPOENA (RULE 45(a))
                                            :
         Defendant(s).                      :
--------------------------------------------x
```

To: _____ [person subpoenaed]

YOU ARE COMMANDED TO APPEAR AT the offices of the undersigned counsel for the defendant, _____, located at _____ Street, Room _____, New York, New York, on _____, at 9:30 A.M., to testify under oath in the case listed above, pending in the United States District Court for the Southern District of New York.

This subpoena has been issued by the United States District Court for the Southern District of New York. You are required to attend and give testimony at the time and place set out above. Should you fail to do so, that failure may be punished as a contempt of court.

The text of subdivisions (c) and (d) of Rule 45 of the Federal Rules of Civil Procedure is attached to this subpoena pursuant to Rule 45(a)(1)(D).

Dated: _____

_____[Firm]

By: _____[Signature]

[Name, Initials, Attorney Number
   of Signatory]
[Address]
[Phone]

Attorneys for _____

To: _____

         _____

         _____

RULE 45. SUBPOENA

* * *

(c) Protection of Persons Subject to Subpoenas. (1) A party or an attorney responsible for the issuance and service of a subpoena shall take reasonable steps to avoid imposing undue burden or expense on a person subject to that subpoena. The court on behalf of which the subpoena was issued shall enforce this duty and impose upon the party or attorney in breach of this duty an appropriate sanction, which may include, but is not limited to, lost earnings and a reasonable attorney's fee.

(2)(A) A person commanded to produce and permit inspection and copying of designated books, papers, documents or tangible things, or inspection of premises need not appear in person at the place of production or inspection unless commanded to appear for deposition, hearing or trial.

(B) Subject to paragraph (d)(2) of this rule, a person commanded to produce and permit inspection and copying may, within 14 days after service of the subpoena or before the time specified for compliance if such time is less than 14 days after service, serve upon the party or attorney designated in the subpoena written objection to inspection or copying of any or all of the designated materials or of the premises. If objection is made, the party serving the subpoena shall not be entitled to inspect and copy the materials or inspect the premises except pursuant to an order of the court by which the subpoena was issued. If objection has been made, the party serving the subpoena may, upon notice to the person commanded to produce, move at any time for an order to compel the production. Such an order to compel production shall protect any person who is not a party or an officer of a party from significant expense resulting from the inspection and copying commanded.

(3)(A) On timely motion, the court by which a subpoena was issued shall quash or modify the subpoena if it

(i) fails to allow reasonable time for compliance;

(ii) requires a person who is not a party or an officer of a party to travel to a place more than 100 miles from the place where that person resides, is employed or regularly transacts business in person, except that, subject to the provisions of clause (c)(3)(B)(iii) of this rule, such a person may in order to attend trial be commanded to travel from any such place within the state in which the trial is held;

(iii) requires disclosure of privileged or other protected matter and no exception or waiver applies; or

(iv) subjects a person to undue burden.

(B) If a subpoena

(i) requires disclosure of a trade secret or other confidential research, development, or commercial information, or

(ii) requires disclosure of an unretained expert's opinion or information not describing specific events or occurrences in dispute and resulting from the expert's study made not at the request of any party, or

(iii) requires a person who is not a party or an officer of a party to incur substantial expense to travel more than 100 miles to attend trial, the court may, to protect a person subject to or affected by the subpoena, quash or modify the subpoena or, if the party in whose behalf the subpoena is issued shows a substantial need for the testimony or material that cannot be otherwise met without undue hardship and assures that the person to whom the subpoena is addressed will be reasonably compensated, the court may order appearance or production only upon specified conditions.

(d) Duties in Responding to Subpoena. (1) A person responding to a subpoena to produce documents shall produce them as they are kept in the usual course of business or shall organize and label them to correspond with the categories in the demand.

(2) When information subject to a subpoena is withheld on a claim that it is privileged or subject to protection as trial preparation materials, the claim shall be made expressly and shall be supported by a description of the nature of the documents, communications, or things not produced that is sufficient to enable the demanding party to contest the claim.

FORM 7—SUBPOENA *DUCES TECUM*

UNITED STATES DISTRICT COURT
SOUTHERN DISTRICT OF NEW YORK

--x
                    :

        Plaintiff(s),   : ___ Civ. ___ (Judge's Initials)

                    :

          - against -   : **SUBPOENA *DUCES TECUM***
                          (RULE 45(a))

                    :

        Defendant(s).   :
--x

To:_____ [person subpoenaed]

YOU ARE COMMANDED TO APPEAR AT the offices of the undersigned counsel for the defendant, _____, located at _____ Street, Room _____, New York, New York, on _____, at 9:30 A.M., to testify under oath in the case listed above, pending in the United States District Court for the Southern District of New York.

YOU ARE FURTHER COMMANDED TO BRING WITH YOU on that occasion the documents listed in the Schedule annexed to this subpoena.

This subpoena has been issued by the United States District Court for the Southern District of New York. You are required to attend and give testimony and produce for inspection and copying all the documents listed on the attached Schedule and to do so at the time and place set out above. Should you fail to do so, that failure may be punished as a contempt of court.

The text of subdivisions (c) and (d) of Rule 45 of the Federal Rules of Civil Procedure is attached to this subpoena pursuant to Rule 45(a)(1)(D).

Dated: _____

_____[Firm]

By: _____[Signature]

[Name, Initials, Attorney Number
      of Signatory]
[Address]
[Phone]

Attorneys for _____

To: _____
         _____
         _____

SCHEDULE TO SUBPOENA *DUCES TECUM*

(1) Documents concerning negotiations that occurred on or about ____ between plaintiff _____ and defendant _____ concerning a proposed arrangement for an investment by defendant in plaintiff's planned commercial development to be built along the riverside at 50th–53rd Streets, New York, New York.

(2) Documents relating to financial projections prepared by plaintiff for any investors in said project prior to _____.

(3) Documents relating to financial projections prepared by plaintiff for any investors in said project subsequent to _____.

(4) Documents regarding a meeting between representatives of plaintiff and representatives of defendant held on or about _____ concerning the said project.

(5) Documents regarding meetings or communications subsequent to _____ between plaintiff and persons or entities other than defendant concerning a prospective investment by said persons or entities in the development referred to above.

RULE 45. SUBPOENA

* * *

(c) Protection of Persons Subject to Subpoenas. (1) A party or an attorney responsible for the issuance and service of a subpoena shall take reasonable steps to avoid imposing undue burden or expense on a person subject to that subpoena. The court on behalf of which the subpoena was issued shall enforce this duty and impose upon the party or attorney in breach of this duty an appropriate sanction, which may include, but is not limited to, lost earnings and a reasonable attorney's fee.

(2)(A) A person commanded to produce and permit inspection and copying of designated books, papers, documents or tangible things, or inspection of premises need not appear in person at the place of production or inspection unless commanded to appear for deposition, hearing or trial.

(B) Subject to paragraph (d)(2) of this rule, a person commanded to produce and permit inspection and copying may, within 14 days after service of the subpoena or before the time specified for compliance if such time is less than 14 days after service, serve upon the party or attorney designated in the subpoena written objection to inspection or copying of any or all of the designated materials or of the premises. If objection is made, the party serving the subpoena shall not be entitled to inspect and copy the materials or inspect the premises except pursuant to an order of the court by which the subpoena was issued. If objection has been made, the party serving the subpoena may, upon notice to the person commanded to produce, move at any time for an order to compel the production. Such an order to compel production shall protect any person who is not a party or an officer of a party from significant expense resulting from the inspection and copying commanded.

(3)(A) On timely motion, the court by which a subpoena was issued shall quash or modify the subpoena if it

(i) fails to allow reasonable time for compliance;

(ii) requires a person who is not a party or an officer of a party to travel to a place more than 100 miles from the place where that person resides, is employed or regularly transacts business in person, except that, subject to the provisions of clause (c)(3)(B)(iii) of this rule, such a person may in order to attend trial be commanded to travel from any such place within the state in which the trial is held;

(iii) requires disclosure of privileged or other protected matter and no exception or waiver applies; or

(iv) subjects a person to undue burden.

(B) If a subpoena

(i) requires disclosure of a trade secret or other confidential research, development, or commercial information, or

(ii) requires disclosure of an unretained expert's opinion or information not describing specific events or occurrences in dispute and resulting from the expert's study made not at the request of any party, or

(iii) requires a person who is not a party or an officer of a party to incur substantial expense to travel more than 100 miles to attend trial, the court may, to protect a person subject to or affected by the subpoena, quash or modify the subpoena or, if the party in whose behalf the subpoena is issued shows a substantial need for the testimony or material that cannot be otherwise met without undue hardship and assures that the person to whom the subpoena is addressed will be reasonably compensated, the court may order appearance or production only upon specified conditions.

(d) Duties in Responding to Subpoena. (1) A person responding to a subpoena to produce documents shall produce them as they are kept in the usual course of business or shall organize and label them to correspond with the categories in the demand.

(2) When information subject to a subpoena is withheld on a claim that it is privileged or subject to protection as trial preparation materials, the claim shall be made expressly and shall be supported by a description of the nature of the documents, communications, or things not produced that is sufficient to enable the demanding party to contest the claim.

FORM 8—MOTION FOR PROTECTIVE ORDER
(SAMPLE 1)

UNITED STATES DISTRICT COURT
SOUTHERN DISTRICT OF NEW YORK

```
----------------------------------------------x
                                              :
          Plaintiff(s),                       :   ___ Civ. ___ (Judge's Initials)

                                              :

                - against -                    :   MOTION FOR
                                                   PROTECTIVE ORDER
                                              :   (RULE 26(c))

          Defendant(s).                        :

----------------------------------------------x
```

PLEASE TAKE NOTICE that, pursuant to Rule 26(c) of the Federal Rules of Civil Procedure, defendant shall move this court, at the United States Courthouse for the Southern District of New York, 500 Pearl Street, New York, New York, Room _____, on the _____ day of _____, for a protective order quashing the notice of deposition dated _____ and served by plaintiff upon defendant on _____ which purported to schedule the taking of the defendant's deposition for _____, on the ground that the taking of said deposition would violate the scheduling order issued by this court dated _____, which order required that any such deposition be completed by _____, after which the defendant would be entitled to take the depositions therein identified. Defendant has commenced and will complete depositions within the schedule ordered by the court.

Counsel for defendant has conferred with counsel for plaintiff in an effort to resolve this dispute without need for the intervention of the court but that effort has been unsuccessful, as demonstrated in the annexed affidavit of _____, Esq.

Dated: _____

_____[Firm]

By: _____[Signature]

[Name, Initials, Attorney Number
   of Signatory]
[Address]
[Phone]

Attorneys for _____

To: _____
       _____
       _____

FORM 9—MOTION FOR PROTECTIVE ORDER
(SAMPLE 2)

UNITED STATES DISTRICT COURT
SOUTHERN DISTRICT OF NEW YORK

```
---------------------------------------------x
                                             :
```

Plaintiff(s),   : ___ Civ. ___ (Judge's Initials)

                                       :

- against -   : **MOTION FOR**
                                          PROTECTIVE ORDER
                                       : **(RULE 26(c))**

Defendant(s).   :

```
---------------------------------------------x
```

PLEASE TAKE NOTICE that, pursuant to Rule 26(c) of the Federal Rules of Civil Procedure, defendant _____ shall move this court, at the United States Courthouse for the Southern District of New York, 500 Pearl Street, New York, New York, Room _____, on the _____ day of _____, for a protective order limiting the production of documents required to be produced by defendant in response to the demand pursuant to Rule 34 made by plaintiff dated _____ on the ground that compliance with Items 11, 14 and 21 of the demand would place an undue burden upon this defendant, and be oppressive and unreasonably expensive, including with regard to the production of computer data called for by each of the said items that can be retrieved only at what is estimated to be a cost of $40,000, as explained in the accompanying affidavit of _____, and on the ground that the information sought by these requests is in any event irrelevant to any matter at issue in this litigation and incapable of leading to the production of relevant information.

Counsel for defendant conferred with counsel for plaintiff in a good faith effort to reach agreement with regard to the aforesaid items of plaintiff's demand. Such agreement could not be reached, however, as explained in detail in the annexed affidavit of _____, Esq., thereby leaving defendant with no alternative other than to seek the intervention of this court.

Dated: _____

                      _____[Firm]

                      By: _____[Signature]

                      [Name, Initials, Attorney Number
                           of Signatory]
                      [Address]
                      [Phone]

                      Attorneys for _____

To: _____
       _____
       _____

FORM 10—MOTION FOR PROTECTIVE ORDER
(SAMPLE 3)

UNITED STATES DISTRICT COURT
SOUTHERN DISTRICT OF NEW YORK

```
-----------------------------------------------x
                                               :
```

Plaintiff(s),	: ___ Civ. ___ (Judge's Initials)
	:
- against -	: **MOTION FOR**
	PROTECTIVE ORDER
	: **(RULE 26(c))**
Defendant(s).	:

```
-----------------------------------------------x
```

PLEASE TAKE NOTICE that, pursuant to Rule 26(c) of the Federal Rules of Civil Procedure, defendant _____ shall move this court, at the United States Courthouse for the Southern District of New York, 500 Pearl Street, New York, New York, Room _____, on the _____ day of _____, for a protective order prohibiting plaintiff from pursuing inquiry, during the course of the deposition of defendant, which is scheduled to be taken on _____ pursuant to notice dated _____, into the processes, data and analyses that comprise this defendant's commercial secret regarding _____ on the ground that, as explained in the accompanying affidavit of _____, the details thereof are unrelated to the matters in dispute in this litigation, but the disclosure of said details would have a significant adverse effect upon the defendant's current business operations and its prospects for the future. Under the circumstances present here, defendant is entitled to a protective order, as shown in the accompanying memorandum of law.

Counsel for defendant initiated discussions with other counsel to this case with a view toward agreeing upon a proposed Stipulation and Order addressing confidentiality that might be submitted to this court. Counsel for all parties other than plaintiff agreed to defendant's proposal, with modest modifications. Counsel for plaintiff, however, rejected it and terminated discussions, as explained in detail in the annexed affidavit of _____, Esq., thereby leaving defendant with no alternative other than to seek the intervention of this court.

Dated: _____

                                        _____[Firm]

                                        By: _____[Signature]

                                        [Name, Initials, Attorney Number
                                             of Signatory]
                                        [Address]
                                        [Phone]

                                        Attorneys for _____

To: _____
           _____
           _____

FORM 11—MOTION FOR PROTECTIVE ORDER
(SAMPLE 4)

UNITED STATES DISTRICT COURT
SOUTHERN DISTRICT OF NEW YORK

---x

                               :

        Plaintiff(s),   :   ___ Civ. ___ (Judge's Initials)

                               :

           - against -   : **MOTION FOR**
                               PROTECTIVE ORDER
                            : **(RULE 26(c))**

        Defendant(s).   :

---x

PLEASE TAKE NOTICE that, pursuant to Rule 26(c) of the Federal Rules of Civil Procedure, defendant _____ shall move this court, at the United States Courthouse for the Southern District of New York, 500 Pearl Street, New York, New York, Room _____, on the _____ day of _____, for a protective order prohibiting plaintiff from taking for a second time the deposition of this defendant, who was previously deposed, pursuant to notice dated _____, on _____, _____ and _____, and in accordance with the scheduling order of this court, whereby, among other things, all discovery in this matter should have been completed by _____, upon the ground that defendant has already been deposed at length on all aspects of this action, for a total of 20 hours, that counsel for plaintiff stated at the conclusion of the last session of the deposition that he had completed all questioning of the defendant, that all depositions were completed pursuant to the scheduling order of this court on_____, and that there have been no new developments in this action since the last session of the deposition of defendant that would justify a second deposition of defendant.

Counsel for defendant has conferred with counsel for plaintiff in an effort to reach an agreement with regard to plaintiff's demand for a second deposition, but that effort has been unsuccessful, as demonstrated in detail in the annexed affidavit of _____, Esq.

Dated: _____

_____[Firm]

By: _____[Signature]

[Name, Initials, Attorney Number
     of Signatory]
[Address]
[Phone]
Attorneys for _____

To: _____

_____

_____

FORM 12—MOTION FOR PROTECTIVE ORDER
(SAMPLE 5)

UNITED STATES DISTRICT COURT
SOUTHERN DISTRICT OF NEW YORK

```
---------------------------------------------x
                                       :
         Plaintiff(s),                 :   ___ Civ. ___ (Judge's Initials)
                                       :
              - against -              :   MOTION FOR
                                           PROTECTIVE ORDER
                                       :   (RULE 26(c))
         Defendant(s).                 :
---------------------------------------------x
```

PLEASE TAKE NOTICE that, pursuant to Rule 26(c) of the Federal Rules of Civil Procedure, defendant _____ shall move this court, at the United States Courthouse for the Southern District of New York, 500 Pearl Street, New York, New York, Room _____, on the _____ day of _____, for a protective order limiting the conditions under which and the means by which the deposition of defendant, scheduled to be taken on _____, pursuant to notice dated _____, shall be taken on the ground that the conduct of a deposition without such limitations would be dangerous to defendant's health and well-being given his advanced age and the precarious state of his physical and emotional condition, which are explained in detail in the accompanying affidavits of _____, sworn to _____, and _____, M.D., sworn to _____.

Counsel for defendant has conferred with counsel for plaintiff in an effort to reach an agreement as to how the deposition should be taken without need for the intervention of the court, but that effort has been unsuccessful, as demonstrated in detail in the annexed affidavit of _____, Esq.

Dated: _____

_____[Firm]

By: _____[Signature]

[Name, Initials, Attorney Number
    of Signatory]
[Address]
[Phone]

Attorneys for _____

To: _____
        _____
        _____

FORM 13—AFFIDAVIT ON MOTION FOR PROTECTIVE ORDER

UNITED STATES DISTRICT COURT
SOUTHERN DISTRICT OF NEW YORK

---x
                                             :
      Plaintiff(s),   : ___ Civ. ___ (Judge's Initials)

                         : **AFFIDAVIT IN SUPPORT**
        - against -   **OF MOTION FOR**
                         : **PROTECTIVE ORDER**
                            (RULE 26(c))

      Defendant(s).   :

---x

STATE OF NEW YORK   )
                       ss
COUNTY OF NEW YORK)

_____, Esq., being duly sworn, deposes and says:

1. I am a member of the firm of _____, attorneys for defendant _____ in the captioned action, and am a member in good standing of the bar of this court. I submit this affidavit in support of this defendant's motion, pursuant to Rule 26(c) of the Federal Rules of Civil Procedure, for a protective order setting limitations with regard to the conditions under which and the means by which the deposition of defendant is taken in view of the advanced age of defendant and the precariousness of his physical and emotional health.

2. The deposition of defendant has been scheduled to take place on _____ pursuant to notice dated _____.

3. Defendant resides in Weatherville, Kansas. He is 85 years old. He suffers from coronary artery disease, senile dementia and Parkinson's disease. Accompanying this motion is an affidavit of Dr. Richard Lake, who is the Chairman of Geriatric Medicine at Windham Hospital in Kansas City, Kansas. Dr. Lake has also been the defendant's personal physician for 35 years. As is explained in detail in this affidavit, the defendant, by

virtue of his age and physical infirmities, has substantial difficulty concentrating for extended periods of time. If required to do so, he becomes disoriented, which cannot be beneficial to the discovery of the facts related to this case. This disorientation causes defendant to become emotionally upset to a substantial degree, which is perilous to his health in view of his coronary problems. Dr. Lake also believes that the presence of strangers would exacerbate the problems for defendant, as would the general stress associated with a deposition.

4. Of course, plaintiff has a right to pursue reasonable discovery in this case, even though we are convinced that at the conclusion of the matter, it will be established that there is no merit to plaintiff's assertions with regard to this defendant. However, we respectfully urge that the entry of a protective order in this case is necessary to safeguard the health of defendant, whose life might otherwise be placed in serious jeopardy, as Dr. Lake expressly concludes. Such an order can be crafted in a way that ensures that plaintiff is afforded a full opportunity to pursue discovery with regard to this defendant.

5. Defendant urges the following. It appears clear that, given defendant's unquestionably limited involvement in the events at issue in this case, the deposition of defendant cannot take longer than six hours. Defendant urges that the court set the following conditions for the taking of the deposition. The deposition should be taken in sessions lasting no longer than two hours each on any one day. Defendant should be deposed from a location near his home. The deposition should be taken by video teleconference. As explained by Dr. Lake, these conditions, which will not impede plaintiff from pursuing the facts, are directly responsive to the medical and emotional problems with which defendant must live and should, it is hoped, avoid any adverse medical consequences for defendant from the deposition. There is a facility near defendant's home from which a video teleconference can be conducted.

6. As explained in detail in the accompanying certificate, my firm sought to reach an agreement with counsel for plaintiff and the other parties in this case regarding the conditions under which the defendant's deposition ought to be taken. All defendants agree with our proposals, but counsel for plaintiff rejected them. Counsel declined to accept our assertions regarding the health of defendant, despite the documentation we offered to provide. Accordingly, defendant has had no alternative but to bring on this motion.

7. For the reasons indicated above, in the other supporting papers and in the accompanying memorandum of law, the motion, it is respectfully submitted, should be granted and a protective order issued setting forth limitations on the taking of defendant's deposition as requested above.

_____
[Name], Esq.

[Notary]

FORM 14—NOTICE OF MOTION TO TERMINATE DEPOSITION

UNITED STATES DISTRICT COURT
SOUTHERN DISTRICT OF NEW YORK

---x
                                             :

       Plaintiff(s),   :   ___ Civ. ___ (Judge's Initials)

                             : **NOTICE OF MOTION**
          - against -   **TO TERMINATE**
                             : **DEPOSITION**
                               (RULE 30(d)(4))

      Defendant(s).   :

---x

PLEASE TAKE NOTICE that, pursuant to Rule 30(d)(4) of the Federal Rules of Civil Procedure, defendant _____ shall move this court, at the United States Courthouse for the Southern District of New York, 500 Pearl Street, New York, New York, Room _____, on the _____ day of _____, for an order directing the officer before whom the deposition of said defendant is being taken pursuant to notice of plaintiff dated _____ to cease forthwith from taking the deposition and awarding to defendant the reasonable expenses incurred in relation to this motion, on the ground that the examination is being conducted in bad faith and in such manner as unreasonably to annoy, embarrass, and oppress the defendant in that, as set forth in the annexed affidavit of _____, Esq., counsel for plaintiff has, during the course of the deposition, abused and insulted the defendant and his counsel, challenged defendant's answers repeatedly and asked numerous questions completely irrelevant to the action in order to embarrass the defendant and reveal sensitive personal information.

Counsel for defendant conferred with counsel for plaintiff during the deposition in an effort to obtain rulings on the matters in dispute and conferred with said counsel subsequent to the deposition session in an effort to resolve this dispute so as to permit the deposition to continue without need for the intervention of the court, but those efforts were unsuccessful, as demonstrated in detail in the annexed affidavit of _____, Esq.

Dated: _____

                         _____[Firm]

                         By: _____[Signature]

                         [Name, Initials, Attorney Number
                           of Signatory]
                         [Address]
                         [Phone]

                         Attorneys for _____

To: _____
          _____
          _____

FORM 15—MOTION TO COMPEL

UNITED STATES DISTRICT COURT
SOUTHERN DISTRICT OF NEW YORK

```
-------------------------------------------x
                                           :
        Plaintiff(s),                      :    ___ Civ. ___ (Judge's Initials)
                                           :
             - against -                   :    NOTICE OF
                                                MOTION TO COMPEL
                                           :    (RULE 37(a))
                                           :
        Defendant(s).                      :
-------------------------------------------x
```

PLEASE TAKE NOTICE that, pursuant to Rule 37(a) of the Federal Rules of Civil Procedure, defendant _____ shall move this court, at the United States Courthouse for the Southern District of New York, 500 Pearl Street, New York, New York, Room _____, on the _____ day of _____, for an order: (i) compelling plaintiff _____, whose deposition was commenced on _____ pursuant to notice dated _____, to answer the questions propounded by counsel for defendant at said deposition and identified in the accompanying affidavit of _____, Esq. and Exhibit C thereto, which questions plaintiff declined to answer; (ii) directing the continuation of said deposition to take place on _____; and (iii) awarding to defendant the reasonable expenses of this motion, including attorney's fees. The ground for this motion is that plaintiff's refusal to answer the identified questions was without any reasonable justification or basis, as explained in the accompanying memorandum of law, and obstructed defendant in the proper discovery of facts bearing upon this action.

Counsel for the moving defendant conferred with counsel for plaintiff during the deposition and after it in an effort to resolve this dispute so as to permit the deposition to continue without need for the intervention of the court, but that effort has been unsuccessful, as demonstrated in detail in the annexed affidavit of _____, Esq.

Dated: _____

_____[Firm]

By: _____[Signature]

[Name, Initials, Attorney Number
   of Signatory]
[Address]
[Phone]

Attorneys for _____

To: _____

           _____

           _____

FORM 16—AFFIDAVIT ON MOTION TO COMPEL

UNITED STATES DISTRICT COURT
SOUTHERN DISTRICT OF NEW YORK

```
---------------------------------------------x
                                             :
        Plaintiff(s),                        :   ___ Civ. ___ (Judge's Initials)
                                             :
                - against -                  :   AFFIDAVIT IN SUPPORT
                                                 OF MOTION TO COMPEL
        Defendant(s).                        :
---------------------------------------------x
```

STATE OF NEW YORK   )
                      ss
COUNTY OF NEW YORK   )

_____, Esq., being duly sworn, deposes and says:

1. I am a member of the firm of _____, attorneys for defendant _____ in the captioned action and a member in good standing of the bar of this court. I submit this affidavit in support of defendant's motion for an order, pursuant to Rule 37(a) of the Federal Rules of Civil Procedure, compelling plaintiff to answer questions posed during the deposition of plaintiff taken pursuant to defendant's notice dated _____, setting a new date for the taking of the deposition, and awarding defendant the reasonable expenses of this motion, including attorney's fees.

2. The deposition of plaintiff took place on _____. This deposition had been adjourned numerous times by counsel for plaintiff prior to that date.

3. During the course of the deposition, counsel for plaintiff was extremely obstructive, hostile, and discourteous. A copy of the transcript of the deposition is annexed hereto as Exhibit A. Annexed as Exhibit B is a listing of the pages of the transcript on which appear instances in which counsel made insulting remarks about counsel for defendant, defendant, or defendant's position in this case. The remarks made were sufficiently

glaring as to lead one to conclude that they were designed to obstruct the deposition.

4. It is against this backdrop that counsel for plaintiff on many occasions directed his client not to answer questions posed during the deposition or prevented the witness from answering the questions by interruptions and statements designed to have that effect. Annexed as Exhibit C is a list of 18 instances in which questions of defendant were circumvented by counsel for plaintiff in these ways.

5. None of the objections or interruptions by counsel for plaintiff was justified. All of the questions were relevant. Indeed, 12 of the instances concerned important meetings at which the transactions that are the subject of the complaint in this action were either planned or analyzed. The other instances concerned communications about key events in this case alleged to have occurred between plaintiff and defendant or other persons also referred to in the complaint (*see* Paras. 24–26). It is not possible for plaintiff with any basis to have objected to these questions on grounds of irrelevance, apart from any other considerations.

6. The questions were not objected to on grounds of attorney-client privilege and the instructions not to answer were not otherwise proper under Rule 30(d)(1). The questions were also not improper as to form.

7. Defendant submits, as explained more fully in the accompanying memorandum of law, that the conduct of counsel for plaintiff identified in Exhibits B and C was solely intended to obstruct, delay and frustrate defendant in the examination of the deponent.

8. As explained in detail in the accompanying affidavit of _____, defendant sought at the time of the deposition and prior to filing and service of this motion to resolve this dispute without the need for the intervention of this court, but counsel for plaintiff rejected defendant's position. There was no alternative available to defendant other than to make this motion.

9. Defendant requests, pursuant to Rules 30(d)(3) and 37(a)(4), that the court award defendant the reasonable expenses of this motion, including attorney's fees. In the accompanying affidavit, defendant supplies details in support of this aspect of the application.

10. Accordingly, it is respectfully submitted that this motion should be granted in its entirety, a new date should be set by the court for the completion of plaintiff's deposition, and defendant should be awarded its reasonable expenses on this motion.

_____

[Name], Esq.

[Notary]

FORM 17—MOTION FOR SANCTIONS

UNITED STATES DISTRICT COURT
SOUTHERN DISTRICT OF NEW YORK

```
-------------------------------------------x
                                           :
          Plaintiff(s),                    :  ___ Civ. ___ (Judge's Initials)
                                           :
              - against -                  :  NOTICE OF MOTION
                                              FOR SANCTIONS
                                           :  (RULE 37(b)(2))
          Defendant(s).                    :
-------------------------------------------x
```

PLEASE TAKE NOTICE that, pursuant to Rule 37(b)(2) of the Federal Rules of Civil Procedure, defendant _____ shall move this court, at the United States Courthouse for the Southern District of New York, 500 Pearl Street, New York, New York, Room _____, on the _____ day of _____, for an order imposing sanctions as follows: (i) directing that matters regarding _____ shall be taken to be established for the purposes of this action in accordance with the claim of defendant; and (ii) directing plaintiff _____ and its counsel to pay to defendant the reasonable expenses, including attorney's fees, caused by the plaintiff's failure to disclose. The grounds for this motion are that plaintiff _____, whose deposition was taken on _____ pursuant to notice of the moving defendant dated _____ and the order of this court dated _____, was required by said order to answer the questions propounded by counsel for defendant at said deposition with regard to _____, but that, notwithstanding the order, plaintiff refused to do so upon the direction of counsel. The specific questions at issue are identified in the accompanying affidavit of _____, Esq. and Exhibit B thereto. The conduct of plaintiff was without reasonable justification or basis, as set forth in the accompanying memorandum of law. The matters that defendant seeks to have this court find to have been established are set forth in the _____ Affidavit, together with an identification of the expenses imposed upon defendant by plaintiff's violation of the court's order.

Counsel for defendant conferred with counsel for plaintiff during the deposition and afterward in an effort to resolve this dispute so as to permit the deposition to continue without need for the intervention of the court, but that effort has been unsuccessful, as demonstrated in detail in the annexed affidavit of _____, Esq.

Dated: _____

                                    _____[Firm]

                            By: _____[Signature]

                            [Name, Initials, Attorney Number
                                of Signatory]
                            [Address]
                            [Phone]

                            Attorneys for _____

To: _____

           _____

           _____

FORM 18—CHANGES TO DEPOSITION (FRCP 30(e))

UNITED STATES DISTRICT COURT
SOUTHERN DISTRICT OF NEW YORK

--x
                                          :

      Plaintiff(s),   : ___ Civ. ___ (Judge's Initials)

                                          :

         - against -   : **NOTICE OF CHANGES
                                             TO DEPOSITION OF**

                                          : _____

      Defendant(s).   :

--x

TO: _____ [officer before whom deposition was conducted]

PLEASE TAKE NOTICE that, pursuant to Rule 30(e) of the Federal Rules of Civil Procedure, _____, a witness in this action, having reviewed the transcript of his deposition taken herein on _____, hereby makes the following changes to the deposition:

1. On page ____, at line[s] _____, the word[s] _____ is/are deleted and the word[s] _____ inserted in place thereof. The reason for this change is _____ [e.g., the reporter misheard the words used and incorrectly typed _____ when the words actually said were _____, which is evident from my testimony on page ___, at lines ____; I misunderstood the question and confused the meeting being inquired about, thinking that it was another. This misunderstanding is evident from my testimony on page ___, at lines ____, as well as from the questions on page ___, at lines _____; these citations demonstrate that there was a misunderstanding and how it came about].

2. On page _____, at line[s] _____, the word[s] _____ is/are deleted and the word[s] _____ inserted in place thereof. The reason for this change is _____.

3. On page _____, at line[s] _____, the word[s] _____ is/are deleted and the word[s] _____ inserted in place thereof. The reason for this change is _____.

Dated: New York, New York

_____

_____

_____

To: _____

_____

_____

FORM 19—PRETRIAL SCHEDULING ORDER

UNITED STATES DISTRICT COURT
SOUTHERN DISTRICT OF NEW YORK

```
-----------------------------------------------x
                                           :
          Plaintiff(s),                    :  ___ Civ. ___ (Judge's Initials)
                                           :
              - against -                  :  PRETRIAL SCHEDULING
                                              ORDER
                                           :
          Defendant(s).                    :
-----------------------------------------------x
```

APPEARANCES:

Plaintiff(s)   by:_____
_____

Defendant(s)   by:_____
_____

(Judge's Name), District Judge:

Do the parties consent to proceed before a United States Magistrate for all purposes, pursuant to 28 U.S.C. § 636(c) and Fed. R. Civ. P. 73?

Yes ___   No ___

Pursuant to Rule 16(b) of the Federal Rules of Civil Procedure, after holding an initial pretrial conference on notice to all parties, it is hereby ordered that:

Except under circumstances agreed to by the Court:

1. No additional parties may be joined after _____, _____.

2. No additional causes of action or defenses may be asserted after _____, _____.

3. **Discovery**: All discovery, except for expert discovery, shall be commenced in time to be completed by _____, _____. Disclosure of expert testimony, if any, will be made at least 45 days before the agreed-to trial month. Evidence intended to contradict or rebut the subject matter of the expert testimony will be submitted within 21 calendar days after the disclosure made by the other party, subject only to further order of this Court. As the Court rarely grants extensions, any delays or disputes in the taking of discovery should be reported to the Court immediately.

4. **Motions**: No party may make a dispositive motion returnable after _____, _____. Either party may request (and will be given a date by Chambers for) oral argument. The above date is the date by which any motion shall be fully briefed (i.e., moving, opposition and reply papers) and a courtesy copy delivered to Chambers.

In deciding the last date to submit fully briefed motions and the trial month agreed to, keep in mind that the Court requires at least 60 days to decide dispositive motions.

5. **Joint Pretrial Order**: A joint pretrial order shall, unless waived by the Court, be submitted by _____, _____. The pretrial order shall conform to the Court's Individual Practice and Rules. Counsel may inquire of Chambers with respect to the filing date(s) for requests to charge, proposed voir dire, and motions in limine, but in no event are they to be submitted less than five (5) business days (fully briefed) before the date set for trial.

6. **Jury** ____. **Nonjury** ____. Estimated number of trial days is _____. **This case is added to the _____ Trailing Trial Calendar**. Counsel should not make any other commitments during this month. As a general rule, all cases will be tried within six to eight months from the date of the first pretrial conference, or earlier if possible.

7. The law clerk assigned to this case is _____, to whom all correspondence should be directed.

8. Upon request to Chambers by either side, the Court will schedule and conduct a settlement conference and/or mediation. The Court will also, upon request, facilitate mediation under the Court Mediation Program or a settlement conference before your Magistrate Judge. In the case of a mediation to be conducted by the Court, all parties must bring their respective clients to the mediation. Keep in mind, closure, for the most part, is accomplished in direct proportion to how early in the litigation the media-

tion occurs. Any ADR procedure must occur within the framework of this order.

9. Whenever a case is resolved, the parties must submit an Order of Discontinuance, signed by all parties. When the parties settle within 48 hours of trial or the filing of a dispositive motion, they *must* notify the Court immediately of such settlement, and fax to the Court no less than 36 hours prior to their planned appearance, an Order of Discontinuance (copy attached), signed by all parties.

10. The parties' signatures below represent their understanding and agreement that this schedule is final and binding upon them unless the Court concludes that extraordinary circumstances warrant an extension with respect to one or more than one of the scheduled dates.

For Plaintiff   For Defendant

SO ORDERED.

DATED: New York, New York

_____, _____   _____
                                                 (Judge's Name)
                                                 United States District Judge

STATE FORMS

FORM 1—NOTICE OF DEPOSITION

SUPREME COURT OF THE STATE OF NEW YORK
COUNTY OF NEW YORK: COMMERCIAL DIVISION

```
-----------------------------------------x
                                         :   Part _____

        Plaintiff(s),                    :   Index No. _____

                                         :

              - against -                :   NOTICE OF DEPOSITION


                                         :

        Defendant(s).                    :
-----------------------------------------x
```

PLEASE TAKE NOTICE that, pursuant to Rule 3107 of the Civil Practice Law and Rules, the defendant will take the deposition upon oral examination of the plaintiff, _____, who resides at _____, New York, New York, at the offices of the undersigned counsel for the defendant, _____, New York, New York on _____, at 9:30 A.M.

Dated: New York, New York

      _____

                        _____[Firm]

                        By: _____[Signature]

                        _____, Esq.
                        A Member of the Firm
                        [Address]
                        [Phone]
                        Attorneys for _____

To: _____
     _____
     _____

NOTE: With regard to the signing of papers, see Part 130 of the Rules of the Chief Administrator.

FORM 2—NOTICE OF DEPOSITION—CORPORATION

SUPREME COURT OF THE STATE OF NEW YORK
COUNTY OF NEW YORK: COMMERCIAL DIVISION

---x
	: Part _____
Plaintiff(s),	: Index No. _____
	:
- against -	: **NOTICE OF DEPOSITION**
	:
Defendant(s).	:

---x

PLEASE TAKE NOTICE that, pursuant to Rules 3106 and 3107 of the Civil Practice Law and Rules, the plaintiff will take the deposition upon oral examination of the defendant _____ Corp. by _____, [title], New York, New York, at the offices of the undersigned counsel for the plaintiff, _____, New York, New York on _____, at 9:30 A.M.

Dated: New York, New York

_____

_____[Firm]

By: _____[Signature]

_____, Esq.
A Member of the Firm
[Address]
[Phone]
Attorneys for _____

To: _____

           _____

           _____

FORM 3—NOTICE OF DEPOSITION—CPLR 3111
DOCUMENT REQUEST

SUPREME COURT OF THE STATE OF NEW YORK
COUNTY OF NEW YORK: COMMERCIAL DIVISION

```
----------------------------------------------x
                                    :   Part _____

        Plaintiff(s),               :   Index No. _____

                                    :

              - against -           :   NOTICE OF DEPOSITION

                                    :

        Defendant(s).               :
----------------------------------------------x
```

PLEASE TAKE NOTICE that, pursuant to Rule 3107 of the Civil Practice Law and Rules, the defendant will take the deposition upon oral examination of the plaintiff, _____, who resides at _____, New York, New York, at the offices of the undersigned counsel for the defendant, _____, New York, New York on _____, at 9:30 A.M.

PLEASE TAKE FURTHER NOTICE that, pursuant to Rule 3111 of the Civil Practice Law and Rules, plaintiff is required to produce at said examination to be marked as exhibits and used on the examination the books and papers in the possession, custody or control of the plaintiff set forth in the Appendix attached to this Notice.

Dated: New York, New York

            _____

                        _____[Firm]

                        By: _____[Signature]

                        _____, Esq.
                        A Member of the Firm
                        [Address]
                        [Phone]
                        Attorneys for _____

To: _____

      _____

      _____

APPENDIX TO NOTICE OF DEPOSITION

(1) Correspondence between plaintiff and any representative of defendant regarding plaintiff's request made in or about _____ for an extension of a loan made by defendant to plaintiff in _____.

(2) Correspondence or other writing reflecting communications between plaintiff and any third party regarding plaintiff's request made in or about _____ for an extension of a loan made by defendant to plaintiff in _____.

(3) Notes or other writings relating to a meeting between plaintiff and representatives of defendant held at the offices of defendant on _____ concerning said request by plaintiff.

(4) Documents embodying or reflecting commitments allegedly made by representatives of defendant in or about _____ regarding extension of a loan made by defendant to plaintiff in _____.

FORM 4—NOTICE OF DEPOSITION— NONPARTY WITNESS

SUPREME COURT OF THE STATE OF NEW YORK
COUNTY OF NEW YORK: COMMERCIAL DIVISION

```
--------------------------------------------x
                                    :   Part _____

        Plaintiff(s),               :   Index No. _____

                                    :

            - against -             :   NOTICE OF DEPOSITION

                                    :

        Defendant(s).               :
--------------------------------------------x
```

PLEASE TAKE NOTICE that, pursuant to Rule 3107 of the Civil Practice Law and Rules, the defendant will take the deposition upon oral examination of nonparty witness _____, who resides at _____, New York, New York, at the offices of the undersigned counsel for the defendant, _____ New York, New York on _____, at 9:30 A.M. Such examination is required because the said nonparty witness is a former employee of the plaintiff who is reasonably believed to possess information regarding the transactions at issue in the action and examination of the witness may lead to the discovery of admissible evidence.

Dated: New York, New York

_____

_____[Firm]

By: _____[Signature]

_____, Esq.

A Member of the Firm
[Address]
[Phone]
Attorneys for _____

To: _____

        _____

        _____

FORM 5—SUBPOENA

SUPREME COURT OF THE STATE OF NEW YORK
COUNTY OF NEW YORK: COMMERCIAL DIVISION

```
----------------------------------------------x
                                    :  Part _____

        Plaintiff(s),               :  Index No. _____

                                    :

              - against -           :  **SUBPOENA**

                                    :

        Defendant(s).               :
----------------------------------------------x
```

The People of the State of New York

To: _____
_____
_____

GREETINGS:

WE COMMAND YOU, that, all business and excuses being laid aside, you attend and give testimony under oath, before a court reporter authorized by the laws of the State of New York to administer oaths, as a witness before trial at a deposition upon oral examination, at the offices of counsel for defendant herein, _____, located at _____, New York, New York, on _____, at 9:30 AM and at any adjourned session thereof.

Failure to comply with this subpoena may be punished as a contempt of court and subject you to a penalty not to exceed $50 and damages caused by the failure to comply as fixed by law.

Dated: New York, New York

_____

    _____[Firm]

By: _____[Signature]

    _____, Esq.

A Member of the Firm

[Address]

[Phone]

Attorneys for _____

FORM 6—NOTICE OF DEPOSITION BY VIDEO

SUPREME COURT OF THE STATE OF NEW YORK
COUNTY OF NEW YORK: COMMERCIAL DIVISION

```
----------------------------------------x
```
	: Part _____
Plaintiff(s),	: Index No. _____
	:
- against -	: **NOTICE OF DEPOSITION**
	:
Defendant(s).	:

```
----------------------------------------x
```

    PLEASE TAKE NOTICE that, pursuant to Rule 3107 of the Civil Practice Law and Rules, the defendant will take the deposition upon oral examination of the plaintiff, _____, who resides at _____, New York, New York, at the offices of the undersigned counsel for the defendant, _____ located at _____, New York, New York, on _____, at 9:30 A.M.

    PLEASE TAKE FURTHER NOTICE that, pursuant to Section 202.15 of the Uniform Rules for the Trial Courts, the examination shall be recorded by videotape. The operator of the recording equipment will be _____ of _____ Corp., _____, New York, New York.

Dated: New York, New York
      _____

                      _____[Firm]

              By: _____[Signature]

              _____, Esq.
              A Member of the Firm
              [Address]
              [Phone]

              Attorneys for _____

To: _____
        _____
        _____

FORM 7—CROSS-NOTICE OF DEPOSITION

SUPREME COURT OF THE STATE OF NEW YORK
COUNTY OF NEW YORK: COMMERCIAL DIVISION

```
---------------------------------------------x
                                  :   Part _____

         Plaintiff(s),            :   Index No. _____

                                  :

              - against -         :   **CROSS-NOTICE OF**
                                      **DEPOSITION**

                                  :

         Defendant(s).            :

---------------------------------------------x
```

PLEASE TAKE NOTICE that, pursuant to Rules 3106 and 3107 of the Civil Practice Law and Rules, the plaintiff will take the deposition upon oral examination of the defendant _____ Corp. by _____, [title], whose address is _____, New York, New York, at the offices of _____, counsel for the defendant, located at _____, New York, New York on _____, commencing upon the conclusion of the deposition of plaintiff scheduled to be taken by defendant at 9:30 A.M. on said date at the same location.

Dated: New York, New York
_____

                              _____[Firm]

                              By: _____[Signature]

                              _____, Esq.
                              A Member of the Firm
                              [Address]
                              [Phone]
                              Attorneys for _____

To: _____

        _____

        _____

FORM 8—NOTICE OF DISCOVERY AND INSPECTION

SUPREME COURT OF THE STATE OF NEW YORK
COUNTY OF NEW YORK: COMMERCIAL DIVISION

```
----------------------------------------------x
                                        :   Part _____

           Plaintiff(s),                :   Index No. _____

                                        :

                      - against -       :   NOTICE OF DISCOVERY
                                            AND INSPECTION

                                        :

           Defendant(s).                :
----------------------------------------------x
```

PLEASE TAKE NOTICE that, pursuant to Rule 3120 of the Civil Practice Law and Rules, plaintiff is hereby required to produce the documents set forth below for inspection and copying at the offices of the undersigned counsel for the defendant, _____, located at _____, New York, New York on _____, at 9:30 A.M.

PLEASE TAKE FURTHER NOTICE that defendant will accept as sufficient compliance herewith the production of complete and fully legible photocopies of all the documents set forth below if delivered to counsel for defendant at least five days prior to the date fixed above for production, together with a notice or letter from counsel for the plaintiff stating that the photocopies constitute complete production of all the documents called for in this Notice.

DOCUMENTS TO BE PRODUCED

With respect to this demand, the following definitions shall apply:

"Documents" shall mean: All records, whether written, typed, copied, transcribed, or otherwise reproduced or maintained, of writing, printing, drawing, images or other forms of communication, including, but not limited to, letters, memoranda, notes, computer files, charts, tables, books, telegrams, statements, bills, messages transmitted by fax or electronic mail, notices, demands, or proposals, together with any drafts or revisions thereof.

"Communications" shall mean: Any and all transmissions of information from one person to another, including correspondence, faxes, electronic mail messages, whether written, printed or transcribed or otherwise reproduced or recorded.

The documents to be produced shall consist of all the following in the possession, custody or control of the plaintiff:

(1) Correspondence or other communications between plaintiff and any representative of defendant regarding plaintiff's request made in or about _____ for an extension of the term of a loan made by defendant to plaintiff in _____.

(2) Correspondence or other record reflecting communications between plaintiff and any third party regarding plaintiff's request made in or about _____ for an extension of the term of a loan made by defendant to plaintiff in _____.

(3) Notes or other writings relating to a meeting between plaintiff and representatives of defendant held at the offices of defendant on or about _____ concerning said request by plaintiff.

(4) Documents embodying or reflecting commitments allegedly made by representatives of defendant in or about _____ regarding extension of the term of a loan made by defendant to plaintiff in _____.

Dated: New York, New York

_____

_____[Firm]

By: _____[Signature]

_____, Esq.
A Member of the Firm
[Address]
[Phone]
Attorneys for _____

To: _____

         _____

         _____

FORM 9—MOTION TO COMPEL

SUPREME COURT OF THE STATE OF NEW YORK
COUNTY OF NEW YORK: COMMERCIAL DIVISION

```
------------------------------------------------x
                                    :  Part _____

            Plaintiff(s),           :  Index No. _____

                                    :  Justice _____

                  - against -       :  **NOTICE OF MOTION**


                                    :

            Defendant(s).           :  Oral Argument Requested
------------------------------------------------x
```

PLEASE TAKE NOTICE that, upon the annexed affirmation of _____, Esq., attorney for defendant, dated _____, and the exhibits thereto, the defendant will move this court at the Motion Support Office Courtroom, Room 130, of the New York County Courthouse, 60 Centre Street, New York, New York, on _____, at 9:30 A.M., or as soon thereafter as counsel may be heard, for an order, pursuant to Rule 3124 of the Civil Practice Law and Rules, compelling plaintiff to produce documents called for in defendant's Demand for the Production of Documents on the ground that plaintiff has, without justification, failed to comply with every item of the Demand.

An affirmation that a good faith effort has been made to resolve the issues raised in this motion without need for the intervention of the court is annexed pursuant to Uniform Rule 202.7.

Pursuant to CPLR 2214(b), answering affidavits, if any, are required to be served upon the undersigned at least seven days before the return date of this motion.

Dated: New York, New York
_____

_____[Firm]

By: _____[Signature]

_____, Esq.

A Member of the Firm

[Address]

[Phone]

Attorneys for _____

To: _____

        _____

        _____

FORM 10—AFFIRMATION ON MOTION TO COMPEL

SUPREME COURT OF THE STATE OF NEW YORK
COUNTY OF NEW YORK: COMMERCIAL DIVISION

---x

                         :   Part _____

        Plaintiff(s),   :   Index No. _____

                         :   Justice _____

           - against -   :   **AFFIRMATION IN**
                                SUPPORT OF
                             :   **DEFENDANT'S MOTION**
                                TO COMPEL

        Defendant(s).   :

---x

_____, Esq., an attorney duly admitted to the practice of law in the courts of the State of New York, hereby affirms the following under penalties of perjury:

1. I am a member of the firm of _____, attorneys for defendant _____ in the above-captioned action. I submit this affirmation in support of defendant's motion to compel discovery pursuant to Rule 3124 of the Civil Practice Law and Rules.

2. On _____, defendant served upon counsel for plaintiff a demand for the production of documents pursuant to CPLR 3120. (A copy of the demand is annexed as Exhibit A.) This demand was served in accordance with the preliminary conference order of this court issued on _____, which order provided that all demands for the production of documents must be served on or before _____. (A copy of this order is annexed as Exhibit B.)

3. Plaintiff failed to serve a response to the document demand on _____ as required by CPLR 3120. Plaintiff neither produced documents nor served objections as required by CPLR 3122. Plaintiff simply ignored the demand.

4. On _____, I sent a letter to counsel for plaintiff, _____, Esq. of the firm of _____, reminding counsel that the deadline for production had passed and requesting a response. (A copy of this letter is annexed as Exhibit C.)

5. Having heard nothing in response to this letter, I sent a second letter to _____ on _____ reiterating the message contained in the first. (A copy of this letter is annexed as Exhibit D.) Once again, no response was received.

6. The deadline for the production of documents having passed without result, on _____, I transmitted to the attorney for plaintiff a letter requesting production in order to avoid motion practice. (A copy of this letter is annexed to the accompanying affirmation as Exhibit E.) No response was received.

7. Thereafter, between _____ and _____, I placed two phone calls to the attorney for plaintiff to discuss the overdue documents. Although I left my name and number with the secretary on both occasions, neither call was returned.

8. On _____, I happened by chance to encounter the attorney for plaintiff in the hallway of the courthouse and took the opportunity to raise the problem with her. She informed me that it was the position of plaintiff that the defendant's response to plaintiff's Rule 3120 demand, which response had been served on _____, was inadequate in that the objections raised to certain demands were baseless and that plaintiff therefore would not produce documents called for in defendant's notice. I inquired whether the problem might be resolved informally if the two of us were to meet at another time and discuss the situation in detail. Counsel for plaintiff stated that the problem could not be resolved except by a ruling of the court and that defendant should make a motion if so advised.

9. Clearly, defendant has attempted energetically and in good faith to achieve a response to the document demand, without result. Defendant had no alternative but to make this motion.

10. Plaintiff has not only ignored defendant's demand, but has violated the preliminary conference order of this court. That order required plaintiff to respond to any demand for the production of documents by _____, the date set forth in defendant's demand.

11. Plaintiff's rationale for ignoring defendant's document demand and the preliminary conference order is without foundation. Pursuant to Rule 3122, defendant was required to produce documents called for by plaintiff to the extent not objected to and to serve objections in accordance with that Rule. Defendant did just that. In a timely manner, defendant objected to parts of two of plaintiff's 18 demands on the ground that the demands

sought information that is completely irrelevant to the issues in this case and is commercially very sensitive.

12. Plaintiff, of course, need not have agreed with defendant's two objections. However, pursuant to Rule 3122, the only proper action for plaintiff to take at that point was to discuss the matter with the attorneys for defendant, and, if an accord could not be reached, to make a motion to compel in a timely manner or to raise the dispute at a conference with the court. Plaintiff's attorneys did not communicate with counsel for defendant about the asserted problems with defendant's objections until the chance encounter of _____. Counsel for plaintiff still has not taken action with regard to the objections.

13. As set forth in the accompanying memorandum of law, it is the position of the defendant that, at this point, plaintiff has waived the right to complain of defendant's objections to the two items in question. In any event, plaintiff has no right to refuse to produce documents in response to defendant's demand. Plaintiff has failed to serve objections as required by Rule 3122 and so has waived any it might have wished to assert. There is no legal foundation for plaintiff to withhold documents purely as a retaliatory device. This tactic is not merely procedurally improper, but it also violates the court's preliminary conference order.

14. The court's preliminary conference order required production of documents in advance of depositions. This scheduling was done so that the parties could fully prepare for depositions in this case, which is a document-intensive one. The court set out a detailed schedule for the taking of depositions, with which defendant has fully complied. However, depositions are required to be completed by _____. Defendant has scheduled the depositions of plaintiff and his accountant and business advisor, _____, for _____. Defendant cannot properly take these depositions without the documents called for in its demand and now long overdue.

15. As demonstrated in the accompanying memorandum of law, the circumstances set forth above, it is respectfully submitted, require issuance of an order of the court compelling plaintiff to produce the overdue documents. It is respectfully urged that said order require plaintiff to produce those documents no later than _____ so that defendant will have time adequately to prepare for the depositions of plaintiff and _____.

_____, Esq.

Dated: New York, New York

_____

FORM 11—MOTION TO DISMISS (CPLR 3126)

SUPREME COURT OF THE STATE OF NEW YORK
COUNTY OF NEW YORK: COMMERCIAL DIVISION

```
---------------------------------------------x
                                    :  Part _____

        Plaintiff(s),               :  Index No. _____

                                    :

            - against -             :  NOTICE OF MOTION

                                    :

        Defendant(s).               :  Oral Argument Requested
---------------------------------------------x
```

PLEASE TAKE NOTICE that, upon the annexed affirmation of _____, Esq., attorney for defendant, dated _____, and the exhibits thereto, the defendant will move this court at the Motion Support Office Courtroom, Room 130, of the New York County Courthouse, 60 Centre Street, New York, New York, on _____, at 9:30 A.M., or as soon thereafter as counsel may be heard, for an order, pursuant to section 3126 of the Civil Practice Law and Rules, dismissing this action for failure of plaintiff to provide discovery as required by previous orders of this court.

An affirmation that a good faith effort has been made to resolve the issues raised in this motion without need for the intervention of the court is annexed pursuant to Uniform Rule 202.7. The circumstances of the failure are set out in detail in the annexed affirmation.

Pursuant to CPLR 2214(b), answering affidavits, if any, are required to be served upon the undersigned at least seven days before the return date of this motion.

Dated: New York, New York

_____

_____[Firm]

By: _____[Signature]

_____, Esq.
A Member of the Firm
[Address]
[Phone]

Attorneys for _____

To: _____
         _____
         _____

FORM 12—AFFIRMATION ON MOTION TO DISMISS (CPLR 3126)

SUPREME COURT OF THE STATE OF NEW YORK
COUNTY OF NEW YORK: COMMERCIAL DIVISION

```
-----------------------------------------x
                                         :  Part _____

        Plaintiff(s),                    :  Index No. _____

                                         :  Justice _____

                   - against -           :  AFFIRMATION IN
                                            SUPPORT OF
                                         :  DEFENDANT'S MOTION
                                            TO DISMISS
        Defendant(s).                    :

-----------------------------------------x
```

_____, Esq., an attorney duly admitted to the practice of law in the courts of the State of New York, hereby affirms the following under penalties of perjury:

1. I am a member of the firm of _____, attorneys for defendant _____ in the above-captioned action. I submit this affirmation in support of defendant's motion to dismiss this action pursuant to section 3126 of the Civil Practice Law and Rules because of plaintiff's repeated violations of this court's orders regarding discovery proceedings.

2. On _____, defendant served upon counsel for plaintiff a demand for the production of documents pursuant to CPLR 3120. (A copy of the demand is annexed as Exhibit A.) This demand was served in accordance with the preliminary conference order of this court issued on _____, which order provided that all demands for the production of documents must be served on or before _____. (A copy of this order is annexed as Exhibit B.)

3. Plaintiff failed to serve a response to the document demand on _____ as required by CPLR 3120. Plaintiff neither produced documents nor served objections as required by CPLR 3122. Plaintiff simply ignored the demand.

4. Attached as Exhibit C is a series of letters sent by me in an effort to obtain compliance with defendant's notice without need for court inter-

vention. Defendant received no response to any of these communications. On _____, the deadline for the production of all documents in the case set in the court's prior order passed without response by plaintiff.

5. On _____, I brought on a motion to compel pursuant to CPLR 3124. On _____, the court granted this motion in a decision, a copy of which is annexed as Exhibit D. This order required plaintiff to produce the documents called for in the demand by _____ and to appear for a deposition on _____. The order also determined that plaintiff had waived any objections he might have had to production of the documents by failing to object in a timely fashion.

6. Plaintiff failed to produce any documents by the _____ deadline. I then sent plaintiff two letters during the following week (copies are annexed as Exhibit E), which were again ignored.

7. I was, therefore, obliged to bring a motion to dismiss by order to show cause. By decision dated _____ (a copy of which is annexed as Exhibit F), the court granted the motion and ordered the dismissal of the case if plaintiff failed to produce the documents called for by _____ and to appear for deposition on _____.

8. Once again, plaintiff failed to comply. Plaintiff produced no documents. Rather, plaintiff ignored the demand and, in a letter dated _____ (a copy of which is annexed as Exhibit G), counsel for plaintiff purported to assert objections to all the requests in the demand and to adjourn the deposition of plaintiff fixed by the court for _____ on the ground that business required that plaintiff be out of the country on that date.

9. Defendant sent a letter to counsel for plaintiff by hand dated _____ (a copy of which is annexed as Exhibit H) stating that, in view of the court's order, defendant would have to bring on the instant motion unless plaintiff both produced the overdue documents by _____ so as to allow defendant time to review them and prepare for the scheduled deposition, and appeared for the deposition as directed by the court. Plaintiff did neither. Defendant attended the deposition on the date scheduled by the court notwithstanding that plaintiff had still produced no documents. Therefore, defendant has had no alternative other than to bring this motion.

10. It is clear that the conduct of plaintiff amounts to deliberate, willful and contumacious flouting of three court orders. There was no justification for failing to produce documents on the ground of untimely objections, nor was the asserted press of business abroad a valid excuse for

failing to appear for deposition as ordered by the court. The court having already issued an order conditionally dismissing this action unless plaintiff complied with its discovery obligations in regard to the documents and the deposition, and the plaintiff having done neither and having offered no reasonable excuse therefor, defendant respectfully requests that the action must be dismissed unconditionally. As made clear in the accompanying memorandum of law, the conduct of plaintiff in so blatantly interfering with the discovery process in this case without any justification merits the sanction of dismissal.

_____, Esq.

Dated: New York, New York

_____

FORM 13—MOTION FOR SANCTIONS (CPLR 3126)

SUPREME COURT OF THE STATE OF NEW YORK
COUNTY OF NEW YORK: COMMERCIAL DIVISION

```
---------------------------------------------x
                                    :  Part _____

        Plaintiff(s),               :  Index No. _____

                                    :  Justice _____

                - against -         :  NOTICE OF MOTION

                                    :

        Defendant(s).               :  Oral Argument Requested
---------------------------------------------x
```

PLEASE TAKE NOTICE that, upon the annexed affirmation of _____ _____, Esq., attorney for defendant, dated _____, and the exhibits thereto, the defendant will move this court at the Motion Support Office Courtroom, Room 130, of the New York County Courthouse, 60 Centre Street, New York, New York, on _____, at 9:30 A.M., or as soon thereafter as counsel may be heard, for an order, pursuant to section 3126 of the Civil Practice Law and Rules, imposing sanctions upon plaintiff and plaintiff's counsel for interference with and obstruction of defendant's deposition of plaintiff and requiring plaintiff to appear for a further deposition session.

An affirmation that a good faith effort has been made to resolve the issues raised in this motion without need for the intervention of the court is annexed pursuant to Uniform Rule 202.7.

Pursuant to CPLR 2214(b), answering affidavits, if any, are required to be served upon the undersigned at least seven days before the return date of this motion.

Dated: New York, New York

_____

_____[Firm]

By: _____[Signature]

_____, Esq.
A Member of the Firm
[Address]
[Phone]

Attorneys for _____

To: _____
           _____
           _____

FORM 14—AFFIRMATION ON MOTION FOR SANCTIONS (CPLR 3126)

SUPREME COURT OF THE STATE OF NEW YORK
COUNTY OF NEW YORK: COMMERCIAL DIVISION

```
---------------------------------------------x
                                    :   Part _____

        Plaintiff(s),               :   Index No. _____

                                    :   Justice _____

            - against -             :   AFFIRMATION IN
                                        SUPPORT OF
                                    :   DEFENDANT'S MOTION
                                        FOR SANCTIONS

        Defendant(s).               :

---------------------------------------------x
```

_____, Esq., an attorney duly admitted to the practice of law in the courts of the State of New York, hereby affirms the following under penalties of perjury:

1. I am a member of the firm of _____, attorneys for defendant _____ in the above-captioned action. I submit this affirmation in support of defendant's motion for an order pursuant to section 3126 of the Civil Practice Law and Rules imposing sanctions upon plaintiff and plaintiff's counsel based upon the misconduct of both plaintiff and plaintiff's counsel that severely interfered with defendant's deposition of plaintiff, and directing that plaintiff appear for a further session of the deposition.

2. On _____, this court issued a preliminary conference order which required that all depositions be completed by _____. (A copy of this order is annexed as Exhibit A.) The deposition of plaintiff was scheduled for _____, but was adjourned numerous times by plaintiff as shown in the correspondence annexed as Exhibit B.

3. Finally, the deposition took place on _____. The conduct of plaintiff and plaintiff's counsel during this deposition was plainly improper and, as demonstrated in the accompanying memorandum of law, in violation of clear principles of law governing depositions in this state. The actions of plaintiff and counsel made a mockery of the deposition process.

4. Attached as Exhibit C is a copy of the deposition of plaintiff. Plaintiff and plaintiff's counsel engaged in a variety of improper actions during the deposition. For ease of reference, the list annexed as Exhibit D identifies, by page and line number, grouped separately by each type of improper action, the various forms of misconduct committed.

5. For example, the attorney for defendant made numerous objections despite the fact that the majority of them were unnecessary since, under prevailing law, they were preserved for resolution at trial. The cumulative effect of all these objections was highly disruptive. One measure of this is the fact that the name of plaintiff's attorney appears on 75 of the 118 pages of the deposition.

6. The attorney for plaintiff used many of these objections as occasions to make speeches on the record. The speeches were irrelevant to the proceedings since the objections, as noted, were largely preserved. To the extent the objections concerned the form of a question, plaintiff's counsel need only have stated that he was objecting on the grounds of form. Having done that, he would have preserved his rights, and if I, as attorney for defendant, had failed to correct the perceived problem, the risk was mine. In fact, I asked counsel to refrain from doing more than objecting in this manner unless I asked for elaboration of the basis of the objection. Counsel ignored this request.

7. On 35 different occasions, identified in Exhibit D, counsel for plaintiff made speeches on the record. Some of these speeches were very extensive. In themselves, they prolonged the deposition and interfered with its flow. Beyond that, they signaled to plaintiff how he should answer the questions asked. In every instance, the answer given by plaintiff followed the signal set forth in the objection, as the court will see from reviewing the record.

8. Counsel for plaintiff also frequently directed that the witness not answer the question posed. In every instance listed in Exhibit D, he did so in violation of the rules that apply.

9. In some instances, counsel for plaintiff objected on grounds of irrelevance. Plaintiff has asserted in this case that representatives of defendant misled him as to the terms of an extension of a loan and engaged in fraud. In this connection, plaintiff has stated that he is not financially sophisticated. I attempted at the deposition to inquire about other analogous transactions plaintiff may have engaged in and to explore the nature of his

business activities in a general way. Counsel for plaintiff objected that such questions were irrelevant and refused to let the witness respond. It is clear that questions concerning plaintiff's business and financial sophistication were proper under the broad standard of relevance that applies to the discovery process in light of plaintiff's own allegations in this case.

10. Counsel for plaintiff criticized many of the questions asked and questioned my competence as an attorney. The witness repeatedly insulted me and abused representatives of defendant on the record. Plaintiff also testified on 18 occasions that he could not recall information and incidents that he had to have remembered since, among other things, he has referred to them in prior affidavits in this case.

11. On several occasions during the deposition, I asked counsel for plaintiff to join me in a conference call to the court to resolve problems during the deposition. Counsel refused to participate.

12. In view of the severe obstruction that occurred, which was so extensive as to render the deposition useless—a review of the transcript reveals that plaintiff provided almost no information on any subject other than general facts about his background—and given my inability to obtain a ruling, I advised counsel that I would be compelled to make this motion and requested that the obstructive conduct end so that the motion would not be necessary. Counsel responded, "Do what you have to do." (Tr. at 106.)

13. Because of the pervasive misconduct, defendant seeks an order directing plaintiff to appear for another session of the deposition and to answer questions in a proper manner, free of obstructive and baseless objections and directions not to answer. Because defendant has wasted time and money in a fruitless effort to depose plaintiff, the defendant further requests that sanctions be imposed on plaintiff's counsel and plaintiff to cover defendant's costs on this motion and in taking the entirely pointless deposition. Annexed as Exhibit E is a breakdown of defendant's costs in detail. This is a true and accurate statement of defendant's expenses occasioned by the misconduct described. In view of this, defendant respectfully urges the court to impose sanctions in the amount of $_____, to be paid to the defendant.

_____, Esq.

Dated: New York, New York

_____

FORM 15—MOTION FOR PROTECTIVE ORDER

SUPREME COURT OF THE STATE OF NEW YORK
COUNTY OF NEW YORK: COMMERCIAL DIVISION

```
-----------------------------------------x
```
	:	Part _____
Plaintiff(s),	:	Index No. _____
	:	Justice _____
- against -	:	**NOTICE OF MOTION**
	:	
Defendant(s).	:	<u>Oral Argument Requested</u>

```
-----------------------------------------x
```

PLEASE TAKE NOTICE that, upon the annexed affirmation of _____, Esq., attorney for defendant, dated _____, and the exhibits thereto, the defendant will move this court at the Motion Support Office Courtroom, Room 130, of the New York County Courthouse, 60 Centre Street, New York, New York, on _____, at 9:30 A.M., or as soon thereafter as counsel may be heard, pursuant to Section 3103 of the Civil Practice Law and Rules, for a protective order against the taking of the deposition of the defendant _____ Corp. by _____, its [title], scheduled by notice to take place on _____, upon the ground that such a deposition would impose unreasonable burden, expense, and annoyance upon defendant and its officials, defendant having already produced for deposition by plaintiff in this action three officials with knowledge of the relevant transactions and events who testified at length.

An affirmation that a good faith effort has been made to resolve the issues raised in this motion without need for the intervention of the court is annexed pursuant to Uniform Rule 202.7.

Pursuant to CPLR 2214(b), answering affidavits, if any, are required to be served upon the undersigned at least seven days before the return date of this motion.

Dated: New York, New York

_____

_____[Firm]

By: _____[Signature]

_____, Esq.
A Member of the Firm
[Address]
[Phone]

Attorneys for _____

To: _____
          _____
          _____

FORM 16—AFFIRMATION ON MOTION FOR PROTECTIVE ORDER

SUPREME COURT OF THE STATE OF NEW YORK
COUNTY OF NEW YORK: COMMERCIAL DIVISION

```
---------------------------------------------x
                                  :  Part _____

        Plaintiff(s),             :  Index No. _____

                                  :  Justice _____

              - against -         :  AFFIRMATION IN
                                     SUPPORT OF
                                  :  DEFENDANT'S MOTION
                                     FOR A PROTECTIVE
        Defendant(s).             :  ORDER

---------------------------------------------x
```

_____, Esq., an attorney duly admitted to the practice of law in the courts of the State of New York, hereby affirms the following under penalties of perjury:

1. I am a member of the firm of _____, attorneys for defendant _____ Corp. in the above-captioned action. I submit this affirmation in support of defendant's motion for a protective order pursuant to Section 3103 of the Civil Practice Law and Rules prohibiting plaintiff from taking the deposition of defendant by _____, its [title], which has been noticed for _____.

2. In compliance with notices served upon defendant by plaintiff and the court's scheduling order issued at the preliminary conference in this case, defendant has produced three of its senior officials for deposition, namely, _____, _____ in charge of the commercial lending division of defendant at the time of the transactions between plaintiff and defendant that are the subject of this action; _____, _____ of defendant, who participated in negotiations with representatives of plaintiff for an extension of the original loan facility between plaintiff and defendant; and _____, _____ in the commercial lending division of defendant who was in charge of the loan facility and handled the extension request for defendant.

3. All three of these officials had knowledge of relevant events in this action. Each testified at length about the transactions at issue in the case. These witnesses answered all of plaintiff's questions with the exception of a few as to which objections were made on grounds of attorney-client privilege. All three witnesses testified that they were the only officials at defendant who had dealt with plaintiff and his representatives in regard to the loan facility and the requested extension.

4. Furthermore, plaintiff in his deposition (relevant portions of which are annexed as Exhibit A) identified these three witnesses as the only persons at defendant with whom he or his representatives had had any dealings regarding the loan facility or the proposed extension. Plaintiff stated in his deposition that neither he nor his representatives had had any communications with Mr. _____ during or about the time of the events at issue in the case. (Tr. at 213.) Plaintiff stated that he did not "know anything whatsoever" about Mr. _____. (Tr. at 215.)

5. Accompanying this affirmation is an affidavit of Mr. _____, sworn to _____. Mr. _____ explains in this affidavit that he was not employed by defendant when the original loan facility was granted and, indeed, did not join defendant until four months before the time when plaintiff, according to his own testimony, first contacted defendant to request an extension. Mr. _____ further indicates that he was obliged to take a medical leave of absence from defendant two weeks before the request was made and that this leave continued for six months, well past the time the negotiations over an extension had collapsed and only two weeks prior to the initiation of this lawsuit. Mr. _____ avers that his medical condition was such that he was unable to handle his professional responsibilities throughout his convalescence on orders of his physicians.

6. As is made clear in the _____ affidavit, Mr. _____ has no knowledge of the events at issue in this case and can provide no useful testimony. Plaintiff's own deposition indicates as much. On the other hand, defendant has already produced three fully knowledgeable witnesses who have testified at length about all aspects of the relationship and dealings between plaintiff and defendant. Plaintiff has made no complaints about the testimony furnished by these witnesses and has not claimed that anyone other than Mr. _____ within defendant has knowledge about this case.

7. Defendant has produced enough witnesses for deposition. It should not have to produce another. As the accompanying memorandum of law demonstrates, to require defendant to produce a fourth witness in the circumstances of this case clearly would constitute the imposition upon defendant of the unreasonable annoyance, burden and expense that Section 3103 was designed to prevent.

8. This conclusion is particularly compelling since it is clear that, in view of his employment history and medical difficulties, the proposed witness cannot supply any relevant information or provide testimony that might lead to the discovery of admissible evidence. If any further testimony were required, Mr. _____ simply cannot supply it and, in fact, according to plaintiff's own testimony, no one else at defendant can do so either.

9. Therefore, it is respectfully requested that defendant's motion for a protective order be granted with regard to the noticed deposition of ____.

_____, Esq.

Dated: New York, New York

_____

FORM 17—ORDER TO SHOW CAUSE FOR PROTECTIVE ORDER—CONTINUATION OF DEPOSITION

At IAS Part _____of the Commercial Division of the Supreme Court of the State of New York, County of New York, at the Courthouse, 60 Centre Street, New York, New York, on the ___ day of _____, 20__.

PRESENT: HONORABLE _____

Justice.

```
------------------------------------------------x
                                  :   Part _____

        Plaintiff(s),             :   Index No. _____

                                  :

            - against -           :   ORDER TO SHOW CAUSE

                                  :

        Defendant(s).             :
------------------------------------------------x
```

Upon the annexed affirmation of _____, Esq., attorney for defendant, dated _____, and the exhibits annexed thereto, and the affirmation of good faith pursuant to Uniform Rule 202.7 of _____, Esq., dated _____,

IT IS HEREBY ORDERED that plaintiff show cause before this court, the Honorable _____, Justice, Commercial Division Part _____, Room _____ at the Courthouse, 60 Centre Street, New York, New York, on the _____ day of _____, _____, or as soon thereafter as counsel may be heard, why a protective order should not be issued, pursuant to Section 3103 of the Civil Practice Law and Rules, prohibiting the plaintiff from continuing the deposition of defendant by _____, the _____ of defendant in charge of the commercial lending division of defendant, on the ground that the questions plaintiff will seek to ask at the continued deposition of the said witness are improper under governing law and the continued deposition would cause unreasonable annoyance, burden and expense to defendant and the witness.

IT IS FURTHER ORDERED that service of this order to show cause and the supporting papers upon _____, Esq., of _____, _____, New York, New York, on or before the _____ day of _____, 20___ be deemed good and sufficient service.

ENTER:

_____

J.S.C.

FORM 18—AFFIRMATION ON ORDER TO SHOW CAUSE FOR PROTECTIVE ORDER— CONTINUATION OF DEPOSITION

SUPREME COURT OF THE STATE OF NEW YORK
COUNTY OF NEW YORK: COMMERCIAL DIVISION

```
------------------------------------------x
                                          :  Part _____

        Plaintiff(s),                     :  Index No. _____

                                          :  Justice _____

                - against -               :  AFFIRMATION IN
                                             SUPPORT OF
                                          :  DEFENDANT'S MOTION
                                             FOR A PROTECTIVE
        Defendant(s).                     :  ORDER

------------------------------------------x
```

_____, Esq., an attorney duly admitted to the practice of law in the courts of the State of New York, hereby affirms the following under penalties of perjury:

1. I am a member of the firm of _____, attorneys for defendant _____ Corp. in the above-captioned action. I submit this affirmation in support of defendant's motion by order to show cause for a protective order pursuant to Section 3103 of the Civil Practice Law and Rules prohibiting plaintiff from continuing the deposition of defendant by _____, its _____ in charge of the commercial lending division of defendant.

2. In compliance with a notice served upon defendant by plaintiff and the court's scheduling order issued at the preliminary conference in this case, defendant produced Mr. _____ for deposition on _____ and _____, _____. Mr. _____ testified for six hours on the first day of his deposition and four hours on the second.

3. During the course of his deposition (a copy of which is annexed as Exhibit A), Mr._____ answered almost all the questions posed by counsel for plaintiff. In accordance with applicable law, the attorney representing Mr. _____ at the deposition, my partner, _____,

Esq. of the firm of _____, interposed only such objections as were strictly necessary. Mr. _____ objected to a number of questions based upon defects in their form, but such objections were proper and well-founded and did not interfere with the plaintiff's interrogation.

4. At a certain point in the deposition, the attorney for plaintiff, _____, Esq. of the firm of _____, began to ask the witness about whether he had any knowledge of a certain meeting. Mr. _____ testified that he did not, having been out of the office for two weeks prior thereto and one week after the date of that meeting. (Tr. at 302.) Upon further questioning, Mr. _____ testified that the absence from the office had been caused by a family emergency regarding some personal difficulties of his son, and that these difficulties had completely distracted him from matters having to do with the office. (Tr. at 304–6.) Mr. _____ sought to inquire into the nature of the personal difficulties. Mr. _____ objected, requesting an explanation as to why Mr. _____ believed the information would be in any way relevant to the case. (Tr. at 309–10.) Mr. _____ unfortunately became abusive, insulted Mr. _____ and provided only a vague assertion of relevance. (Tr. at 313—15.) ("This has to do with the credibility of the witness in relation to the meeting, and anyway this is my deposition and I get to call the shots.") Mr. _____ directed the witness not to answer the question on the ground that the questions counsel sought to ask were palpably irrelevant and prejudicial. (Tr. at 318.)

5. At this point, Mr. _____ requested that counsel for plaintiff join him in a call to the court to seek a ruling on the objection. Mr. _____ refused to do so, saying that "this is my deposition and I can ask what I want and you have to answer, and I refuse to dignify your incompetent objections, which are designed simply to obstruct and to prevent plaintiff from achieving justice given the fraud committed on him by defendant." (Tr. at 320.) Counsel for plaintiff then proceeded to issue an unfortunate stream of invective directed at the witness and Mr. _____, to which Mr. _____ objected in a polite manner. (Tr. at 322–26.)

6. Later in the deposition, counsel for plaintiff sought to ask questions about relations between defendant and real estate investors in New York City who, like plaintiff, had borrowed money from defendant. Mr. _____ allowed plaintiff some leeway in this area. However, it became apparent from clear statements by Mr. _____ (Tr. at 355–56) that he intended to conduct extensive inquiry, which he described as "three hours worth of questions" (Tr. at 366), regarding defendant's dealings with

other investors. At this point, Mr. _____ objected and requested that counsel for plaintiff join him in a call to the court for a ruling on the line of inquiry, which Mr. _____ believed to be palpably irrelevant to the issues in the case. Mr. _____ refused to take part and again gave way to a stream of invective and insults directed at defense counsel and the witness. (Tr. at 371–74.) Defense counsel stated that he had no choice but to direct the witness not to answer the questions until he could seek a protective order from the court.

7. As shown in the accompanying memorandum of law, the inquiry was properly objected to. The complaint in this case (a copy of which is annexed as Exhibit B) raises issues concerning defendant's alleged fraudulent conduct in relation to an extension of a loan facility requested by plaintiff. Plaintiff claims that defendant's representatives misled and defrauded plaintiff by making certain promises to him and his representatives that the facility would be extended, upon the basis of which plaintiff engaged in certain transactions. When the extension was not granted, plaintiff claims that the transactions collapsed, causing him substantial losses.

8. Defendant has denied the key allegations of the complaint. (Annexed as Exhibit C is a copy of the answer of defendant.) But even if the representations alleged by plaintiff had occurred, the issue in the case is whether the alleged fraudulent conduct of defendant in making those representations was such that plaintiff could have relied upon the representations. It is completely irrelevant to that question in view of provisions in various documents, including the loan agreement, what dealings defendant did or did not have with other real estate investors in the city, who are not parties to this case and had no involvement in any of the events or transactions at issue here. Furthermore, were this to become an acceptable subject for discovery, the dimensions of this case would expand exponentially.

9. Defendant's Mr. _____ has answered all the questions posed by plaintiff for 10 full hours except those described above. The objections raised were entirely proper. Defendant should not have to bear the burden and expense of producing Mr. _____ yet again to answer these improper questions, particularly when the witness and his attorney may well be subjected to improper harassment and abuse by counsel for plaintiff. This is especially the case since defendant attempted on several occasions during the deposition to obtain rulings of the court on the matters in dispute, but counsel for plaintiff refused to participate. Therefore, it is

respectfully requested that the defendant's motion for a protective order against the continued deposition of Mr. _____ be granted.

_____, Esq.

Dated: New York, New York

_____

FORM 19—MOTION FOR COMMISSION

SUPREME COURT OF THE STATE OF NEW YORK
COUNTY OF NEW YORK: COMMERCIAL DIVISION

```
-------------------------------------------x
                                    :  Part _____

        Plaintiff(s),               :  Index No. _____

                                    :  Justice _____

                - against -         :  NOTICE OF MOTION


                                    :

        Defendant(s).               :

-------------------------------------------x
```

PLEASE TAKE NOTICE that, upon the annexed affirmation of _____ _____, Esq., attorney for defendant, dated _____, and the exhibits thereto, the defendant will move this court at the Motion Support Office Courtroom, Room 130, of the New York County Courthouse, 60 Centre Street, New York, New York, on _____, at 9:30 A.M., or as soon thereafter as counsel may be heard, for an order, pursuant to Article 31 of the Civil Practice Law and Rules, authorizing the issuance of a commission for the taking of a deposition on oral questions outside the State of New York.

Pursuant to CPLR 2214(b), answering affidavits, if any, are required to be served upon the undersigned at least seven days before the return date of this motion.

Dated: New York, New York
        _____

                                    _____[Firm]

                                    By: _____[Signature]

                                    _____, Esq.
                                    A Member of the Firm
                                    [Address]
                                    [Phone]
                                    Attorneys for _____

To: _____
           _____
           _____

FORM 20—COMMISSION

SUPREME COURT OF THE STATE OF NEW YORK
COUNTY OF NEW YORK: COMMERCIAL DIVISION

```
---------------------------------------------x
                                 :  Part _____

           Plaintiff(s),         :  Index No. _____

                                 :  Justice _____

                  - against -    :  COMMISSION


                                 :

           Defendant(s).         :
---------------------------------------------x
```

THE PEOPLE OF THE STATE OF NEW YORK:

To: _____

           _____

           _____

GREETINGS:

KNOW YE, that we, with full faith in your prudence and competency, have appointed you Commissioner, and do hereby authorize you to serve as the officer before whom shall be taken the examination upon oral questions, under oath, of _____, residing at _____, as a witness in the action captioned above pending in our Supreme Court of the State of New York, New York County, Commercial Division, pursuant to Article 31 of the Civil Practice Law and Rules of the State of New York.

We therefore request of you or any other duly authorized person who may administer oaths pursuant to the laws of the State of _____ that at a certain time and place to be by you appointed, you do cause the aforesaid witness, by proper and usual process, to come before you, or before some competent person appointed by you for that purpose, and to be then and there placed under oath and to answer the questions put to the said witness by the attorneys for the parties hereto; that the testimony of the witness be then and there recorded and that it be reduced to writing, subscribed by the witness, and certified to be correct and proven before you; and that you return the transcript of the testimony to the Clerk of the Supreme Court of the State of New York, County of New York, 60 Centre Street, New York, New York 10007, by certified or registered mail with all convenient speed. And you are to be governed in the premises by the applicable law of the State of New York.

WITNESS, the Hon. _____, one of the Justices of our Supreme Court, this _____ day of _____, 20___.

BY THE COURT:

_____

J.S.C.

FORM 21—AFFIRMATION OF GOOD FAITH
(UNIFORM RULE 202.7)

SUPREME COURT OF THE STATE OF NEW YORK
COUNTY OF NEW YORK: COMMERCIAL DIVISION

```
---------------------------------------------x
                                    :   Part _____

        Plaintiff(s),               :   Index No. _____

                                    :   Justice _____

                    - against -     :

                                        AFFIRMATION OF
                                    :   GOOD FAITH
                                        (UNIFORM RULE 202.7)
        Defendant(s).               :

---------------------------------------------x
```

_____, Esq., an attorney duly admitted to the practice of law in the courts of the State of New York, hereby affirms the following under penalties of perjury:

1. I am a member of the firm of _____, attorneys for defendant _____ in the above-captioned action. I submit this affirmation pursuant to Section 202.7 of the Uniform Rules for the Trial Courts.

2. In a separate affirmation submitted in support of defendant's motion to compel pursuant to Rule 3124 of the Civil Practice Law and Rules, I set forth the circumstances that have required defendant to make the motion. In particular, I explain that the plaintiff has failed and refused to produce documents called for in defendant's demand pursuant to CPLR 3120, which documents are required by defendant to prepare for depositions that must, pursuant to a preliminary conference order issued by this court, be completed by _____.

3. The deadline for the production of documents having passed without result, I transmitted to the attorney for plaintiff a letter requesting production in order to avoid motion practice. (A copy of this letter is annexed to the accompanying affirmation as Exhibit A.) No response was received.

4. Thereafter, on _____ and _____, I placed two phone calls to the attorney for plaintiff, _____, Esq. of the firm of _____, to discuss the overdue documents. Although I left my name and number with the secretary on both occasions, neither call was returned.

5. On _____, I happened by chance to encounter counsel for plaintiff in the hallway of the courthouse and took the opportunity to raise the problem with her. She informed me that it was the position of plaintiff that the defendant's response to plaintiff's Rule 3120 demand was inadequate in that the objections raised to certain demands were baseless and that plaintiff therefore would not produce documents called for in defendant's notice. I inquired whether the problem might be resolved informally if the two of us were to meet at another time and discuss the situation in detail. Counsel for plaintiff stated that the problem could not be resolved except by a ruling of the court and that defendant should make a motion if so advised.

6. Defendant has attempted in good faith to resolve the discovery dispute between the parties without resort to motion practice, but has been unsuccessful and, accordingly, has had no alternative but to bring on the accompanying motion.

_____, Esq.

Dated: New York, New York

_____

FORM 22—REQUEST FOR JUDICIAL INTERVENTION

REQUEST FOR JUDICIAL INTERVENTION   UCS-840 (REV 1/2000)

COURT, _____COUNTY INDEX NO. DATE PURCHASED:

	For Clerk Only
PLAINTIFF(S):	
	IAS entry date
DEFENDANT(S):	
	Judge Assigned
	RJI Date

Date issue joined: _____ Bill of particulars served (Y/N): [   ] Y   [   ] N

NATURE OF JUDICIAL INTERVENTION (check **ONE** box only **AND** enter information)

[   ] Request for preliminary conference

[   ] Note of issue and/or certificate of readiness

[   ] Notice of motion (return date:_____)
        Relief sought _____

[   ] Order to show cause
        (clerk enter return date:_____)
        Relief sought

[   ] Other ex parte application (specify:
        _____)

[   ] Notice of petition (return date:_____)
        Relief sought _____

[   ] Notice of medical or dental malpractice
        action (specify:_   )

[   ] Statement of net worth

[   ] Writ of habeas corpus

[   ] Other (specify: _____
        _____

NATURE OF ACTION OR PROCEEDING (Check **ONE** box only)

MATRIMONIAL

[ ]	Contested	-CM
[ ]	Uncontested	-UM

COMMERCIAL

[ ]	Contract	-CONT
[ ]	Corporate	-CORP
[ ]	Insurance (where insurer is a party, except arbitration)	-INS
[ ]	UCC (including sales, negotiable instruments)	-UCC
[ ]	*Other Commercial	-OC

REAL PROPERTY

[ ]	Tax Certiorari	-TAX
[ ]	Foreclosure	-FOR
[ ]	Condemnation	-COND
[ ]	Landlord/Tenant	-LT
[ ]	*Other Real Property	-ORP

OTHER MATTERS

[ ]	*_____	-OTH

TORTS

Malpractice

[ ]	Medical/Podiatric	-MM
[ ]	Dental	-DM
[ ]	*Other Professional	-OPM
[ ]	Motor Vehicle	-MV
[ ]	*Products Liability	-PL
[ ]	Environmental	-EN
[ ]	Asbestos	-ASB
[ ]	Breast Implant	-BI
[ ]	*Other Negligence	-OTN
[ ]	*Other Tort (including intentional)	-OT

SPECIAL PROCEEDINGS

[ ]	Art. 75 (Arbitration)	-ART75
[ ]	Art. 77 (Trusts)	-ART77
[ ]	Art. 78	-ART78
[ ]	Election Law	-ELEC
[ ]	Guardianship (MHL Art. 81)	-GUARD81
[ ]	*Other Mental Hygiene	-MHYG
[ ]	*Other Special Proceeding	-OSP

<u>Check "YES" or "NO" for each of the following questions</u>:

Is this action/proceeding against a

YES	NO		YES	NO	
[ ]	[ ]	Municipality (Specify_____)	[ ]	[ ]	Public Authority: (Specify_____)

YES	NO	
	[ ]	Does this action/proceeding seek equitable relief?
	[ ]	Does this action/proceeding seek recovery for personal injury?
	[ ]	Does this action/proceeding seek recovery for property damage?

Pre-Note Time Frames:
(This applies to all cases except contested matrimonials and tax certiorari cases)

Estimated time period for case to be ready for trial (from filing of RJI to filing of Note of Issue):

Expedited: 0-8 months   Standard: 9-12 months   Complex: 13-15 months

Contested Matrimonial Cases Only: (Check and give date)

Has summons been served?   No   Yes, Date _____

Was a Notice of No Necessity filed?   No   Yes, Date _____

ATTORNEY(S) FOR PLAINTIFF(S):

<u>Self Rep.*</u>	<u>Name</u>	<u>Address</u>	<u>Phone #</u>

ATTORNEY(S) FOR DEFENDANT(S):

<u>Self Rep.*</u>	<u>Name</u>	<u>Address</u>	<u>Phone #</u>

*Self Represented: parties representing themselves, without an attorney, should check the "Self Rep." box and enter their name, address, and phone # in the space provided above for attorneys.

<u>**INSURANCE CARRIERS**</u>:

<u>**RELATED CASES: (IF NONE, write "NONE" below)**</u>:

<u>Title</u>	<u>Index #</u>	<u>Court</u>	<u>Nature of Relationship</u>

      I AFFIRM UNDER PENALTY OF PERJURY THAT, TO MY KNOWLEDGE, OTHER THAN AS NOTED ABOVE, THERE ARE AND HAVE BEEN NO RELATED ACTIONS OR PROCEEDINGS, NOR HAS A REQUEST FOR JUDICIAL INTERVENTION PREVIOUSLY BEEN FILED IN THIS ACTION OR PROCEEDING.

Dated:

_____
(SIGNATURE)

_____
(PRINT OR TYPE NAME)

_____
ATTORNEY FOR

ATTACH RIDER SHEET IF NECESSARY TO PROVIDE REQUIRED INFORMATION

FORM 23—NOTE OF ISSUE

NOTE OF ISSUE

Calendar No. (if any) _____

Index No. _____

_____ Court,

_____ County

	For use of clerk

---x

       Plaintiff(s),   :   Name of Assigned Judge

                                :   _____

          - against -   :

                               :   **NOTICE FOR TRIAL**

                               :

       Defendant(s).   :

---x

_____ Trial by jury demanded _____ of all issues; _____ of issues specified below; _____ or attached hereto

_____ Trial without jury

Filed by attorney for _____

Date summons served _____

Date service completed _____

Date issue joined _____

Nature of action or special proceeding:

Tort:

    Motor vehicle negligence _____

    Medical malpractice _____

    Other tort _____

Contract _____

Contested matrimonial _____

Uncontested matrimonial _____

Tax certiorari _____

Condemnation _____

Other (not itemized above) _____ (specify)

Special preference claimed under _____ on the ground that _____

Indicate if this action is brought as a class action _____

Amount demanded $_____

Other relief _____

Insurance carrier(s), if known: _____

Attorney(s) for Plaintiff(s) _____
Office and P.O. Address:
Phone No.

Attorney(s) for Defendant(s) _____
Office and P.O. Address:
Phone No.

NOTE: The clerk will not accept this note of issue unless accompanied by a certificate of readiness.

FORM 24—CERTIFICATE OF READINESS

**CERTIFICATE OF READINESS
FOR TRIAL**

(Items 1–7 must be checked)

For use of clerk

	Complete	Waived	Not Required
1. All pleadings served.	_____	_____	_____
2. Bill of particulars served.	_____	_____	_____
3. Physical examinations completed.	_____	_____	_____
4. Medical reports exchanged.	_____	_____	_____
5. Appraisal reports exchanged.	_____	_____	_____
6. Compliance with § 202.16 of the Rules of the Chief Administrator (22 NYCRR 202.16) in matrimonial actions.	_____	_____	_____
7. Discovery proceedings now known to be necessary completed.	_____	_____	_____

8. There are no outstanding requests for discovery.

9. There has been a reasonable opportunity to complete the foregoing proceedings.

10. There has been compliance with any order issued pursuant to section 202.12 of the Rules of the Chief Administrator (22 NYCRR 202.12).

11. If a medical malpractice action, there has been compliance with any order issued pursuant to section 202.56 of the Rules of the Chief Administrator (22 NYCRR 202.56).

12. The case is ready for trial.

Dated: _____

_____ (Signature)

Attorney(s) for: _____
[Office and P.O. Address]

Honorable Harold Baer, Jr.

Harold Baer, Jr., is a United States district court judge. He resigned from the New York State Supreme Court in 1992 after ten years of service. For two years before his induction as a district court judge, he was the executive judicial officer at JAMS/Endispute, where he supervised and did dispute resolution work. Prior to his election to the supreme court, he was for a decade in charge of litigation in a Wall Street law firm. He was assistant U.S. attorney and headed the Organized Crime and Racketeering Unit of that office in the 1960s; he returned as first assistant U.S. attorney and chief of the Criminal Division in 1970. Judge Baer served on the Mollen Commission, a special unit of the New York State Commission of Investigation, and the State Commission on the Governmental Operations of the City of New York.

He has been active in the New York State Bar Association and various city and county bar associations, chairing committees for each, and he served as a trustee of the Federal Bar Council. He is the founder of the Network of Bar Leaders and former president of the New York County Lawyers' Association. In addition to hundreds of published opinions, he has written extensively on legal topics, with some 50 books, pamphlets and articles to his credit. He graduated *magna cum laude* and Phi Beta Kappa from Hobart College and from the Yale Law School in 1957.

Robert C. Meade, Jr., Esq.

Robert C. Meade, Jr., graduated from Fordham University School of Law, where he was a managing editor of the law review. He served for two years as a law clerk to Hon. William Hughes Mulligan, United States Court of Appeals for the Second Circuit. He was in private practice thereafter, including as an associate at a major commercial law firm. He was law secretary to Hon. Harold Baer, Jr., Supreme Court, New York County, and to Hon. Walter M. Schackman, Commercial Part 14 and Commercial Division, Supreme Court, New York County. Since the establishment of the Commercial Division in 1995, Mr. Meade has served as the director of the division in New York County, as well as deputy chief clerk of the Supreme Court, Civil Branch, New York County.

He is a member of the Advisory Committee on Civil Practice of the Chief Administrative Judge of the State of New York. He is also a member of The Association of the Bar of the City of New York and the New York County Lawyers' Association, where he was co-chair of the Committee on the Supreme Court.

CASES

STATUTES, RULES AND REGULATIONS

FEDERAL

Federal Rules of Civil Procedure

Federal Rules of Evidence

United States Code (U.S.C.)

STATE

Civil Practice Law & Rules

Judiciary Law

N.Y. Comp. Codes, R. & Regs.